Real Visual Basic

Real Visual Basic

A Practical Approach to Enterprise Development in the Corporate World

Dan Petit

ADDISON-WESLEY

An imprint of Addison Wesley Longman, Inc.

Reading, Massachusetts • Harlow, England • Menlo Park, California
Berkeley, California • Don Mills, Ontario • Sydney
Bonn • Amsterdam • Tokyo • Mexico City

The publisher offers discounts on this book when ordered in quantity for special sales. For more information, please contact:

AWL Direct Sales
Addison Wesley Longman, Inc.
One Jacob Way
Reading, Massachusetts 01867
(781) 944-3700

Visit AWL on the Web: www.awl.com/cseng/

Library of Congress Cataloging-in-Publication Data
Petit, Dan
    Real Visual Basic : a practical approach to enterprise development in the corporate world / Dan Petit.
        p.   cm.
    Includes bibliographical references and index.
    ISBN 0-201-61604-1
    1. Microsoft Visual BASIC.   2. BASIC (Computer program language)   3. Application software—Development.   I. Title.

    QA76.73.B3 P48 1999
    658'.055268–dc21   99-058356

Acquisitions Editor: Gary Clarke
Editorial Assistant: Rebecca Bence
Production Coordinator: Marilyn E. Rash
Cover Design: Simone Payment
Design/Composition: Ruth Maassen

ISBN 0-201-61604-1
Text printed on recycled and acid-free paper.

1 2 3 4 5 6 7 8 9 10 –CRS– 03 02 01 00 99
First printing, December 1999

To the memory of my father, Charles Petit

Contents

List of Myths

Foreword

As a professional software developer, you are responsible for writing software to automate business processes. If you do your job correctly, your software becomes the engine that makes your company both successful and competitive. However, creating an effective business system in today's environment is no trivial task. You really have to know what you're doing to move through the various stages of a software development project.

Transforming your ideas from a whiteboard in the design phase into source code, and then into executable code for production, can be incredibly challenging. It takes many different skill sets to bring a large-scale software development project to fruition. There's increasing pressure to keep projects on time and under budget. And in the end, it's critical that an application does what it was originally designed to do.

In this book, Dan Petit unearths and explains the critical skills required for writing large software projects with Visual Basic. When you compare VB to other languages, there are many opportunities and there are also certain limitations that you must fully understand. This book dispels many myths about VB and shows you how to make the most of what you have. You'll learn how to manage the life-cycle of a large-scale Visual Basic project. You'll see best-practice design techniques for making the most of VB's unique blend of object-oriented programming features. And although no one book will give you a complete in-depth understanding of a tool as vast as VB or a platform as complicated as Windows, Dan does a great job pointing you to the best resources on many related topics.

If every project manager and software developer in our industry fully understood the principles clearly described in this book, we would have many more software projects completed on time and under budget. And, most important, the software would always do what it was originally written to do. It would allow its users to get their jobs done quickly and effectively.

Ted Pattison
Manhattan Beach, CA

Preface

According to Microsoft's Web site, there are more than three million Visual Basic users in the world. Although computer languages come and go, with this wide a user base, it is safe to say that VB is here to stay for quite some time. Many of these users are computer hobbyists and students who are drawn to VB for its inherent simplicity compared to other languages. The others are primarily professional developers who use VB to create enterprise solutions. Moreover, since Microsoft began aggressively pushing the language in the corporate world with version 4 and the release of Windows 95, VB has managed to root itself firmly in the realm of corporate development.

Students find that practical corporate development differs greatly from the classic academic approaches in many regards. Whereas academic programming concentrates on thoroughness of process and sound programming technique, the almighty dollar drives corporate programming. When it comes to accountability, failure in the academic world can lead to a bad grade; in the corporate world, it can lead to financial collapse. The problem is that many corporate programmers get their start in academic circles or as hobbyists, working on interesting yet typically trivial examples. Their skills may be adequate for simple programs, but they get a serious reality check when, as professionals, they receive their first real VB project. All the rules change.

Even seasoned professionals can find the rigors of corporate development challenging, however. Companies expect a lot from Visual Basic programmers and managers, yet companies rarely provide the training they need to do their jobs successfully. There is also a tendency to choose VB as a tool for the wrong reasons and, consequently, end up expecting too much from the language. This book is intended to flush out common misconceptions and provide practical examples, pointing out those areas where companies make the biggest mistakes. While it may seem irreverent to criticize corporate practices in a book aimed at companies, the intention is to help corporations get the most out of Visual Basic as a tool and get the most bang for their buck. This is unlikely to take place without changing a few fundamental corporate beliefs and practices.

What This Book Is About

Real Visual Basic explores the important *practical* aspects of Visual Basic development in the corporate world. It concentrates on answering questions such as, "How do I do that?" and "Why does VB do that?" as they pertain to various VB technologies. More important, though, it provides down-to-earth advice, answering perhaps the most important question of all, "Should I do that?" Because what may make sense on paper may not make sense in practice, this book offers solutions to real-life problems in corporate development. In the end, the goal is to help make your Visual Basic projects more successful.

Because many of the problems companies have with VB development stem from misunderstandings, *Real Visual Basic* addresses and dispels myths of corporate software development, particularly those that relate to Visual Basic. The goal is not to defend or attack Visual Basic (though I will do both), but rather to explore and expose the practical view. Many of the myths drive misguided practices. Many are general beliefs in the world of software development that are exacerbated by the inclusion of Visual Basic into the equation.

More than anything else, this book is about my experiences as a developer in the corporate world. While I make a living using Microsoft products, I don't feel obligated to protect them, and I am more than willing to point out their faults. To this end, I provide numerous anecdotal discussions, mostly in sidebars, drawn from my experiences, both good and bad, working as a professional developer. My goal in presenting this information is to provide real-life examples of practices I know work and do not work on VB projects. I hope these sections will help prevent you from making the same mistakes I did and will make your life as a VB professional that much easier.

This book covers a variety of topics, from database design to project management to hardcore VB coding (see Road Map section that follows). It may seem odd to include such a disparate array of topics, but this mixture represents the various aspects of software development that many VB developers and managers are exposed to in a corporate environment on a daily basis. They all contribute to the success or failure of VB projects.

This Book's Audience

This book is intended primarily for developers and development team leads, but there is also a substantial amount of material about project management and quality assurance that technical managers will find useful. Moreover, as the corporate managers of tomorrow, programmers will find the project management topics invaluable as well. I assume that those readers who are programmers know the language well and that managers and team leaders have experience with managing Visual Basic projects. The major code examples are clear but nontrivial, and the discussions of management issues assume some level of expertise. Although some of the specific code materials are aimed at a more advanced audience, much of the material will be accessible to most programmers.

However, because even the basic aspects of project management and software design are challenging without a couple of years of experience, this is not a book for complete beginners. Software design, database modeling, and most of the other topics covered here are complex. To avoid repeating introductory materials that is presented better in other sources, *Real Visual Basic* assumes that the reader has a firm grasp of VB's capabilities as a language and defers to other sources when the material is either too introductory or too detailed to present here. Each chapter ends with an annotated "Further Reading" list, and a complete bibliography appears at the end of the book.

What This Book Is Not About

Although it covers a wide array of topics, there are nevertheless a number of subjects beyond the scope of this book. Many of the topics not covered relate to corporate development but have received adequate treatment elsewhere. Others, while still important, have little connection to the corporate world, and I have omitted them for the sake of cohesion.

Bookstore shelves are absolutely covered with books about Internet development. It is one of the hottest topics around these days, and one that is best suited to individual treatment. Therefore, beyond a discussion of system architecture, no substantial Internet-related topics are explored. You will not learn how to make a browser; you will not learn about WebClasses, IIS, ASP, HTML, or XML; and you will not find out how to deploy Internet applications. If you are looking for a discussion of these topics, try another book.

Windows API programming is also a complicated topic, again deserving of separate treatment. Windows API (Win32 API) discussions appear only in the context of solutions to specific problems—no overviews or guidelines are provided, and this book is in no way an API reference. Detailed discussions of other APIs (MAPI, TAPI, DirectX, ODBC, etc.) are omitted as well. Authors have devoted entire books to these topics, and a chapter or two here would not do them justice.

Furthermore, you will see little in the way of COM internals. I'll present a few IUnknowns, an IDispatch or two, but mostly a whole lot of IDontCares.

COM is far too vast a topic to include in detail here; so, instead, I concentrate on what makes COM important and practical to corporate VB programmers and spend very little time on what makes it tick under the hood.

Finally, Microsoft Transaction Server (MTS) and Microsoft Message Queue (MSMQ) are relatively new technologies that are becoming popular in corporate settings. While you will see how you can leverage these tools in designing system architecture, I will not explore the mechanics of using them in any detail.

Road Map to the Book's Contents

This book consists of the following four parts:

Part I, Development Prerequisites, introduces project management techniques and development lifecycles that form the structure of the remainder of the book. To help make your projects successful, the material in this section concentrates on avoiding common problems. Much of the material is not VB-specific, but rather focuses on Rapid Application Development (RAD) tools, of which VB is the most common, and general project misconceptions. This part also looks at requirements gathering and project documentation—two areas that are both neglected and critical for VB projects.

Part II, Designing Visual Basic Software, provides a detailed discussion of the ins and outs of designing VB software. This part starts from the outside, looking at architectural concerns, then moves on to creating user interfaces and designing software and databases.

Part III, Implementation, turns to more code-oriented topics. It covers solid, general VB coding practices and advanced data access coding implementations before turning to some advanced VB coding topics, including creating ActiveX controls and controlling asynchronous program flow. Finally, this part takes a detailed look at how to debug your VB applications.

Part IV, Testing, Reviewing, and Distributing Software, covers the loose ends, including quality assurance and the things that typically take place after coding. This part looks at various ways to test VB applications and to measure their quality. Then there is an in-depth discussion of creating and enforcing coding standards, from naming conventions to commenting practices. The final chapter addresses ways to distribute your finished software.

On-line Materials

Many of the code examples discussed in this book are much too long to include in their entirety. However, complete code examples, including Visual Basic project files, can be found on-line at

http://www.awl.com/cseng/titles/0-201-61604-1

In addition, this is where you can find any updates to this book, including errata and new material. The coding standards template mentioned in chapters 19 and 20 can be found here too. You will also find links to VB resources and tools, including Standards Master, plus author contact information.

Acknowledgments

First things first. Hi, Mom.

At Addison Wesley Longman, numerous folks on both coasts contributed to this book. Many thanks to Gary Clarke, Rebecca Bence, Marilyn Rash, Eric Droukas, Tasha Schlake, Robin Bruce, Chanda Leary, and Kate Saliba. It was a pleasure to work with such a supportive team.

I have been very fortunate to have the help of several technical reviewers who verified the book's technical accuracy, reviewed its flow, and critiqued my writing style. Their feedback was indispensable, and along the way they caught many blunders and goofs that otherwise might have found their way into the final version. Any remaining blunders and goofs are mine alone. Many thanks to Derek H. Lawless and John P. McCartan of Solutech, Inc.; Ben Baird; Joseph LeVasseur; and William R. Epp.

My good friend Robert Patterson served as both a formal reviewer and an informal critic. Over the last year, we have had numerous discussions of the material in this book, and he consistently provided the honest and often blunt criticisms my work needed. He also holds the distinction of being the individual responsible for convincing me to become a professional developer. The world may never forgive him.

And, finally, I would like to thank my wife, Dee, who somehow managed to put up with my head being buried in research materials and my computer for a year while I wrote this book. She's my strongest supporter and without her this book would not have been possible.

PART I

Development Prerequisites

This part addresses aspects of software development that traditionally take place before formal programming begins. In chapter 1, we start with some general topics and see why Visual Basic is usually a good choice of tools for most projects at most companies and then see when and why it is not. Although VB is a tool that facilitates Rapid Application Development, we will also discover how and why most software projects fail, even with the advantages RAD technologies provide. Chapter 2 turns our attention to software lifecycle models to decide whether they make sense for your Visual Basic projects.

Chapter 3 introduces requirements gathering and use case analyses. Here we'll discover how to drive a project from user requirements to finished product, integrating quality assurance into the whole process. Finally, chapter 4 takes a look at the "big picture" of the software development process and describes how to plan and estimate VB projects.

Chapter 1

Rapid Application Development with Visual Basic

This chapter lays the groundwork for the rest of the book. We will begin by introducing Rapid Application Development and explaining its impact on corporate development. Then we will explore Visual Basic (VB) as a tool, comparing it to other languages and describing the types of business applications for which it is most applicable. We'll end with an extended look at why software projects fail and learn how to avoid key pitfalls.

Rapid Application Development

As a professional in the software industry, I am constantly noticing the strain on software development to better itself, especially corporate software development. Indeed, the last twenty years have seen companies struggle with software that is both too difficult to use and unnecessarily cumbersome to create. Recently, however, software development as a whole has been making very visible signs of progress. For example, the shift toward more friendly user interfaces (in the form of GUIs) and the emergence of component-based software development (based on COM or CORBA, for example) are two clear indications that software *should be* both easier to use and simpler to create than it was even just a few years ago. Unfortunately, it seems that as the technologies improve the demands placed on the industry intensify. Rather than moving forward by leaps and bounds, the industry is treading water to stay afloat, even with the recent progress. Software development has fallen into a vicious cycle: the better it gets, the more people expect of it.

Enter the *Rapid Application Development* (RAD) process. RAD simply means to develop software quickly, especially more quickly than you do now (McConnell, 1996). However, in practice, this phrase has become somewhat loaded, and it is often difficult to pin down an exact definition. Many people refer to it as any process involving new fourth-generation visual programming tools such as Delphi, PowerBuilder, and, of course, Visual Basic. Others think of RAD as a method of building software out of preexisting, reusable pieces (components), and there are still other definitions. However, no matter what the intended meaning, most companies want to say they are a part of it.

Because of the popularity of RAD, the term usually carries more power than it really deserves. Companies want to believe that RAD is the silver bullet for their software development troubles (Brooks, 1995). Panicked software managers will often relax under its spell, believing it will magically solve all of their problems. In reality, for most companies, it is little more than a placebo, providing a false sense of security, setting unrealistic expectations, and causing undue scheduling pressure. Because of the complacency it encourages, RAD can often create more problems than it solves. Simply put, RAD is overrated: even with its effective use, software construction remains complicated and inconsistent (Krutchen, 1999).

Visual Basic is certainly the most popular and pervasive RAD tool, and in many circles, particularly dedicated VB shops, the two are synonymous. Consequently, Visual Basic picks up many of the trappings of the phrase Rapid Application Development. Throughout this book, we shall work to overturn these misconceptions and put both RAD and especially VB in a new perspective. We shall see that they cannot *automagically* make up for poor managerial practices or fix failed methodologies. On the contrary, they can make the methodologies fail faster. We will discover that Visual Basic is not the software savior and that it has its fair share of weaknesses. Nevertheless, we shall also see that VB, when used properly, has many strengths and that it can be a wonderful all-purpose tool.

Picking the Right Tool for the Job

Because economics drive companies to try to complete software projects as quickly as possible and because Visual Basic has the reputation of being *the* Rapid Application Development tool, it follows that many corporations choose VB as their default tool. Consequently, it has become a one-size-fits-all language. This all-purpose nature is both its strongest and its weakest feature.

Indeed, VB *can* do most of the tasks that companies need it to do. However, a screwdriver *can* do many of the things a carpenter needs to do as well. It can drill a hole, hammer a nail, cut a board, measure a length, and even drive in a screw. Yet, it would be ludicrous to expect a carpenter to have only a screw-driver in his toolbox. While screwdrivers are good at driving in screws, they are quite bad at measuring lengths and hammering nails (though on occasion I have tried!) and are exceptionally bad at drilling holes and cutting boards. Like-wise, it is ludicrous to think that companies would flatly consider only one tool. Yet this is precisely what they do, and more often than not, VB is that tool.

So why is it that companies often do not look beyond VB? There are a num-ber of good and not so good reasons. Consider the following:

- Microsoft has been pushing VB as an enterprise-level solution since ver-sion 4. Its release roughly corresponded with the release of the much-anticipated Windows 95, and it got an extra push because of the timing. Microsoft's marketing is influential, to say the least.

- Companies like stability, and Microsoft is a stable, reliable company that is likely to be here tomorrow. With the quickly changing landscape of the software industry, it is difficult to say this about many tool providers. For example, rumors of instability plagued Borland, and even with its strong tool set, the rumors were damaging.

- VB is a good general-purpose programming tool, and some companies may not feel that they need a more involved tool set to accomplish their goals successfully.

- Other tools (especially C and C++ based tools) are more difficult to use, even if they are more reliable and more powerful. Therefore training is more expensive, and software development takes more time with them in most cases.

- There are over three million VB programmers in the world, and it is gener-ally accepted to be the most widely known computer language, making it easier to find programmers who can work in VB than in Delphi or C++.

- Some companies mistakenly believe that VB programmers rarely require training and whatever training is required is cheaper than it would be for other tools.

- Caught up in buzzwords, corporations want a RAD tool, and VB is the most popular.

Visual Basic versus Other Tools

Given the opportunity, Visual Basic can complement other tools quite well. For example, Visual Basic works well with the other tools in Microsoft's Visual Stu-dio. There is a great deal of overlap between the feature sets of each tool, but each has its own strengths and weaknesses. As a good general-purpose language, Visual Basic is ideal for creating user interfaces and small- to medium-scale applications. On the other extreme, Visual C++ can create solid ActiveX components and is a very powerful tool, but is quite difficult to use because of the overhead involved with learning the workings of the Microsoft Foundation Classes (MFC) or ActiveX Template Library (ATL). It is typical to find VB used for the user interface and client-side development and VC++ used for controls, business components, and server-side applications.

Table 1.1 compares Visual Basic, Java-based tools (like Visual J++), Delphi, and Visual C++. Each is a general-purpose tool to some degree. Delphi, which descends from the language Pascal, and Visual Basic are generally the two easiest to use, though in different ways. As Bruce McKinney put it, "Visual Basic makes the easy things easier; Delphi makes the hard things easier" (McKinney, 1999a). Visual C++ is arguably the most powerful: in the Windows world, if you cannot do it in VC++, it can't be done. This is certainly not true of Visual Basic, though VB can do what most companies need a tool to do. I think Java has gotten more hype than it deserves, and since it is such a young language it remains to be seen how pervasive it will be as a corporate development tool.

When training is an issue, Visual Basic usually wins out over Visual C++. In my experience, the learning curves of Visual Basic and Visual C++ vary dramatically. Although actual development times for the two languages are difficult to pin down because it is rare to find them being used for exactly the same purpose, I have summarized my findings in Figure 1.1, which compares the learning curves of Visual Basic and Visual C++ as they relate to program complexity and time. On the graph, the time to learn to program a task appears on the hor-

TABLE 1.1   Major Programming Tools Compared

Tool	Pros	Cons
Visual Basic	Easy to use Great for creating user interface Can edit code while running	Slow code Buggy IDE General instabilities
Java-based tools	Platform independence (sort of) Strong Internet capabilities	Slow code Limited functionality Not yet well-suited for desktop apps
Delphi	Easy to use Very fast code Outstanding string manipulation Elegant language (Pascal)	Small user base More difficult to find developers
Visual C++	Extremely powerful Very fast code	Difficult to use More complicated code Longer development time (typically)

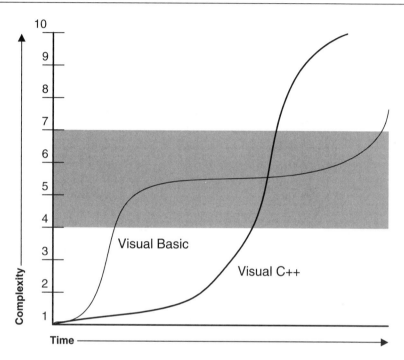

FIGURE 1.1   Learning Curves for Visual Basic and Visual C++

izontal axis, in arbitrary units. The complexity of the task appears on the vertical axis. It covers a range of 1 to 10, where a 1 is a program of the "Hello
World!" variety and a 10 represents an extremely complicated application. I
have found that, in practice, most corporations do the bulk of their development in the middle ground of complexity, between 4 and 7 (shaded), though
there are exceptions on either extreme. The learning curves themselves are
based on individuals with little or no programming experience.

As Figure 1.1 shows, with Visual Basic, you can learn to code programs of
moderate complexity relatively quickly, whereas even simple Visual C++ programs take a while to learn to write. VB's simple Integrated Development Environment (IDE) allows developers to jump right in, whereas the overhead of
learning MFC stifles VC++ developers. Visual C++ programmers also tend to
have a hard time learning about pointers, something that most VB programmers
never have to face. Eventually, however, for very complex programs, VC++ actually becomes easier to learn as a tool, because of Visual Basic's learning curve's
characteristic "dead spot." As a language, Visual Basic attempts to hide much of
its inner workings from the developer. For simple projects, this is a blessing,
since the programmer can concentrate more on the big picture and less on the

details of implementation. However, as a program's complexity increases, this crutch becomes a frustrating nightmare. Consequently, a plateau appears in VB's learning curve (the dead spot), and with complex programs it can take some time and experience to figure out how to make VB work for you rather than against you.

Note that Microsoft has dramatically improved the IDE for VC++ over the last few releases and may continue to do so, making it easier to learn and use. I heard rumors that Microsoft wanted to give all tools in Visual Studio the same (or a similar) IDE, but this has yet to materialize. If it does, I hope it is as intuitive as the existing VB IDE (are you listening, Microsoft?).

Because of the babying that Visual Basic provides to programmers, many developers (especially hardcore C++ developers) consider it a "toy" language. Since VB is capable of accomplishing nontrivial tasks, this is obviously a myth. The same developers who think writing a 10,000-line "Hello World!" program is the ultimate sign of machismo typically are the ones who hold this belief. I think it is more masochism than machismo. While C++ is certainly a more powerful language, companies often do not need that extra power to complete their projects. The bottom line is that when used correctly, VB can produce simple, highly maintainable code in a short amount of time.

Myth 1
Visual Basic is a "toy" language that cannot be used for serious software development.

Choosing a Version of Visual Basic

There are now three major versions of VB in common use: versions 4, 5, and 6. (Version 3 is still around, but I am aware of very little new development still using it.) Version 4 was a milestone in the history of Visual Basic, since it was the first to introduce object-oriented functionality and allow the creation of 32-bit applications. However, the performance of VB 4 applications was atrocious, and very large applications were extremely difficult, if not impossible, to create. Trade magazines in 1996 were littered with stories about companies with high hopes for their large VB 4 projects that ended up switching to another tool, sometimes in the middle of the project.

Version 5 helped performance immensely by improving form loading and adding native code compilation. It also added a handful of new object-oriented features, changed the IDE, and began the movement to push VB into the world of web development. VB 6, the latest version, improves server-side features and adds new wizards. For me it is a disappointing release because, server features aside, for the most part it is a lot like version 5, only with more bugs. It would have been nice to see some real features added to the language (such as inheritance, which has been talked about since version 4.0), rather than all of the gloss.

So which of these versions is right for you? The answer depends on your projects. Generally, for new projects either VB 5 or VB 6 is the best choice, though VB 5 is certainly the more stable of the two. VB 6 is great for Internet applications, but for general client-side development is still not as reliable as VB 5 because of the bugs. In addition, some of VB 6's new client-side features (string functions, new controls, etc.) are not all they are cracked up to be. Be sure to review the discussion of the new features of VB 6 in chapter 12. In short, if you already have VB 5, there is probably no great need to run out and get version 6 for your new projects.

If you are looking to upgrade from an earlier version, be sure to look before you leap. Upgrading successfully from version 3 to a later version usually requires quite bit of code tweaking, and you will need to replace all VBXs (16-bit controls) with 32-bit OCXs. However, to truly take advantage of the object-oriented features of the later versions, you will probably have to redesign your applications from scratch, and in the end it may not be worth the trouble. Directly porting VB 3 applications to a later version is unlikely to solve many problems, though it will make the tool set current.

Converting from version 4 to version 5 or 6 is less painful, but still not automatic. In general, most VB 4 applications port well, and the new features in versions 5 and 6 make the transition well worth the effort. If you want to upgrade from VB 5 to VB 6, remember that VB 6 offers very few new features for client-

---

◆ Upgrading Visual Basic

If you are considering upgrading to a higher version of Visual Basic, remember these points: Each new release can read most of the code created with earlier versions, but the reverse is obviously not true, so be sure to have a backup plan if the transition ends up causing too many problems. I have worked on VB 4 to VB 5 conversions for companies that had to restart the conversion process several times before actually succeeding. Also, installing two versions of VB on the same PC (with one operating system) is a delicate process, and you are likely to run into significant problems with the earlier version. This has been true of every major version upgrade and is one of the most striking problems with the series.

Furthermore, Visual Basic does not uninstall well, so it is virtually impossible to downgrade the version of VB on a PC without reinstalling the operating system. I recommend keeping the different versions of VB on completely separate PCs, or at least on a dual-boot system, while making the transition. Last, even seemingly innocent service packs can cause transition problems, so be sure to time your upgrades wisely.

side development. Should you take the plunge? I generally recommend upgrading from VB 5 to VB 6 only if you need to take advantage of VB 6's new Web features—the other features aren't worth the trouble. I expect many companies will skip VB 6 altogether and transition from VB 5 to VB 7 when it is released.

Business Tasks Best Suited for Visual Basic

We have seen how Visual Basic stacks up against some of the other tools on the market and have reviewed the different versions of VB. Now let's look at the types of tasks for which it is especially well suited. Luckily, as mentioned earlier, there is a strong correlation between what VB does well and what companies need a tool to accomplish for them.

User Interface Creation

The strongest feature of Visual Basic is the ease with which it can create Windows user interfaces. It is arguably the best tool available for this task. For client applications that are of small or medium complexity, VB is generally the only tool needed and can handle data access, business logic, and user interface elements well. For larger or more complex applications, it is best used in conjunction with other tools (e.g., C++, MTS). In these situations, VB provides the user interface and interacts with the other tools, which handle the bulk of grunt work.

Client/Server Development

Visual Basic is also a fine tool for general data access in client/server applications. When used in conjunction with MS SQL, Oracle, Access, or some other Relational Database Management System (RDMS), VB can provide elaborate editing and querying functionality. It is suited for single-user and multiuser applications, and for both pessimistic and optimistic locking. See chapter 13 for a discussion of data access.

Legacy System Rewrites

One of the prevalent types of applications companies develop today is the legacy system rewrite. These legacy programs are typically host-based applications with propriety databases running on some system developed long before any members of its current support staff were born. They are often slow, difficult to learn, expensive to maintain, and impossible to expand. Many corporations, fearing repercussions from the Year 2000 problem, or seeking to add some sex appeal to their applications, choose to rewrite these systems in a specialized client/server architecture. Visual Basic is often the tool of choice for the front end of such rewrites, for the reasons just described. The introduction of OLE DB and ADO makes it even easier for Visual Basic to access proprietary data sources consistently. Refer to chapter 14 for a detailed discussion of OLE DB, OLE DB providers, and ADO.

The main problem with using Visual Basic for legacy system rewrites is that sometimes companies do not fully realize what they are getting themselves into. Falling into the silver bullet trap discussed earlier, they think that VB will solve all of their problems. In reality, the transition from a hosted system to a client/server system or *n*-tier system involves a *fundamental change* in the way companies use, develop, and maintain software. It requires an entirely different support structure and is not something that can be done casually. With an appropriate plan of action, though, legacy system rewrites with Visual Basic can be very successful.

ActiveX Controls

If you are considering writing custom ActiveX controls, Visual Basic can simplify things, provided the control is not too complex. VB is especially good at creating controls derived (subclassed) from existing controls. If your controls need extensive drawing, require elaborate API messaging, or are exceedingly complicated, consider another tool. Chapter 15 discusses custom control creation further.

Business Tasks Not Suited for Visual Basic

There are also a number of tasks for which Visual Basic is not the ideal choice. This is not necessarily to say that VB cannot do these tasks, but rather they are not its forte, and you are typically safer considering another tool. Level of performance and degree of reliability are usually the deciding factors when determining what tool to use for a task, and in the following situations, VB receives low marks.

Generally speaking, server-side applications, especially Windows NT services, are unreliable in Visual Basic. This includes both isolated daemon-type programs with no interaction with other applications and more elaborate remote servers (using DCOM and MTS, for example). While it is possible to create Windows NT services in Visual Basic, Microsoft does not recommend it because of some peculiar behavior. With this warning presented, we will explore Windows NT services and server-side components in chapter 16. If your server-side component does not need to be 100 percent reliable, Visual Basic may be a viable solution, and there has been some improvement in the creation of MTS components.

Applications that are load-intensive or need to run as quickly as possible are best created with another tool, since VB does not handle either of these requirements well. Similarly, graphics-intensive applications, especially ones with a great deal of animation, such as games, are difficult to pull off with Visual Basic.

Applications that must be 100 percent reliable (for the medical industry, for example) are also difficult to do in Visual Basic, since there are so many potentially serious points of failure in the language that are beyond the control of the programmer. Furthermore, as a fourth-generation language, Visual Basic's easy-to-

TABLE 1.2 Suitability of Visual Basic for Common Projects

Task/Project Description	*Suitable for VB?*
Creation of any type of Windows graphical user interface	Yes
Graphics-intensive applications or applications with extensive animation	No
General client-side applications, of low to medium complexity and scale	Yes
General client-side applications, of high complexity and large scale	No
Server-side applications and services	No
Mission-critical applications requiring high performance and reliability	No
General client/server data access	Yes
Extensive low-level file access	No
Legacy system rewrite (specialized client/server, accessing a proprietary database)	Yes
Simple ActiveX controls, created through subclassing.	Yes
Complicated ActiveX controls	No
Add-ins for Visual Basic	Yes

use file capabilities are typically not sophisticated enough for serious file access considerations, as in a homegrown database management system (DBMS).

To summarize these points, Table 1.2 lists common projects and tasks required of software tools in the corporate world, along with a very general recommendation of whether Visual Basic alone is a suitable tool for the job. Again, just because Table 1.2 lists a task or project as not suitable for Visual Basic does not necessarily mean that VB is incapable of rendering a solution for it. Rather it means that you would probably be better off implementing it with another tool, perhaps in conjunction with VB.

Project Failure

Successful projects are those that meet the functional requirements, are delivered on time, and cost no more than originally anticipated. However, practical dogma suggests that it is reasonable to expect at least one corner of this "time–cost–quality" triangle to miss the target. Companies may dub these projects successful nevertheless. This is especially true when one or two of the corners miss the target, but the third does better than expected (e.g., it may have been late, but it was cheap).

While in some cases these partial successes may be acceptable, outright failures never are. Since it is usually easier to pin down what makes a particular project fail as opposed to what makes one succeed, let's look at an extended example, in the sidebar "Project Failure," of an unsuccessful project that fails on all three counts. We will use this example as a point of reference in the remainder of this section. In situations like this, the projects are usually late or canceled. Everyone comes away from the experience with a bit of animosity, blaming everyone else for the failure. Morale is destroyed, and money is wasted. It is not a pretty sight, but it is typical.

While the sidebar example of a failed project is fabricated, in the real world most projects *do* fail. According to the Standish Group's infamous CHAOS report,

◆ Project Failure: An Example

XYZ, Inc., decided to create a new application, GizmoApp, to help streamline many of the manual processes its business community followed on a daily basis. The project did not have a strong sponsor, and the user community did not devote much attention to defining the requirements of GizmoApp. They eventually slapped together some sample screens and simple functional requirements, and handed the project over to the development team.

Because of the user community's apathy, the development team got the requirements for the software late. Since they were already behind, they decided to get to work immediately. The scope of the project was large, but since they had just finished a similar project, they were convinced that with enough hard work it could be done. While the previous project was both late and over budget, they believed they knew what they had done wrong and were not about to repeat their mistakes.

First, they started with some design—just enough to get a good feeling about the project and to say that the design had been done. They really did not feel they needed to do more, and they were pressed for time anyway, so they jumped right into coding.

They worked on the user interface first. The programmers spent a good deal of their time polishing its appearance, moving buttons and searching the Internet for pretty icons, leaving the difficult algorithms and data access for later. Consequently, it looked like they were making a lot of progress because the most highly visible aspect of the system, the user interface, looked great.

Halfway through, the users reviewed the project during a dog-and-pony show. The beauty of the screens stunned the users, and they happily reported all was well to their superiors. Encouraged by the users, the programmers continued to crank out the code.

Sadly, it did not take long for concerns to arise. They ran into serious problems late in the development cycle when they realized that their simple design was flawed and that they had completely missed a couple of key requirements. Some of these requirements had to be omitted, since the amount of rework it would have taken to include them was astounding. Everyone continued to work lots of overtime to keep patching the numerous holes.

To complicate things further, the users decided to change the user interface completely, and all of the work the developers had done on it was for nothing. Although they eventually did finish, the project was a failure. They missed the delivery schedule, ran over budget because of the delays and the overtime, and had to leave out features that the design could not support.

in large companies, less than 10 percent of projects are on time and on budget. The study shows that 31.1 percent of projects are canceled prior to completion and that 52.7 percent of projects end up costing 189 percent of their original estimates. Things are better for smaller companies, but still remarkably disappointing (The Standish Group, 1995). Other studies have yielded similar results.

So, what are all of these projects doing wrong? Sources covering software project management are loaded with examples of "worst practices," covering everything from poor coding techniques to managerial blunders. We'll discuss good and bad programming habits in chapter 11. As for other causes of project failure, my own top-ten list appears in Exhibit 1.1. In creating this list, I drew on the existing writings in the field and my own experience (Booch, 1999; Maguire, 1994; McConnell, 1996, 1998; Royce, 1998). I will discuss these ten causes in detail. You may also refer to the sources listed at the end of the chapter for further discussion of these and other issues.

Most of the items in the list apply to software development in general, but in some cases, using Visual Basic as a tool potentially makes them worse. Where appropriate, VB-specific problems are noted in the discussion that follows. Much of this book revolves around preventing and solving these problems.

EXHIBIT 1.1 Top Ten Reasons for Software Project Failure
_____

1. Failure to assess and manage risk
2. Lack of appropriate quality assurance mechanisms
3. Poor understanding of the requirements
4. Poor communication, especially between primary stakeholders and developers
5. Unrealistic goals
6. Lack of or poor design
7. Arbitrary or artificial assessments of progress
8. Weak team members
9. Lack of employee focus
10. Promotion of talented technical people out of their roles

---

Failure to Assess and Manage Risk

In my experience, poor risk assessment and management is the single most common mistake made in corporate development, and it is also the most devastating to project success rates. By risk, I mean any potential problem that could affect the project, from ill-conceived requirements to problematic personnel. For a variety of reasons, many of the players involved in the creation of software are often unwilling to be the bearers of bad news. This is true at all levels of the corporate hierarchy. Consequently, they hide or ignore risk early in the development process, relying on hope rather than formal risk management. Even in cases in which everyone is forthcoming about the *known* risks, there rarely is a proactive mechanism for detecting *unknown* ones. Worst of all, there is seldom a contingency plan, or a way to deal with the risk when it manifests itself as a full-scale problem. Many project plans have extra time built in for a couple of "Oh, my Goshes" and a "Holy Cow!" but this is not proactive risk management. Note that the later a risk is discovered in the process, the more likely it is that it will become a damaging problem. Therefore, early risk detection and management are *critical*.

When it comes to the programming aspect of a project, using Visual Basic as the development tool can make risk detection more difficult. This is because VB makes it very easy to create attractive user interfaces that give the appearance of progress on the project. In reality, the user interface is often only dressing, and its sexiness can detract from other more important issues. In the "Project Failure" sidebar, the users had no reason to question the status of the project, since they were very impressed with the user interface. The positive feedback encouraged the developers, and the serious defects went unexplored. In effect, VB pulls the wool over everyone's eyes.

Visual Basic can also be a fun language to work in, and sometimes programmers are blind to potential problems in their code because they are having so much fun. I remember a humorous list of ways to shoot yourself in the foot in various programming languages that circulated on the Internet. For Visual Basic, the gist was that you can shoot yourself in the foot, but you have so much fun doing so that you don't even realize it. Who wants to worry about assessing risk when you are having fun?

Lack of Appropriate Quality Assurance Mechanisms

When many companies think of quality assurance, they imagine a small group of their more experienced users testing the software when it is finished. However, to be most *effective*, successful quality assurance mechanisms must pervade *every aspect* of development. Though it is common occurrence in corporate development, formal quality assurance cannot be relegated to the last 5 or 10 percent of the project's time, no matter how small the project. Ideally, the primary stakeholders, typically the users, should become involved even in those areas that they traditionally shy away from: analysis and design. With proactive quality assurance throughout the process, teams detect problems early, making them easier (and therefore cheaper) to fix.

This book covers several aspects of quality assurance that are often neglected by members of the development team, including the following:

◆ *Debugging and units testing:* Coders often make the worst testers. Although they may know how to break the code, out of a sense of personal

◆ Stakeholders

Throughout this text, I use the term *stakeholder*. A stakeholder is any individual who has, directly or indirectly, some degree of vested interest in a project. As you would expect, the amount of personal stake in the project a person has varies from individual to individual. Members of the user community are often quite vested, and I refer to them as *primary stakeholders*. Any individual who is actively concerned about the project is a primary stakeholder. *Secondary stakeholders* may include managers and developers. Management is often too busy with many other projects to become vested in any one in particular, while developers, out of sheer pride, tend to become at least moderately vested in any project they get involved with.

This is not to say that on occasion developers are not primary stakeholders or that users always are. I present these cases as examples. The important point is that primary stakeholders will tend to be more adamant about the project because they are more attached to it. Such involvement makes for interesting office dynamics.

pride they want to avoid finding bugs. Yet, developers can prevent many bugs with thorough unit testing and debugging habits, as discussed in chapters 17 and 18. With Visual Basic, it is especially difficult to develop good debugging habits because programmers can code so quickly that they do not think their work is complicated enough to merit thorough debugging.

◆ *Formal testing:* Chapter 18 provides an overview of solid testing procedures. It covers most types of testing that should take place during a project, including unit testing, batch testing, integration testing, system testing, beta testing, and regression testing.

◆ *Code reviews:* Code reviews are designed to provide a mechanism for ensuring that source code is up to the company's standards. They also provide a great opportunity for developers to examine one another's code and to spot potential problems before they become issues. Coding standards and code reviews are covered in chapters 19 and 20.

Poor Understanding of Requirements

This problem applies not only to the technical teams involved in the project, but also to the user community that spearheads the creation of the requirements. Obviously, the programmers and technical managers need to have a firm grasp of what it is they are trying to do. These individuals can miss the boat for many reasons, including poor communication. In many cases, the technical people are the ones who are ultimately responsible for the success or failure of the project. Because of this, it is crucial that technical teams verify that the users really know what they are asking for, so that everyone is clear. Moreover, the users often are not sure what they want, even if they claim that they do. The users may even ask for features that do not make sense technically. When this happens, it is the responsibility of the technical teams to review the requirements and let the users know the potential consequences of their requests (increased cost, unexpected behavior, etc.). I mention all of these points not to belittle technical managers or make dolts out of users, but to stress that requirements are tricky business. All involved parties need to be sure that they are proactively helping the process, not hindering it. Ultimately, you need to know what the problem is *before* you can solve it. Employing use cases and scenarios (chapter 3) can help.

Poorly defined requirements can be very costly to a project. For each requirement that is misunderstood, poorly documented, or omitted, you will pay 50 to 200 times more to correct it during coding as you would to get it right the first time (McConnell, 1998). With such penalties, a project with poorly considered requirements is all but doomed to failure.

A related issue is the misguided belief that the requirements of a project can be set in stone before work begins and will remain fixed for the duration of the project. Most projects will experience at least *some* scope creep. Taking more time to define the requirements can help prevent this or at least minimize it. However, companies still must build mechanisms for dealing with changing scope into their development processes and learn to adjust project plans accordingly. For an excellent discussion of change control, see Steve McConnell's *Software Project Survival Guide* (McConnell, 1998).

Poor Communication, Especially between Primary Stakeholders and Developers

I have heard many developers say to users, "If that's what you wanted, why didn't you say so in the first place?" Typically, misunderstandings are the result of poor documentation or a lack of a common language for defining problems and goals. Remember that when discussing the solution to a problem, developers and other stakeholders tend to look at things from entirely different angles. Whereas business managers may see the benefits of expanding a particular solution to fit other parts of the business, programmers are already thinking of the coolest way to implement it. Some simple processes can help bridge this communications gap. See the discussion of the Unified Modeling Language (UML) in chapters 3 and 9.

Besides stakeholders and developers, it is typical to find other instances of poor communication as well. For example, development teams working as separate groups on different parts of the same system often work in communication silos, hoping to integrate their respective parts magically when they are finished. As outsourcing becomes a more popular option for software development, this problem becomes more serious. Issues with communication may also exist between members of the same team, especially between management and the people in the trenches. Proactive measures designed to open communication channels, such as short status meetings, can help.

Unrealistic Goals

Corporations do not make software because it is fun. The business community at companies treats IT/IS (where most corporate software development takes place) as providers of an important service, but not as the primary drivers of the business. The business community typically spearheads development and usually pays for it. Moreover, there is an economic reason for virtually every decision made during the lifetime of a software project.

Most companies are overly ambitious and expect projects to live up to unrealistic goals in the areas of time, cost, or scope. Project parameters are rarely based on estimates of *how long* it will really take, *how much* it will actually cost, or *what features* can really be included. Rather, these thresholds are dictated by business priorities; that is, they *substantiate the needs* of the business community. First the business community defines the target parameters, and then the project's estimates (time, cost, scope) are put into place to fall into line with the target. The rationale for such "fudging" may be to win a proposal or funding—a seemingly positive result in the eyes of most parties involved (Royce, 1998). Nevertheless, the real result is that the business community may have unrealistic expectations of the project. Initial estimates in the areas of time, cost, and scope are typically way out of line, but are as generous as possible from the standpoint of business needs.

Furthermore, when those creating the estimates know that Visual Basic is the tool, they may be tempted to cut the estimates. Since Visual Basic is so simple to code in, many believe development should be able to happen more quickly. Sometimes this is the case, but VB is not a silver bullet for all scheduling problems.

Insisting on unrealistic goals can also damage morale. Whereas sales and marketing teams may be motivated by impossible goals, developers tend to be more logical and pragmatic. Realizing that the goals are unachievable, they lose motivation (McConnell, 1998).

However, what is perhaps most problematic about unrealistic goals is that even when a company comes to the conclusion that the original estimates were unrealistic, they still are reluctant to change them. Sometimes people are afraid that their superiors might construe such backpedaling as an admission of failure, so they shun it like the plague. To avoid this problem, companies need to modify estimates aggressively as a project progresses. This allows realistic expectations to be set. Initial estimates are provisional, and they should feature a built-in margin of error, for example, "it will take between ten and sixteen weeks" (McConnell, 1996). As the project moves forward, proof-of-concept analyses can help generate estimates that are more precise (see chapter 4). These issues are related to risk management (see Exhibit 1.1, reason 1) and communication (see reason 4).

Lack of or Poor Design

As I will mention throughout this book, I believe that 90 percent of the benefit of doing something comes from the process of doing it, not from the result. This is most certainly true of design. Most companies simply *do not spend nearly enough* time on design. According to Barry Boehm, it is 100 times more costly to fix a problem after delivery than in the design phase (Royce, 1998). This statistic alone makes it clear that design is a critical element in economic success.

It is common to find shortcuts being taken with design. Managers may know that design should be done and ask the programmers to do it. Lazy programmers may produce as simple a design document as possible, believing that their managers will not know the difference. The managers feel better because they have done their job in demanding a design, and the programmers are happy because it did not take very long to fake it. The result is that everyone is content, but a thorough design is still lacking.

With Visual Basic, there is a strong temptation to forgo design and jump right into coding. Programmers do this because VB programming can be fun. Managers often do this because they do not think that VB is a serious enough language for VB projects to warrant design. Whatever the reason, a lack of design can have very damaging results. Part II of this book is devoted to designing Visual Basic solutions.

Myth 2
Visual Basic projects do not require serious design.

Note that too much design, though uncommon, is also a problem. Over-engineering results in increased cost and overhead: not only does it take more time to design the system, but usually it also takes longer to implement and costs more to maintain. Furthermore, all interactions with the system (new subsystems, integration with other systems, etc.) become unnecessarily complicated, so its condition spreads. While it may be interesting to explore exotic and innovative solutions to a problem, in almost every instance the simplest solution is the best solution.

Arbitrary or Artificial Assessments of Progress

Most users and project managers (and their bosses and their bosses' bosses) have a more distant view of the actual status of a project than the coders working in the trenches. Often they refer to the most highly visible aspects of the system as indications of the status of the whole project. A quick dog-and-pony show of the application is typically enough to satisfy the curiosity of management, who feels better about the project because they have seen something tactile. The problem is that simple checks of the visible aspects of the system, such as the user interface or polished documentation, are misleading and are not accurate status indicators for the whole project (McConnell, 1996).

To gain a realistic depiction of the status of the system, a thorough understanding of the requirements and an accurate schedule are required. Prototypes and proof-of-concept models can help reveal weaknesses in the system and may be used as baselines for measuring the progress of the project itself.

Weak Team Members

On occasion, every development team finds itself with one particularly weak team member. This individual may be a contractor or a full-time employee, a new member or a veteran. He or she may be a weak member for any number of reasons, such as the following:

- Poor technical skills
- Poor work ethic
- Unusually poor communication skills
- Inability to work effectively with other members of the team (disruptive behavior/attitude problems)

Project leaders should remove weak team members as quickly as possible. They are typically easy to spot, though sometimes their weaknesses become apparent only through the grumbling of the other team members, who are often reluctant to complain directly to management. Removing a team member does not necessarily mean firing him or her; perhaps the individual's skills are more suited to another project or another team. The important thing is to act quickly, since the longer a poor team member remains on the team, the more legitimacy he or she receives (McConnell, 1996).

Poor team members can damage more than just the morale of a team. I heard a true story of one domineering team lead with a team of four talented but young, quiet programmers. Their assignment was to code a large subsystem of a huge system. On paper, the team lead was an experienced developer, and he carefully controlled every aspect of his team's progress. The team worked hard for almost a year, producing only a few deliverables along the way. Throughout the year, the other teams grumbled about the poor state of the code, and the number of bugs dismayed the testing staff. In spite of his credentials, everyone knew it was because of the ineptitude of the team lead, but management did nothing about it, worried that any change of direction on the already late project would mean certain doom. After about a year, when the subsystem was supposed to be finished, the code was in such poor shape that another team had to completely rewrite it. The more than 10,000 man-hours spent by the original team were utterly wasted. In this case, management's failure to act sooner cost the project hundreds of thousands of dollars and put the entire schedule in jeopardy.

Lack of Employee Focus

In the world of Rapid Application Development, it is common to find individuals working on several projects simultaneously, often referred to as multitasking. In and of itself, multitasking is not necessarily a bad thing: the individual may play an important, but ancillary role on all of the projects. It becomes a problem only when team members are the main potential points of failure for more than one project. An individual is a potential point of failure when one project requires 100 percent of his attention for it to have a good chance of succeeding. Obviously, a person cannot devote 100 percent of his or her time to more than one project, so something has to give. Consequently, when someone multitasks, all projects the individual works on suffer an increased chance of failure. This situation is best avoided simply by keeping the multitasking people out of roles that make them the main potential source of failure for a project. This is often easier said than done, since these important individuals typically have domain knowledge that is essential to all projects.

In addition to scheduling conflicts, other factors can affect the focus of the employees. These include environmental distractions, such as a noisy office or an inefficient workspace (McConnell, 1996), and other company distractions, such as unnecessary dog-and-pony shows for upper management, meetings not related to the project, and others.

Promotion of Talented Technical People Out of Their Roles

In IT/IS circles today, it is common to find limited options for the promotion of technical people. Consequently, the best developers quickly reach the top of the pay scale for their positions. Then they are promoted into positions of management, roles that are usually much less technical and that may not be suited for their skill set. In some cases, the promotion occurs only to be able to offer the talented developer more money in order to prevent attrition. The problem is that if the promoted developer makes a poor manager (and many do), *the company puts itself in double jeopardy:* not only has it lost a good developer, but it has also stuck itself with a poor manager.

There is no simple solution to this problem, and discussions of salary and corporate pay scales are always touchy. Companies need to strive to provide better ways of offering pay increases to senior members of their staff in order to keep the talented people who want to retain their technical roles.

To summarize, it is clear that a project can fail for many different reasons. Bad code can cause its fair share of problems. However, ultimately the most dangerous problems are related to weak development and managerial practices. Ironically, bad code is relatively easy to fix. Weak processes and management techniques are more delicate and difficult to correct. The next chapter discusses standard software development lifecycles that can help put projects on the right track from the start.

Further Reading

Steve McConnell, *Code Complete* (1993).   Although it concentrates primarily on coding practices, this book also covers software management processes to some degree. Much of the project management material here appears in *Rapid Development* in expanded form.

Steve McConnell, *Rapid Development* (1996).   This is an outstanding general reference about software management. His list of "Best Practices" echoes many of the solutions presented here.

Steve McConnell, *Software Project Survival Guide* (1998).   He's three for three. While this book also covers a lot of the material already presented in *Code Complete* and *Rapid Development*, there are some fresh twists. This is a relatively short book and makes for an easy, but valuable weekend read.

Bruce McKinney, "Hardcode Visual Basic: A Hardcore Declaration of Independence" (1999a).   This on-line article discusses McKinney's choice to leave Visual Basic and summarizes his experimentation with Delphi.

Walker Royce, *Software Project Management* (1998).   Part I of this book provides an outstanding assessment of the poor state of software development and introduces methods for preventing the problems plaguing traditional software management and development.

The Standish Group, *The CHAOS Report* (1995).   This report is available on-line and provides hard data stressing the poor state of software development.

Chapter 2

Software Lifecycle Models

So you are ready to begin that next big project. You have sharpened all of your pencils, cleaned off your whiteboard, and polished your monitor. But where do you really begin? As a developer or technical manager, you may have come onto the project long after it has been approved. Yet, your boss expects you to hit the ground running and provide a quality solution in a short amount of time for very little money. This sounds like a job for Visual Basic. You had better get started.

In this chapter, we'll look at how having a plan of action in the form of a solid project lifecycle model can help make your Visual Basic project a success.

Lifecycles

At the minimum, all software development involves two fundamental steps: defining the problem and implementing its solution. These two items need to happen in roughly sequential order, since it does not make sense to work on the solution of a problem before you have defined the problem. However, in practice, developers sometimes throw common sense out of the window and try to save time by trying to do both simultaneously. I'll never forget the first time one of my team leads came to me and said, "You go start coding, and I'll go figure out what they want." Nevertheless, for a software project of any complexity to be successful, there must be some kind of organizational guidelines—a plan of action giving structure to the realization of the two steps just named. A project's evolution from inception to completion is called its *lifecycle*. A description or illustration of the general plan of action guiding the evolution is a *lifecycle model*.

Employing a good lifecycle model is one of the essential steps in adopting a positive, proactive attitude toward software development. Good lifecycle models and the processes driving them are the cornerstones of successful projects. Besides helping to define the entire development process, there are three primary reasons to use such a model:

1. Without a formal plan of action as described by the model, software schedules cannot be predicted.

2. Software lifecycle models help to standardize the specific individual processes that comprise the overall development process. This gives users and developers alike a common frame of reference for discussions.

3. Applying a thorough lifecycle model helps improve the success rates of projects, since the model defines a practice that is potentially both successful and repeatable.

Table 2.1 details the steps involved in defining a problem and implementing a solution. A new software project usually begins because someone gets an idea. This person is often a member of the user community (a primary stakeholder) who seeks to simplify a manual process or to expand on software already in existence. With some help from the development team, the user community refines the idea. They ultimately generate a formal statement of what it is they want; in other words, they define the requirements of the system. Eventually someone performs a reality check to see if the project makes sense.

This proof-of-concept analysis serves to answer questions such as the following:

- *Money-related issues:* Is the project cost-effective? What kind of return on investment does it offer? Can we afford to do this?

- *Time-related issues:* When do we need it? Does the project have a feasible time frame?

- *Scope and quality issues:* How "polished" does the software need to be? Are the requirements realistic?

- *And most important, a simple gut check:* Do we really want to do this?

Once the stakeholders formally define the problem, they usually commit it to paper in the form of some kind of documentation, whether it be a proposal, a formal requirements listing, or something else.

TABLE 2.1   The Steps of Software Development

Steps	*Details*
Defining the Problem	Inception (the "idea")
	Requirements gathering (defining the problem's scope)
	Analysis of the problem (proof-of-concept)
	Documenting the problem
Solving the Problem	Technical analysis (estimating, scheduling, and staffing)
	Design (architecture, user interface, application, and database)
	Implementation (coding)
	Quality assurance (debugging, reviewing, and testing)
	Deployment
	Maintenance

While the user community continues to play a role throughout the development process, for the most part, technical teams (managers, developers, testers, etc.) take over during implementation. They do their own reality check, determine whether the project is technically feasible, and then begin the process of designing and implementing the solution. Quality assurance, which in the best lifecycle models permeates each step of the process, gets a strong push toward the end in the form of rigorous testing. Last, the team prepares the programs for deployment and continues with ongoing maintenance.

The details listed in Table 2.1 cover all of the important aspects of software development, although people may give them slightly different names. Some models omit or elide certain of these steps, and they may even present the details in a different order. I am not presenting these stages here to describe all models in detail, but rather to provide familiar terms for a frame of reference. We shall refer to these steps during our discussions in this chapter. Note also that the bulk of this book is organized around these detailed procedures. You may use them as guidelines as you adopt or create your own plan of action.

Common Lifecycle Models

Traditionally, software development has followed one of three general lifecycle models or some hybrid of these models. The models include the detailed steps in Table 2.1, and each has its strengths and weaknesses. The first, which I call the *brute force* approach, lacks a defining plan and is included here to provide an example of what not to do. The second, the *waterfall* model, is popular and relatively simple. The third, which I call the *spiral* model, builds on the waterfall, but adds iterations for a more robust model.

Brute Force (a.k.a. Code-Like-Hell)

If you were to ask even the greenest of rookie programmers and managers how one is *supposed* to write a program, they would typically give you some kind of summary of the steps in Table 2.1. However, although most may know what they are supposed to do, all too often they do not know how to do it. Alternatively, sometimes they do not have enough time. Faced with an impossible schedule and a demanding array of requirements, many teams eschew formal plans and roll up their sleeves. Sometimes the developers have gained a false sense of security from success on past similar projects. They mistakenly believe that if they did it before they can certainly do it again. On most projects, rather than relying on a proven methodology, development teams attack the problem with brute force. They work insane hours, fighting fires constantly. This model has also been referred to as the *code-and-fix* model or the *code-like-hell* model.

Myth 3
Brute force projects are repeatable, especially in Visual Basic.

If this sounds like a project you have worked on, you are not alone. Many of the projects I have been involved with did not follow a rigorous plan, and I have heard horror stories about disastrous projects from nearly everyone I have worked with. Most of these projects were doomed to failure from the beginning.

Steve McConnell (1996) discusses the problems with the brute force approach in *Rapid Development*. Some of his points are summarized in the following list:

1. *It provides a false feeling of accomplishment.* When using brute force, it seems like you are getting more done than you really are.
2. *It has a great deal of risk.* Brute force projects have a large failure rate even when done as efficiently as possible.
3. *It is unrepeatable.* The inconsistent nature of brute force makes it especially difficult to develop repeatable processes.
4. *It causes motivational problems.* People hate to work on projects that consistently fail.
5. *It wastes people's time.* All of the senseless overtime pulls people away from their lives.

Yet, individuals will often rigorously defend their decision not to use a formal lifecycle plan. Although most excuses are just panicked rationalizations, there are a few good ones as well. For example, it is time-consuming and costly to research and adopt a formal plan, since there is training to do and an infrastructure that must be laid down. With these constraints, it is sometimes difficult to find a project team willing to take on the challenge. Teams feel they do not have the time or resources to lay down this infrastructure themselves. In truth, the work need only be done once for all subsequent projects to gain some benefit from it. In short, while it may initially seem not worth the effort, in the end having a formal plan (a development philosophy) in place really pays off.

Rather than present an excuse for not having a formal model, sometimes projects fake it. They employ a very simple model (like design, code, fix), which is really nothing more than brute force with fancy trim. They may do this only to be able to say that they followed a plan, or they may believe that their project was too small or too time-constrained to devote more time to the process. When teams are using a plan only because they feel they have to, they may give the individual steps in the plan only cursory treatment. For example, in the design-code-fix model just mentioned, the entire design phase may in reality end up being a simple document thrown together without much thought. When they cut corners because of constraints in time, teams gain little benefit from the trimming they have added to the brute force model.

Myth 4
A project can be too small to merit use of a formal lifecycle model.

Though typically destined for failure from the start, projects relying on brute force sometimes can miraculously succeed. These exceptions usually involve some type of heroic, superhuman effort on the part of a few essential players. Ultimately, however, brute force projects are not predictable. The heroics of one project are seldom repeatable on another, and, as a result, brute force as a development technique is entirely unreliable.

Waterfall (a.k.a. Linear)

Many software projects employ some variation of what has become known as the waterfall model. The model gets its name from its appearance when depicted graphically, as in Figure 2.1. Starting from the upper left corner, the model features well-defined steps, which closely parallel those in Table 2.1. There are many styles of waterfall models. Some allow movement in both directions; others in only one. Some have overlapping steps, while others have isolated steps. And some have a different number of steps than shown here.

Waterfall models are popular because they feature individual steps in which work on an isolated aspect of the system (its design or the implementation, for

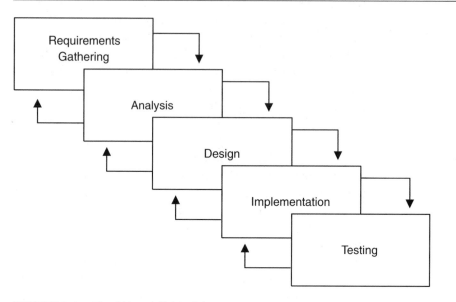

FIGURE 2.1 The Waterfall Model

example) can take place. Usually teams produce some type of deliverable at the end of each step, whether it is code, an object model, or written documentation. Waterfall models are also popular because they lend themselves well to simple project plans, which tend to be temporally linear. In general, work on one section of the model is finished before moving on to the next, though, as Figure 2.1 shows, there may be some overlap. For example, it is common to begin coding some parts of the system before others have been thoroughly designed.

Disregarding the potential overlap, waterfall models are inherently linear. A project progresses down the waterfall from step to step until it is completed. Note that, as Figure 2.1 shows, it is also possible to move back up the waterfall to the previous step. In practice, however, this proves to be difficult, just as it is much more difficult to travel up a real waterfall than down one (just ask a salmon). Also, note that because it is linear, it is not practically possible to skip steps, though they can be given a cursory treatment.

The biggest problem with the waterfall model is that it does not have inherent early risk detection. Furthermore, waterfall-based projects tend to gather too much momentum, and it is difficult to change the course of development late in a project. With these two factors combined, it is common to find problems in a project (for example, a flawed design or misunderstood requirements) too far into the time line to be able to do much about them.

Even with these weaknesses, the waterfall model is far better than no model. It is especially well suited for shorter projects of limited scope—projects with simple, well-defined requirements. Spiral models, discussed next, build on the basic waterfall design to address its weaknesses. They are more useful on more complex projects.

Spiral (a.k.a. Iterative)

The term *spiral* describes inherently iterative lifecycle models. Like waterfall models, spiral models get their name from their graphical appearance, which resembles the spiral of a nautilus shell, as shown in Figure 2.2. There are many varieties, and the term *spiral* really refers to a class of similar models. The model depicted in Figure 2.2 is a simple example—others are more complicated. The exact steps involved in each iteration are some variation of the basic steps of the waterfall model. For example, Figure 2.2 uses "Gathering Requirements and Analysis," "Design," "Implementation," and "Testing and Planning." Spiral models break apart large projects into smaller subprojects to be completed roughly sequentially via a number of iterations. Throughout each iteration,

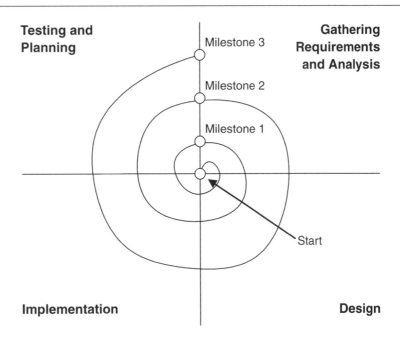

FIGURE 2.2 The Spiral Model

there is constant risk assessment and proactive planning. The spiral model is preferred among many circles at Microsoft.

With a typical spiral model, each iteration builds on the previous one until the software is completed. The first few iterations are usually quite small in scale and duration and are followed by more and more involved iterations as time goes on. The nautilus spiral depicts this well, since the innermost loops of the spiral, which take place first, are shorter than the outer ones, which occur later. To read a spiral model, start from the center and follow the steps listed along the circumference of the spiral, working your way outward. When you have completed the four steps, you have completed one iteration and you are back where you started, except one step further up the axis from the origin of the spiral.

Like waterfall models, iterative processes are goal-oriented. A deliverable is usually produced for each milestone in the project. Many projects declare milestones after every iteration or so (as shown in Figure 2.2), while others have fewer. There may also be various degrees of importance put on milestones. For example, the milestone "beta testing complete" is likely to be more important than "prototype finished."

Spirals models are also sometimes called *terraced waterfalls*, as shown in Figure 2.3. This model demonstrates more clearly the relationship to traditional waterfall models. Again, the exact steps in the process will vary from model to model.

Besides individual iterations, it is common to find other defining super-structures attached to spiral models as well. For example, a complete softward development process from Rational Software, the *Rational Unified Process*, introduces four basic, self-explanatory phases (Jacobson et al., 1999), as follows:

1. Inception
2. Elaboration
3. Construction
4. Transition

Each phase consists of one or more iterations, and each iteration consists of the following sequential steps:

1. Requirements Analysis
2. Design
3. Implementation
4. Integration

This sequence of steps is a variation of those defined in Table 2.1. The resulting model is both iterative and hierarchical. Moreover, the focus of the iterations

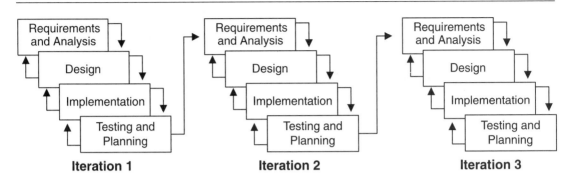

FIGURE 2.3   The Terraced Waterfall Model

shifts as the project progresses through the phases. For example, during the construction phase, the implementation step in each iteration receives more attention than it does during the inception phase (Kruchten, 1999).

Note that spiral models rarely specify the number of iterations to use for a project. In general, it is best to use as many as needed, but no more. However, even a small number of large-scale iterations are useful. These can result in such milestones as a prototype, an alpha version, a beta version, and a final version. The best plans are thorough, but avoid iterations for the sake of iterations.

Various model designers have attached many other superstructures to the basic spiral as well. While these are sometimes helpful, it is easy to go over-board. Certain superstructures may apply only to specific types of projects, and they end up appearing artificial or decorative on others. Moreover, complicated superstructures may end up interfering with the basic strengths of the approach. In short, be wary of spiral models that have extremely elaborate designs; they may add too much weight to the spiral foundation, weakening its overall effectiveness.

Lifecycle Models Compared

So what really makes iterative models better than traditional waterfalls? The most important feature is certainly early risk mitigation. In addition, by starting small and gradually building momentum, development teams can keep projects more manageable. It is much easier to make minor course corrections. Furthermore, iterative approaches provide constant, realistic assessments of the project—the process has built-in mechanisms for both providing reassurance and raising issues. An iterative process goes a long way toward addressing some of the ten fundamental reasons for project failure described in chapter 1 (Exhibit 1.1).

However, there is a drawback associated with this thoroughness. By their very nature, iterative processes are more time-consuming because there is more overhead in the process itself. In larger projects, the overhead is typically absorbed unnoticed, but in smaller projects, the process can get in the way if not managed carefully.

It is interesting to note how quickly the iterative model has worked its way into the sources on project management and planning. Since its introduction by Barry Boehm (1988), numerous variations have appeared. In addition to its integration into the Rational Unified Process described earlier, the spiral model appears as part of methodologies recommended by Royce (the "modern" method in *Software Project Management*, 1998) and McConnell (1996), as well as others. In fact, it is difficult to find sources written after 1990 that still suggest only the traditional waterfall model.

Which lifecycle model should you use? The answer will depend on the maturity of your corporate processes, the size of the project, and the project's time line. Overall, the spiral model is best for most projects and is especially well suited for VB projects that take advantage of VB's strong prototyping capabilities. Even so, waterfall models can be useful for shorter projects. However, you should remove brute force from consideration immediately. If your company currently has no formal software processes in place (i.e., brute force is the primary weapon) or only trivial ones, an elaborate spiral model is probably going to be too much to handle. Unless you can devote adequate time to developing its infrastructure, the spiral model may bury the project in process. Table 2.2 provides a summary of these points. Ultimately, you may wish to consider a hybrid of these models.

Hybrids

In addition to the basic lifecycle models just described, there are numerous and common hybrids, formed by combining the best parts of these models. We have already talked about a simple example, the brute-force-with-design model (a.k.a. design-code-fix), which is a weak hybrid of the waterfall model and brute force. More often, the hybrids meld parts of the basic waterfall and spiral models. One common approach is to include the rigors of the iterative model early in the requirements gathering and design stages, followed by a simple waterfall for the remainder of the project. This approach keeps the overall process simple while emphasizing the risk-detection aspect of the iterative model early in the process, when it can be of most use. Sometimes use of this hybrid is planned from the start. Other times it happens because the time line of the project becomes cramped, and a full spiral model is shortened to a simple waterfall late in the project (McConnell, 1996).

Steve McConnell presents several other hybrids. These models combine the more esoteric aspects of existing methods. The evolutionary prototyping

TABLE 2.2   Lifecycle Models Compared

Model	*Strengths*	*Weaknesses*
Brute force	No time spent on process	Highly unpredictable Very poor success rate Wastes people's time Unrepeatable
Waterfall	Well-defined steps Goal-oriented	Difficult to change direction of project Late risk detection
Spiral	Early risk detection Well-defined steps Goal-oriented	Very process intensive

model features constant refinement of the conceptual aspects of the system, like many spiral models. In this model, a simple prototype (usually just a user interface) becomes more advanced as the feature set becomes more defined. It is useful for simpler projects that have poorly defined requirements or shifting requirements.

McConnell's staged delivery model is similar, except control of the deliverables is tighter. In this model, the customer receives the system in pieces, rather than in one big chunk when finished. When a tight schedule pushes the time line of the project, the staged delivery can become the design-to-schedule model, whereby the constraints of actually finishing the project are removed. The users prioritize the deliverables, define some minimum feature sets, and then assume that they will get the more advanced features only if the schedule allows.

There are alternatives to a rigorous model as well. First, you can decide that you will include only features in your applications that are already provided by the specific software tools you have (VB, Office, etc.), thereby avoiding new software development altogether. This is McConnell's design-to-tools strategy, which is perhaps best exemplified by a custom Microsoft Office solution using Access or Excel only. Another strategy is to purchase some third-party solution off the shelf. Under certain circumstances, both of these solutions can be practical (McConnell, 1996). However, it is likely that you will have to make concessions on the exact functionality your apps will have because of limitations in the constituent tools.

Further Reading

Barry Boehm, "A Spiral Model of Software Development and Enhancement" (1988). When it comes to iterative lifecycle models, this article started it all.

Grady Booch et al., *The Unified Modeling Language User Guide* (1999). Appendix C of this book provides a brief introduction to the Rational Unified Process.

Ivar Jacobson et al., *The Unified Software Development Process* (1999). Rational Software's Unified Process receives its most thorough treatment in this book. It discusses the rationale behind using a use case–driven, iterative approach to software development. While there is a good deal of overlap between the material in this book and in Kruchten's *The Rational Unified Process*, the two books take slightly different approaches.

Philippe Kruchten, *The Rational Unified Process* (1999). This book provides a detailed introduction into the Rational Unified Process. It stresses iterative processes, different work flows, and the relationship of the various workers on a project.

Steve McConnell, *Rapid Development* (1996). McConnell discusses various lifecycle models in detail and provides valuable information about work environments.

Walker Royce, *Software Project Management* (1998). This is another outstanding general reference about software management, similar in scope to *Rapid Development*. It is a bit more up to date, however, and has an obvious connection to Rational Software's cornerstones: the UML and the Rational Unified Process.

Chapter 3

Requirements Gathering and Documentation

This chapter discusses those aspects of a software project that usually occur before formal design and coding begin. Overall, it concentrates on how to set expectations of project scope. We begin by examining the relationship between users and developers as it pertains to the requirements of the project. This section concludes with an introduction to use case models, one of many mechanisms for creating requirements documentation. The importance of use case models continues to be stressed in the rest of the chapter. Our discussion then turns to the formal analysis of the requirements. Here we focus on proof-of-concept analyses, estimates, and planning the day-to-day activities of the implementation. The last section explores formal documentation, introducing the various types of documentation commonly found and the target audience. This section also stresses documentation as a living process.

Many of the techniques discussed here are applicable to projects using any programming language. Where appropriate, the text discusses the specific effects of choosing Visual Basic as a tool.

Requirements Gathering

The requirements-gathering stage of the development process has two primary goals: first, to rigorously define the problem in question; and, second, to ensure that all parties involved have a common understanding of that definition. Only with a clear grasp of the problem can the implementation of its solution begin.

As discussed in chapter 2, projects traditionally fall short both in defining the problem and in coming to a common definition. In this section, we will explore some solid practices for reaching these goals.

To begin, the requirements of a project are rarely clear-cut. In practice, the scope starts off quite fuzzy and shifts a great deal during this stage, growing and shrinking as the problem becomes better understood. With hard work and a bit of luck, eventually something relatively concrete emerges. In most cases, the stakeholders document this initial plan and pass it along to the development team. The developers essentially own the project from that point forward. However, constant scope creep, miscommunication, and unclear goals usually plague the process.

In the ideal world, at the end of the requirements phase everyone involved would have a similar set of expectations. In the real world, this is rarely the case. As mentioned in chapter 1, an aggressively iterative requirements-and-analysis phase can help. Primary stakeholders need to refine the requirements proactively, being certain to take the time to create a thorough and accurate description of the problem. All too often, the user community understands the typical uses of the system quite well, but pays little or no attention to the secondary items on their wish list. They end up defining the main sections well, but are less thorough with the remainder of the system.

In an iterative lifecycle, the development team can help define and solidify scope by questioning the users to be sure they really know what they want. This questioning can take the form of interviews, conducted directly with the users to define the scope of system. These interactive checks usually also include a preliminary technical analysis to verify that the problem is technically solvable. Again, this process involves a lot of give and take between the two groups, and clear communication is critical. However, with an aggressively iterative approach, the ultimate result is that the users expect something the developers can actually deliver. Moreover, the users not only get what they ask for but also get what they really want.

◆ **Requirements—Functional or Otherwise**

Bear in mind that the term *requirements* refers not only to what the system needs to do from the standpoint of the user (functional requirements) but to all other guidelines as well. For example, a system may be expected to support anywhere from 1 to 1000 users, and thus scalability would be a requirement. Similarly, you might expect it to perform well on any of several platforms, so portability would be a requirement. While such expectations are not functional in nature, they are nevertheless important requirements and must be included in any thorough investigation of what a system is supposed to do.

Use Case Models

This iterative process may be elegant on paper, but in practice user groups and technical teams usually lack a common language with which to discuss the project. In addition, different stakeholders in the user community may even have fundamentally different views of the same project. Any advantage provided by the iterative process gets lost in translation. In the end, traditionally it is rare to find a system that is both well defined and clearly understood by all parties. Use cases defined with the Unified Modeling Language (UML) can help remove this obstacle, and I strongly recommend using them. The UML is a simple but thorough graphical language for visualizing, specifying, constructing, and documenting systems (Booch et al., 1999). We will discuss various aspects of the UML throughout this book, but for now, we will introduce its ability to produce consistent use case models.

A *use case* describes how one aspect of a system is used. A single use case describes a single way of using the system. *Use case models* are both graphical depictions of the behavior of a system (use case diagrams) and textual descriptions of scenarios involving the system. These two views complement one another to create a complete definition of the problem—from the point of view of the *user* community. Most important, use cases allow a team to talk about the system in terms consistent with the business domain driving the project.

Use case diagrams depict the various actors (actual users or perhaps other systems), the things the actors do (the use cases themselves), how actors interact, and even how the system responds. Use cases were popularized by Ivar Jacobson and his colleagues in *Object-Oriented Software Engineering* (Jacobson et al., 1992) and since have become an integral part of many iterative methodologies. For example, the Rational Unified Process, introduced in chapter 2, relies heavily on use case analyses in its inception phase.

A good use case model stresses what the system is supposed to do (its intended behavior) without indicating how it is actually done (its implementation). Consequently, by their very nature, use case models are requirements-centric. They allow the designer to focus on the definition of the problem itself, pushing the details of the solution aside for later. They help answer the question "what do I want to do?" rather than "how do I do it?"

Individual use case diagrams rarely attempt to describe an entire system. Rather, a number of interlaced diagrams describe different parts of the system, often from different points of view. The diagrams may refer to one another or summarize the detail of a different diagram with an elided version of it. Taken altogether, these diagrams can provide a detailed description of the whole system. You should explore all potential use cases in a system to gain a complete picture of it. Furthermore, use case analyses help create traceable software. That is, with software defined from use case analyses, you can always trace any particular bit of functionality back to the use case that determined it as a requirement. This also means that the ramifications of changing the use cases late in a project can be predicted (Rosenberg, 1999).

In addition to many other types of diagrams, the UML provides the syntax and vocabulary for creating easy-to-understand use case diagrams. Though it is a language, it is not a computer language and is not intended solely for developers or technical people. Nontechnical users should not cringe at its very mention. On the contrary, the UML is perhaps most beneficial for these people. It is simple, yet provides a rigorous framework for describing problems where such a framework is traditionally lacking. Communication gaps between the user community and the development teams are frustrating, and the UML fills these gaps.

If all of this diagramming seems entirely new, think again. Classic flowchart diagrams are still around, called *activity diagrams* by the UML. These charts feature the decision points that shape the flow of the system. As one of several potential types of supporting diagrams, activity diagrams document the specific actions that constitute a particular use case. In some cases, activity diagrams represent the final version of the system before user interface design begins. In fact, the flow of an activity diagram often closely resembles the steps a user follows while interacting with the system via the user interface.

Creating Use Case Diagrams

So how do you get started creating use case diagrams? A full-scale explanation is well beyond the scope of this book, but the introduction here provides a simple overview and should be enough to get you started. You may refer to the "Further Reading" section at the end of this chapter for a list of alternative sources containing more detailed discussions. Depending on your experience with object-oriented design and analysis, start small with a simple system, perhaps one you know well or have already completed (Booch et al., 1999). While knowledge of the UML is not required to create meaningful use case models, it does help immensely. You need only be familiar with the basics of the UML to begin designing use cases for your system with it. Of course, you can always create use case diagrams without the UML if you would like.

Fundamentally, there are three steps in the creation of a use case model:

1. *Define the boundaries of the system.* This is a general description of the system, often only a sentence or two. It is designed to set the stage for further examination. From this description, it should be clear what is and is not involved in the system. It is common to use the vocabulary of the problem's domain when creating this description.

2. *Identify the actors in the system.* What things describe the system? Who interacts with the system? What other systems interact with the system? Most important, what roles do these actors play? These are the nouns in the system, answering the question, "who?" or "what?" Be sure to describe the actors fully, listing them separately. Initially you will identify more actors than you will really need to define the system, but it is best to be thorough from the start. Extraneous actors can always be removed.

3. *Define the use cases themselves.* What do the actors do? What is the system supposed to do from the standpoint of each actor? These are the actions and are derived from verbs. Again, be as thorough as possible, being certain to describe the actions fully. The combinations of the actors and the actors' actions are the use cases of your system.

Note that these steps are general by design. The goal is to communicate the requirements clearly, so use simple English and avoid techno-jargon—there will be plenty of time for that later.

As these steps are repeated for each piece of the system, the whole system itself begins to take shape, albeit in very general form. With this skeleton in place, it is simpler to fill in more detailed descriptions of the subsystems. You may add diagrams as needed. With more and more iterations, a complete specification of the requirements emerges.

Use Cases: An Example

As a simple and familiar example, let's consider two activities that are commonplace at a bank: making a deposit and making a withdrawal. This model is commonly used to discuss system dynamics, and its simplicity and familiarity make it a good example here. This system describes the mechanism by which a banking customer performs either transaction, interacting with a bank teller as needed. Note that this is not a real application—any software developed from this model would not be used by any of the actors in the system. Rather, it is a simulation of a system with which we are all familiar. Here is a brief description, defining the system's boundaries:

> We want a system that simulates two simple bank transactions: a withdrawal and a deposit. When a customer wants to make a deposit or a withdrawal, he goes to the bank and fills out either a deposit slip or a withdrawal slip. This slip indicates the amount of the transaction and the customer's account number. He then stands in line, waiting for an available teller. When it is his turn, he hands the slip to the teller, along with the funds if it is a deposit. The teller verifies the transaction against the customer's account and hands the customer a receipt if it is a deposit or the funds if it is a withdrawal.

Two actors emerge immediately from the description: customer (account holder) and teller. These are clearly the two most important nouns in the description. But what about the others? We should also consider bank, deposit slip, withdrawal slip, account, account number, queue of customers, funds, and receipt. However, these actors play an ancillary role in the system, so we will omit them here for the sake of simplicity. In a more elaborate treatment, we would consider each in turn, determining the relationships among them. Often you will end up omitting several of your noun types anyway on further analysis (Rosenberg, 1999). Alternatively, you may opt to include them as entities in your class diagrams (see chapter 9) during the formal design phase.

The use cases themselves are simple, as in this example: make a deposit or make a withdrawal. There are many other verbs in the description. Consider "go to bank," "fill out deposit slip," "fill out withdrawal slip," and "stand in line." These actions are part of the system, but are clearly ancillary.

Digging a little deeper, we can formalize our findings in simple use case descriptions and diagrams, as in Exhibit 3.1 and Figures 3.1 and 3.2. Even without an elaborate introduction to the UML, basic use case models and activity diagrams are very easy to understand. For instance, Exhibit 3.1 shows the two use case descriptions depicting our visit to a bank teller. The use case diagram itself is shown in Figure 3.1, and a simple activity diagram for making a withdrawal appears in Figure 3.2. This example, while trivial, demonstrates the simplicity and effectiveness of the technique.

To reiterate, these are simple, well-defined descriptions of the requirements of the system. We have not discussed anything about the solution in our description and have not begun thinking about the design. With this simple skeleton in place, we can go back to our analysis and add more functionality by creating more use case descriptions, revolving around the actors and actions deemed less important initially. It is important to stress that secondary use cases are not something you can ignore. In fact, if not thoroughly explored and

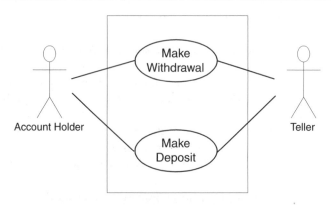

FIGURE 3.1 A Simple Use Case Diagram

EXHIBIT 3.1   Use Case Descriptions

Use Case I: Make a withdrawal.

Summary: A customer with an account fills out a withdrawal slip and hands it to the teller. If funds are available, the teller deducts the amount from the customer's account and hands the customer the funds.

Actors: Account holder (customer), teller

Preconditions: The customer has an account at the bank.

Flow of Events:

1. The customer fills out a withdrawal slip, indicating account number and amount of the withdrawal. This slip is given to the teller.

2. If funds in the account are available, the teller enters the deduction from customer's account and gives the customer the funds.

3. If funds are not available, the teller informs the customer. The customer may then fill out another withdrawal slip for a different account or different amount.

Postconditions: If the customer receives funds, the customer's account is properly debited.

Use Case II: Make a deposit.

Summary: A customer with an account fills out a deposit slip and hands it to the teller, along with the deposit. The teller verifies the deposit materials (checks and/or cash) and adds the amount to the customer's account. The customer also receives a receipt.

Actors: Account holder (customer), teller

Preconditions: The customer has an account at the bank.

Flow of Events:

1. The customer fills out a deposit slip, indicating account number and amount of the deposit. This slip is given to the teller along with the funds to deposit.

2. The teller verifies that the amount of the deposit is correct and that the checks have been endorsed. The teller enters the deposit into the customer's account and gives the customer a receipt.

Postconditions: If all checks in the deposit clear, the customer's account is properly credited and updated.

documented, they are left to the whims of the programmers. Programmers are usually more than willing to implement a weakly defined use case, but will implement only the basic idea with whatever specifics fit their fancy (Rosenberg, 1999). If this happens, you will have inconsistent functionality and software that rarely performs as it should.

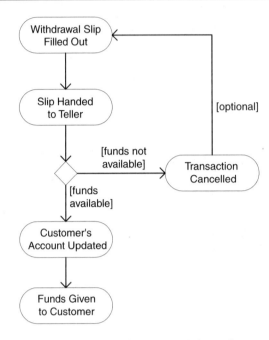

FIGURE 3.2   Activity Diagram for Making a Withdrawal

Don't be misled by the apparent simplicity of the process. Developing use case analyses for a nontrivial system is a very time-consuming process. The extra time spent up front is well worth it, because it can save a lot more time over the course of a project. Be careful not to get too carried away, though. It is a good idea to distribute the time spent proportionally to the importance of the item being investigated.

Use Cases and Visual Basic

When using Visual Basic, use case models and supporting diagrams provide a solid foundation on which to base simple prototypes. Because user interfaces are so easy to create with VB, you may even opt to include simple screen layouts in your supporting activity diagrams. By doing so, your documentation not only shows what each use case is supposed to do, but also approximates what the actions look like to the user. The whole system becomes easier to understand when the model includes something as tangible as preliminary screen shots. With a series of diagrams containing basic screen shots, a simple prototype for the system is only a few steps away. We'll discuss prototyping in detail in chapter 7.

This discussion has omitted many of the details involved in creating more thorough use case analyses, including preconditions and postconditions for use cases, use case extensions, and others. We also have not explored any of the advanced applications for use case analyses. I strongly recommend Jacobson's *Object-Oriented Software Engineering* (1992) and Rumbaugh's *OMT Insights* (1996) for a theoretical overview, as well as the practical discussions of use cases in *Applying Use Cases* (Schneider and Winters, 1998) and *Use Case Driven Object Modeling with UML* (Rosenberg, 1999).

Drawbacks of Use Case Analyses

Use case analyses are among the most consistent and thorough means for defining the requirements of a system. However, there are a number of drawbacks to them. If a company has no experience with use cases, it can be difficult to get started. Furthermore, old habits die hard, and people are reluctant to try a new approach. Developing use case models is also time-consuming. Stakeholders spend much of this time defining basic elements of the system, and for many people it seems like a complete waste of effort. Moreover, there is a strong temptation to stop the process prematurely once the basics of the system are clearly documented. In my view, however, *taking the time* to think and talk about all of the requirements is more important than any resulting artifact. Furthermore, incomplete use case models can give a false sense of security to the project. This occurs when the incomplete model is mistakenly assumed to represent the whole system.

To make matters worse, the process of creating use case analyses has no built-in pop-up thermometer to let you know when you have investigated the requirements fully, though robustness analyses can help (see Rosenberg, 1999). As a result, it is up to the analysts to verify their own progress. To this end, use case analyses do not necessarily provide a surefire way of describing a system. The analysts still need to ask the right questions. The use case analyses act merely as a quality assurance mechanism to ensure that the answers to the questions fit the system as a whole. Because of this flaw, use case analyses (and processes that revolve around them) often end up as scapegoats. Failed project leaders look back on the process of creating use case analyses and blame it for the failure of the whole project. Though the conclusion is misguided, it makes them feel better.

However, although sometimes the immediate benefits of use case models are not obvious, in the end they can facilitate subsequent steps in the development process. For example, consider the role of use cases in the following stages of development:

1. The analysis stage relies on accurate use case models to perform proof-of-concept analyses. The models define the "concept" in the term "proof-of-concept" (see chapter 4). They can also help with scheduling and estimating.

2. Documentation teams will refer to the use case diagrams when creating the end user documentation, such as training materials (see next section). Doug Rosenberg takes this idea a step further by suggesting that a use case driven approach to software development is like writing the user manual first. This reinforces the notion that the design of this system mirrors the functional requirements of the system from the standpoint of the users (Rosenberg, 1999).

3. Designers perform constant checks against the use case models. Often designers deliberately make the actors subsystems in the code, and as a result the use case model becomes a high-level design. In a sense, class models come from more detailed analyses of the entities in use cases.

4. Coders and testers refer to use case diagrams to perform quality assurance. A well-implemented system should behave as it does in the use case diagram. In addition, writers of test scripts often derive test plans and other checks directly from scenarios based on the use case diagrams.

Documentation

Documentation is a general term that refers to written materials in a variety of forms, including on-line HTML files, bound manuals, simple "how-to" instruction sheets, stacks of papers in unmarked binders, or my favorite, notes scribbled on a napkin. Documentation is created to explain how something works: how to put it together, how to polish it, how to turn it on, and so on. It pervades our day-to-day lives, so it is not surprising that it plays an important role in software development as well.

On software projects, there are three basic kinds of documentation, as distinguished by their intended audience, though the boundaries defining audiences can be fuzzy. The three kinds of documentation are as follows:

1. *Marketing documentation.* This category includes all documentation intended for people who currently have no direct involvement with the system. It is typically created to appease upper-level management or attract potential customers. This type of documentation talks about what a system is supposed to do, rather than how the system does it. Marketing materials are usually very nontechnical, except when the technology itself is a selling point. Examples include marketing pamphlets (often referred to as *glossies*), simple presentations, and even interactive tours (dog-and-pony shows). Since it is designed to sell the need for the system, marketing documentation is often weak on content and high on gloss.

2. *End user documentation.* This is documentation aimed at the users of a system. It includes on-line help, tutorial materials, and written manuals.

3. *Technical documentation.* This documentation is intended for internal use by programmers and administrators in creating and maintaining the system. It includes use case diagrams, system schematics, database models, object models, and other types of information that programmers and business analysts may find useful.

While important in its own right, beyond saving a few screenshots, marketing documentation rarely requires the involvement of the development team, so we will pass over it here. Let us briefly consider both end user documentation and technical documentation.

End User Documentation

Documentation directed at end users should facilitate their use of the system you have created. In the world of Windows programming, users rely on a combination of written manuals and on-line help. Ideally, a system should be so easy to use that formal documentation is not required for the user to do most tasks. You accomplish this by polishing the user interface to such an extent that any user with a little domain knowledge can figure out what to do. We will look at how to accomplish this in our discussion of user interfaces in chapters 6 and 7.

From the perspective of the user, there is no such thing as too much documentation. Yet, most of the computer users I know hate to read manuals. They pull the manual out only when they are frustrated trying to figure the problem out on their own. Clear user interfaces and carefully constructed manuals can reduce their frustration.

No matter what the project, the principles of creating the documentation remain the same. Here are some suggestions for making your end user documentation the best it can be:

1. *Factor in the type of software you are creating.* Is the application a shrink-wrapped product for sale or is it an in-house tool for simplifying labor-intensive aspects of day-to-day business? Shrink-wrapped software may need more thorough documentation than the in-house tool.

2. *Understand the average target user's computer skills.* For in-house applications aimed at inexperienced users and other applications with a novice user base, you may have to include some very rudimentary introductory materials explaining Windows and basic Graphical User Interface concepts. However, unless you are creating a tutorial-style application, teaching computer skills should not be the focal point of the documentation. Remember that most people have at least a basic understanding of GUI interfaces, so be sure not to force them to read this introductory material if they don't need it. Present it in such a way that it can be skipped by more advanced readers. When creating shrink-wrapped software, it is reasonable to assume that users who are savvy enough to choose your software are savvy enough to use Windows.

3. *Consider the average target user's domain knowledge.* Beyond basic Windows skills, what are you expecting your users to understand about the domain of the application? If you have written software to help run a bank, are you confident that the users understand how a bank works? Provide this information if appropriate, perhaps in a separate manual. A manual for a shrink-wrapped software package that illustrates this is the manual for the accounting software Quickbooks. In addition to teaching the user how to use Quickbooks itself, it provides some basic accounting training.

4. *Take into account the age group and reading level of the intended audience.* If you are writing software for children, write a manual for children. If you are writing software for adults, be sure not to sound condescending and don't make the prose more flowery or technical than it needs to be. Clear communication is critical, and that involves knowing your audience.

5. *Use screen shots appropriately.* One of the biggest advantages to using Visual Basic is that you can create very appealing interfaces easily. Take advantage of this fact by showing them off whenever possible, especially in your documentation. However, remember that it is possible to overdo this. While screen shots are certainly helpful, be sure your documentation does not simply reproduce information readily available on the forms themselves, especially if the user interface is already clear and simple. Also, be sure to describe the actions the user can perform while working with a particular screen. The results of choosing menus, buttons, and clicking other parts of a screen are difficult to visualize from a static screenshot alone.

6. *Augment traditional manuals with context-sensitive help when appropriate.* Context-sensitive help will allow users to explore the application on their own without referring to a written manual. They can move along from form to form, referring to the on-line help when the functionality is not obvious from the user interface. Context-sensitive help is difficult to do well. It must be consistent: don't provide help for every control on one form and for no controls on another. This type of help can also be frustrating to use for some people. Murphy's Law of Context-Sensitive Help says that the item you need help with will always return "help not available." Review your context-sensitive help to avoid this problem.

7. *When creating on-line help, stick to standard help formats.* Many users find it annoying to install software only to find that they need to install some other bit of software to read the on-line manuals. You can avoid this by sticking to Windows standard help file formats, like .HLP files or the new HTML help files. Only use formats that require supporting software (like Adobe PDF files, which need the Acrobat Reader) as a backup to the printed manual. To make your life easier and to ensure consistency, consider using one of the many help file generation tools available.

8. *Use interactive guides for work flow.* For a polished presentation, consider including on-line wizards or even something like MS Office assistants to help walk a person through tasks. While power users often turn them off immediately, many novice users find these to be cute, easy to use, and very helpful. Some even feature "natural language" searching capabilities. Distribute these in conjunction with standard-context sensitive help.

9. *Include "Quick Start" information.* This may take on the form of a simple one-sheet explanation of the basics or a more elaborate "Quick Start Guide." In short, don't expect your users to read the full manual, especially if it is bulky. Providing a simple overview can help many users, especially those who don't (or won't) read lengthy manuals. The material presented here should summarize important points of the more detailed manual. Remember that more often than not, people will take the shortest route to getting started with the software, especially if it means not reading anything. Simple tutorials are ideal.

Creating end user documentation often means coordinating the efforts of people from several departments in your company. In larger companies, there is usually a documentation department with technical writers who design and write the bulk of the materials, including the on-line help. They base their material on the work of business analysts. Programmers often participate to help hook any context-sensitive help to the forms in the user interface. Carefully created requirements documents and rigorously applied user interface standards can simplify the creation of documentation.

Technical Documentation

Technical software documentation is written for internal use in the corporation. This definition usually covers almost every document every person generates. When pressed for a more concise definition, I include only documents of substance, not those created to satisfy the administrative paper trails associated with software projects (time sheets, request forms, trivial status reports, etc.). The purpose of technical documentation is to detail the internal workings of the system.

The main point of writing end user documentation is to create something for the user to read. The finished document must be practical, since practicality is central to the whole concept of creating the documentation in the first place. We write it, they read it—it is a simple dichotomy. However, with technical documentation things are not quite so clear. Here writing documentation is an exploratory process, and there is much to be gained from simply taking the time to do it. In fact, with technical documentation, companies stand to benefit more from the exploration than from the resulting document.

It is interesting to note that some developers find it tedious to create documentation, avoiding it whenever possible. Yet ironically, they are usually the first to complain about the lack of documentation when asked to support a system without it. Technical documentation is written by technical people for technical people, and what goes around comes around.

Documents as Artifacts

It is helpful think of technical documents as *artifacts* of the development process. An artifact is something of artificial character usually created by external (and extraneous) intervention. In other words, it is something residual, a by-product of human effort.

Artifacts are snapshots of the system from which they are born. A particular snapshot may be an accurate depiction of a past state of that system. As the system evolves, however, its snapshots become stale immediately. In short, artifacts show the way things may have been, but not necessarily the way they are now.

Many companies believe the physical deliverable—whether it be a word processor file, some printed materials, or something else—is all that matters when producing technical documentation. I disagree. *Companies need to learn to treat technical documents as artifacts*. The focus should not be on creating some pile of paper but rather on the process of exploring what they are documenting. The very reason we undergo the documentation process should not be to have its by-product, a piece of paper, but to learn about the system.

When the focus shifts from the physical artifacts to the process of creation, companies can even benefit from some rather peculiar practices. For example, traditionally, the very notion of creating documentation just to throw it away is considered absurd. However, with the emphasis on the process of creation rather than on the finished product, this practice is much more reasonable, since so much is gained from the creative process itself. As an example of this, consider the creation of use case diagrams. It is often helpful to explore alternative views of the system and far-out "what if" scenarios. The resulting documents may not be very meaningful, but may help focus future documents by pointing out potential problems, holes, or other issues.

I am not saying that the resulting document is never important. On the contrary, it is essential for knowledge transfer (especially when direct conversations are not feasible). For example, when companies are faced with high attrition rates, accurate documentation can help save the day. Without it, nobody knows what to do when so-and-so leaves the company and takes her precious domain knowledge with her. Solid documents can also help train new hires in the particulars of systems. Furthermore, as a system becomes more fixed, new documents are less likely to become stale and therefore are more valuable. This is perhaps best exemplified by postmortem documents, specifying the *way we did it*.

However, I am discouraged by companies that produce documents for the sake of documents. These are reports, work requests, write-ups, diagrams, and so forth, that are never read (and probably never will be), generated solely to satisfy some arbitrary requirement or policy whose real intention is long forgotten. These also include documents requested by people who are too lazy to read existing documents to find the information they need. I have worked with many people (especially managers) who are infamous for this. Rather than taking a couple of minutes to see if their questions have already been answered by the pile of unread documentation on their desks or folders full of unread e-mail, they request yet another document. In short, if there is nothing new to be gained from the document itself or the process of writing it, why bother?

Types of Technical Documents

Programmers and leads are often called on to produce documentation during various stages of the development process. Both waterfall and iterative lifecycle models typically include some type of documentation at the end of each stage as a deliverable. Table 3.1 lists some typical types of technical documentation for each stage of development. Note that in practice, the type of documentation actually needed will vary from project to project.

The documentation of each stage of development has different goals and different advantages. In the requirements gathering and analysis stages, the goal is to ensure that the software's role is well defined and that it solves the problem in question. Here a lot of documentation is produced, much of it superfluous, to be discarded. When the smoke clears, you should have documents that can explain the system to someone unfamiliar with it. The design stage also

TABLE 3.1   Typical Technical Documentation for Each Stage of Development

Stage	*Documents*
Requirements gathering	Use case models
Analysis	Use case models, prototype summaries, activity diagrams, robustness diagrams, etc.
Design	Object diagrams, class diagrams, use case diagrams, system architecture diagrams, state diagrams, etc.
Coding	In-code comments
Testing	Test plans, use case diagrams
Maintenance	Postmortem analyses (the way we did it)

produces a lot of documentation, which should explain how the system will be constructed. During the actual coding, very little external documentation is usually required, though it is common to explain complicated algorithms and formulas through comments in the code. The testing stage's documentation can be derived from the materials generated earlier. The goal here is to develop test plans to use as a frame of reference to ensure that the implementation meets the requirements. Last, postmortem analyses help to summarize the project, its successes and its failures.

To get the most out of your documents and to make them as consistent as possible, I strongly recommend using a standard language (like the UML). This is especially helpful for diagrams and other visual aids. It can be confusing to see classes and objects presented one way on one diagram and in an entirely different fashion on another.

Further Reading

Grady Booch et al., *The Unified Modeling Language User Guide* (1999).   This is the main text for learning and using the UML. It describes all aspects of the language (including extensions) in gory detail. It is definitely not light reading, but worth the effort if you are serious about using the UML on your projects.

Ivar Jacobson et al., *Object-Oriented Software Engineering* (1992).   Like Rumbaugh's OMT, Jacobson's OOSE has been absorbed into the Unified Modeling Language. However, this volume remains one of the most important sources on use case analyses around.

Ivar Jacobson et al., *The Unified Software Development Process* (1999).   The central role of use cases in software development is described in this book, although it does not present a thorough process for creating them. See Schneider and Winters and Rosenberg for a more practical explanation.

Deborah Kurata, *Doing Objects in Microsoft Visual Basic 5.0* (1997).   Kurata presents a solid overview of the process of developing software.

Steve Maguire, *Debugging the Development Process* (1994).   This is a compilation of anecdotes from Maguire's experience working for Microsoft. While his points are sound, his anecdotes tend to get in the way. Luckily, he summarizes whole sections of the book with a single sentence at the end of the section.

Doug Rosenberg, *Use Case Driven Object Modeling with UML* (1999).   This book promises a down-to-earth explanation of how to perform use case analyses and how to create software from them. It is based on Rosenberg's early melding of the techniques of Jacobson, Booch, and Rumbaugh.

James Rumbaugh, *OMT Insights* (1996).   Though now eclipsed by OMT's inclusion in the Unified Modeling Language, this book offers insight into use case analyses and many other aspects of object-oriented design and analysis.

Geri Schneider and Jason P. Winters, *Applying Use Cases* (1998).   This book provides a very solid introduction to use cases, concentrating on the first phase of the Rational Unified Process (inception). It is informal in tone and relatively short, making it accessible to just about anyone.

Chapter 4

Analysis

This chapter takes an extended look at *analysis*, the examination of a complex structure through its constituent elements. The analysis stage of software development breaks down a complex problem as defined by the requirements and examines its constituent elements. In doing so, it accomplishes two primary tasks. First, it verifies the completeness of the problem's definition by performing iterative checks and proof-of-concept analyses. Second, once the scope is as near to complete as possible and as stable as it can be, it provides the background for comprehensive planning.

The term *analysis* is often coupled with the word *design*. In fact, many people use the terms interchangeably, without realizing the important difference between them. Analysis involves verification of a proposed solution as defined by the requirements of the system. Design is the first step in implementing the solution. While analysis takes place throughout a project, even during the design phase, here we will be referring only to the analysis that takes place before formal design begins. In this stage, it is imperative not to put the cart before the ox. For our purposes, the analysis stage does not involve creating objects, properties, events, methods, classes, components, or any other type of object-oriented thing: we will consider those activities when we discuss the design stage.

Proof-of-Concept Analyses

To verify the requirements of a system, it is helpful to simulate its functional performance on paper. By putting the system through its paces, you can uncover problematic sections, find important but missing functionality, and learn to handle the unexpected. More important, you can verify that the requirements really make sense. By verifying that the proposed system indeed solves the right problems, you prove the concept.

If you have created use case models and activity diagrams for your system, then you are halfway home. To perform proof-of-concept analyses, you will need a solid idea of what the system is supposed to do. Use case models are ideal for this. What remains is to create detailed scenarios involving the users of the system (actors) and to enact them on paper to be sure the system behaves as expected. There are two types of scenarios you should be sure to consider, primary and secondary.

First, verify the main flow of the system with primary scenarios. Primary scenarios are defined by the "typical" conditions. Sometimes this is the general flow that the users follow most of time. On the other hand, it may be a flow involving no errors or unexpected behavior. You will need to create several primary scenarios, one for each use case. Taken together, all primary scenarios typically involve most of the functionality of the system.

To create the primary scenarios, annotate the steps of what you expect to happen (or would like to have happen) in each use case. You may use almost any type of written style to present your scenarios, from informal text to numbered lists of steps to pseudocode logic (Schneider and Winters, 1998). Whatever you decide, the important thing is to be consistent. When verifying that the system supports a scenario, identify the state of the system before you begin testing it. As you continue test driving the system, annotate problems for correction during the next pass. When finished, verify the state of the system again to be certain everything is as expected.

When your primary scenarios all check out, begin working on the secondary scenarios. These verify exceptional situations—the "what ifs." They test the error-handling mechanisms and other nonstandard cases. Often there are far more secondary scenarios than primary.

If you discover a problem with any scenario, revise your requirements accordingly. After a few iterations, you should have a system defined that does what it is supposed to and actually solves the problem it is trying to solve. When finished, the models you have created can provide the basis for end user documentation and formal test plans. You can also feel confident that the system's requirements are adequate and reasonable—the first step in a successful project. For a final, more tangible indication of the completeness of the requirements, consider developing a prototype of the user interface to help you visualize the flow of your scenarios (see chapter 7).

Estimating, Scheduling, and Staffing

Once you have defined and verified the requirements, you can begin to create estimates for planning the remainder of the project. Be aware that initial requirements, even those defined rigorously, are rarely set in stone. A friend of mine once told me that it seems like the requirements for the projects he works on do not become finalized until about three weeks after the projects are finished! Since requirements are always in motion, all planning must be considered preliminary, with a wide margin of error.

There are three types of estimate you will need to address to gain a better picture of the project. First, you will need to gain an understanding of the size of the project. This estimate is usually in lines of code or function points. With an idea of the size of the project, you can then estimate the effort (usually in man-months) required to complete the project. Last, you apply this effort to a calendar and a team of developers to generate an estimated schedule.

Estimating Size

An estimate of the size of a project is very important, primarily because you will use it to create other estimates and errors may become compounded. Unfortunately, size estimates are also the most difficult to generate, because they involve taking an abstract entity like a requirements goal and converting it into something concrete and empirical.

So how do you create a size estimate? There are two basic approaches. First, you can rely on experience, perhaps with a similar project, and make a ballpark estimate as to the number of lines of code or function points required. This is what I call a *guestimate*. While inherently imprecise, these guesses are often better than nothing. Another approach is to use one of several formulaic algorithms to derive size from scope. Let's look at each of these approaches in turn.

Guestimates

If you have worked on a similar project and know how much work it ended up being, you have a good basis for guessing. Alternatively, you can use the size of parts of other familiar projects in combination to size up the current one. You might think that this is the poorest of approaches, and when not done properly, you would be right. However, in my experience, the ballpark estimates generated by seasoned developers and team leads are generally reasonably accurate. These guestimates simply need to be stated in a way that shows their inherent imprecision. It is only when they are considered to be more aggressive and precise than they should be that they become a problem. We will discuss presentation styles and setting expectations later in this chapter.

The biggest problem with guestimating the size of Visual Basic projects is that it is often difficult to judge how much work will actually have to be done by the developers and how much of the functionality can be leveraged from existing components. VB relies heavily on components, from elements of the

◆ **Function Points versus Lines of Code**

For many years, the measurement of the number of lines of code (LOC) in an application was the only way we had of describing how big an application was. In fact, LOC measurements are still in wide use today. However, they present many problems. First, it is not always clear how to count the number of lines of code (are comments included? what about white space?). Second, the number of lines of code required to complete a given task depends heavily on the language in use. Third, different programmers given the same task to implement in the same language will often produce wildly different-sized programs. Though there are numerous other problems, these simple examples show that LOC measurements are inconsistent at best.

To address these and other problems, A. J. Albrecht of IBM created function points in the 1970s. Several revisions of his findings followed throughout the 1980s, and use of function point measurement has now become widespread. Rather than relying on a count of lines of code, function point analyses look at the inputs, outputs, and files in a system. It weights these according to the complexity of the system to produce a number of function points. Since the implementations themselves are not considered, function point analyses are language-independent and present a more consistent measurement of size. For a complete discussion of the history and uses of function point counts (see Capers Jones's *Applied Software Measurement,* 1996).

user interface (controls) to data access and transaction management. VB itself includes dozens of standard controls and components. In addition, your company may use third-party components, or perhaps you have custom-built reusable components. All of these can greatly reduce the number of lines of code or function points in a project, if they are applicable to it. However, it is not always obvious whether your components are robust enough (or generic enough) to suit your needs, and consequently they leave you with a big question mark in your estimate.

Formulaic Estimates

Another approach for estimating the size of a project is to use some kind of formula to calculate the size given specific requirements. There are many types of formulas available, and several are included in software packages. Using software has the advantage of removing human error from the calculations and generally makes the estimation process run more smoothly.

The approach outlined by Schneider and Winters (1998), derived from the work of Gustav Karner, is to base size estimates on use case models. You begin by weighting the actors involved, rating them as simple, average, or complex. By multiplying each actor by a numeric value for its weight and tallying the results, you end up with a total actor weight for the system. You then follow a

◆ Accuracy versus Precision

Although they are often used as synonyms, the terms *accuracy* and *precision* have a subtle, but important difference in meaning. Accuracy is conformity to fact. An accurate answer is a correct answer. Precision refers to the degree of exactness. There is something of a sliding scale to the meanings of both words—they are not typically absolutes. Therefore, one result may be both more accurate and more precise than another.

On the other hand, an estimate can be accurate but not precise. For example, if an estimate states that a project will take between 2 and 20 months and it actually ends up taking 10, it would be accurate but not very precise. However, if the estimate states that the project will take 6 weeks but ends up taking 20, it is precise but not accurate. If it states that a project will take 6 weeks and it does indeed take 6 weeks, the estimate is both precise and accurate.

similar set of steps for weighting use cases, resulting in a total use case weight. These two totals taken together form a raw number for use in some simple equations. These equations also involve technical factors (e.g., portability, ease of use, level of security, etc.) and environmental factors (e.g., motivation, stability of requirements, etc.). The result of all of this manipulation is a number representing the number of Use Case Points (UCP) on the project. This number is a raw representation of size that can then be used to compute the total man-hours required.

Function point analyses take a slightly different approach (see sidebar "Function Points versus Lines of Code"). Function points are language-independent logical elements of code that are often more informative than the count of the lines of code. Like use case estimates, function point analyses typically rely on weighting various aspects of the system. The number and complexity of items such as inputs, outputs, and files roll together to determine the function point total for a system. As with use case based estimates, with Visual Basic as your tool it may be difficult to determine size completely without a thorough understanding of how much reusable functionality in your components you can leverage (Jones, 1996).

When considering specific weights in any formulaic approach, bear in mind that a single number by itself is essentially meaningless (frequently the weighting numbers assigned do not have a unit of measure). Only when taken together as a population of numbers does some clearer image of the project's size emerge. These approaches are a lot like expressionistic paintings. Up close and in detail they are fuzzy and unclear. Only when you take a step back and look at the big picture does something meaningful appear.

Moreover, in those approaches that involve applying numerical weights to subjective elements, the process of judging the weights is more important than

◆ Fuzzy Input, Concrete Answers

Neural networks may help make all of the messy math involved in estimating more digestible. Fuzzy logic thrives on the inherently imprecise and subjective nature of initial data. Neural networks are complicated systems that accept fuzzy inputs and produce concrete answers.

The big difference between neural networks and equations fed with raw data is that neural networks can be trained to produce consistent results, given accurate training data. In the end, this is preferable and will likely be more consistently accurate. There are no such approaches in common use today, but the avenue does appear promising. Who knows?—maybe in a few years expert systems using neural networks that generate estimates will revolutionize the software industry.

the weights assigned. By taking the time to examine the individual subjective elements closely, you invariably end up with a better gut feeling for the system as a whole. You can better understand differences in complexity between various pieces of functionality and generally can develop a clear picture of the size of the project. Ultimately, any formulaic estimate that does not *feel* right will not (and probably should not) be trusted.

Some people consider using a formulaic approach to be unnecessarily complicated or otherwise suspect, and they may be right. All such approaches to size estimation are at the mercy of the raw data entered. This data is inherently subjective and often a bit fuzzy. As with any equation, the results are only as good as the inputs. This is not to say that such approaches are not useful, but rather that they must be taken for what they are, at face value. Written equations and fancy numbers can provide a false sense of credibility to an estimate, since you can point to your notepad and show your work. In short, do not put more stock into an estimate than it deserves, and remember that even the best estimates are subject to a great deal of unknowns.

Setting Expectations

In the end, all size estimating is imprecise, even if it is presented with seemingly precise numeric values such as number of lines of code or number of function points. It is therefore critical to set expectations for the estimate immediately and present it in such a way that it explicitly demonstrates the imprecision. Clear communication is necessary, so stick to your guns. There is a tendency in the software industry to lean toward the best-case estimate. Furthermore, primary stakeholders typically want very precise and accurate estimates from the start, which is impossible. Consequently, software schedules are often overoptimistic, because they are based on unrealistic best-case estimates presented with artificial precision. It is wise to explain estimates in a style that reflects their inherent imprecision while stressing their accuracy (McConnell, 1996). Ranges (four to seven man-months) and plus-or-minus qualifiers (5 man-months, +3 man-months, −2 man-months) are helpful. They are accurate (there is a very good chance that the actual value will fall within the range provided) and as precise as possible. In short, when generating estimates, strive to be 100 percent accurate, but only *as precise as you really can be*. This is all anyone can reasonably hope for.

Since estimates are imprecise, constant refinement is the best weapon to keep your projects on track (McConnell, 1996). With refinement throughout the life span of the project, the size estimate can become more precise, and the ranges and size of the qualifiers will become smaller. Moreover, the range of error in the target estimate for a project becomes smaller as the project moves toward completion, as shown in Figure 4.1.

Estimating Effort

As with estimating size, estimating effort can happen in many ways. Guestimates again are useful, particularly if you know the habits of your programmers and the level of process maturity your company can handle. For a more refined approach, consider Barry Boehm's Constructive Cost Model (COCOMO) or its updated version, COCOMO II (Boehm, 1981). (A word of warning: as presented in *Software Engineering Economics*, COCOMO can be a bit daunting. Refer to appendix B of Royce's *Software Project Management* (Royce, 1998) for a streamlined explanation of COCOMO and COCOMO II.) In either case, base your estimate of effort on your estimate of size.

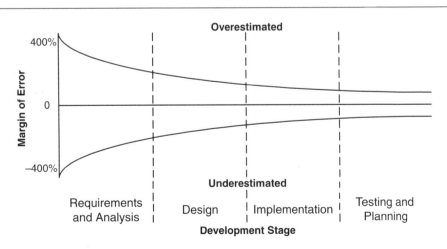

FIGURE 4.1 Precision of Software Estimation over a Project's Life Span

Source: Adapted from Royce, 1998.

No matter what your approach, you will end up with some kind of figure representing the amount of work it will take to complete the project, typically in man-months or some similar unit. Your next goal is to staff the project, then spread the work out among the staff to determine how long it will actually take to complete the project.

Before looking at the creation of the schedule itself, let us again consider how choosing Visual Basic as a tool can affect effort estimates. Because user interface creation is one of VB's strong points, it is realistic to expect programmers to be able to complete a user interface faster with VB than with a language like C++. As a result, it is likely the time estimate for this will be rather short. However, at the same time, there are a number of tasks that VB is rather poor at, and these should be taken into consideration as well. Complicated mathematics, animation, and fast code are all weak points for Visual Basic. Unfortunately, because the desire is to make the estimate as small as possible, estimates of size consider the time saved by VB's strengths but forget all about the additional time required to account for its potential weaknesses.

There is also a general belief that RAD languages like Visual Basic are magically faster to work with and therefore the whole estimate can be cut. In truth, there is very little clear-cut data suggesting that VB or other fourth-generation languages substantially reduce the time of development. Too many other factors come into play (McConnell, 1996). However, it is reasonable to believe that there is at least the *potential* for some increased development speed from these languages, especially if the project uses a proactive, iterative, risk-assessing lifecycle model. Only by eliminating and managing risk can this potential even begin to be realized.

Myth 5
Using Visual Basic usually substantially reduces the overall time of development for a project.

Scheduling

In the simplest of terms, the amount of actual time it will take to finish a project can be calculated using Equation 4.1. Here, the estimate for effort, spread across the available resources, yields the calendar time. Note that a similar equation can also help determine the number of people needed on a project, if the calendar time is known and fixed. This is shown in Equation 4.2.

Equation 4.1 Computation of Schedule from Effort and Number of Workers

Time (Hours) = Effort (Man-hours) / Number of Workers

Equation 4.2 Computation of Number of Workers
from Effort and Schedule

```
Number of Workers = Effort (Man-hours) / Time (Hours)
```

These equations show that calendar time and number of workers on a project are intertwined. In theory, the fewer the people, the longer it will take to do the work. Because of this relationship, it is theoretically possible to stack one parameter or the other to accommodate your needs. For example, if you have only four people on your team, you should plan for a longer schedule than if you had ten. Taken literally, the equations show that adding people to a project shortens its calendar schedule. Many corporations estimate schedules with these equations religiously.

However, though these equations are simple, their practical applicability is exceedingly suspect. They rely on the following assumptions:

- People can always work simultaneously and independently.
- People produce the same amount and work as quickly as one another.
- The actual amount of work always remains constant and is independent of the number of people assigned to the project.

In practice, all these assumptions are wrong. First, projects of any complexity have internal dependencies that prevent certain parts from being developed before others. Thus, people cannot always work simultaneously, since they may have to wait for someone else to complete a dependent piece. Even without the dependencies, rarely can the work be spread evenly enough to keep all workers busy at all times.

Second, every programming team has its stronger and weaker players. It has been shown that the discrepancy in productivity is large and that some individuals are an order of magnitude more productive than others are (Brooks, 1995). It is ludicrous to think that somehow the discrepancies in productivity and talent all average out in the end. Therefore, the whole notion of a *man-hour* is itself suspect, since it represents an averaged, theoretical unit that in practice is impossible to evaluate. Unfortunately, it is the best unit we have.

Last, even excluding obligatory scope creep, projects rarely remain fixed in size. Adding people to a project invariably adds to the amount of work. This work takes the form of increase managerial overhead and additional interpersonal communication. The fallacy that the project's size remains fixed in spite of changes in team size is one of the key points in Frederick Brooks's essay "The Mythical Man-Month" (in Brooks, 1995). Mathematically, the number of potential paths of communication grows exponentially as the team's size increases. Equation 4.3 shows the recursive formula for determining the number of paths. For a team with two members, the number of potential communication paths is 1. For a team of 40 people (large for a Visual Basic project), there are an astonishing

780 potential paths of communication! The more interpersonal communication there is, the more time it takes and the greater the overall amount of work. More important, there is also a greater opportunity for miscommunication. While it is true that not everyone on the team will need to communicate with everyone else, there is at least the potential. In practice, a clearly defined team hierarchy can reduce the actual number of paths.

Equation 4.3 Computation of Potential Paths of Communication

$$c(n) = (n-1) + c(n-1)$$

where

c = communication paths and n = number of team members

The moral of the story is that there comes a point when adding more bodies to a project ceases to shorten its schedule. If a project is already resource heavy, this point comes much more quickly than most companies realize. There is a practical limit to the number of people who can work effectively on a project. In practice, this limit is very close to the number of people who are actually assigned to the project. However, when a schedule begins to slip, the first instinct is to throw more bodies at the project. Unfortunately, adding more workers breaks the practical threshold and often ends up making the problem worse because of the increased overhead caused by extra training and orientation and increased communication needs. If the project is already late, the results are disastrous. Always remember Brooks's Law (Brooks, 1995): "Adding manpower to a late software project makes it later."

Myth 6
Adding more members to a development team always shortens the delivery schedule.

Shortest Possible Schedule

Since time is of the essence, companies tend to seek the shortest possible calendar schedule for their projects. This is the schedule derived from the most aggressive estimates of size and effort, and it stacks as many people as is productively possible onto the team. It also assumes that the scope is reasonably stable and the processes used by the team are as efficient as they can be. Practically, however, there will be scope creep, changes in the team (thus increasing overall effort), and potential weaknesses in the team's processes. This means that the shortest possible schedule is rarely achievable.

This being said, it is disconcerting to note that primary stakeholders not only tend to take the shortest possible schedule as *the* schedule, but also frequently insist that it is not good enough. From the standpoint of the business case, there may be important restrictions, perhaps even externally imposed, that dictate a drop-dead date that is much sooner than the estimated completion date in the shortest possible schedule. Because of this pressure, the stakeholders demand the finished product sooner. However, the naive view that somehow *the shortest possible schedule can be shorter adds confusion, frustration, and pressure* to the process and invariably makes the situation worse. The urgency of the stakeholders is not going to miraculously change the fundamental basis for calculating the shortest schedule (Brooks, 1995). While it may be difficult to be the bearer of bad news, proper communication of this fact is the key to preventing misunderstandings (see "Setting Expectations" section). The bottom line is that, if the desired project scope and schedule are impossible, something must change or you should reconsider doing the project at all. See the discussion of unrealistic goals in chapter 1.

Myth 7
The shortest possible schedule can be shorter.

Estimating the Schedule
The process of creating the schedule involves applying the work to a calendar, thus generating a *schedule estimate*. Equation 4.4 will generate a reasonable schedule estimate from the effort estimate (Boehm, 1981; McConnell, 1996).

Equation 4.4 Computation of Schedule from Effort
$$\text{Schedule in months} = 3.0 * \text{Man-months}^{1/3}$$

With this equation, if you have an estimate of 50 man-months of effort, you can expect the project to actually take about 11 months ($3.0 * 50^{1/3}$) of calendar time. Taken together with Equation 4.2, you can also estimate the size of the team (see "Staffing" section later in this chapter). There are various opinions as to the exact makeup of the equation (for example, Boehm uses 2.5 for the constant and 0.38 for the exponent), but unless you have strong internal data to suggest otherwise, it is a good place to start (McConnell, 1996). Like all estimates, your results from this equation must seem reasonable for the estimate to be meaningful. In other words, if the value does not seem right according to your gut instinct, find out why. Avoid applying this equation without a saltshaker handy. Finally, Equation 4.4 is reasonable for most projects, but be cautious when applying it to very large or very small projects, since its margin of error increases.

Creating the Schedule
Most project managers begin scheduling a project by breaking the system down into logical chunks of work and assigning bodies to them until every-

thing is covered. This is a good way to proceed, since in basic terms, assigning workers to portions of the system is the only way to create the actual project plan. Managers usually have some awareness of the talents and skill levels of the members of the team and a good understanding of how to put together software. However, development managers rarely have the same priorities as the user community. Consequently, the breakdown of workers generated by technical managers may be quite different from those envisioned by the user community. Managers may consider some bit of functionality to be obscure and unimportant and therefore delegate it to late in the schedule, while the users may consider that functionality critical.

In general, a technical manager's schedule is not a problem if the project runs smoothly. If there are delays, however, the user community may want partial functionality delivered anyway, including the obscure stuff not finished in the manager's version of the schedule. In short, managers may take an all-or-nothing approach to the schedule for efficiency, but end up stuck without anything to present to the users if the project runs into scheduling trouble.

With use cases, it is possible to create a meaningful, evolutionary project schedule that considers user priorities. To begin, create a list of the use cases generated for the project. This list summarizes the functionality of the project and from a scheduling standpoint represents the project's "to do" list. Prioritize the use cases, remembering to consider any dependencies one may have on another. Also, be certain to consider any scenarios generated during the use case analysis. The user community should drive decisions for prioritizing functionality.

It is often true that the primary scenario of a use case is far more important to the users than the secondary scenarios. Therefore, different scenarios of the same use case may end up with different importance ratings. When finished

◆ Aggressive Scheduling

An aggressive schedule is a requirement in today's high-pressure world of software development. It seems that it is impossible to finish a project too soon, and team leads are forced to turn up the heat on the schedule, especially when it begins to slip. As Steve Maguire points out, though, an overly aggressive schedule can destroy team spirit and ultimately affect the quality of their work. Realizing that there is no chance of hitting the goal, teams become discouraged. Worse, when the deadline approaches, they throw common sense to the wind and do sloppy work with false hopes of finishing on time.

As Maguire writes, it is imperative not to discourage or demoralize a team by driving it through an unrealistic schedule toward what may be an arbitrary completion date. Make the schedule as aggressive as needed to keep the team focused, but be sure it is attainable. Break apart large spans of time as needed to create more manageable, meaningful schedules (Maguire, 1994).

with the examination, you may have several levels of importance in your prioritization, so group similar use cases by level. As a simple example of this process, Table 4.1 shows a list of potential use cases for a typical project along with their scenarios. Table 4.2 shows the same list prioritized, ready for scheduling.

Create the schedule by considering the most important group of use cases first, then the next, and so on. In the example shown in the tables, the primary scenarios of Use Case I and Use Case III would come first on the schedule, since they are of importance level 1, as shown in Table 4.2.

With this approach, the software schedule, like the software itself, evolves out of the use case analyses. The sections important to the stakeholders, as determined in use cases, are written first, followed by the others. This simple approach is generally useful, but it has its potential problems as well. Because the schedule is vertical by use case, it may lack the underlying benefits of a horizontal schedule that finds commonalties among the disparate portions of functionality. These commonalties may help reduce the workload by exploiting potentially reusable portions of code. Use case approaches define a schedule from the point of view of the users, and this is not necessarily the best way to proceed with implementation. A particular secondary scenario may, in fact, be rather complex to design and code. Therefore, it makes sense to address secondary scenarios early in the process to be certain their design is consistent

TABLE 4.1   List of Use Cases and Scenarios for a Sample Project

Use Case	Scenario
Use Case I	Primary Scenario
Use Case I.	Secondary Scenario
Use Case II	Primary Scenario
Use Case II	Secondary Scenario 1
Use Case II	Secondary Scenario 2
Use Case III	Primary Scenario
Use Case III	Secondary Scenario

TABLE 4.2   Prioritized List of Use Case and Scenarios for a Sample Project

Use Case	Scenario	Importance Level
Use Case I	Primary Scenario	1
Use Case III	Primary Scenario	1
Use Case II	Primary Scenario	2
Use Case I	Secondary Scenario	2
Use Case II	Secondary Scenario 1	3
Use Case II	Secondary Scenario 2	3
Use Case III	Secondary Scenario	3

with the rest of the system. In short, consider use case ratings as guidelines, not as the final word.

Software packages such as Microsoft Project can help simplify schedule management greatly. These packages can make the process of dividing tasks and assigning workers much easier, and most can produce GAANT charts or other reports to help you visualize the schedule. Be sure the overhead involved in learning the software is incorporated into the project plan, since some scheduling software packages have a steep learning curve.

Staffing

We have talked about how adding more bodies to a staffed project to shorten its completion time has its practical limits. But how should the project be staffed in the first place? As noted by Equation 4.2, the number of people on a project is the result of the estimated effort on the project (in man-months) divided by the schedule (in months). According to this equation, given a 50-man-month project and an 11-month schedule, the best team size is about 4 or 5 people (50 man-months / 11 months = 4.5 team members).

Again, use the number derived from this equation as a guideline. You may need to adjust the actual team size given the project's complexity and the strength of the team. If you have an exceptionally strong team or a simple project, you may be able to do without a member. If you have a young, inexperienced team or a more complicated project, you may need extra help. In addition, in highly iterative lifecycle models, it is common to staff up and down during various stages as required. All these factors can change the ideal size of the team.

Once you have an idea of how many people will be needed, you need to consider the skill sets required by your project, that is, the constitution of the team. Many sources have talked about team makeup, specifically about the defining characteristics of the roles team members play on a project (Brooks, 1995; Krutchen, 1999; McConnell, 1996). Other sources concentrate on the kinds of team models available. Steve McConnell consolidates many of these common team approaches in *Rapid Development* (McConnell, 1996). Some of his more useful findings are summarized in Table 4.3.

Although specific approaches to team member roles and whole team models are great in theory, corporations often do not have the luxury of having qualified, talented people with particular skill sets available as needed, if they have them at all. The economy influences resource availability greatly. At the time of this writing (early 1999), Visual Basic programmers are in high demand, as are just about every other kind of technical worker. This has been the case for a number of years and is likely to continue to be true for quite some time.

The laws of supply and demand reign supreme. When supply is low and demand is high, compromises in quality can be expected. Consequently, it is com-

TABLE 4.3 Teams Models

Team Model	*Description*
Business Team	This team features a group of developers of equal status, led by a technical lead. Team members are differentiated by area of expertise (database, UI, etc.). This is the traditional business model and is quite common.
Chief-Programmer Team	In this model, introduced by Harlan Mills, one or two superstar programmers do the bulk of the design and coding, leaving other team members to work on specialized portions of the system. Brooks calls this the surgical team (Brooks, 1995).
Skunkworks Team	This team is a group of independent developers, segregated from the day-to-day activities of the company to allow them to focus on highly creative solutions. They typically govern themselves. These teams can be very intense and highly motivated, but are difficult to manage. It also can be difficult to assess the progress of such a team.
Feature Team	In this model, one or two developers from a company's traditional hierarchy (development, quality-assurance, documentation, etc.) are assigned to a project to handle their corresponding functionality.
Search-and-Rescue Team	This type of team is used to track down and resolve problems, especially emergency issues.
SWAT Team	This is a group of highly skilled people who are experts in a particular tool. They work together to solve a problem from within the confines of the tool set. In many companies, Visual Basic development takes place with SWAT teams, since they are responsible for solving the problem with VB alone.

mon to find inexperienced rookie programmers, database administrators, and designers working on relatively important and complicated pieces of functionality, because more qualified resources are not available. For companies that are struggling to find employees, a warm body that programs is better than nothing. When times are tough, companies have to make do with what they have.

What makes this problem worse is that because of resource constraints, Visual Basic developers are often called on to do things they would not be expected to do if more specialized resources were available. These tasks may include development of the database and object designs, formal testing, and documentation. While these developers may be fine coders, they could be terrible database designers and poor writers. The lack of qualified resources affects the quality of the project as a whole.

When a company does not have the resources available internally, there are a number of alternatives. First, the teams can be augmented with contractors. Although some companies abhor contracted work, others find it highly beneficial.

However, it can be difficult (and expensive) to find truly skilled contractors to bring onto a project. Corporations can also consider outsourcing a project completely, or substantial portions of it, though again for some companies this is beyond consideration. A third option is training the developers to be better at the tasks they are expected to do. I recommend object-oriented design training for all Visual Basic programmers and their project managers. A solid foundation in database design can be crucial as well. In fact, one of the fundamental premises of this book is to expose both programmers and project managers to topics with which they traditionally would have no formal experience.

To summarize, staffing a project is a complicated balancing act. There are no clear-cut answers to most staffing problems, so creativity is of paramount importance. Project managers and team leads need to have their fingers on the pulse of the team to ensure things are running smoothly. Changes in team dynamics, motivation, and morale can all affect the performance of the team, and it is common to have to make adjustments in personnel, even in midproject.

Further Reading

Barry Boehm, *Software Engineering Economics* (1981). This book provides a detailed analysis of estimating costs and schedule for software with the COCOMO model.

Frederick P. Brooks Jr., *The Mythical Man-Month* (1995). This is *the* classic book on software engineering. Although the examples and anecdotes are noticeably dated (first published in 1975), many of the principles are still sound today. The book's anniversary edition has four new essays and a new preface.

Capers Jones, *Applied Software Measurement* (1996). In addition to discussing function points, this book provides more information than you would ever want to know about measuring software. Trust me.

Philippe Kruchten, *The Rational Unified Process* (1999). This book provides some excellent guidelines for balancing your team.

Deborah Kurata, *Doing Objects in Microsoft Visual Basic 5.0* (1997). Chapter 3 covers requirements gathering and preliminary analyses.

Steve Maguire, *Debugging the Development Process* (1994). Maguire's comments about overly aggressive scheduling are among this book's highlights.

Steve McConnell, *Rapid Development* (1996). McConnell covers several estimating techniques, in addition to team management and creation.

James Rumbaugh, *OMT Insights* (1996). Though now eclipsed by its inclusion into the Unified Modeling Language, this book offers insight into use case analyses and many other aspects of object-oriented design and analysis.

Geri Schneider and Jason P. Winters, *Applying Use Cases* (1998). The discussion of generating estimates from use case analyses presented in the book is short and clear; definitely a worthwhile read.

PART II

Designing Visual Basic Software

This part examines the practical elements of designing software solutions in Visual Basic in detail. We'll start with a comparison of logical and physical architectures, and we'll also see how COM helps make implementing flexible, scalable software architectures easier in chapter 5.

For many corporate programmers, Visual Basic is the primary means of creating Windows user interfaces. Chapters 6 and 7 explore what is involved in designing and implementing a solid user interface. These chapters cover general user interface concepts, practical tips, detailed form design, and prototyping.

Next, in chapter 8, we turn to one of the more neglected aspects of Visual Basic development, object-oriented analysis and design. We'll start with a look at standard object-oriented concepts and learn to what extent Visual Basic utilizes them. Then chapter 9 discusses how to leverage VB's object-oriented features when designing VB software.

Finally, most corporate applications are data-centric, and most rely on relational databases in a client/server or multitiered architecture. Visual Basic developers must work with these databases on a regular basis, so in chapter 10 we will look at how to design a solid database. We'll look at table design, constraints, stored procedures, views, triggers, and the like.

Chapter 5

Architecture and COM

Before you focus on the lower-level details of designing Visual Basic applications, it is a good idea to have a large-scale plan of attack for the system as a whole. In this chapter, we will look at system architecture—the "big pieces" of your VB applications. We'll start by looking at the relationship between logical and physical architectures and by examining several of the most commonly used architectural approaches.

Since Microsoft Transaction Server (MTS) is an important tool for developing multitiered applications, we'll discuss its strengths and weaknesses, in the hopes of making it easier for you to decide if it is the right tool for *your* system. Finally, Microsoft's Component Object Model (COM) and system architecture are very closely related, so we will explore what makes COM so powerful and how it makes designing, programming, and deploying Windows applications smoother.

System Architecture

Creating software involves consolidating many seemingly disparate tasks. Some are obvious and relatively straightforward, like writing the code itself and testing the finished product. Others are more difficult to define, like establishing requirements and creating an object model. System architecture falls into the second category.

When you develop software, it is important not only to focus on the low-level details of the system, but also to step back and look at software development from a distance to help identify, in the most general of terms, the responsibilities of the system. Even the simplest of business applications potentially consist of many logical groups of functionalities, as described in Table 5.1. Each of these areas of responsibility is unique, yet there is often some overlap between the actual code that provides the functionality. User interface validation and business rule enforcement are very closely related, for example. Also, security often pervades every aspect of the application and thus is difficult to isolate. Taken separately, each area of responsibility represents a service for the application and can be grouped into one of three general service types—*user interface* services (also known as *presentation* services), *business* services, and *data* services. Sometimes the words *tier* or *layer* replace the word *services*, but the idea is the same. Not all applications have all of these types, but most are present for business applications of even medium complexity.

Common System Architectures

The nature of the deployment of these responsibilities in a system is the system's *logical architecture*. In Windows development, each area of responsibility may reside in its own component (ActiveX DLL or ActiveX EXE), or the areas may share components as needed. The system's *physical architecture* maps various logical components to physical pieces of hardware. The important point to remember about physical architecture is that adding more hardware to a system provides more flexibility but also makes the system harder to maintain. As we will see later in this chapter, COM makes it easier to write components that can live on any networked machine, but there are trade-offs to consider.

For now, let's look at various ways to distribute the responsibilities across components and typical ways to deploy those components. Table 5.2 presents a grid illustrating how several common architecture types divide the services among executable components and where these components commonly reside. Note that this table is by no means an exhaustive list of possibilities. Virtually any combination is possible—these are just among the most popular and the most familiar to VB developers.

Monolithic Applications

The simplest architecture in Table 5.2 is the monolithic application, which is depicted in Figure 5.1. Here there is one client-side executable handling all aspects of the system, including data access via flat files. This architecture is compact and easy to code, and the approach is fine for stand-alone applications of medium complexity or applications with very few users. The downside is that it is not very scalable, even when the flat files reside on a shared server for multiple users to access. Note that it is also common to deploy monolithic applications on shared file servers for multiple clients to access at the same time.

TABLE 5.1 Software Responsibilities

Responsibility	*Description*
User Interface Services	
User Interface Presentation	With very few exceptions, Windows applications written in Visual Basic have user interfaces. In fact, the ease of creating user interface elements helps make VB such an attractive tool for many companies in the first place. ActiveX controls and forms are at the center of user interface presentation, though ASP, HTML, XML, and other technologies are on the rise.
User Interface Validation	It is one thing to present a series of forms to a user, but it is quite another to develop logic that validates the user's interaction with a system. User interface validation straddles the fence between user interface presentation and the enforcement of business rules. It encompasses not only what the user does on a particular form, but also what underlying business logic needs to validate that action.
Business Services	
Business Rule Enforcement	Corporate development is loaded with complex logic, which is the essence of the business application being developed. The rules cover everything from validation of simple data elements (e.g., the *name* field can only be twenty characters long) to complex data processing (e.g., compute the subtotal, including all applicable taxes).
Security Enforcement	It is also common for applications to have secured elements. This is usually an all-encompassing feature—it pervades every aspect of the system, from the lowliest data elements to individual fields on the user interface.
Data Services	
Access to Data Storage	Again, with very few exceptions, business applications store data permanently for subsequent retrieval. The system therefore needs access to a way of getting at the data that needs to be stored. This can be something as simple as a flat file or as complex as a data mining engine.
Data Relationship Rule Enforcement	At a very low level, there are specific fundamental rules that pertain to the data being stored (data types, field lengths, relationships to other bits of data, etc.). While the logic to validate the data sometimes falls under the Business Rule Enforcement responsibility, it is frequently complex enough to merit separate treatment under data services.

TABLE 5.2 Common Logical/Physical Architecture Configurations

	User Interface Services		Business Services		Data Services	
Architecture Type	*Present User Interface*	*Validate User Interface*	*Enforce Business Rules*	*Enforce Security*	*Provide Data Access*	*Enforce Data Rules*
Monolithic	Main App (on client)	Main App (on client)	Main App (on client)	Main App (on client)	Main App (flat files, perhaps shared)	Main App (on client)
Simple Client/ Server	Main App (on client)	Main App (on client)	Main App (on client)	Main App (on client)	DBMS (embedded SQL on client)	DBMS (embedded SQL on client)
Robust Client/ Server	Main App (on client)	Main App (on client)	Separate DLL (on client)	Main App (DBMS)	DBMS (stored procedures on DBMS)	DBMS (stored procedures on DBMS)
n-Tier Example I	Main App (on client)	Main App (on client)	Business Logic Server EXE (on app server)	Main App (DBMS)	DBMS (stored procedures on DBMS)	DBMS (stored procedures on DBMS)
n-Tier Example II	Main App (on client)	Separate DLL (on client)	Business Logic DLL (on app server with MTS)	Windows NT, MTS, and DBMS	DBMS (stored procedures on DBMS)	DBMS (stored procedures on DBMS)

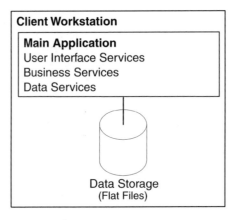

Client Workstation

Main Application
User Interface Services
Business Services
Data Services

Data Storage
(Flat Files)

FIGURE 5.1 A Simple Monolithic Application

Doing so makes upgrading the application's files easier, since individual desktops may not need to change.

Client/Server Architectures

Client/server architectures improve on this design by substituting a database management system (DBMS) for direct flat file manipulation (see Figure 5.2). The database usually lives on a separate physical server accessible by many simultaneous users. With such an architecture, you can separate data access and validation logic from the main application (via stored procedures), thus improving the scalability of the system. In relational database management systems (RDMSes), the SQL language provides a common mechanism for data access, making it easier to create different applications that need to access the same data. Furthermore, most relational database systems (e.g., Oracle and MS-SQL Server) have built-in multiuser control and security, removing this burden from the developer.

Client/server systems have been very popular over the last few years. They are relatively easy to create and support, and are moderately scalable. For most multiuser systems, a client/server architecture is usually all that is needed. As busi-

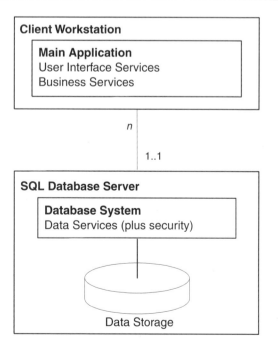

FIGURE 5.2   Simple Client/Server Architecture

ness systems get larger and more complicated, though, the inherent weaknesses with the client/server approach become apparent, including the following:

◆ Usually, each client workstation requires its own connection to the database. Furthermore, it must have all of the necessary data access drivers installed (ODBC, OLE DB, ADO, etc.).

◆ Multiple clients often need to access the same data repeatedly, putting unnecessary stress on the database. While some database engines can cache and optimize the queries, this is not always possible.

◆ Common business validation logic (which often goes hand in hand with data access) must be repeated in every different client application accessing the same database, making for redundant code. Stored procedures help by consolidating some of the data validation rules (denormalization, etc.), but do not solve the problem entirely.

◆ In cases in which the data required to run the application resides in more than one data source, the situation can get very complicated. Now the same client application must access several data stores and presumably will establish and maintain a connection to each. This can get messy quickly.

◆ Changing business logic means changing the main application, which traditionally means updating desktops.

n-Tier Architectures

With *n*-tier systems (also called multitier systems), the business services reside in a component all their own, usually on a separate physical server (often called an application server). They are separate from both data services and user interface services (though it is also common to find the middle tier on the same server as the database). The most common *n*-tier systems have three tiers, though other configurations are certainly possible. As Figure 5.3 shows, with an *n*-tier architecture, applications can share executable code. The middle tier acts as a layer of abstraction between the user interface tier and the data tier.

In theory, *n*-tier systems are a major improvement over traditional client/server architectures. The separation of business logic from the user interface layer and data layer allows multiple user interfaces to access the same middle tier business components. With multi-interface applications becoming more common (e.g., a desktop application and a Web-based application accessing the same data), this is an important benefit. Furthermore, applications frequently need to access information from many different sources of data. Centralizing this logic in a separate tier facilitates making changes to the system.

Security potentially is also improved. While RDMSes provide some built-in security for the data in the system, a separate middle tier makes it easier to

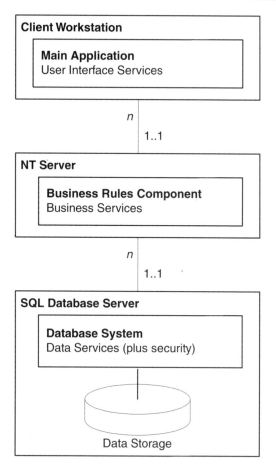

FIGURE 5.3 *n*-Tier Logical Architecture

enforce security on an object's actions against that data as well. For example, you may have a business rule dictating that only managers may void invoices for more than $1000. If all applications needing to enforce this rule use components on the middle tier, this security measure is centralized. Without a middle tier, you would have to enforce this rule either on every client application or at the database level in SQL, which is awkward to say the least.

Problems with *n*-Tier Systems At first glance *n*-tier systems are so powerful and flexible that you may wonder why any company would use a different approach for large projects. Microsoft certainly wants everyone to believe that this approach is best—they have even dedicated a whole suite of products to supporting it and a new marketing term to advertise it (DNA, Distributed inter-Net Applications Architecture). In theory, they are right, but there are important trade-offs to take into account.

The first problem is that although dividing the system's responsibilities into separate layers makes the system itself more scalable, in practice it can also make it much more difficult to maintain and harder to develop. In theory, it should be easier: when you need to make a change to business logic, you simply update the middle tier and everything else remains unchanged. But unfortunately, this is one of those areas where theory and practice diverge greatly. In practice, it is rare to find that a substantial change in business logic does not *affect both* the data services and the UI services. Admittedly, it is *possible* in well-designed and well-separated systems, but I wouldn't rely on it. In the end, rather than changing one application (as you would with a monolithic architecture or a client/server architecture), you end up changing three layers.

Myth 8
In practice, multitier architectures are easy to maintain.

A second problem is that deployment is also more difficult. Since there is more complexity to the system, it must be maintained and managed differently from a client/server system. Multitiered architectures are still new enough that few companies have personnel with substantial experience working with this architecture. Moving and registering middle-tier components and then verifying that all clients can access them is a daunting task. As we will see later in this chapter, MTS can help with this issue.

Third, when designing business objects, I find it helpful for a particular object to know everything about itself. That is, it should understand not only business logic (business rules, property validation for the user interface, etc.), but also its own database representation (i.e., given a connection, it can read and write itself from a database). With *n*-tier architectures, these two aspects of the object are at odds with one another, and the physical distance between layers can complicate the issue. The business logic validation belongs closer to the user interface layer (for flagging invalid fields, etc.), while the data-aware aspects should be closer to the database. Since it is common to deploy the middle tier on a separate server, you often have to choose between one side and the other. You can get around this problem by deploying the component containing the class in question in multiple places, but this partially defeats one of the main purposes of using an *n*-tier architecture in the first place: to localize and consolidate business logic. We'll see in a moment why this sacrifice may be worth it.

Network Boundaries and Serialization Pushing the distance problem a little further, although COM helps make physical deployment more transparent, ultimately the combination of logical and physical deployment can greatly impact how you design your applications. For example, most developers know that passing a variable by reference to a method on an in-process object is faster than passing it by value, and therefore it is common practice, even when they are not expecting to receive a meaningful return value. However, moving that object into another process creates a problem: now COM must marshal the argument both to and from the calling object, across a process boundary. We'll look at marshaling more in chapter 16. For now, suffice it to say that this round trip is very expensive, and it becomes particularly so when the server object resides across a network. To work around this issue, developers must think about minimizing the number of calls made to objects living across a network boundary and must also minimize the amount of data sent back and forth.

One solution to this problem is *serialization* of data. In a nutshell, serializing data means to pack it together into one long stream so that it may be transferred more easily. For example, with in-process objects, it is common to set properties individually, as follows:

```
Dim oMyObject As New clsMyObject
With oMyObject
    .sName = "MyObjectName"
    .nCount = 2
    .bActive = True
End With
Call oMyObject.DoSomething
```

This code is easy to read and performs well when oMyObject resides on the same machine. But it actually makes four separate calls to the object. With an object living across a network boundary, compacting the information into one call is more efficient, as shown:

```
Dim oMyObject As Object
Set oMyObject = CreateObject("MyComponent.clsMyObject", "MyServer")
Call oMyObject.DoSomething("MyObjectName", 2, True)
```

Of course with this approach, you must be sure the method DoSomething is prepared to receive all of the data as parameters (which is sometimes awkward when there is a lot of a data), but the performance benefit is often worth the effort.

There is also a way to pack the entire state of an object into a string (regardless of actual variable types) to send in one trip across the network boundary to an awaiting object. This is very useful when you have business components in a DLL that resides both locally and on the destination server, as

I mentioned earlier. You create the object on the client, pack its state into a string, and then create another object of the same type on the server. You can then pass the packed state to the server-side object for it to populate itself.

Listing 5.1 illustrates this serialization technique. The key is to define all of the properties you wish to pack in a user-defined type (UDT). You then create another user-defined type to act as a buffer and use LSet to force the contents of one into the other (this is similar to a union in C). Because it is both faster and easier to maintain, this approach is far better than the commonplace technique of providing a SelfCopy(roDestinationObject) method in which you copy each property one at a time from an object to another object of the same type passed by reference. When you copy each property one at a time, it is easy to forget to update the copy routine when adding a new property to the class itself. With the UDT trick in Listing 5.1, you cannot forget, since you actually declare the property as part of the UDT, which gets copied wholesale in one call. You must remember to update the length of the buffer UDT, but a simple run-time assertion can verify this, as shown.

Note that in VB 6, UDTs can be public members of classes and can therefore act as function return values and procedure parameters. You could pass the UDT around as the container holding the object's state, but using a packed string offers better encapsulation and is more portable.

Listing 5.1   Packing Object State into a String from a UDT

```
Private Type MyType_type
    'You must use fixed length strings for
    'the LSet trick to work. Use any type except
    'variants, including arrays.
    sName As String * 20
    lSeqID As Long
End Type
Private Type Buffer_type
    'The size of the buffer should be the same as the
    'size of the whole udt defined above.
    sBuffer As String * 24
End Type
Private mtMyAttributes As MyType_type

'For all properties, simply delegate to the UDT. For example:
Public Property Get sName() As String
    sName = mtMyAttributes.sName
End Property

'Define a property get and let to provide a serialized
'version of the object's data (state) by string.
'With these 2 properties, you may copy the state of one
'object onto another like so:
'oObject2.sMyState = oObject1.sMyState
Public Property Get sMyState() As String
```

```
        Dim tBuffer As Buffer_type
        Debug.Assert (Len(tBuffer) = Len(mtMyAttributes))
        LSet tBuffer = mtMyAttributes
        sMyState = tBuffer.sBuffer
End Property

Public Property Let sMyState(rsNewValue As String)
        Dim tBuffer As Buffer_type
        Debug.Assert (Len(tBuffer) = Len(mtMyAttributes))
        tBuffer.sBuffer = rsNewValue
        LSet mtMyAttributes = tBuffer
End Property
```

It is also practical to take this serialization approach one step further and pack multiple objects together into one string. The example "Packer," which comprises several projects and is included on-line (see "On-line Materials" in the preface for more information), demonstrates the basic technique. The key to the solution is to create a generic data moving class (clsDataMover) that can be instantiated on the client, given objects to pack, and then told to send the data to another similar object living on a remote server. The first object serves as the packer, and the second object as the unpacker. The unpacker receives the string containing all the packed data, splits it apart, instantiates the appropriate business objects, restores their states, and performs whatever function is needed. If the unpacker is a Microsoft Transaction Server (MTS) object, it can even create the appropriate transaction in which to wrap the business objects. The code in clsDataMover need not know anything about the business objects it carries (other than the class name, which it gleans from the data itself), making this technique highly scalable. The Packer example is simple but powerful, and can be expanded easily into a full-scale data transfer solution.

MTS

Recently, Microsoft introduced the Microsoft Transaction Server, a Windows NT service designed to provide a common solution to some of the problems associated with developing *n*-tier applications. As one of the core DNA services, MTS works well with other Microsoft technologies, such as Windows NT (and Windows 2000), MS SQL Server, Microsoft Message Queue (MSMQ), Internet Information Server (IIS), Systems Management Server (SMS), and Exchange. It really should have been called Microsoft Component Server because, although MTS makes cross-platform transaction management easier, clearly its main use is to serve up objects in components registered with it.

Numerous sources cover MTS in detail (see the "Further Reading" section at the end of the chapter): indeed, it has become one of the hottest topics around. As a result, we won't cover using it in detail here. Rather, we'll just touch on some of its strengths and weaknesses.

◆ **Serialization with XML**

I have also heard of developers using XML to create robust data trees to send object data across a network boundary in one trip as well. Using XML has the advantage of working with a standard, popular language, and the data can be sent to a variety of sources that understand XML. On the downside, you have to create XML trees one property at a time (making it easy to forget to add properties), and the resulting string is much bigger than it needs to be, since in addition to your data, it also has all of the XML markup. Still, you may find it better to stick with a standard technology than to exploit a homegrown approach, like the one the Packer example demonstrates.

MTS Strengths

Improved Security In many cases, business objects act as information containers, and access to this information frequently needs to be wrapped in security protocols. MTS leverages the Windows NT security model and provides its own roles for validating security.

Database Connection Pooling One of the biggest advantages of having a middle tier controlling business logic is that it presents the opportunity to reduce the number of database connections. In most client/server applications, the client needs to access the database only for short periods of time, but since opening and closing a connection is time-consuming, many developers opt to leave the connection open even when not in use. With a middle tier, it is easy to add logic to balance the load of database transactions across fewer actual connections. In effect, the clients share connections. MTS handles this (along with ODBC) by adding "closed" connections to a pool of available connections rather than actually closing them when the application calls the connection's Close method. When a new connection is needed, MTS searches for an unused one in the connection pool and uses it rather than creating a new one. While it is certainly possible to implement such pooling by hand in a COM server (in fact, it really isn't that hard), the MTS model is robust and already written.

Simplified Component Deployment As already mentioned, deployment of middle tier applications can be particularly frustrating. MTS simplifies the process with a user-friendly interface in the form of the MTS Explorer. Adding middle tier components becomes simply a matter of dragging the component to the proper MTS package, which you can create easily from within the MTS Explorer as well. MTS also provides robust analysis tools for looking at statistical information pertaining to your packages, making troubleshooting problems much easier.

Cross-platform Transaction Management Another big advantage of a middle tier is the ability to access multiple data sources from a common location. In a typical scenario, the client application makes data requests from the middle tier, which decides where and how to access the information needed. Later, when the client needs to write data, the middle tier can worry about handling transactions. MTS facilitates the creation of cross-database transactions in an Online Transaction Processing (OLTP) system by creating objects in the context of a transaction. The objects collectively form the whole transaction, and each has a vote on whether or not the transaction should succeed. Behind the scenes, MTS tallies the votes and either commits or aborts the transaction across all platforms involved. Thus, the client application can work with any number of middle tier objects without having to worry too much about how cross-platform transactions behave.

Object Pooling Finally, middle tiers can benefit from object pooling, wherein a given object is not actually destroyed when its client releases it, but rather is added to a pool of objects and selected for reuse when a new object is needed. Like connection pooling, in theory object reuse helps reduce the overhead of the system, since the system does not have to repeatedly suffer the hit involved with actually creating the object. With Visual Basic, MTS does not currently (and may never) support object pooling, but it does have the `CanBePooled` property on its `ObjectControl` interface as a stub for future enhancement. Each class implementing this interface has an opportunity to let MTS know whether its objects are poolable.

MTS Drawbacks

As helpful as MTS is in the creation of *n*-tier architectures, there is nevertheless still a fundamental challenge. While MTS does allow you to have state*ful* objects (i.e., objects that hold their properties over a substantial lifetime) within the context of a transaction, it prefers state*less* objects. (Stateless objects will be easier to pool, if that MTS functionality ever materializes.) The MTS philosophy is that an object should be created, used, and thrown away as quickly as possible. This is directly at odds with the fundamental paradigms of object-oriented programming, since abstraction and encapsulation suggest that objects should maintain their state. We'll look at these concepts in detail in chapter 8. MTS wants developers to treat objects more like packages of methods to be called one at a time, without storing state in between calls. To me, this seems like a huge step backward from the elegance of object-oriented programming.

Nevertheless, though it has a few problems, MTS helps resolve some of the common problems with creating *n*-tiered systems by providing a series of important services making middle-tier management simpler. Note that MTS is by no means required for creating *n*-tier applications, but Microsoft is clearly pushing it. It is the future of COM (COM+), like it or not. Still, in many cases, a simple client/server architecture is all that a company needs to satisfy business requirements. There is a tendency for companies to use MTS and *n*-tier development for a project just because they are in fashion. If this decision is not weighed carefully, it can lead to unnecessary troubles in development and maintenance because of increased architectural complexity.

COM and VB

Microsoft's Component Object Model is both the lifeblood and the bane of the Visual Basic world. VB programmers use it everyday, but few even realize that it is there or understand (or even care) how it really works. As Don Box put it, in the several years COM has been around, no two people have completely agreed on exactly what COM is (Pattison, 1998). On the surface, COM provides the everyday tools that allow Visual Basic programmers to work. Under the hood, COM is a wonderfully complex conglomerate of stuff that few programmers in any language really understand.

Although COM is like black magic to many, it is transparent—you do not need to know very much about it to use it successfully. Yet many authors of books on Visual Basic have felt obligated to try to enlighten the VB programmers of the world with all of the gory details. This material has its place, but this book is not it. Rather than present a long, involved description of how the intricacies of COM work, we'll look at what makes COM practical in day-to-day corporate development. Those wishing to dig deeper should refer to the Further Reading section at end of the chapter.

Exhibit 5.1 lists several of the features of COM that make it important to VB development at corporations. Many of these features are important no matter what the language, but these are especially important to VB, which makes a point of hiding the details of a lot of what it is doing. More often than not, the magic VB brews under the hood is the result of COM. Let's look at each of these features more closely.

EXHIBIT 5.1   Important Features of COM

Component creation

Language independence

Leveraging of object-oriented concepts

Separation of interface and implementation

Automatic object lifetime management

Location transparency

Component Creation

Though people often think of Visual Basic as a tool only for rendering user interfaces, ultimately Visual Basic's ability to create and use COM components helps make it multipurpose. A component is a bit of reusable executable code used as a building block for larger software solutions. COM components follow a specific set of standards, providing them with the ability to communicate with one another for maximum flexibility.

In addition to being able to create COM components, Visual Basic provides the glue for sticking them together. It controls their interaction with one another and the users' interactions with them. Components are the Lego's of the software world, allowing you to create large, complex applications out of relatively small, simple parts (though, as I remember it, Lego's were a lot more fun).

Language Independence

In theory, you can use COM components created in Visual Basic from within any language supporting COM and vice versa. The COM specification accomplishes this minor miracle by requiring that all COM components support a standardized binary block of memory (called the *vtable*), which lives at the beginning of the component. This table is really just a bunch of pointers to other functions that implement the standard COM interfaces. This allows the implementations themselves to be written in virtually any language. As long as the component supports the *vtable*, it is a COM component. Luckily, the VB compiler takes care of all of this messy COM work for us, generating the *vtable* entries that make VB components COM ready. Compilers in many other languages offer the same features, though there are unfortunate souls out there who have had to complete this drudgery by hand.

For the most part, the language independence feature of COM works well, but Visual Basic still has some trouble with certain data types, especially pointers and unsigned integers and longs, which are common in C++. If you are writing your entire application in Visual Basic, the ability to use your components from within another language is probably not that important to you. However, if your company is one of the many developing mixed-language solutions (e.g., VB for the UI layer, VC++ for the business layer, and perhaps Java for Web development), such interlanguage reusability is critical. If you plan to share your components among languages and platforms, plan your choice of data types accordingly.

Leveraging of Object-Oriented Concepts

Prior to COM, Windows development was not terribly object-oriented. Old-fashioned DLLs contained functions, not objects (the DLLs in the Win32 API itself fall into this category). COM components allow developers to instantiate *objects* from the executable code in the component, thus opening the door for encapsulation, polymorphism, and inheritance in software solutions (see chapter 8). As anyone who has ever had to figure out complicated API declarations by hand can testify, traditional DLLs, while offering the potential for reuse, are a pain in the rump. The abstraction possible with objects created from COM components makes software not only easier to design, but also easier to code.

Separation of Interface and Implementation

As we will see in chapter 8, because Visual Basic does not have implementation inheritance, interface inheritance is one of the key mechanisms VB developers have for creating elegant polymorphism. COM is really all about interfaces—more specifically, about separating an interface from its implementations. Since Visual Basic sits on top of COM, it follows that it would mimic COM's behavior. It does so by allowing the developer to create an interface with one class and to implement it in another. See the discussion of polymorphism in chapter 8 for more information.

Automatic Object Lifetime Management

COM objects take care of their own lifetimes. They do so by tracking the number of references that are pointing to them. The object remains "alive" while there is at least one reference to it, and when the last reference disappears, the object destroys itself.

On the whole, this automatic lifetime management is a helpful feature of COM. Tracking object lifetimes (explicitly allocating memory, keeping track of references, and releasing the memory) by hand in any language is a chore and in VB would be a complete nightmare (if it were even possible). We are fortunate that COM and VB internals handle this. Automatic object lifetime management does have its problems, though. For example, although VB is supposed to clean up after itself, you can nevertheless generate nasty memory leaks by creating circular references to objects. (In chapter 17 we'll learn how to avoid and debug these instances.) With automatic lifetime management, setting a reference to an object to Nothing does not guarantee that the object will be destroyed, which can make code more confusing.

Location Transparency

Even just a few years ago, companies designed most Visual Basic applications to run entirely on one workstation, usually accessing an external SQL database for information. The applications themselves were often monolithic—one giant executable containing all the code needed. When application suites needed to share code, developers placed the common code into a DLL for all applications to access as required. This approach yielded relatively fast in-process code, was reasonably easy to program, and was ideal for small- to medium-sized applications.

As mentioned earlier, more recently enterprise applications have gotten larger and much more complicated. Consequently, the trend has been to break apart the applications both logically (by creating different functional layers—a UI layer, a business layer, etc.) and physically (UI services running on a workstation with business logic executables residing on a shared server, for example). With such radically different approaches to architecture, you would think that developers would have to code programs entirely differently. But this is not the case with applications built on COM.

COM (and its partner in crime, Distributed COM, a.k.a. DCOM) makes it possible to treat calls to in-process objects the same as calls to objects living out of process and even to objects living across a network. Thus, with COM, the actual location of the object is not very important. This means that you can activate any COM component in basically the same way, no matter where it actually lives. You can therefore distribute logical layers across almost any combination of physical systems with very little effort or change to code.

However, we have already seen that in practice, you will always want to know whether you are calling across a process boundary and especially when you are making calls across a network. Coding techniques designed to improve the performance of in-process servers can actually hinder the performance of the system when scaling to a cross-process approach. Note that this is more an artifact of design, not coding—the mechanisms for creating and using objects remain the same.

Further Reading

Don Box, *Essential COM* (1998).   This is one of the best explanations of COM I have found. It covers the basics cleanly and moves on to more advanced topics for those wishing to dig deeper.

Guy Eddon and Henry Eddon, *Programming Components with Microsoft Visual Basic 6.0* (1998).   This book provides a general overview of MTS, in addition to a solid explanation of creating ActiveX components.

Alex Homer and David Sussman, *Professional MTS and MSMQ with VB and ASP* (1998).   As its title states, the focus of this book is MTS and MSMQ. Like Lhotka's *Visual Basic 6 Business Objects*, this book presents a large-scale practical example, which is developed to illustrate the book's main points.

Rockford Lhotka, *Visual Basic 6 Business Objects* (1998).   This book provides practical examples of how to develop applications with MTS. Lhotka introduces a video store example, taking the reader through various logical architectures with the same application to demonstrate just how flexible COM really is.

Ted Pattison, *Programming Distributed Applications with COM and Microsoft Visual Basic 6.0* (1998). Pattison provides an in-depth look at creating *n*-tier applications in Visual Basic. Of particular interest is his discussion of transactions in MTS. This is a must-read for anyone who wants to create MTS applications.

Dale Rogerson, *Inside COM* (1997). Though its focus is clearly on COM from the perspective of C++, this book provides an excellent detailed look at what COM really is all about, and many Visual Basic programmers will find it indispensable.

Chapter 6

User Interface Design I:
UI Concepts

Because user interfaces can be created so easily and quickly with Visual Basic, user interface design is almost always neglected. The tactile nature of the VB development environment has a tendency to encourage developers to jump right into coding, often without proper planning and design. To help you steer clear of these problems, this chapter provides some guidelines for developing well-designed user interfaces.

We'll start by looking at some of the basic elements of a good user interface. We will see how use case analyses can drive the design of your application's user interface. We'll then turn to the different UI models available to you with a discussion of form types and interface styles.

Elements of a Good User Interface

In his humorous and painfully accurate book *The Design of Everyday Things*, Donald Norman discusses some of the foibles of modern computer systems. Norman insists that designers of computer systems seem particularly oblivious to the needs of users and that computers provide a treasure trove of examples of how *not* to design systems (Norman, 1990). Since the user interface of your application is the medium through which your users will, in fact, *use* the application, avoiding simple mistakes when creating your UI is imperative.

From a general standpoint, there are actually only a small handful of features users want in all software they use, regardless of what the software is supposed to do. Consider the following:

◆ Users want to be able to learn the software quickly, without too much reliance on manuals and help files. They feel it should be obvious how to perform the primary tasks in the application. Remember that users hate reading manuals almost as much as you probably do. Your app should be designed in such a way that it allows them to learn through exploration.

◆ They want to be forgiven for minor mistakes and warned politely before they make major ones. Your software should not beep loudly or crash when the user does something questionable. Nor should it allow them to perform deleterious tasks without some kind of prompt.

◆ They want error messages and other forms of feedback to be meaningful, accurate, and easy to understand. "Run-time Error 91: Object or With Block Variable Not Set" does not qualify as a meaningful, accurate, or easy to understand error message, yet I have seen error messages like this one pop up too many times in production business applications.

◆ They want the software to work. This may seem obvious, but sometimes marketing departments can get carried away and promote features that either are missing or do not behave as promised. Often there is little a developer (or even a project leader) can do to prevent this, but it is still annoying and likely to be blamed on developers anyway.

◆ They don't want to be completely bored. Your application should not be tedious to use. Nor should it be so entertaining that it detracts from the tasks at hand (unless, of course, you are writing a computer game).

◆ But, most important, they want to feel empowered by the software. That is, it should make their lives easier and enable them to work more efficiently. I can still remember the computer system my father purchased for his business back in the 1980s. He struggled to get it set up and running, but found it so difficult to use and maintain that it was eventually abandoned in favor of the old, manual system, becoming very expensive furniture. Clearly the system did not empower him or enable him to work more efficiently.

These general principles provide a good foundation for designing a user interface. No matter what your application does from a business perspective, it should provide these features. However, there is much more to creating a user interface. You also need to be sure that the application does what it is supposed to do and that the UI is applicable to the business model being implemented. Ultimately, the guidelines just listed are not a starting point, but rather represent something of a quality assurance checklist for you to measure your UI against as you design, develop, and test it. To begin the meat-and-bones portion of UI design, turn once again to your use case analyses.

User Interface Design and Use Cases

When we first looked at use case analyses back in chapters 3 and 4, we saw that they give you an understanding of the requirements of the system from the perspective of the user. Along with supporting diagrams such as activity diagrams, your use case analyses should provide everything you need to identify the actions and processes your users can perform with the application. From there it is a small step to creating very simple mock-ups of the forms driving the main processes, including menu commands and a general layout of the information needed by the user. In fact, this information is often included as part of an activity diagram.

User interface design is one of the best opportunities software projects have for group development. For most systems, a few group design sessions and a printable whiteboard are all you will need to come up with the basic design of your UI. Depending on the complexity of the system, this usually consists of a few main forms, along with guidelines (the look and feel) for creating supporting forms. As you iterate through several UI development sessions, you will gradually weed out the bad ideas and emerge with a clear understanding of the look and feel of your application. This takes time, but is still practical in a group setting.

Throughout your design sessions, always keep your use case analyses in mind. Concentrate on the primary scenarios first to be sure your application

◆ Group Design Caveats

Be careful not to turn your group UI design sessions into group application design sessions. While you are likely to find some issues with the use case analyses you are working with, the task at hand is not to fix them, but to leverage them in the creation of the user interface. If you have issues with certain aspects of the requirements of the system, don't waste time trying to design a user interface for them—hand them back to the individuals responsible for requirements definitions. I have seen group interface design sessions take months because of lack of focus.

As for the makeup of the group, be sure to include users, business analysts, and technical leads (or developers) to get as many different points of view as possible. User interfaces created by developers look very different from those created by business analysts. Ones created by users are different still. All are usually not quite right, so strive for a blend of these three perspectives, even if they are contradictory.

has a smooth "best case" flow to it. Generally speaking, the tasks that encompass your primary scenarios will be the ones your users will perform most frequently and therefore should be considered very carefully. Once your application supports the primary scenarios, begin working on the secondary scenarios, adding UI elements to support them as needed.

Document-centric versus Task-centric Models

Most business applications work primarily with data. However, users rarely understand data outside of the context of the tasks they perform on that data. To a user, a *thingamabob* itself is not as important as the task of *erasing a thingamabob*. This is the basis of a task-centric system. For example, I once worked on the front desk module for a hotel management system, and one of the most important tasks in such a system is checking in a guest. From the standpoint of the users (the front desk clerks), it is a simple process: find the guest's reservation and check the guest in (at one point, the system I worked on did this with the press of one button). The clerk is concerned primarily with actions involving a guest. Behind the scenes, the application has to worry about guest records, inventory (which room the guest will stay in), credit cards, billing, housekeeping status, and just about everything else. This amounts to a lot of data that the user may know is out there but cannot really understand outside of the context of operations on that data (i.e., checking in a guest).

However, while most business applications can support a task-driven approach well, others have data that has some degree of autonomy to it. The data is self-contained, and the users understand it and work with it as a document (a document-centric approach). Thus, the downside to designing your user interface only from use cases is that you will have a more difficult time with document-centric applications. As we will see later in this chapter, these programs tend to lend themselves well to Multiple Document Interfaces (MDI), which are otherwise rare in business applications. Even in these instances, though, your use cases will help mold the menus, command bars, and toolbars that users have access to when working with the document. Ultimately, there is a fine line between task-driven and document-driven perspectives, and applications often blend them as the situation dictates.

Form Types

Once you know basically what you want your user interface to accomplish, you can turn to the process of putting it together. Since all user interfaces are made up of one or more forms, understanding form types can make design decisions easier. There are two fundamental types of forms your application can have: modal and modeless (sometimes called nonmodal). Modal forms must be dismissed before the user can return to the calling form, while modeless forms allow the user to switch between windows at will. Most programmers are very familiar with these types of forms and know the rules associated with using them (you cannot open a modeless form while a modal form is visible, for example).

Because modeless forms provide the user with more flexibility, Microsoft recommends using them whenever possible over modal forms (Microsoft, 1995). However, as we will see, this is often easier said than done. In fact, it is rare to find modeless forms in applications, even in those by Microsoft (document forms are the exception, as noted later). For example, consider Microsoft Word. Of the dozens of forms the application is capable of displaying, only a few are actually modeless.

Microsoft's suggestion is well taken, though. To illustrate the potential inflexibility of modal forms, imagine a user working with a modal form that an application presents for entering customer information. If the user needs to look up the customer's phone number in another part of the application, he will have to cancel the current operation. He will lose whatever information has already been entered and will have to reenter it once he finds the phone number. This can be a frustrating situation. While modeless forms may help prevent this, it is more complicated to synchronize them and validate the data they contain. In short, there is a constant trade-off between flexibility and ease of implementation.

As you work on your user interfaces, remember that there are some cousins in the form family that are less commonly found, but nevertheless add to the palette of tools for creating a user interface. Let's take a look at an extended list of form types, from the most obtrusive to the most flexible. The five most common form types are listed here; we'll look at each in more detail in the following sections.

- System Modal
- Application Modal
- Always-on-Top Modal
- Floating Modeless
- Modeless

System Modal

The most attention-grabbing form type is system modal. When an application displays a system modal form, it not only stops execution in the application until the form is dismissed, but also interrupts all other applications as well. You should use system modal forms *only* when you are certain you want to suspend the execution of all other applications on the user's system. For corporate environments in which the users are running only software approved by the company, there are circumstances where this is useful, such as to alert the user of a pending system or network failure. For shrink-wrapped applications, system modal dialogs are in poor taste.

To implement a system modal dialog, use the `vbSystemModal` flag of the `MsgBox` function. Under 16-bit Windows, there was a simple API call that allowed you to designate a custom form to be system modal, but I have not found a good equivalent in 32-bit Windows.

Application Modal

Standard modal forms are also called application modal forms. They are the most common type of form in applications and are used primarily for main application forms and to handle short-term, input-sensitive tasks. They are also useful for displaying error messages and informational warnings to the user. Since they must be dismissed before the user can continue using the application, they are more direct than status bar messages. Therefore, use them when you want to be certain the user has seen your message (though whether they actually read and understand the message is another story).

Modal forms are also useful when you want a user to enter very explicit information as part of a rigid process or work flow. By not allowing the user to move off a form until all necessary information has been entered and validated, you force the user to proceed down the path offered by the work flow or abort the process altogether. Generally speaking, such tightly controlled work flows should be avoided, but when unavoidable, modal forms can simplify the implementation.

Always-on-Top Modeless

While modeless forms allow the user more freedom to move within a system and stand out less, there are nevertheless ways of making them more prominent. One of the simplest techniques is to change a modeless form's Z order (its depth) so that it always appears on top of other windows. Like system modal forms, modeless forms set to appear at the top of the Z order will display on top of all other forms in the system. However, they do not have to be dismissed before the user can move on to another form. They are useful for systemwide reminders that you want to be persistent but nonrestrictive. I have used them in applications that display broadcast messages to all users, such as "Database will shut down in 5 minutes. Please save your work and exit." With such a dialog (fitted with a countdown clock for added drama), the users can see the reminder, but continue to work. Note that such dialogs are of less use in shrink-wrapped applications.

As a rule of thumb, do not make these dialogs very large. The main reason for using them is to allow the user to keep working, which is difficult to do if your form blocks most of their screen. Also, if possible, position them in a corner of the screen or some other location that is out of the way. If you want to be sure the user has seen your message, position the form in the center of the screen, but allow them to move it. Because the very act of moving the form is a type of acknowledgment, be sure your users do not have to move the form more than once.

To create always-on-top forms, use the `SetWindowPos` API function. As shown in Listing 6.1, you can add code to the `Form_Load` event to force the form to the top of the Z order the moment it is loaded. (Interestingly, there is no easy way to make a form always-on-bottom.) The debugging class presented in chapter 17 uses this technique to force the custom debugging window to appear on top of your application's windows. Remember that since only one window can physically be on top, using this API on more than one form may defeat the purpose of using it in the first place.

Listing 6.1   Using `SetWindowPos` to Create an Always-on-Top Form

```
Private Const HWND_TOPMOST = -1
Private Const SWP_NOMOVE = &H2
Private Const SWP_NOSIZE = &H1
Private Const SWP_FRAMECHANGED = &H20
Private Const SWP_DRAWFRAME = SWP_FRAMECHANGED

Private Declare Function SetWindowPos Lib "user32" _
    (ByVal hwnd As Long, ByVal hWndInsertAfter As Long, _
    ByVal x As Long, ByVal y As Long, ByVal cx As Long, _
    ByVal cy As Long, ByVal wFlags As Long) As Long

Private Sub Form_Load()
    Call SetWindowPos(Me.hwnd, _
        HWND_TOPMOST, 0, 0, 0, 0, _
        SWP_NOSIZE Or SWP_NOMOVE Or SWP_DRAWFRAME)
End Sub
```

Floating Modeless

If you want your modeless form always to appear on top of just one window, you can create a floating modeless form. These forms are attached to a particular form (called a *parent* form) and will always appear to float over that form. They will not prevent other forms from coming to the foreground, though, so are extremely flexible. The classic example of a floating modeless form is a Find dialog that hovers over a parent document window. Such an arrangement allows the user to work with the Find dialog until she needs to edit something on the document. Clicking on the parent document window activates the window, but does not move it on top of the Find dialog. This is most helpful when one of the forms is smaller and can be hidden (like the Find dialog). If it didn't float, the user would have to move the bigger form to get back to the smaller one.

To create a floating modeless form, you need to attach it to the parent form using the SetWindowLong API function, as shown in Listing 6.2. This example loads a second form (mfrmFloatingForm) from within the Form_Load event of a first form. Pressing the cmdFloat button toggles the floating state of the second form. Don't forget to restore the original parent with SetWindowLong when you are finished floating the form.

Listing 6.2   Creating a Floating Modeless Form with SetWindowLong

```
Private Const GWL_HWNDPARENT = (-8)
Private Declare Function SetWindowLong Lib "user32" Alias _
    "SetWindowLongA" (ByVal hwnd As Long, ByVal nIndex As Long, _
    ByVal dwNewLong As Long) As Long

Private mbFloating As Boolean
Private mhWndOriginalParent As Long
Private mfrmFloatingForm As frmFloat

Private Sub cmdFloat_Click()
    If mbFloating Then
        'Restore the form
        mbFloating = False
        Call SetWindowLong(mfrmFloatingForm.hwnd, _
            GWL_HWNDPARENT, mhWndOriginalParent)
    Else
        'Float the form
        mhWndOriginalParent = SetWindowLong( _
            mfrmFloatingForm.hwnd, GWL_HWNDPARENT, Me.hwnd)
        mbFloating = True
    End If
End Sub

Private Sub Form_Load()
    Set mfrmFloatingForm = New frmFloat
    Load mfrmFloatingForm
    mfrmFloatingForm.Show
End Sub

Private Sub Form_Unload(Cancel As Integer)
    Unload mfrmFloatingForm
    Set mfrmFloatingForm = Nothing
End Sub
```

Modeless

True modeless dialogs are used almost exclusively for documents. That is, they represent a single editable entity. Since you can have as many modeless forms displayed at the same time as you would like, they give you the flexibility to provide your user with a separate window for each entity being viewed or edited.

If your application follows the paradigm of *one entity equals one form* (document-centric), creating applications using modeless forms is not very difficult. This is the approach taken by just about every application in the Microsoft Office suite. However, it is also possible (and sometimes convenient) to have different modeless forms provide different views of the same data, thus violating the paradigm. This poses a problem with synchronization of the data on the various forms. For example, consider a personal finance software package, complete with checkbook register and a bunch of financial reports. If you are viewing a transaction summary report in one modeless window and then open another modeless window and edit a transaction included in the report, what should happen to the data in the now stale report window? Presumably, you would want the report window to update automatically when you have saved the transaction in the transaction window. Alternatively, you could provide the user with a Refresh button on the report window, which recalculates the data on the report when pressed. In the end, if the stale view is read-only, the worst that can happen is that the user gets a bit confused by the discrepancies.

However, if more than one modeless form *edits* the data from the same object, you have a genuine problem. Returning to the financial software example, let's assume you retrieve a transaction for editing and change its transaction category from *Dining* to *Groceries*. Then, before saving the change, you switch to a modeless category listing and delete the *Groceries* category. In this situation, you are likely to have some strange validation issues.

These issues are similar to those posed by multiuser applications in which more than one user can read or update the same data. But since you are working from within the same application, you can design a robust mechanism for notification, similar to those used by asynchronous activities (see chapter 16 for a discussion of notifications). The most common technique is to have your modeless forms respond to events raised by the objects controlling the changed data. When one form changes the data, the data controller notifies any and all forms listening to it of the change, and they can update themselves accordingly.

Interface Styles

We now turn to how to use form types to create a particular style of interface. The style of your application's interface shapes not only the app's generally usability, but also its scalability and robustness. Most VB programmers are familiar with the two main styles of interfaces: the Single Document Interface (SDI)

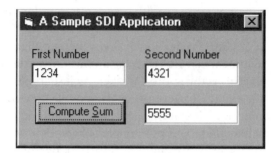

FIGURE 6.1   Example of a Single Document Interface

and the Multiple Document Interface (MDI). As with form types, though, there are hybrid cousins worth exploring. While really just variations on these two principal styles, these hybrids have become so widely used that it is helpful to think of them as styles in their own right. Let's look at each style in turn.

Single Document Interface

The SDI is the most common style of interface, and includes any application whose main forms are primarily modal and independent. Most of the Windows Accessories (Notepad, Calculator, Solitaire, etc.) are SDI applications. Traditionally, SDI applications have one central form, with supporting forms as needed (see Figure 6.1).

SDI applications are useful when your application does not (or cannot) work with individual documents simultaneously. They help lock your user into a more stable flow of tasks (work flow), which is useful for applications with complicated business logic. Unfortunately, many applications with Single Document Interfaces rely too heavily on the "button-form" interface design, in which a button on one form brings up another form, which brings up another, and so on. When these forms are modal, the user can quickly find himself under a pile of windows, making the application difficult to use. Furthermore, it is easy to create an SDI application that is difficult to navigate, especially when the program has restrictions placed on navigation based on complicated business logic. In the end, even though you may want your users to be restricted in movement at certain times, strive to make your SDI applications as flexible as possible.

True Multiple Document Interface

While MDI applications had a strong start in early versions of Windows, this style of interface is becoming exceedingly rare. MDI applications feature one main form with any number of child forms contained within the main form. Each child form usually corresponds to a single document. A common example of such an interface is Microsoft Word 97 (or just about any other word processor), which allows you to work with multiple documents simultaneously. See Figure 6.2 for a generic example.

Applications using the MDI style *should* follow the example set by other MDI applications. More specifically, they are document-centric: child windows are, for the most part, documents. The documents usually correspond to files with a specific extension. Incidentally, double-clicking on one of these files *should* launch your application and open a new document window, or, if your app is already running, just open a new window. MDI applications *should* feature homogeneous child forms, providing the same view of different data. This is a fundamentally different approach from the one taken by SDI applications, which often present different views of the same data, albeit in a more restrictive manner. The child forms *should* also be completely resizable (see "Resize Well, or Don't Resize at All" sidebar) and include maximize and minimize buttons.

My use of the word *should* is an indication that these practices are not always followed. Admittedly, there are probably instances when it is practical to bend the rules to achieve a certain effect. But bending the rules too much defeats the purpose of using this style in the first place: to provide a consistent

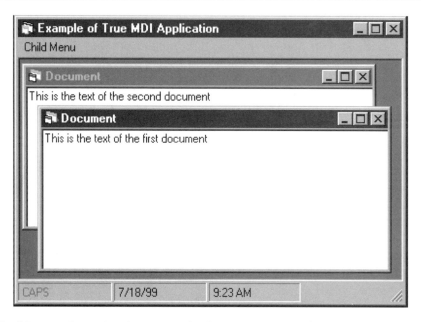

FIGURE 6.2 Example of a True Multiple Document Interface

look and feel your users may already be familiar with from other MDI applications. For example, if none of your child forms are resizable, the application simply won't have the right look and feel. When the user maximizes the MDI parent form, your app creates ugly, empty real estate that goes to waste. Furthermore, the user is likely to have portions of the child form disappear as the form is moved out of the parent's window. (See the sidebar "Resize Well, or Don't Resize at All" for more information.)

But, the biggest mistake designers make when choosing an MDI style is doing so only to gain better window management. While VB does make it rela-

---

◆ Resize Well, or Don't Resize at All

As a user of software, I find nothing more frustrating than an application that does not behave according to Windows standards. While minor issues (such as extraneous "Are you sure…?" dialogs) are merely a nuisance, more serious ones make me want to stop using the software. Several of the most common and frustrating violations of standards deal with resizing forms.

The only reason a form needs to be resizable is to force the resizing of one or more of the controls on that form. Usually the resizing increases or decreases the acreage of a view or editing box. If none of the controls change size, resizing the form just creates wasted space or cuts off controls that do not fit. Remember that resizing includes not only manually dragging the sides or corner of a form, but also using its maximize and minimize buttons. Unfortunately for VB developers, the default BorderStyle for forms is 2-Sizable. Since this is rarely what developers actually want, more often than not they have to change this property.

Creating forms that resize well is not an easy task. You need to define the smallest practical dimensions for your form, as well as how the form should behave when it is made arbitrarily large. This means defining (and, usually, coding) size changes for every

control on the form. Some controls will grow or shrink (text boxes usually do), while others (such as buttons) remain fixed as the form changes size. Luckily, there are some third-party controls that make creating resizable forms easier. You still have to figure out how you want the form to behave, though.

I also find it frustrating to use an application that maximizes or minimizes a form automatically (using WS_MAXIMIZE or WS_MINIMIZE styles) when I perform some action, especially if the application is coded so that I have no choice but to accept the new state. I have even seen the strange behavior of minimizing a form when the close button is clicked (I won't mention any names, but the product's initials are PVCS), leaving the user with no obvious way to close the form.

The moral of the story is that you do not *have* to create resizable forms—in many cases it is perfectly acceptable to fix a form's size. You just need to be sure that the form will fit on your users' screens (800-by-600 resolution is pretty safe these days). For commercially released applications, resizable forms are a good idea, since they are more flexible. However, they are disastrous if not done well. If you cannot make a form resize well, do not make it resizable at all.

tively simple to control MDI child forms with the Arrange method, you should not choose an interface style based solely on this fact. All too often MDI applications have a mishmash of unrelated child forms sharing a common container. Such applications are usually awkward, ugly, and confusing. My rule of thumb is to refer once again to practical examples: if you cannot find a similar construct of forms in Microsoft Office, you are probably on the wrong track in your UI design.

MDI applications are by no means dead, but they are dying. Microsoft's *The Windows Interface Guidelines for Software Design* mentions a handful of practical substitutes, including workspaces, workbooks, and projects (Microsoft, 1995), and these have gained some popularity. However, in Office 2000 even Microsoft has moved away from true MDI applications and variations toward MDI applications without a containing parent.

MDI through Modeless Forms

Applications such as Microsoft Outlook and many of the applications in the Office 2000 suite boast a newer style of interface that is more flexible than a traditional MDI interface. You can still edit multiple documents at the same time, but rather than living within a main form, each document resides in its own modeless window, complete with toolbars, menus, and the like. This approach removes many of the potential problems with true MDI applications and is among the most flexible of styles. While you must do without the tiling ability provided in the true MDI style, this is not much of a loss. The new style allows you to mix and match modeless and modal forms as needed to accomplish the task at hand. And like the traditional MDI style, you can drive your application from a central, modeless form, though this is not a requirement. Because it doesn't have a main form, the style is very similar to SDI, with multiple instances of the same form available simultaneously. See Figure 6.3.

An Explorer-style Interface

The final common style of interface is really just a specific type of SDI, the Explorer-style interface (see Figure 6.4). Named for the Windows Explorer application, interfaces of this type feature both a hierarchical view of data and a detailed view of data at the same time. Windows Explorer achieves this by including a treeview control on the left to display hierarchical information (the directory tree) and a listview control on the right for details (folder contents), separated by a dragable split bar. While these controls are among the most popular for creating such an interface, they are by no means required—it is the dual view provided by this interface that makes it a powerful tool.

Even though Explorer-style interfaces are popular, they are not well suited for many applications. The style focuses on the hierarchical nature of your data,

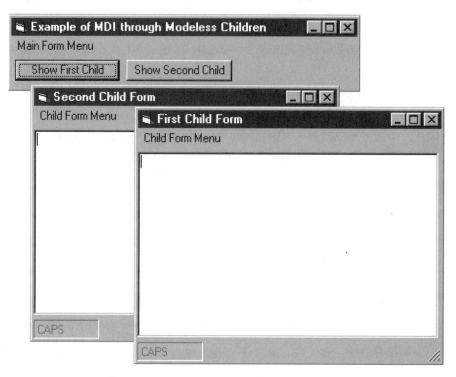

FIGURE 6.3 A Multiple Document Interface Using Modeless Forms

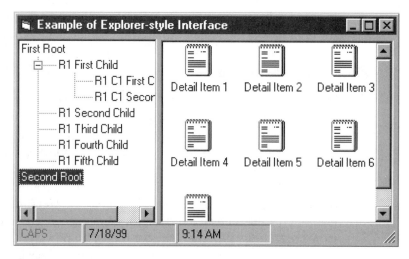

FIGURE 6.4 Example of an Explorer-style Interface

but your users may not care about the data's organization: they are more interested in tasks. They care more about what they can do with a particular business entity than what its relatives are. Developers, on the other hand, strive for neat, crisp hierarchies in data elements, often at the expense of practical usage. There is a tendency for these developers to want to present the data hierarchically, even if the users could not possibly have a conceptual understanding of that hierarchy. When deciding whether to use an Explorer-style interface, always consider whether the hierarchical nature of the data is an artifact of the business that the users will understand or the whim of the developer. If it is the latter, consider another interface style.

If you do decide to use an Explorer-style interface, try to make the interface as flexible as possible to accommodate the skill levels and personal preferences of your users. Microsoft Outlook, for example, accomplishes flexibility by having two different hierarchical sides to its interface. One is a treeview showing multiple levels of the hierarchy, and the other is a simple listbar with icons representing the highest levels of the hierarchy. Some users prefer the tree structure, while others find the simplified list easier to work with—Outlook lets the user decide. If you think your advanced users will benefit from having the full data hierarchy tree but your novice users won't, consider this customizable, dual approach. Most important, be sure to prototype your choice and get feedback from users.

Further Reading

See chapter 7 for further reading suggestions on user interface design.

Chapter 7

User Interface Design II:
Forms and Prototyping

In the last chapter we looked at some of the important topics in user interface design. In this chapter we will continue our discussion by digging a little deeper into the specifics of form design. We'll discuss the steps involved in laying out the forms in your application to achieve the smoothest interface flow, from choosing controls to polishing forms with gloss and help information.

We'll also look at the ten dos and don'ts of user interface design for practical advice in making your user interfaces user-friendly. Finally, we'll look at the art of prototyping, concentrating not only on prototyping as a form of quality assurance but also on common pitfalls associated with prototyping at corporations.

Detailed Form Design

Once you have decided on the general appearance of your user interface, you can turn your attention to designing the details of the forms themselves. Exhibit 7.1 lists several steps for designing the details of your forms, in roughly the order in which you should address them. Don't be surprised or dismayed if the first few forms developed in your project design are awkward in the eyes of the users—there is often a discrepancy between how developers and users approach the same problem. The important principles are iteration and refinement. Getting the user interface "right" is only half the battle; having the understanding to determine whether it is right is just as difficult. By constantly comparing your user interface against user expectations, not only do you refine

EXHIBIT 7.1   Steps for Creating Detailed Form Designs

1. Assign tasks to forms.
2. Determine form navigation.
3. Choose control types.
4. Lay out the form.
5. Define menus.
6. Add gloss.
7. Define help elements.

your interface more carefully, but also you are likely to discover holes in the requirements long before they become expensive mistakes (see the "Prototyping" section in this chapter).

Let's look at each of the design steps in more detail.

Assign Tasks to Forms

The first and most critical step in designing a form is to determine what the form is supposed to do, or more precisely, what the user is supposed to do with the form. Begin by assigning tasks defined by use case scenarios to a form or group of forms. Document or diagram your decisions (in fact, if you have done sequence diagrams or activity diagrams, you probably already have a good feel for how the most important tasks in the system relate to a user interface). Continue refining your interface until the tasks associated with every scenario on every use case in the system are assigned to at least one form.

When you have finished assigning tasks to a form, you may perform a mental usability check by reversing engines and trying to derive the tasks from your form descriptions. For each form, ask, "what is the purpose of this form?" You should be able to determine what the user is supposed to be able to do on every form. As you are performing this sanity check, you should also gain a better understanding of the complexity of your user interface. If you find that a particular form does too many things, reconsider the assignments. You should strike a balance in your interface. Avoid both one complex form that does too much and many simpler forms that appear simultaneously or in tight succession, stifling the user.

Determine Form Navigation

For every form in your system, you should determine not only how the user arrives at the form but also what the application does when the user dismisses the form. You may want your users to be able to get to a particular form from more than one path, so you need to assess how this flexibility affects the overall work flow of the system. Simple flowcharts (called *activity diagrams* in the UML) can help you visualize and document navigation.

There are two general guidelines for creating the navigational flow of your user interface. First, make navigation trees as shallow as possible (i.e., avoid recursive "button-form" interfaces). Complicated work flows are difficult to follow and hard to abort, two factors that make them unpopular with users, so plan complex tasks accordingly. Second, keep forms for commonly performed tasks close at hand and provide a simple mechanism for accessing them (like a toolbar or a menu). Likewise, make navigation to less important or infrequently performed tasks less direct. However, never bury functionality too deeply within an application.

As an example of these points, consider the customizable user interfaces available on many point-of-sale stations in bars and restaurants. The people who customize these interfaces place the most commonly ordered food and drink items in the most accessible places (usually only one button press away), while the less popular items are relegated to submenus that are not central but are still readily accessible. Deborah Kurata uses a hospital room analogy to describe this behavior. The more commonly used items are in plain sight (tongue depressors, gloves, and swabs), and those that are less frequently needed (or that are dangerous, like scalpels) are locked away (Kurata, 1997).

Choose Control Types

Assigning tasks to forms and determining form navigation help define a form's place within the overall user interface. However, the real work on the form itself begins with choosing control types. Choosing the appropriate types of controls can be a difficult task. You must decide whether the information you want to display to the user belongs in a list-like control, in a formatted grid, in a gauge or status bar, in an editable field, or in some read-only tag, to name but a few of the control types. You must also determine how the user will initiate actions. Will it be through choosing buttons, toolbars, or controls supporting drag-and-drop transference?

Note that at this stage you really do not need to worry too much about deciding on a specific control—you should be more interested in the type of control required. That is, concentrate on what the user is supposed to be able to do with the control rather than what specific control you want to use. Choosing a specific control is an aspect of implementation, not design, though obviously there is a gray area here. In the end, if you lock yourself into using a particular control early in the design phase, you will limit your opportunity to explore other possibilities (including, perhaps, employing custom controls or third-party controls). As we will see later in the chapter, visual prototyping in Visual Basic directly can help pinpoint actual controls.

I recommend reviewing Microsoft's *The Windows Interface Guidelines for Software Design* (1995) for guidelines in helping you choose control types. In general, the key questions to ask yourself as you choose your control types are the following:

◆ What is the basic function the user will perform with the control? The most common answers are view data (including status information and instructions), edit data, choose an item, or initiate some action.

◆ How is the hierarchical nature of the data best displayed? Does the user care about the hierarchy? The answer to this question will help you decide whether a treeview or multidimensional grid is applicable.

◆ Is the text appearing on each field editable, read-only, or possibly either? This will help you choose between text boxes and labels.

◆ For each list of items, does the user need to be able to select more than one item?

◆ Are there few enough items in each list to display them all at the same time, or will the user need to scroll through the options?

Lay Out the Form

Once you have an idea of what control types you will need, arrange them on a form. Different perspectives are important for this process, so I suggest working in a group. I recommend using a whiteboard or even cutout pictures with tape so that you can move things around easily. Pick a sizable iconic representation of your control type for easy recognition. Alternatively, attach an overhead projector to a computer and have a developer mock up changes directly from within VB. This is usually slower, but provides the best this-is-what-it-will-look-like perspective.

Begin laying out the form by determining which controls should be the form's focal points. Most forms have controls that are more important than others (labels for text fields are rarely as important as the text fields themselves, for instance). You will want the user's attention to be drawn to these controls immediately, so place them prominently on the form. (There are many ways to make a control more prominent, including placing it in a strategic location, making it slightly larger than others, or decorating it with color or an icon). Also define the grouping of the controls you intend to put on your form. Differentiate groups with additional space, frames, or lines.

As you arrange your controls you need to consider both the placement and relative size of each. You might find yourself making an editable field or a list of items much too narrow for practical use if you do not consider size carefully. Again, Microsoft's *The Windows Interface Guidelines for Software Design* (Microsoft, 1995) offers practical guidelines.

Also, consider the actions a user may have to perform to use the form, especially complicated actions like drag-and-drop transference. Actions that require the user to work with more than one control or group of controls will demand careful control placement (you do not want the user to have to drag an item from source to destination across several other controls, for example).

Finally, consider the user's journey through your form carefully. Common sequential tasks (like editing multiple text boxes to enter name and address information) should flow easily. Setting tab order can help, but even a good tab order cannot make a hopelessly confusing form flow well. Be sure all actions are fluid and are as obvious as possible. If you cannot make your form flow well, you likely have chosen bad control types, or the form is too complicated. Verify your choices by reviewing the "Choose Control Types" section earlier in this chapter.

Define Menus

Defining your menus is a relatively simple task that you will probably have to redo several times during the course of designing and implementing your user interface. The slightest change to a user interface can impact the entire menu structure, so do expect some rework. Later, when you begin coding, avoid placing too much code directly in menu handler routines—delegate this workload to other methods or functions. Doing so will lessen the impact of changes to menus.

Since menus are almost always used to drive navigation and perform tasks, you will need to be comfortable with your results from numbers 1 and 2 of "Steps for Creating Detailed Form Designs." You will also want to address how your menu options will interact with the controls you have chosen, especially if you plan to use pop-up menus to perform tasks on items in the controls.

Be sure to follow all Windows standards when creating menus, and use simple common sense. It is a good idea to avoid cascading menus if possible, especially those that cascade more than one level. Also, never place commonly needed menu items in a cascading menu, but do provide keyboard shortcuts for such items. Finally, if you are working with a true MDI application, plan how you want menus of child forms to behave when they are propagated to the parent form. What may look appropriate on the child alone may be confusing when added to the parent form.

Add Gloss

As you complete your user interface design, you should have a very solid understanding of what each form is supposed to do and how each control helps the form accomplish its purpose. You will certainly think of associations you can make between the task a form or control performs and a graphical representation of that action. The most common graphical example is a toolbar with icons, like those used in almost every Windows application. Such icons conserve space and offer a quick reminder about what the particular toolbar button does. Behind such icons are strong cognitive associations (press the picture of the printer to print, or the slanted "*I*" for italics, etc). You can even create an association out of the overall appearance of your application. For example, most spreadsheet packages look like manual spreadsheets; word processors have rulers and tab settings like their manual counterparts; and the Windows calculator looks like a calculator.

It is easy to take adding gloss too far, though. One of the common mistakes made when designing user interfaces is to concentrate too much on the glossiness too early in the process. Creating, finding, and adding graphics can be fun and gives the impression of getting a lot of bang for your buck. However, there is a tendency to want to sculpt the design of a form around a particularly compelling graphical item, often at the expense of the purpose of the form (remember step 1?). I recommend adding gloss late in the overall process.

I have little artistic talent when it comes to creating images for use in software, so I rely heavily on "borrowing" images from the Internet, other applications, and published collections of images. The strategy works well for me, and I recommend it to most developers, though you will have to watch out for copyright violations and applicable licensing fees. For large applications or ones that need very specific icons, consider hiring the services of a graphics designer.

Define Help Elements

The last step in designing your user interface is to determine to what extent your forms require on-line help. You must consider both domain help (an explanation of business rules and logic) and mechanical or technical help (how to perform a given task within the context of a form). Remember that your users probably will not want to read on-line documentation (but will complain bitterly if it is omitted), so be as thorough and concise in your help files as possible. Since help elements are defined in part by the controls on your form and its general layout, do not begin adding them until your user interface design is relatively stable. If your user interface ultimately reflects your use cases, the help materials should be straightforward (in fact, if they are not straightforward, it is likely a sign that your use cases or your forms are somehow flawed).

When designing for your actual implementation, do not forget to consider all of the help mechanisms the user might need, including tool tips, "What's This?" items, and items available via context-sensitive on-line help. I find that

◆ Resource Files and Design

If your application must support international settings, be sure to plan for them as early in the design stage as possible. Leave plenty of room on your forms for verbiage (captions, labels, etc.) in various languages. You will probably want to choose icons and other images that are universal, or expect to pick different ones for each of the locales you intend to support. Place your changing cursors, bitmaps, icons, and textual information into resource files (not directly on the forms) to be loaded at runtime.

tool tips alone often can provide enough information to keep the user happy, but this depends on the complexity of the system. Most important, be consistent in your design. For example, if you add context-sensitive help for a task on one form, be sure all forms that allow the user to perform the same task have the same help.

Practical Implementation Tips

Exhibit 7.2 is a practical list of various tips, tricks, suggestions, and guidelines for creating effective user interfaces. There is no order or overriding organization. Many are lessons I learned the hard way from working with software I found difficult to use when it did not need to be. Once you have worked through your detailed form design, review these items to double check the usability of your interface as a whole. Let's look at each of the dos and don'ts in more detail.

EXHIBIT 7.2   Ten Dos and Don'ts of User Interface Design

- ◆ DO consider all your users.
- ◆ DON'T make the same mistakes twice.
- ◆ DO create cancelable and reversible tasks.
- ◆ DON'T ask unreasonable questions.
- ◆ DO trust your users.
- ◆ DO be consistent.
- ◆ DON'T forget preferences.
- ◆ DON'T provide meaningless error messages.
- ◆ DO make your UI stateful.
- ◆ DO simplify complicated forms using progressive disclosure.

DO Consider All Your Users

Be sure to design your forms in such a way that they are usable by both beginners and power users. Power users like pop-up menus, multiselect options, drag-and-drop transference, and extensive keyboard shortcuts. Many novice users do not have the mouse and keyboard control to perform these advanced actions (especially if the action combines mouse and keyboard, like multiselecting and drag and drop). You will need to provide simplified mechanisms for accomplishing the same tasks for these users. (It is always a good idea to be sure users can accomplish every task in the application without a mouse, since a faulty mouse could make your application unusable.) At the same time, making an interface geared too much toward novice users is likely to annoy power users. Also, do not forget to include hooks to help disabled users, if required.

DON'T Make the Same Mistakes Twice

Many Visual Basic projects are rewrites of legacy systems. These old systems usually have some kind of text-based display accessed through an emulator or a dumb-terminal. Creating sexy new user interfaces for such systems is often the main goal for converting them to Windows, and VB is the perfect tool. It is therefore mind-boggling to find VB systems that are essentially recreations of the ugly text-based systems being replaced. The only reason I can think of to do this is to provide continuity to the users of the system, but I think this is a terrible excuse. Granted, experienced users often refer to the functionality of legacy systems by the look of the screen or the obscure keyboard commands that drive them. (I can clearly remember a user once telling me that I just needed to "pull an F4 = 3 = 5 report and compare it to the F7 = 9 = F4 = 4 screen for discrepancies." What!? No wonder they needed to rewrite the system.) But a poor user interface ported into Windows is just a shinier poor user interface. The moral of the story is, do not reproduce the problems inherent in text-based interfaces in Windows. In the end, you are not doing anyone a favor.

DO Create Cancelable and Reversible Tasks

Even the most experienced users make mistakes from time to time. Providing your users with the ability to undo a mistake (or cancel an action before it becomes a mistake) makes the application more robust. You do not necessarily have to have an undo stack dozens of levels deep, but at least provide a way for the users to undo their last action. If a particular action is not undoable, be sure to alert the user with an appropriate warning, especially if the operation is deleterious in some way. See appendix C of *The Windows Interface Guidelines for Software Design* (Microsoft, 1995) for more information.

DON'T Ask Unreasonable Questions

Do not flood your users with questions they cannot answer (or that they should not have to), especially when they are first learning your application. This includes asking them for information about how their system is configured, bizarre or meaningless business questions, and redundant questions. For example, I have worked with systems that expected a user to enter a complicated network path (like \\ntdevsvr\vol08\apps\bin) before beginning to use the application. Needless to say, most users did not have a clue what to enter when prompted. Often such settings can be determined at the time of installation, or you can just provide default settings and allow the user to change them in an options or preferences dialog. If you must get such information from a user, provide a "getting started" dialog, listing possible choices in an easy-to-understand format. The introductory dialog of Microsoft Access is a good example of this.

DO Trust Your Users

In my experience, there is often a tendency for developers of corporate applications to treat users like imbecilic, second-class citizens. While it is true that most corporate users are not as technically savvy as the developers writing the software, they are the reasons for writing the software to begin with and deserve respect. Furthermore, users can be very resourceful; that is, they will find shortcuts for their favorite actions that you never even considered and will develop their own habits when using your software. They are also likely to discover their own workarounds for your application's limitations. Allow them this flexibility. While you clearly need to lock down sensitive areas of the system with security measures, you should not force users through a series of handholding questions every time they perform an action. I have seen a number of systems that assumed the users were complete idiots and babied them through every task with gratuitous wizards, informational dialogs, and extraneous "Are you sure?" messages. Sometimes a little babying is helpful—it can assist complete novices and prevent users who know just enough to be dangerous from damaging data. But don't assume that all of your users are beginners—it can be downright insulting. Trust them, and they will develop confidence not only in themselves, but also in your system.

DO Be Consistent

Consistency is the key to user interface design. Simply put, creating a consistent look-and-feel to your user interface allows users to develop learned behaviors and associations. Here are some suggestions to help make your user interface consistent.

- Choose a small number of fonts and stick with them. Use bold and italic formatting consistently.

- Limit the number of colors your application uses as much as possible. In the era of 16-million-color computers, it is ironic that business applications rarely need more then 16 or perhaps 256, unless they are graphics-intensive.

- When you have chosen your control types (see "Choose Control Types" section), pick representative controls for the implementation and use them in all applicable places. I have seen many applications that use GridXYZ on one form and GridABC on another. Remember, too, that control sizes are important. Make the similar controls (all buttons, list boxes, etc.) on all of your forms the same size unless there is a specific reason not to.

- Choose a limited number of icons and bitmaps and use them consistently. Remember that many icons have specific meanings in applications other than yours. Be sure not to confuse your users by using standard Windows icons for nonstandard purposes.

- Try to standardize the general layout of your forms as much as you can. If you use a simple toolbar on one form but not on similar forms, you are not being consistent.

- Provide your users with *affordances* (graphic representations of how something should be used) to help them understand the activities they perform in your application. For example, the resizing grip in the lower right corner of many forms looks like something the user should manipulate. Slider controls look like they should be slid. And buttons look like they should be pressed. If your application requires the user to perform a task that may be confusing, explaining the operation with supporting affordances can help. For more information on affordances, see *The Design of Everyday Things* (Norman, 1990).

- Once you have determined the specifics of your application, create a standards document to state your consistencies.

DON'T Forget Preferences

I know I have spent too much time at a particular bar when I walk in and the bartender has my favorite indulgence waiting for me. Still, it is remarkably convenient and a pleasant reminder of my importance to the business. As your users become more familiar with your application, they will move windows and toolbars around, customize menus and toolbar options (if they can), and work with the same data files repeatedly. Allowing them to save this information and restore it will increase the usability of your application. Features such as this separate the truly polished applications from the average ones.

DON'T Provide Meaningless Error Messages

I mentioned the point about meaningless error messages at the beginning of chapter 6 as one of the features users don't want in software; it is important enough to mention again here. You should be certain to create messages that are meaningful to the user within the context of the application. Use critical, question, and informational icons as appropriate. Consolidate a series of messages into one message box (or custom form) so that the user does not have to dismiss too many message boxes. Users are most interested in error messages that let them do something to resolve the problem, so be as explicit as possible. Finally, be sure the tone of your messages is appropriate for the context: avoid using first person (e.g., "I have saved the file"), it can give the impression of talking down to the user.

DO Make Your UI Stateful

In addition to information messages, you can provide your users with other visual cues that can help them work more efficiently and recognize error conditions. For example, consider a modal form the user fills out to add customer information to a database. Your form is likely to have mandatory fields (like first and last name) and fields requiring the user to enter the information in a specific format (like a phone number). If the form has Ok and Cancel buttons, disabling the Ok button until the state of the form is good (that is, until the user has entered all required information in the right format) lets the user know that the information is not valid without displaying a single error message. I have even seen this technique taken a step further by adding multistate captions to the text boxes, alternating between bold (invalid) and normal (valid). As the user tabs through the form filling out information, these captions change to indicate the new status.

You can also add other visual clues to your application to provide feedback. For example, status bars entertain the user during long tasks; hourglass mouse cursors let the user know when the system is busy; and different drag/drop cursors let a user know what actions are valid.

DO Simplify Complicated Forms Using Progressive Disclosure

If you have a group of related tasks that you would like to place on one form and some of the tasks are performed much less frequently than others, consider using progressive disclosure (Microsoft, 1995). Add a More>> button or an Advanced>> button that when pressed expands the form to reveal the less frequently used (or more advanced) tasks. Alternatively, consider grouping your tasks onto different tabs on the form. Tabs are an ideal way to create more real estate when the user may have to perform several smaller, essentially unrelated tasks in the context of a larger task. Complex options dialogs rely heavily on this strategy. Whatever you decide, avoid dialogs that try to do too much and tasks that require too many forms to complete.

If you do decide to use progressive disclosure, be sure the items on the advanced part of the form are not needed often. If you place a common or required item on the advanced part of the form, your users will end up pressing the advanced button all of the time, effectively making the process more complicated rather than simpler.

Prototyping

As you work through the ideas discussed in this chapter in your projects, you will reach the point when you feel it is time to start building something tangible. This is where prototyping comes into play. A *prototype is a visualization* of the user interface of the application you intend to create. However, prototyping is a form of quality assurance, not preliminary development. The goal of a prototype is to *verify the assumptions* you have made during the course of designing your user interface. It therefore is an important tool for developers and designers alike. It also provides the ideal medium through which to solicit feedback from the user community. By providing a way for the users to test-drive your application, you create another opportunity to verify that the users are getting not only what they ask for, but also what they really want. In fact, prototyping is likely to be an ongoing endeavor as you work through and verify your user interface design iteratively. You define a few standards, then create a simple prototype to try them out. Rinse and repeat.

Interestingly, it is the secondary goal of prototyping—to provide a demonstration device—that often serves as its primary driver. Prototypes are the perfect addition to any dog-and-pony show, serving to impress a prospective client, generate excitement in the user community, or placate the demanding manager.

Besides these advantages, prototyping has several other perks that can make it an attractive strategy for many companies. Foremost among these is that prototyping gives junior programmers not directly involved in the design of the user interface something to do when they might otherwise be idle. As the design team finishes a form, they can hand it off to the programmers for coding. This type of task is ideally suited for junior developers. Creating forms in Visual Basic is trivial but fun. User interface creation is also a wonderful confidence builder. Novice programmers get immediate gratification and can see the fruits of their labor almost at once. Many junior programmers are anxious to get involved and want to jump right in and start coding something. Having them work on a prototype satisfies this craving. You have to watch out for overzealous developers, though, who want to make a mountain out of a molehill. They may have aspirations of turning the prototype into a fully functional application. We'll look at this pitfall in detail later in this section.

The task of prototyping is also a fine opportunity to train expert users and business analysts in the fundamentals of Visual Basic. Most computer-savvy people can learn to drop controls onto a form, set bitmaps and other simple properties, and arrange everything into a neat presentation with very little training. Involving such individuals in the development of the prototype helps remove the "we/they" boundaries that often separate the user community from the development community at corporations. Ultimately, the more comfortable your business analysts and power users become with the system, the more likely they will be able to use it to do what the business needs it to do.

Creating a Prototype

There are many ways you can create a prototype. Perhaps the simplest is to draw the user interface with a tool like Visio or PowerPoint, and many such tools have specific templates for just this purpose. Doing so has the advantage of yielding relatively portable prototypes for sharing among coworkers and requires no specialized programming skills (though both software packages mentioned require a certain proficiency to be productive). However, if a picture is worth a thousand words, then an interactive picture must be worth more. Ultimately, you gain the most benefit from your prototype if it is somewhat interactive. Windows is a very tactile environment, and the "feel" part of the expression "look and feel" is very important. Even the simplest of prototypes that allow the user to click and press (or otherwise play) is more effective than those that just sit there. In the end, Visual Basic is one of the best Windows interface prototyping tools around, since it makes creating interactive prototypes easy.

So how far should you take prototyping? As mentioned earlier, it is easy to get carried away with prototyping, especially when using a tool like Visual Basic that seemingly begs developers to take that next step. There generally is no problem with polishing your prototype with custom icons, bitmaps, and other visual candy. I also suggest populating list boxes, combo boxes, and grids with dummy data and adding simple navigation code to take the user from form to form. Doing so makes the prototype look more like the final product and helps remove ambiguity. However, do not add substantial business logic or data access (even from a local database) to your prototype because it is likely to be wasted effort. Tooltips and gratuitous message boxes can help explain missing underlying functionality and help maintain the appearance of a work in progress.

The Perils of Prototyping

Prototyping is not without its drawbacks, though. Advocates of prototyping at companies must be very careful about how they show off the prototype. There is the temptation to give lots of demonstrations, with the goal of gathering the kudos the team so rightly deserves. The prototype is often the first tangible evidence of progress upper management sees. There is a temptation for everyone to make more out of it than it really represents, and this can raise false expectations.

However, by far the biggest mistake companies make when prototyping is attempting to polish the prototype into the actual application. I have never seen a company successfully polish a prototype of an application of moderate complexity into a working application, though I have seen it tried numerous times. The reasons for attempting to do so are many, but they are all bad. One common reason is that bored or renegade programmers often invest too much time in the prototype, developing a vested interest in their work. If unchecked, they are unlikely to throw away what they have worked on. Another common reason is schedule. When pressured for time, management thinks that every little bit of leverage counts, so they might figure it would be easier to modify the prototype than to code the application separately. Under some circumstances, they may even want to shorten the project's schedule, naïvely thinking that the prototype represents an early version of the software and that they are somehow miraculously ahead of schedule. Users and nontechnical managers often cannot (or choose not to) grasp the magnitude of difference in complexity between a prototype and working application. From their standpoint, the user interface *is* the application, so a well-done prototype represents a completed (or nearly so) application. It is not an accurate indicator of progress, but it has the appearance of one.

Myth 9
A prototype should be used as the code base for the actual application in order to save time and even shorten the schedule.

However, in truth the only feeling of security a prototype should give is the reassurance that the software does what the users need it to do. Though it may look impressive, a prototype does not represent a working application, and it is naïve to think that the frail code supporting the UI of the prototype can be expanded in a meaningful way. If you followed my suggestions, much of the prototype is likely to have been done by junior programmers or even business analysts trained to work with Visual Basic forms—in other words, not the individuals you want constructing the foundation of the application.

To be fair, you can usually reuse the prototype's form modules in your actual applications. Lots of enthusiasm probably went into finding the right graphics and icons and positioning controls just right. However, destroy any and all code underneath these forms, and take the time to rename all of the controls according to your project's naming conventions (see chapters 19 and 20).

In summary, be certain to advertise your prototype as only a prototype and be sure everyone who sees it understands that it represents one of the green flags required to *begin* development, not substantial development progress. As Steve McConnell puts it, prototyping is a "useful dead end" (McConnell, 1998). If you treat your prototype as being completely disposable, you can avoid setting false expectations and resist the temptation to reuse it.

Further Reading

Alan Cooper, *About Face: The Essentials of User Interface Design* (1995).   Alan Cooper is sometimes referred to as the father of Visual Basic, and he has a lot to say about user interface design, Visual Basic's forte. On the whole, he does quite a bit of complaining, but the book is nevertheless well worth reading.

Alan Cooper, "14 Principles of Polite Apps" (1999).   This article discusses some very straightforward ways of making your applications more user-friendly.

Deborah Kurata, *Doing Objects in Microsoft Visual Basic 5.0* (1997).   In chapter 6 there is an excellent discussion of the fundamental philosophies of user interface design. The material draws heavily from Cooper's *About Face*.

Steve McConnell, *Software Project Survival Guide* (1998).   In chapter 8, McConnell covers using prototypes as drivers and baselines for user requirements.

Microsoft Corporation, *The Windows Interface Guidelines for Software Design* (1995).   This book is *the* reference on the Windows 95/98/NT interface. It was released to correspond with the advent of Windows 95 (and later, NT 4.0), and it covers the nitty-gritty of creating visual interfaces for Windows applications. This book should be required reading for anyone working on anything other than the simplest of Windows applications. While it provides an excellent high-level introduction to the basic structures in a Windows application (menus, forms, controls, etc.), it also contains detailed information aimed squarely at the graphic artist (including how to create shadowing and three-dimensional effects, etc.).

Donald A. Norman, *The Design of Everyday Things* (1990).   This book contains a theoretical and psychological view of designing things to be used by people. Most of the material applies to the creation of software interfaces, even though the section on computers is rather short.

Chapter 8
Object Design I: Concepts

In this chapter we will look at some of the important elements of object-oriented analysis and design (OOAD) as it pertains to Visual Basic. Since VB has its own strengths and weaknesses as an object-oriented language, the material centers on techniques that are well suited for it.

We will begin by diving into a discussion of object-oriented concepts, including abstraction, encapsulation, polymorphism, and inheritance. We'll see the benefits of each of these concepts and how VB handles them. We will also see how in practice they can both clarify software design and make it more confusing. Finally, we'll turn to a discussion of just how object-oriented Visual Basic really is.

Object-Oriented Concepts and Visual Basic

In recent years, there has been a decided shift in focus in the computer programming industry from procedural programming to object-oriented programming. Though object-oriented concepts have been around for many years, even just a few years ago it was difficult to find colleges and technical trade schools that taught them, let alone people using them practically in the corporate world. Nowadays it is more commonplace. It is no coincidence that the trend has corresponded with the dissemination of graphical user interfaces (Windows, the Mac OS, XWindows, etc.). GUIs thrive on things that the user can point to, click on, move, and so on—or simply put, graphical *objects*.

Computer industry trade magazines have reflected the shift in emphasis as well. Over the last ten years content has moved from discussions of algorithms and creating better abstract data types to object-oriented topics (especially as they pertain to the C++ language, which has emerged as one of the industry favorites). In recent years, topics have included discussions of inheritance and polymorphic classes; graphical user interfaces; and, most recently, reusable executable components.

In this chapter, we will look at the fundamental building blocks of object-oriented solutions. But before moving on, I'd like to present one of the myths of Visual Basic that raises the most eyebrows: that Visual Basic is not an object-oriented language. We'll see exactly why this is a myth throughout the next section. If you want the fast-and-dirty answer, refer to the sidebar "Object-Oriented versus Object-Based Programming" in this section. For now, consider it food for thought.

Myth 10
Visual Basic is not an object-oriented language.

Abstraction: The Overriding Principle

So what exactly is object-oriented programming? Entire books have been written to answer this question, but in my opinion it really comes down to one high-level feature: *abstraction*. Abstraction is the mechanism that allows people to think of something as a general entity, without worrying too much about its internal workings. With abstraction, they recognize and group those traits of something that make it unique and meaningful in a given context. They choose not only the level of detail with which to work, but also which traits of the entity they find important at the time. It is entirely perspective-based, depending not only on the context, but also on who is abstracting.

For example, consider George, a father who runs his own business and coaches Little League baseball. To the kids on his team, he is a *coach*. To his children, he is a *father*. To his employees, he is a *boss*. Coach, father, and boss are all abstractions of the same individual from different perspectives. His Little League team members are most concerned with those traits that make George their coach (he brings the equipment, wears a coach's hat, and buys ice cream after the games). His children think of him as a father (an authority figure and provider), while his employees recognize him as their boss (the man in charge and the man who pays them). Given a context and a point of view, certain of George's traits combine to make him a coach, a father, or a boss.

In software development, abstraction allows you to think about the solution to a problem in terms taken from the problem's domain, not in unrelated computerese. This is obviously a more natural approach: it does not make sense to talk about a *linked list of address records* when you can use the more appropriate term *mailing labels*. From the standpoint of the business domain, mailing labels are important; linked lists are not. Moreover, as you can see, abstraction ties in neatly with the concept of use case driven software development (see chapters 3 and 4). When you define requirements with use cases, you describe the system in question with entities derived from the problem space of the system. When you do object-oriented analysis and design, you work with many of the same entities defined by the use cases, creating a very natural relationship between the requirements of the software and its design.

That being said, let's get some vocabulary out of the way. An *object* is an abstracted entity, defined by its appearance and behavior, in other words, its methods, properties, and events. An object is defined and implemented by a *class*, which contains the actual code. In short, an object is an *instance* of a class. I like to think of classes as the blueprints for objects. A given class can provide any number of instances of objects.

Note that at the procedure level, there is little difference between the code you see in traditional procedural applications and that built on object-oriented paradigms. Inline code is inline code, plain and simple. It is only as you back away to higher levels of code organization that the differences become readily apparent. In procedural programming, lines of code are grouped into subroutines, but in many cases this is where the meaningful organization stops (though sometimes related routines are grouped by physical file). For example, in C, where all routines are created equal, it is very difficult to glean a program's structure from the routines alone. In object-oriented programming, lines of code are grouped into subroutines as well, only now the subroutines become methods and properties that together define a class as an entity. Often similar classes are grouped into the same file (though this is not possible in Visual Basic) or into the same component. Once you take a step back from the code in an object-oriented solution, you can begin to see the high-level organization of the code in the form of the classes defined.

Although it is a powerful concept, abstraction itself is not a feature of languages—it is the goal of other features. Commonly, there are three things computer languages can provide to help make abstraction possible: encapsulation, polymorphism, and inheritance. Let's look at each of these in turn to see what they are in general and how they relate to Visual Basic.

Encapsulation

The evolution of *abstract data types* into classes perhaps best summarizes the trend of using object-oriented techniques in lieu of traditional procedural programming. Serious procedural programming requires using abstract data types,

---

◆ Object-Oriented versus Object-Based Programming

There has been a long-standing argument in the world of programming that has stirred emotions almost as much as the infamous *GoTo* debate. The discussion centers on the difference between *object-oriented* languages and *object-based* languages. In a nutshell, it seems that some users of languages that have extensive object-oriented features (Smalltalk and C++ advocates are the biggest culprits) want to reserve use of the term *object-oriented* for their pet language, insisting that less purely object-oriented languages (Visual Basic invariably makes their lists) are merely *object-based*. The problem arose as object-oriented concepts became central in the world of computers because every language started adding its own object-oriented extensions, and in the end the term became little more than a marketing ploy. .

Clearly this is an argument of semantics. In truth, the degree to which a language offers object-oriented features is secondary to the *programmer's ability* to use those features productively. In my experience, most companies barely scratch the surface of object-oriented development concepts, or they go way overboard. Languages like C++ and Smalltalk certainly offer the full gamut of object-oriented features, but with all of that firepower it is still ironically common to find poor object-oriented solutions in these languages. The problem is that although these languages let developers do everything they might want to do featurewise, they also let developers do everything they really don't want to do (even if they think they do) and those things they shouldn't do (but somehow manage to do anyway).

---

which are data structures and the predefined operations performed on that data. The problem with abstract data types is that there is no intrinsic connection between the structure holding the data and the predefined operations. It is up to the programmer to hide the data, which can often be very difficult to do in procedural languages. In most implementations, the data is relatively exposed, visible not only to the predefined routines that *must understand* the structure of the data, but to other code as well, code that *doesn't need to understand* the data's structure or even be allowed to. From the perspective of the programmer who needs to work with an abstract data type, the focus should be on how to use the type to solve the problem at hand (usage), not on figuring out how it is put together (implementation), yet this is rarely the case. With poorly implemented abstract data types (which are, unfortunately, all too common), the separation between implementation and usage is often almost nonexistent, resulting in code that is difficult to maintain and not very reusable.

The ability to hide data and internal operations on that data is known as *encapsulation*. In object-oriented programming, classes replace abstract data types. With classes, scope qualifiers provide intrinsic control over visibility. In most languages with classes, class-level data is private by default. That is, it is not visible to code outside of the class. Similarly, *methods* (the operations on that data) are also private by default, allowing a class to hide its implementation. Of course, a class with completely private features is essentially useless, so classes allow the developer to expose only the data (via public variables and properties) and operations (via methods) that need to be exposed. Together, these methods and properties define the class's *interface* (we'll look at interfaces in detail later).

Thus, with encapsulation, one object never works with another object's data directly. This fact allows a developer to think of the object as an abstraction of a business entity and ignore how it behaves internally, at least in theory. It also allows for better reuse, since multiple objects can be instantiated from the same class. Ultimately, classes are more natural than abstract data types—they create code that more closely models the way things behave in real life.

Visual Basic does a wonderful job of allowing the developer to hide data and the implementation of functions. The `Private` keyword forces variables, properties, and methods to be local to the class, and it is a good idea to make as much data private as possible. However, in all cases you will want to expose certain methods and properties, and you have two choices that allow you to do so. First, you can make the method or property completely visible with the `Public` keyword (notice I did not say make the class variable itself public—I have yet to find any good reason to do so). Or if you want to expose them to only a select few entities, use the `Friend` keyword. However, unlike C++, VB does not allow you to specify exactly which objects are friends with other objects, so you will have to settle for the default, which makes the `Friend` methods and properties visible to all code in the project.

While encapsulation has its obvious advantages, it is also not without its problems. In theory, hiding a class's implementation and data is an elegant solution to the problems posed by abstract data types, and in practice it is usually successful. However, there are instances when a developer needs to know how something is put together to understand better how to use it. This is almost always the case when optimizing the performance of an application. For example, if a particular method takes a substantial amount of time to run, a developer optimizing for performance should be certain that method is not called within tight loop structures, and so on. In practice, only by understanding exactly what an object does under the hood can you create a truly robust system. In the end, you should not have to know, but you will often want to.

Polymorphism

Polymorphism has something of a confusing definition and usage. It literally means the ability to have many shapes. In programming, it has two different, but related meanings. First, polymorphism *is the ability of a consumer object to use any provider object that matches some standard*. For example, an animal doctor (consumer) knows how to treat any kind of domestic dog (provider) equally well, no matter what the specific breed. In this case, dog is the standard, so the vet can examine Saint Bernards and toy poodles in much the same way. The animal doctor might also be able to work with house cats, but differently from dogs.

Second, polymorphism refers to *an object's ability to show more than one face to the outside world*. For example, my laptop computer meets all of the standards associated with *computers*, but also those normally associated with *paperweights*. Thus, a person could use my laptop as a computer or as a paperweight. The same object can have many shapes.

Polymorphism via Late Binding

In Visual Basic, you have two ways of implementing polymorphic objects that satisfy both of the definitions. First, you can use late binding. Simply declare your object variable to be of type `Object` and call `CreateObject` to instantiate an instance of a particular class. You can then use the object as you would an early bound object (see Listing 8.1). This satisfies definition number one, since your code can work with any object (as long as it contains the appropriate methods and properties). Note that you can also treat the object as more than one abstraction at a time just by calling different methods, satisfying the second definition.

Listing 8.1   Polymorphism via Late Binding

```
Dim oFirstObject As Object
Dim oSecondObject As Object
Dim sObjectType As String
'Get the class name
sObjectType = InputBox("Enter the type of the first object:")
'Create the object
Set oFirstObject = CreateObject(sObjectType)
'Use it
Call oFirstObject.Method1
Debug.Print oFirstObject.Property1
'Destroy it
Set oFirstObject = Nothing

'Repeat for second object
sObjectType = InputBox("Enter the type of the second object:")
Set oSecondObject = CreateObject(sObjectType)
Call oSecondObject.Method1
Debug.Print oSecondObject.Property1
Set oSecondObject = Nothing
```

Late binding has the advantage of allowing you to work with an object whose exact type name (the name of the application concatenated with the name of the class, separated by a period) is not known until runtime. However, late binding has numerous disadvantages as well. Besides being well over ten times slower than early binding, late binding provides no compile-time check of the existence of the class of the object, or the methods and properties you call on the object. For example, you may be expecting your late bound object to have five methods, but if for some reason only four are implemented, a call to the missing method (which may only happen under the strangest of circumstances in your code) will generate a runtime error. If the class specified in the `CreateObject` command cannot be found, you will also get a runtime error. This means that you have to litter your code with specialized error trapping, and you do not benefit from the VB IDE's automatic member listing and quick info features.

In VB 4, late binding was the only way to implement polymorphism. Under VB 5 and 6, you can use a second technique, an interface.

Polymorphism and Interfaces

In my opinion, the most powerful new feature of VB 5 was its ability to create a class that implemented a predefined interface. An *interface* defines the characteristics of an object. It is the object's "face," that is, the methods, properties, and events that object exposes to the world. Another way to think of an interface is that it constitutes a contract between an object and the code that uses it. The individual public methods and properties are the terms of the contract; the object agrees to provide them, and the calling code agrees not to try to call anything else. And just like the real world, if either party breaks the contract, bad things can happen. As we saw, with late binding there is no explicit contract. The calling code must trust that the object will indeed provide the methods and properties it calls.

COM is built around interfaces. In fact, its key internal functions help explain what methods and properties an object has (it queries the object for its interface using, appropriately enough, the standard `QueryInterface` method). When developing COM components, it is common to separate an interface definition from its implementation(s). This allows you to define an interface once, but implement it many times, thus creating polymorphism, according to the first definition. This technique is sometimes called *interface inheritance*. VB is built on COM and allows you to create and use COM interfaces easily. Furthermore, since COM is a binary standard, you can use the interfaces you create in VB in any language platform that supports COM.

In Visual Basic, you define an interface by creating a class and adding the public methods and properties you wish to be part of the interface. The class's instancing property is best set to `PublicNotCreatable`, but `MultiUse` works as well. Do not add inline code to the class, however, since its purpose is not to provide functionality but rather to define (in writing, like a contract) what the functionality will be. Classes designed to define interfaces traditionally have the prefix I, as in `IUnknown`, to distinguish them from classes with implementations.

To turn your interface classes into COM interfaces, you can compile them into a DLL, then reference the DLL from within projects that need access to the interfaces. Alternatively, you can have VB generate a type library file (i.e., a file with a .TLB extension) and reference it instead of the DLL. Type libraries have less overhead and are more of the COM way of doing things, but are a little more complicated to create. To generate a type library, add the interface classes you wish to have in the library to a DLL project. Name the project appropriately and check the infrequently used "Remote Server Files" option under the project's component properties (this dialog appears in Figure 8.1). With this option checked, when you compile the project into a DLL, VB generates the type library file for you. You can unregister and delete the DLL itself—it is no longer needed. Note that if you are comfortable with C-style types and header files, you can also create a type library file manually. See the sidebar "Manual Type Library Creation" for more information.

Once you have defined your interface, there are two ways to use it. First, you will want one or more classes to implement the interface. This is accom-

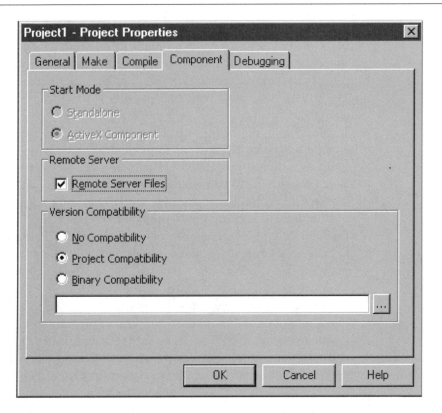

FIGURE 8.1 Project Properties, the Component Tab

◆ Manual Type Library Creation

To create a type library from scratch, you create an interface source code file in either IDL (Interface Definition Language) or ODL (Object Description Language). These two languages are very similar, though IDL is becoming more of the standard, since it is the choice of hardcore C++ programmers doing low-level COM programming. Each has its own compiler (`midl` and `mktyplib`, respectively), and both are a bit quirky to use.

Though it is possible, the only good reason I have found to create type libraries by hand is if you intend to use them with languages other than Visual Basic (C++ or Delphi, for example). Handmade type libraries are more flexible. But remember that it is possible to create type libraries by hand that are unusable by VB, so make your decision whether to do so or not wisely. To get a good feel for what a VB-friendly type library looks like, examine a few of the interface type libraries you have created in VB with the application `oleview.exe`, which ships with Visual Studio.

While a complete discussion of IDL and ODL is beyond the scope of this book, *Programming Distributed Applications with COM and Visual Basic 6.0* (Pattison, 1998) and *Hardcore Visual Basic* (McKinney, 1997) can point you in the right direction. I would also recommend searching through the Books Online, even though the documentation is a bit light and there are few examples.

---

plished with the `Implements` keyword. Simply reference the interface you wish to implement in your project's references and then add a new class to the project. This class will implement the interface, so include the `Implements` keyword followed by the name of the interface at the top of the class's code module (see Listing 8.2). When you do so, the interface name appears in the "Object" dropdown combo on the code pane (the one on the left). When you select the interface in this list, the methods and properties you are expected to implement appear in the "Procedure" dropdown (the one on the right).

This behavior should be familiar—it is how you code handlers for events raised by controls. You must select each of the methods and properties listed in the dropdown and must add at least one line of code to each of the routines (though it may be a comment). Visual Basic will not let you compile an implementation of an interface unless you have provided code for all of the interface members. At the same time, however, VB optimizes your code, stripping out routines without code, so you must add a comment to prevent it from doing so.

Listing 8.2 Polymorphism via an Interface

Code for IDog Class:

```
Public Sub Bark()
'No implementation should go here
End Sub
```

```
Public Property Get sName() As String
'No implementation should go here
End Property
```

Code for class implementing IDog:

```
'This line will make the class look like an "IDog"
'object regardless of what its actual class name is.
Implements IDog

Private Sub IDog_Bark()
'Implementation goes here
End Sub

Private Property Get IDog_sName() As String
'Implementation goes here
End Property
```

When you select a procedure to implement from the dropdown, it appears as a Private routine with the name IMyInterface_AMethod, where IMyInterface is the name of the interface in question and AMethod is the name of the method (note the free underscore, just as with events). If this seems strange at first glance (especially the fact that it is Private by default), don't worry—it is strange at second and third glances as well. We'll look at why VB does this shortly.

Once you have implemented the interface in one or more classes, you can use the interface name to refer to any actual implementation of that interface and access methods and properties as needed. Simply declare a variable to be of the interface type and then use the Set command to attach the reference to an object that implements the interface, as in Listing 8.3.

Listing 8.3   Calling Implemented Methods via Interface Reference

```
'Declare interface reference and create two implementation
'objects.
Dim oDog As IDog
'These 2 classes implement IDog
Dim oPoodle As New clsPoodle
Dim oStBernard As New clsStBernard

'Attach oDog to the first instance of
'the implementation
Set oDog = oPoodle
'Use oDog - this will actually call oPoodle
oDog.Bark   'Poodle Barks

'Attach oDog to the other instance of
'the implementation
Set oDog = oStBernard
'Use oDog - this will actually call oStBernard
oDog.Bark   'St. Bernard Barks
```

```
'Cleanup
Set oDog = Nothing
Set oPoodle = Nothing
Set oStBernard = Nothing
```

Thus, with interfaces, your code can treat all objects that are implementing the same interface the same way. Since the consumer object only understands an object by its interface and since Visual Basic requires that you implement the entire interface, you have an elegant mechanism for creating polymorphism (definition one). Note that when a class implements an interface, it is not restricted to the interface's methods and properties. It can add as many behaviors as it needs, including implementing other interfaces. Thus, an object has the ability to show more than one face to the world. Refer to the on-line example `IntFcTst.vbp` for a complete example of how to create objects that implement more than one interface (see "On-line Materials" in the preface).

Of course, using interfaces to create polymorphic objects is not without its drawbacks. First, once you have implemented an interface, you cannot change it. Ever. Actually, Visual Basic allows you to, but doing so would be a violation of the COM contract described earlier. We all know how COM rules work when changing a DLL: you can add public methods, but may not remove public methods or change their parameter lists. But with interfaces, this rule does not really apply, unless you have total control over every component that accesses or implements the interface. Visual Basic takes special care to insist that you implement every aspect of an interface, and changing the interface after the fact undermines this effort. Imagine the problem you would have when some calling code working with a new definition of an interface attempted to call code on an object implementing an old version of the interface. In short, if you need to change an interface, create an entirely new interface with a different name.

Second, while objects may implement more than one interface, calling code can work with only one of those interfaces at a time. Let's return once again to our friend George. If George were a class, its name would be `clsGeorge`, implementing the `ICoach`, `IFather`, and `IBoss` interfaces, as we described before. However, since VB makes all methods and properties implemented as part of an interface private (and, as we have seen, changes their names), `clsGeorge` actually has no public methods or properties. This means that you cannot call `oGeorge.BuyIceCream` or `oGeorge.PayMe`, since these are actually part of the `ICoach` and `IBoss` interfaces. To access these methods, you need to create a reference to `ICoach` and `IBoss` and set them equal to an instance of `clsGeorge`, as in Listing 8.4. (For an extended example of how to work with objects that implement multiple interfaces, refer to the code in `IntFcTst.vbp`. See "On-line Materials" in the preface for details.)

Listing 8.4   Working with Objects That Implement Multiple Interfaces

```
'clsGeorge implements both ICoach and IBoss
Dim oGeorge As New clsGeorge
Dim oCoach As ICoach
Dim oBoss As IBoss

'While George is at work...
Set oBoss = oGeorge
Call oBoss.PayMe
'Note: We cannot call oGeorge.PayMe

'While George is coaching...
Set oCoach = oGeorge
Call oCoach.BuyIceCream
'Likewise: We cannot call oGeorge.BuyIceCream

Set oCoach = Nothing
Set oBoss = Nothing
Set oGeorge = Nothing
```

This seems like a lot of extra work, especially if the calling code knows that George is a coach, a father, and a boss and wants to call methods from these interfaces in mixed order. Ideally, you would want to be able to refer to *either* oBoss.PayMe or oGeorge.PayMe, as the situation required. Of course, you could add the public methods and properties of all the interfaces to clsGeorge and delegate their implementations internally to the interface implementations, but doing so defeats the purpose of polymorphism. For a discussion of delegation, see the "Inheritance" section that follows. You could also change the private methods implementing the interfaces to public, but again this is merely an awkward hack, not an elegant solution.

Although it is strange, there is a reason for this behavior. If you have two different interfaces that have a method with the same name (ICoach and IFather may both have a BuyIceCream method, for example), how would you know (or specify) which method to use when you called oGeorge.BuyIceCream? It is this very paradox which forces Visual Basic to change the names of the interface methods as you implement them. By itself, BuyIceCream is ambiguous, but ICoach_BuyIceCream and IFather_BuyIceCream are not. For those of you familiar with C++, this is one of the classic problems with multiple inheritance.

Combining Late Binding and Interfaces

Actually, there is a third way to implement polymorphism in VB, though it is really just a combination of the late binding and interface implementation techniques. From within VB, you can declare a reference to the interface, then set that reference to an instance of an object created at runtime. This provides the best of both worlds: you do not have to know the exact type name of the class that will be used until runtime, and you still can use the object by working with an early-bound reference to the interface the object implements. You get the flexibility of late binding with the performance and other benefits of early binding. Listing 8.5 illustrates this technique. Note that if the late-bound object does not implement the interface in question, VB will generate a runtime error, so you can know immediately if the object meets the criteria defined by the interface, not when a call to some obscure method is made, as you would with late binding. This is because an object implementing an interface *must* implement the entire interface. Visual Basic enforces this when you use the Implements keyword and compile an implementation.

Listing 8.5 Combining Late Binding and Interfaces

```
Dim oDummyObject As Object
Dim oDog As IDog
Dim sObjectName As String

'Get the object type from the user.
sObjectName = InputBox("Enter Breed of Dog:")
'This line creates the object at runtime. This
'is late binding by definition.
Set oDummyObject = CreateObject(sObjectName)
'This next line sets the early-bound reference to the
'interface to the object just created. If oDummyObject does not
'implement IDog, this call will fail with a runtime error.
'Note: We can also use TypeOf function to check ahead as so:
'If Not TypeOf oDummyObject Is IDog Then
'Do some error code here
'End If
On Error Resume Next
Set oDog = oDummyObject 'i.e., clsStBernard works, clsCat fails
If Err.Number <> 0 Then
    'Do some error code here - the object does
    'not implement the interface
End If
'Now we can destroy the reference to the dummy object
'and work exclusively with the early bound reference.
Set oDummyObject = Nothing
Call oDog.Bark    'Make the dog bark
Debug.Print oDog.Name    'Show the dog's name
Set oDog = Nothing
```

Inheritance

If there is a single language feature that Visual Basic developers have asked for repeatedly only to have their pleas ignored by Microsoft, it is inheritance (though rumor has it, once again, that inheritance will be included in the next release of VB). In fact, VB's lack of inheritance has probably done more damage

◆ Interfaces and Events: A Lesson in Frustration

I once designed a system that had to configure itself extensively at runtime. Specifically, it needed to work with one of any number of components that all looked the same, but could not determine which one was needed until it retrieved some information from its database at runtime. This sounded like a job for polymorphism via an interface and late binding—in fact, I was convinced it was the ideal solution (and still am). I defined the interface with an interface class, adding the appropriate methods, properties, and events, and compiled the project into a DLL. I then wrote the code that needed to work with the different components and finally began coding several of the components needed to implement that interface.

I was about halfway through implementing the first component when I discovered that although I could define events in an interface, Visual Basic provides no way to raise events defined in an interface from within a class implementing that interface. In the code that used the interface, I was able to declare a variable using the type of the interface and the `WithEvents` keyword and expected to be able to trap the events, but since my implementation could not raise the events, the event handlers would never fire.

At first, I thought I was making some simple mistake, but after hours of staring at the problem, I was convinced my approach was sound. Surely VB would not let me define an interface with an event only to deny me from using it, or would it? Thinking that maybe it was some VB DLL quirk causing the problem, I ditched the interface DLL and had VB generate a type library, then implemented the interface as defined in the type library. Again, there was no way to raise the events defined, even though they were plainly visible in the object browser. Of course the documentation offered no help, so I was on my own. After sacrificing most of a weekend, I gave up, and I know now that what I was attempting to do is just not possible in Visual Basic, for a variety of reasons that relate more to how C++ and COM work than Visual Basic.

What was most frustrating was that my proposed solution was exceedingly elegant and would have allowed for a scalable and maintainable system, yet I was forced to use an arcane hack to work around the problem. Under my intended solution, other developers could have added new, robust components simply by implementing a predefined (and relatively simple) interface. As it turned out, they had to implement the interface and make calls to a late-bound object to raise the events.

to the language's reputation than any other omission. It is the main roadblock that prevents VB from being a "true" object-oriented language in the eyes of VB critics (see sidebar, "Object-Oriented versus Object-Based Programming," on page 124). Let's see what all the fuss is about.

Inheritance and Reuse

Inheritance in software development is like inheritance in real life. It is the ability of a descendant (sometimes called a child) to gain or *reuse* the features or benefits provided by ancestors (sometimes called parents). In object-oriented software development, a class can inherit the methods and properties of another class, *along with their implementations*. This is known as *implementation inheritance*. The child class can also override the parent's implementation and even add new functionality all its own. Simply put, this makes the child a more specific type of the parent (an "is a" relationship). When the child relies on the parent to implement part of its behavior, you have created reusable code. Note that it is also possible for a child class to directly inherit code from more than one parent. This is known as *multiple inheritance*.

For a simple example of inheritance, consider the class `clsStBernard`. It inherits all of the features of `clsGiantBreed`, which inherits all of the features of `clsDog`, which inherits all of the features of `clsPet`, and so on. Put another way, a St. Bernard *is a* giant breed, which *is a* type of dog, which in turn *is a* kind of pet. When you call the property `clsStBernard.sName`, you are actually calling code that resides in `clsPet`. Figure 8.2 illustrates these relationships. Incidentally, diagrams like the one in Figure 8.2 are known as *inheritance trees* or *class hierarchy diagrams*.

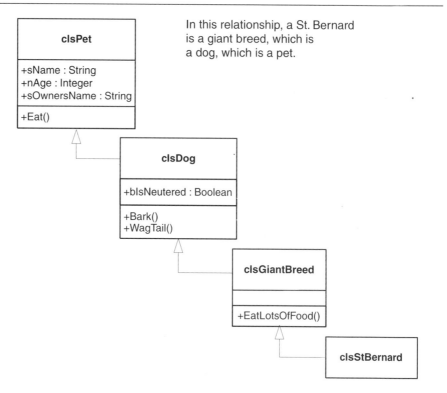

FIGURE 8.2 A Simple Inheritance Tree

Inheritance without Reuse: Defining Behaviors

While the main point of inheritance is to reuse code that lives in a parent class, it is also used to make types of classes, in other words, classes that look like the parents, but do not behave like the parents. In C++, parent classes with methods that have no implementation (virtual methods) are known as abstract classes. When a child inherits from an abstract class, it implements the virtual methods itself. Thus, while it and all of its siblings look like the parent, their individual behaviors are unique. In the end, this is really just a way to implement polymorphism (in fact, it is a very good way, known as *interface inheritance*, introduced earlier), since the net result is that the children are essentially interchangeable (see the first definition of polymorphism earlier in this chapter), though they behave differently.

Let's look at a simple example of this kind of inheritance, concentrating on the process of creating the inheritance tree. Note that the process is the same whether you are trying to create truly reusable code or simply defining the appearance of related objects. To begin, look for commonalties among your objects (both attributes and behaviors) and extract and group them, repeating the process as needed. In many cases, there will be some obvious commonalties to get you started, but don't be afraid to use trial-and-error to dig out other, more subtle, similarities. Eventually, you will have defined several interfaces, which you can then use to implement actual behaviors.

For example, consider three shapes: a rectangle, triangle, and an ellipse (see Figure 8.3). Though they are very different, there are some commonalties among them. For example, each can be drawn, is likely to have a `Draw` method, and will probably have a `lLineWidth` property as well. We can extract this common behavior and the common trait and place them into a separate interface class (`IShape`). Digging a little deeper, triangles and rectangles are polygons and therefore share the `nNumberOfSides` property (`IPolygon`). Rectangles have `lLength` and `lWidth` properties (`IRectangle`), and a triangle might have a `bIsRightTriangle` property (`ITriangle`). Ellipses do not have sides, but do have an `Origin` (`IEllipse`).

Once we have defined the interfaces, implementing a given shape is as simple as implementing all of its ancestral interfaces. For instance, to implement a square, we would create a class called `clsSquare` and implement the `IShape`, `IPolygon`, and `IRectangle` interfaces. To create a circle, we would define `clsCircle` and implement `IShape` and `IEllipse`. We can create many other shapes this way as well.

Note that in this example, there is no code reuse—we couldn't possibly have a circle draw itself the same way as a square. We simply want both `clsCircle` and `clsSquare` to be shapes. Ultimately, by going through the process used to create inheritance trees, we have defined templates for creating polymorphic objects. Thus, in this sense, inheritance and polymorphism are closely related.

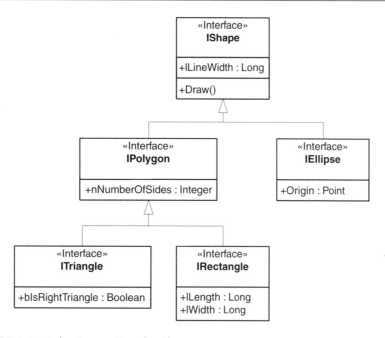

FIGURE 8.3 Inheritance Tree for Shapes

Drawbacks of Inheritance

As we saw in the earlier discussion of polymorphism, VB has a solid mechanism for creating and implementing interfaces. However, achieving actual reuse through inheritance is not an option for VB programmers, since VB does not have inheritance.

But perhaps VB's lack of inheritance is a blessing in disguise. The biggest problem with inheritance is that it is easy to get carried away with what appear to be elegant designs. Specifically, there seems to be an especially strong temptation to overengineer solutions by creating elaborate, but essentially meaningless inheritance trees that offer no practical benefits. This can be caused by a poor understanding of the requirements or by developers wanting to flex their technological muscles, to name but a few of the causes. No matter what the reason, complex hierarchies seldom are necessary and can confuse an otherwise elegant solution.

For example, in our shapes hierarchy just described, we could easily have added `IClosedShape` (with property `dblArea`), `IParallelogram` (with properties `radAngle1` and `radAngle2`), and numerous other interfaces that would have made implementing `clsSquare` a nightmare. Yes, a square is all of these things and more, but if the system only needs to treat it as a shape, the extra detail confuses the issue. I have seen, in one particular case, C++ inheritance trees with so many branches and generations that the software was impossible to maintain. Changing one of the grandparents or great-grandparents in the tree had a huge (and ironically, usually unpredictable) impact on the system. Over time, the programmers on this system ended up having to create whole new classes (copying the bulk of the code from existing classes) to make minor changes to the software, thus defeating the whole point of using inheritance in the first place: to facilitate reuse.

I find that in most cases a shallow inheritance tree, no more than two or three generations deep, allows for optimal reuse and flexibility. I also tend to avoid multiple inheritance, when the ancestors share an ancestor themselves. This type of genealogical inbreeding can be very difficult to follow logically and even harder to implement without the benefits of built-in inheritance. If you find yourself extracting too many ancestors, rethink your strategy. Concentrate less on the grandparents and more on the uncles, aunts, nephews, and nieces.

In short, it is a fallacy to assume that inherited code is somehow magically reusable by default. In the end, the developers and designers need to know what they are doing. They must still design their apps with practical reuse in mind. Inheritance simply makes it easier (in some cases) to implement their reuse strategy.

Myth 11
Code with inherited functionality is always practically reusable.

Reuse through Delegation

Although Visual Basic does not have inheritance, you can simulate implementation inheritance, though it is tedious. The most common approach is to use *delegation*. With delegation, Object A reuses the code in Object B by calling Object B's methods and properties while passing them off as its own. Object A usually contains a module-level reference to Object B, created during Object A's initialization and destroyed upon termination. For an example refer to Figure 8.4. Here, clsPayroll needs to retrieve the employee's and employer's addresses. First it calls oEmployee.GetAddress. This routine delegates the call to clsAddress, which prompts the user for the address information. Similarly, when clsPayroll calls oEmployer.GetAddress, clsEmployer delegates the call once again to clsAddress. Both clsEmployee and clsEmployer have a GetAddress method, but clsAddress does all of the work, thus its code is reused.

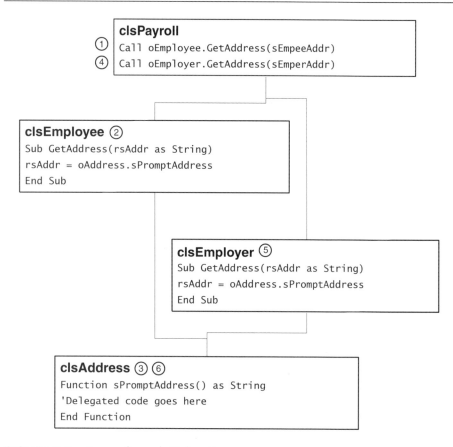

FIGURE 8.4 Reuse through Delegation

Delegation is commonly used when ActiveX controls are created in Visual Basic. In many cases, a homegrown control consists of several constituent controls. The composite control often calls methods and properties on these child controls to do the real work (see chapter 15 for more information on creating ActiveX controls).

Myth 12
Without inheritance, you cannot create reusable code.

Visual Basic's Object-Oriented Features

To summarize, let's take a look at what Visual Basic offers in the way of object-oriented features, along with practical workarounds for overcoming its shortcomings.

Abstraction

Visual Basic allows creation classes with methods, properties, and events, so abstraction is something VB handles well. In addition, because it allows only one class per physical file, VB makes classes seem even more individual and autonomous, which can aid in abstraction.

Encapsulation

Visual Basic earns high marks for encapsulation. It allows developers to hide any amount of data they wish by creating private members. They can provide access to the data with property lets and gets as needed. Furthermore, VB's let syntax ([Let] oDog.sName = sNameVar) allows programmers to treat what is essentially a function as if it were actually a variable. This is syntactic sugar that I find to be more natural in form than the property assignment syntax in most other languages, which often requires awkward functions such as oDog->SetNameValue(sNameVar).

The biggest drawback with the way VB handles encapsulation is that although developers can create Friend functions, they cannot specify who a function's (or class's) friends are. Also, I see no need for public variables at the class level—Microsoft would do well to phase them out and force developers to use property lets and gets.

Polymorphism

By allowing the creation and implementation of interfaces, VB classes can be made to satisfy both definitions of polymorphism presented early in this chapter. That is, a consumer object can use any object implementing a specific interface, and a class can implement as many interfaces as needed. Furthermore, by combining late binding and interfaces, developers can even work with specific implementations in objects whose types are not known until runtime.

VB does not allow programmers to raise events defined in an interface in a class implementing that interface, though. Conceptually, this would be a powerful feature, allowing the creation of types of classes (even controls) with dramatically different implementations.

Inheritance

Although VB does not have a built-in mechanism for creating reusable code with inheritance (a serious drawback in the eyes of many), delegation simulates such reuse, but the technique is tedious and manual. Also, with interface inheritance, developers can create classes that behave like abstract classes in other languages, with minor quirks. Overall, VB does not prevent developers from benefiting from the features of inheritance, but it does not make it easy to do so.

Further Reading

Deborah Kurata, *Doing Objects in Microsoft Visual Basic 5.0* (1997). Kurata provides a brief introduction to OOAD, focusing on object relationships and standard object-oriented concepts.

Rockford Lhotka, *Visual Basic 6 Business Objects* (1998). Lhotka's book provides a solid introduction to designing and creating business objects in Visual Basic. He covers object relationships, traditional object-oriented concepts, implementing interfaces, and creating consistent behavior across business objects. Most of the examples are drawn from a single large example used as the centerpiece of the book.

Bruce McKinney, *Hardcore Visual Basic* (1997). This book provides a detailed look at how Visual Basic uses COM to create components. The author also tackles the issue of how object-oriented Visual Basic really is, and is quick to point out VB's shortcomings in the area.

Ted Pattison, *Programming Distributed Applications with COM and Microsoft Visual Basic 6.0* (1998). This book presents one of the best introductions to how Visual Basic uses COM. While the emphasis is certainly on distributed applications, this book takes the time to discuss polymorphism, interface and implementation inheritance, and creating and implementing interfaces in Visual Basic.

Chapter 9

Object Design II: Relationships and Design

In the last chapter we discussed the fundamental concepts of object-oriented programming in detail. In this chapter we will continue our discussion with an extended look at object relationships. We'll see the various ways that objects can relate to one another and discuss practical ways of implementing these relationships from within Visual Basic.

Because relationships are difficult to describe in words, we will then take a quick look at the Unified Modeling Language, which offers a method of defining these relationships clearly. We will concentrate on the various models the language defines and discuss which ones are most suited for annotation and documenting your programs.

Finally, to summarize the concepts in both chapters 8 and 9, we'll discuss the important steps in actually creating an object-oriented solution. The techniques presented are simple, but practical and effective, and should allow you to create robust object models for your VB applications.

Object Relationships

As part of the process of defining the requirements for your software, you will need to describe relationships between the actors or entities in your system. In fact, such relationships are typically the foundation of the whole system. If your use cases contain the words *owns, has, creates, contains, consists of, is a,* or *is a kind of,* or similar words, you are probably describing a relationship between two entities.

The relationships described in your use case analyses should be directly applicable to your object model. The object model is likely to contain more granularity, but the premise is the same. Every object-oriented theorist seems to have his or her own idea of what the different kinds of relationships between objects are and how to annotate them. Overall, though, there is a great deal of overlap between views, the differences being primarily in vocabulary or in level of granularity. Table 9.1 summarizes the four types of relationship that appear most often.

Let's look at each of these in more detail. For each type of relationship, we'll discuss general uses, and I'll present a simple graphic example (with symbols from the UML) and a VB code listing for clarification.

Collaboration

The simplest type of object relationship is *collaboration*, which is sometimes referred to as the "uses" relationship, or as dependency. With collaboration, two or more peer objects interact, usually for a short period of time. In most cases, one object uses the services of the other, then destroys the other object. For example, if you have an object that needs to call a method on another object in a routine, the first object simply creates an instance of the second, calls the method in question, and destroys the object when finished with it.

Listing 9.1 demonstrates this simple process. Here an object (`clsInvoice`) creates and uses an instance of `clsTax` to compute the tax associated with a sale. Figure 9.1 shows this relationship graphically, with notation from the UML.

TABLE 9.1   Types of Object Relationships

Relationship	Keywords	Description
Collaboration	"uses a"	Two objects interact, but are otherwise peers. Typically, one object instantiates the other, uses its services, and destroys the object. The object used is not part of the first object's interface.
Generalization	"is a" "is a kind of"	One object is a type of another object.
Ownership	"owns" "has"	One object owns another object. This is a typical parent–child relationship, most often used to define collections of objects.
Aggregation	"is made of"	One object is composed of other objects, in whole or in part. Usually the constituent objects are properties of the main object, but not always.

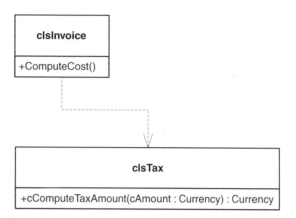

FIGURE 9.1   Graphical Representation of a Collaboration Relationship

Note that if the object being used is actually a member of the object using it, the relationship becomes more like ownership or aggregation, as we'll see in the next section.

Listing 9.1   A Simple Collaboration

```
' In clsInvoice, ComputeCost:
Dim oTax As clsTax
Dim cTotalCost As Currency
' ...
'Add the taxes to the amount
Set oTax = New clsTax
cTotalCost = cTotalCost + oTax.cComputeTaxAmount(cTotalCost)
Set oTax = Nothing
```

As Listing 9.1 shows, collaborations are not very complicated, and you are likely to define many of them in your object diagrams. The biggest caveat is that because one object depends on the behavior of a second object, changing the second object may affect the behavior of the first. However, this is a typical scenario in software development, and most developers are keenly aware of it and understand how to predict (and limit) changes caused by changing dependent objects.

Generalization

Generalizations are used to describe situations in which one object is a kind of (type of, in the generic sense) other object. We have already seen a simple example of a generalization in our discussion of inheritance in the last chapter:

a St. Bernard is a giant breed, which is a type of dog, and so on. The significant trait of generalizations is that the more specialized object in the relationship is substitutable for the more generalized one. For example, you can refer to a St. Bernard in any context in which you can refer to a giant breed. Thus, generalizations demonstrate inherited behavior. Consequently, implementing predefined interfaces (interface inheritance) is one of the easiest ways to create a generalization. Delegation (a workaround for creating implementation inheritance) is also useful. Figure 9.2 illustrates our friend George, whom we met in chapter 8 (see Listing 8.4). As you recall, George is a father who coaches Little League and runs his own business, and thus has three distinct abstractions. Here an instance of clsGeorge may be used wherever a coach, father, or boss is needed.

As an aside, although this kind of relationship is almost always referred to as a generalization, I think the term *specification* is probably a better choice. In practice you are really more concerned with the fact that object A is a more *specific* kind of object B, not that object B is a more general kind of object A.

Ownership

An ownership relation occurs, simply enough, when one object owns another object. It is also commonly referred to as a parent–child relationship. Sometimes the parent owns a single instance of a child object, but more often there is a collection of children. (In the UML, you can specify the precise number of children graphically as needed. This is known as *multiplicity*.) While the child objects are sometimes private to the parent (i.e., they are not published as public properties), parents usually grant public access to the children, though there

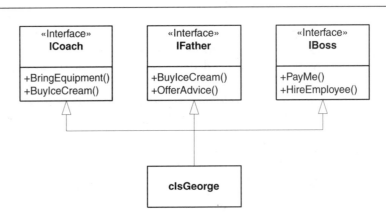

FIGURE 9.2 Graphical Representation of Generalizations

are some caveats to doing this in Visual Basic (see next section). It is also common for the parent to provide a reference to itself to each child, so that the child objects can access the parent's methods and properties as needed. Finally, there are circumstances where joint custody (more than one parent owns the same child for a period of time) is helpful, but such relationships are very difficult to maintain. Figure 9.3 illustrates a simple ownership relationship.

Controlling Child Lifetimes

To own an object completely, the parent must control its lifetime. That is, the parent actually instantiates the object (rather than receiving an external reference to it) and monitors its lifetime explicitly. When the parent intends to destroy the child, it should actually be destroyed. In Visual Basic, realizing this can be something of a problem. Since VB's COM objects create and destroy themselves, in reality, a parent object has no explicit control over the lifetime of its child. Instead, a parent must monitor references to child objects and restrict access to its children as much as possible in order to control its lifetime. Ultimately, diligent attention to the ownership of child objects helps to prevent VB memory leaks caused by circular references (see chapter 17 for more information).

Although monitoring the reference to child can be very difficult, the parent should always have final authority over the state of the children. At any given time, the parent should be able to invalidate a child, even if the child object itself remains alive. To facilitate this, I usually add methods to all child objects to initialize and terminate them explicitly. When the parent instantiates a child object, it calls the object's `Initialize` method (not to be confused with the `Class_Initialize` event on the class), which handles setting up defaults, and so on. When finished using the child, the parent calls the `Terminate` method, which clears module-level data, effectively invalidating the child.

The benefit of explicitly initializing and terminating child objects is that doing so forces you to think more carefully about how objects get passed around to external sources. If an external object obtains a reference to a child and attempts to access the child after the parent has called `Terminate`, bad

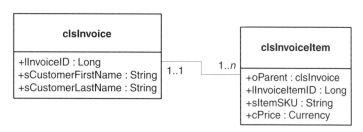

FIGURE 9.3 Graphical Representation of Ownership

things can (and should) happen. When debugging particularly complex object code, I have even put a module-level flag in each child object to indicate whether or not the object has been terminated. At the beginning of each method, the child object checks its terminated flag to see whether the operation is legal. This is a simple but powerful technique that is easy to implement and can save hours of debugging time. It is best if you think about adding such a mechanism while defining the relationships between objects, which is why I mention it here.

Uses for Ownership

Ownership object relationships are commonly used to mirror the implementation of header/detail tables (one-to-many table relationships) in a database (see chapter 10). A parent object holds the data for one row in the header table and owns several child objects, one for each of the rows in the detail table. Thus the parent behaves like a collection of objects, but also usually has information all its own. One common technique for realizing this in Visual Basic is to make the parent class behave just like a VB collection. Refer to the discussion of collections in chapter 12 for an example of how to do this.

To implement an ownership relationship, simply declare a module-level reference to a child object (or a collection of child objects), as shown in Listing 9.2, which declares two singleton objects and a separate collection of children. At some point, instantiate the child object and, if desired, give it a reference to its parent. This usually takes place in the Class_Initialize event of the parent or in some method whose sole purpose is to create and populate the child objects. With the child instantiated, the parent code can access its methods and properties as needed. When finished with the child, the parent destroys its reference (see Terminate). Again, be cognizant of the child object's real lifetime. If external references are still active when the parent destroys its reference, the ownership relationship will be compromised.

Listing 9.2   A Simple Ownership Relationship

```
Private moChildObject1 As clsChild1
Private moChildObject2 As clsChild2
Private mclOtherChildren As Collection

Public Sub Initialize()
    Dim iOtherChild As Integer
    Dim oOtherChild As clsOtherChild

    If moChildObject1 Is Nothing Then
        Set moChildObject1 = New clsChild1
    End If
    'Do something to populate child object, like:
    Set moChildObject1.Parent = Me
    moChildObject1.PopulateSelf
```

```
        'Repeat for other singleton child, moChildObject2
        '...
        'Load OtherChildren collection
        Set mclOtherChildren = New Collection
        For iOtherChild = 1 To mnNumberOfOtherChildren
            Set oOtherChild = New clsOtherChild
            Call oOtherChild.PopulateSelf(iOtherChild)
            Call mclOtherChildren.Add(oOtherChild)
            Set oOtherChild = Nothing
        Next iOtherChild

End Sub
'. . .
'Code to use the child objects lives throughout the parent class.
'When finished, call Terminate.
'. . .
Public Sub Terminate()
    Set moChildObject1 = Nothing
    Set moChildObject2 = Nothing
    While mclOtherChildren.Count > 0
        mclOtherChildren.Remove 1
    Wend
    Set mclOtherChildren = Nothing
End Sub
```

With singleton child objects, ownership is the underlying relationship that allows for inheritance through delegation. Since the child objects commonly provide functionality needed by objects external to the parent, it is customary for the parent to use delegation to access the child's functionality, especially when passing off the functionality as its own.

Aggregation

The last type of object relationship is an *aggregation*. Here, an object is really made up of one or more subobjects, though the parent object can also have properties of its own. This is very much like ownership, and many object-oriented philosophies group them together. The difference is that with aggregation, the owner object ceases to be that kind of object if its children are removed from the picture, whereas with ownership, children are optional. An example of aggregation would be a car, which is made up of an engine, a chassis, seats, a steering wheel, and other parts. While the individual parts are unique entities, they combine to form the aggregation we call a car. Without the parts, the car does not exist.

As with an ownership relationship, you can implement aggregation by declaring and instantiating child objects, shown in Listing 9.2. Figure 9.4 illustrates a simple aggregation, some of the parts of a car. A complete diagram would include every aspect of a car that makes it a car.

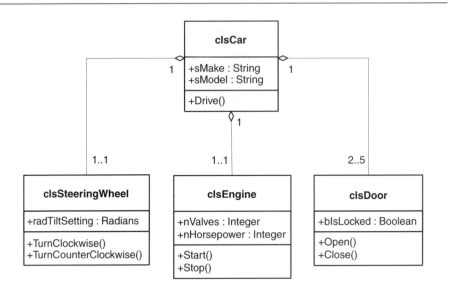

FIGURE 9.4 A Graphical Representation of Aggregation

Overview of the Unified Modeling Language

Although it seems to have the center stage in the corporate world today, object-oriented analysis and design are actually still very much the new kids on the block. Serious, practical OOAD techniques did not really surface until the late 1980s. By the early 1990s the number of methods increased dramatically, but three theories had managed to eke out the most prominent positions. They were Grady Booch's "Booch Method," which focused most heavily on object design as it pertained to code construction; Ivar Jacobson's Objectory process (often referred to as OOSE from its reference in Jacobson's book *Object-Oriented Software Engineering*), which relied heavily on requirements derivation with use cases; and James Rumbaugh's Object Modeling Technique (OMT), which took a more data-centric approach to analysis. There was a great deal of overlap among these three approaches, and each had its own notational system. In the mid-1990s the three amigos, as the authors came to be known, began a concerted effort to unify their approaches. Part of the result is the Unified Modeling Language. To paraphrase its oft-quoted definition, the UML is a language for visualizing, specifying, constructing, and documenting software systems (Booch et al., 1999). It combines the best aspects of each method, provides a standardized notation and language, and improves on all three methods. With the UML, the whole is indeed more powerful than the sum of the parts.

The biggest advantage of the UML is that it provides a nearly universal standard for object-oriented analysis and design. When I first learned OOAD several years ago, I reviewed numerous texts, often coming away more dazed and confused than enlightened. The UML is powerful, yet simple, and it is easy to learn, allowing developers to concentrate on the problem at hand, rather than on figuring out a notation strategy. It is also readily accessible by nontechnical people, making it useful not only in design, but also in requirements gathering.

UML Diagrams

Certainly the most visually striking aspect of the UML is its use of many kinds of diagrams. The list in Exhibit 9.1 shows the nine major types of diagrams defined by the UML proper (there are numerous extensions as well). The diagrams fall into two categories: static diagrams, which show structure, and dynamic diagrams, which describe behavior. While there is some overlap between these types, the first four (class, object, component, and deployment diagrams) are generally considered to be static diagrams, while the others (use case, sequence, collaboration, statechart, and activity diagrams) are dynamic.

EXHIBIT 9.1   UML Diagrams and Their Uses

- Class diagram
- Object diagram
- Component diagram
- Deployment diagram
- Use case diagram
- Sequence diagram
- Collaboration diagram
- Statechart diagram
- Activity diagram

Class Diagram
This is arguably the most common kind of diagram you can create with the UML, and every serious software project needs at least one (usually several). Class diagrams are static diagrams that show the relationships between the classes in your system, along with important methods, properties, and interfaces.

Object Diagram
Object diagrams are a lot like class diagrams. Like class diagrams, they show a static view of the system. However, unlike class diagrams, they describe the relationships between actual (or typical) instantiated objects in the system at a

given point in time. Class diagrams work with classes; object diagrams work with instances of the classes.

I find object diagrams most useful when class diagrams alone are not sufficient to describe the interaction of the entities in the system. Object diagrams are useful for clarifying specific runtime scenarios. However, do not feel obligated to model every object in your system at every state—the class diagram will usually suffice.

Component Diagram

A component diagram shows the relationship between the logical components of your system. It typically contains references to all the applications (EXEs), in-process and out-of-process servers (ActiveX DLLs and EXEs), and supporting entities (Web pages, database packages, etc.). If you have adopted a multitiered logical architecture for your system, component diagrams are indispensable for visualizing how all of the pieces fit together, and they are easy to create.

Deployment Diagram

Whereas component diagrams show the logical layout of your system, deployment diagrams show the physical layout. They are often called *system architecture diagrams*. In these diagrams you can specify the relationships among the various pieces of hardware (actually, everything that is not software) running your system, from PCs to servers, networks and the like. I find it helpful to overlay component diagrams and deployment diagrams—doing so makes it easier to see how scalable a system really is.

For systems written using Visual Basic, deployment diagrams often contain more than just the hardware the VB components touch directly. Legacy servers, mainframes, databases, and networks usually come into play, even if the VB applications do not interact with them directly.

Use Case Diagram

Use case diagrams are among the first diagrams created in many applications. They are generated during the requirements-gathering process to help identify (and document) the system's various actors and their relationships. They are indispensable for modeling the behavior of an application. We looked at use case analysis in detail in chapters 3 and 4.

Use case diagrams are interesting in that they are both static and dynamic. That is, they show the rough organization of the system in terms of its actors (a static trait), but concentrate primarily on defining the behavior of the actors, which is clearly a dynamic trait.

Sequence Diagram and Collaboration Diagram

Collaboration diagrams and sequence diagrams annotate the messages of a system. They are collectively known as *interaction* diagrams. Simply put, interaction diagrams describe "who calls what" in your application. Sequence diagrams are ordered realizations of a series of messages as they occur over time (first A calls B.DoSomething, then B calls C.DoSomethingElse, and so on.). Collaboration diagrams are similar, except they focus more on the entities sending the messages than on the order of the messages. Whereas sequence diagrams depict all details, collaboration diagrams concentrate primarily on the key interactions of the system.

Sequence diagrams are among the most difficult UML diagrams to create and understand. They can pack a lot of information into a small area. However, once you have a good idea of how your classes will interact at a high level, sequence diagrams help to flush out all the methods and properties your classes will need. As for collaboration diagrams, I have found very few practical uses for them—if you can create a sequence diagram you have all of the information a related collaboration diagram has as well.

Statechart Diagram

Statechart diagrams help to pinpoint and trace (in order) the states of a particular aspect of the system (usually an object or related group of objects) over time. As external elements interact with the objects you are modeling, the objects will change state, going through transitions that may have importance in certain circumstances.

Statechart diagrams are most useful when you are modeling entities whose main purpose is to act as a pop-up thermometer for some aspect of the system. For example, expert systems relying on neural networks are entirely reliant on the state of the network. Generally, the network fluctuates as it receives input, ultimately reaching some threshold state that allows it to make a "decision." Statechart diagrams help when modeling such systems, and in any other cases where changes in state are important.

Activity Diagram

Activity diagrams are much like the traditional flowcharts common in the days of procedural programming. They map the flow of control from object to object within a system, depicting the decisions and conditions that control the flow. They are useful when defining user interface work flow and for documenting user interface validation rules.

UML Caveats

One of the biggest mistakes developers make when working with the UML is thinking that they must generate every kind of diagram under the sun. The UML is only a language, not a divine directive, and there is no need to use all of the tools it has to offer. On Visual Basic projects, where relatively simple client-side applications still reign supreme even in the days of distributed systems, a small subset of diagrams will usually suffice. I have found that, in practice, class diagrams, use case diagrams, and activity diagrams are indispensable. Component diagrams and deployment diagrams are useful and easy to make, but client-side systems written in VB are usually not complicated enough to merit elaborate component and deployment documentation. Sequence diagrams can help define the behavior of particularly complicated classes, and statechart diagrams trace changes in object state, but for simple applications both are often just a waste of time. Finally, I use object diagrams sparingly, only in circumstances in which the number of objects in existence at a given point in time is important. However, I have never run across a situation in which a collaboration diagram was worth the trouble. This is not to say that these lesser-used diagrams are inherently less important in general—they are usually just less applicable to typical VB business applications.

An important point to remember about UML diagrams is that they should be highly interactive, living documents. For example, as you work through system requirements with use case analyses, you will be doing the preliminary legwork for your class diagrams. Once you begin class diagrams in earnest, you are bound to find holes in your requirements. Treating the use case documents as fixed, dead artifacts will not plug the holes you find. For maximum benefit, visit and revisit your diagrams iteratively. In fact, the sure sign that you have a clear understanding of the requirements and the design of your system is when you discover that fewer and fewer corrections to the "finished" diagrams are needed as you continue to work. Also, since the process of creating diagrams is even more beneficial than the diagrams themselves, don't be afraid to abandon them when they are no longer of any use. In general, I find it helpful to keep use case diagrams and class diagrams as up-to-date as possible, since these remain useful long after they have been completed. However, I do not see the need to spend much time updating sequence diagrams once most of the methods and properties are fixed.

UML Modeling Tools

Though diagrams are indispensable for serious projects, creating them by hand can be a tedious undertaking, even with the UML. Luckily there are several software packages available to make the process easier. The professional edition of Visio offers UML stencils out of the box, making the creation of static diagrams simple. While Visio contains all of the standard UML shapes and constructs you should need, it also has everything else available to Visio, meaning that you can use other shapes if the UML shapes do not quite meet your needs. (Note that the UML itself is extensible, opening the door for you to use custom shapes when appropriate.)

There are also tools that generate source code from your diagrams. The Visual Modeler that ships with the Enterprise Edition of Visual Studio allows you to create class diagrams, component diagrams, and deployment diagrams. As you fill out the details of your classes, Visual Modeler will generate VB (or VC++) code for you, leaving you with stub routines to finish coding. You unfortunately have to put up with its numerous "##ModelId" tags inserted as comments into the code, but these are required for making the translation from diagram to code and back. Visual Modeler is actually a watered-down version of Rational Software's Rational Rose, which includes all of the bells and whistles. Rational Rose allows you to do just about everything that can be done in the UML, and it contains a scripting language that allows you to generate models from other models, and so on. Entire books have been written about modeling with Rational Rose, and it is well worth the investment if you are going to do serious modeling.

Designing Objects

The release of Visual Basic 4 stirred up quite a bit of interest in object-oriented analysis and design. Everyone wanted to be called an object-oriented developer, so armed with a new, albeit limited tool, developers rushed headfirst to create object-oriented programs. Unfortunately, there was a tendency to equate object-oriented software development strictly with the use of objects, regardless of how the objects were constructed. Many developers simply ported their old VB 3 (and earlier) applications to VB 4, dumping procedural code into classes and calling the solution object-oriented. VB developers were not the only ones guilty of doing this. I can remember a coworker who wanted to learn C++ (she was already a fine C programmer), so she studied the syntactic differences between the two languages and for all intents and purposes understood C++. She never did grasp object-oriented analysis and design, though, and ended up becoming a wonderful C programmer who worked in C++ (as the old saying goes, a good Fortran programmer can write good Fortran code in any language). Clearly there is more to object-oriented analysis and design that porting old applications and reusing existing language skills.

As time has gone by, though, developers have come to realize that although object-oriented coding and procedural coding are very similar at the code level, there is a fundamental difference in the way procedural programs and object-oriented programs are designed. Simply put, to be successful, projects using object-oriented languages need thorough object-oriented analysis and design from the start.

Unfortunately, it is common for companies to cut corners on their projects in favor of the demands of a schedule. (We looked at some of the problems associated with this back in chapter 1.) Arguably the most dangerous work to cut out is design, yet it is often one of the first things to go. I have met professional VB developers with years of experience who have *never* worked on a project with a substantial design phase. Companies skip design for a lot of reasons, ranging from the fact that the design phase often offers few indications of visible progress to a general lack of understanding of its importance. In my experience, by the time the design phase of software development begins in earnest in a given iteration, the project is already usually behind, and it is time to play catch-up. Also, few developers have a lot of design experience (software design is rarely taught in schools and developers receive little incentive from their companies to learn it on their own). Consequently, they become frustrated and bored very quickly and have a tendency to panic, especially when their managers are breathing down their necks for tangible results. They are more comfortable working with code, so they jump into writing source code as soon as they can.

In retrospect, developers sometimes look back at problems and point to poor design as the root of their troubles (managers often single out poor use cases). In fact, it is usually not a poor design that causes the problems—it is the utter lack of a design. It may seem wrong after spending so much time describing object-oriented concepts in this chapter to blame all of the troubles of companies on lack of design, but bear with me. *In my experience, 90 percent of the benefit of doing object-oriented analysis and design comes from the process of doing it, not from the resulting documents.* This is not to say that just any design will always do, but rather that taking the time to do a design is bound to yield better results than a code-like-hell approach without design. I find VB project leaders schedule only about 15 to 20 percent of the project's time for design, and they rarely actually spend even that much. In my view, 30 to 40 percent is more realistic. Overall, design should consume as much of the schedule as coding.

To this end, let's look at a basic approach for creating business objects. Now that we have explored the tools available for creating an object-oriented solution, we can see how to derive the object model itself. Exhibit 9.2 lists and describes the general steps involved in creating an object-oriented design. This is not intended to be an exhaustive look at OOAD, but rather to provide simple, practical steps that can help you to create solid object designs for the typical VB business project.

As you review these steps, keep a few points in mind. First, every project is different, so the steps I provide are as general as possible while still being practical. Second, iteration is the key to successful OOAD. Don't be afraid to work your way through the steps and then backtrack as needed—the order defined here is flexible. Third, do not stop analysis and design until you are fairly comfortable. Only doing half of a design means that you will only benefit from half of a design.

EXHIBIT 9.2   Steps in Creating an Object-Oriented Design

1. Identify the high-level entities in your use case analyses. These are the actors and other major entities that describe the behavior of your system from the standpoint of the users.

2. Fill out the entities by providing them with properties and methods derived from the use cases. You will likely need to break the system's functionality into several pieces, and these will become your first round of classes. At this stage, concentrate on abstraction and encapsulation. That is, be sure the classes define meaningful entities (they abstract well) and that they hide their data and implementations as much as possible. Strive for a balance in the size and complexity of your classes. If you have a class with only one or two properties, think about combining it with a related class. Also, consider breaking apart very complex classes to make them more manageable. Finally, begin to think about where a particular class will eventually live in your logical architecture. Of primary concern here is the separation of user interface elements from business objects and data access objects.

3. Refine the resulting entities from step 2 by stripping out and consolidating commonalties in behavior and appearance. That is, find polymorphic objects and objects that can benefit from inheritance. Look through each object on a case-by-case basis and determine whether the object needs to inherit the actual functionality (implementation inheritance via delegation) or just the appearance (interface inheritance with COM interfaces). If you find that you have no common behavior among your entities, consider rethinking your class definitions, because you may have missed something (you may need more detail). Likewise, if you discover that most of your objects participate in some kind of inherited relationship, refine your model, especially if you have deep inheritance trees. In this case, you likely have too much detail, which will eventually stifle coding efforts.

4. Determine relationships among the classes found. This is one of the hardest aspects of OOAD, since a variety of solutions are usually possible, even with the same set of classes. Some indicators to rely on are whether you need to inherit or delegate functionality (generalization), whether you have classes that are supposed to behave like collections (ownership and aggregation), and whether there are other general interactions between objects (collaboration). Be sure your classes have the necessary methods and properties for realizing your relationships. In the end, every class should have some kind of relationship to another class, but be wary of classes that seem to be related to everything—they will likely be very difficult to code and maintain.

5. Finish grouping classes and their functionalities into logical components. You may have to rethink some of the classes you have defined to be sure they fit neatly into a particular logical component. For example, if you have a class whose main purpose is to support the user interface, you will

continued

probably want to remove any data access logic (if there is any) so that the system is more logically segregated and ultimately more scalable.

6. As your class model becomes more stable, begin thinking about how objects created from these classes will interact as your system runs. Making the move from static to dynamic modeling helps to refine your design. For example, create activity diagrams for complicated tasks and algorithms, and sequence diagrams to explain "who calls what" in complicated processes. The biggest caveat here is not to spend too much time on dynamic modeling until your system's static model is fairly well defined and stable. Creating elaborate behavioral diagrams can be a waste of time if the classes are constantly in flux. The main purpose of the diagrams is to help flesh out details, but they require a solid foundation.

7. As the design becomes more stable, document your classes and all assumptions you have made. If you are using the UML to create various diagrams, consider adding descriptions and annotations directly to the diagrams. If this is not possible, attach notes that refer to external documentation.

8. Do it all again. Remember, iteration is the key.

Following the steps in Exhibit 9.2 will not guarantee a wonderful design, but it is difficult to create a solid design without considering them at all. Again, the goal is to learn more about the system in question and to expose potentially problematic areas while there is still time to fix them. There is no right or wrong design as long as it meets the system's requirements (all functionality is in place, the system is maintainable and scalable, etc.). Good Luck.

Further Reading

Grady Booch et al., *The Unified Modeling Language User Guide* (1999). This is the key source for understanding the elements of the UML. It draws heavily from the UML specification (available on-line at *www.rational.com*), and it provides the most thorough overview around. Unfortunately, it is a bit short on practical examples.

Rockford Lhotka, *Visual Basic 6 Business Objects* (1998). The examples in this book use the UML, and the book includes a brief introduction to the UML in an appendix.

James Rumbaugh et al., *The Unified Modeling Language Reference Manual* (1999). This is the companion to *The Unified Modeling Language User Guide*. It provides reference information about the elements in the UML.

Chapter 10

Database Design

Because Visual Basic is considered a jack-of-all-trades tool, companies often expect VB programmers to be jack-of-all-trades developers. This often means that the developers are expected to be able to understand, query, update, modify, and even create complicated databases. Indeed, most business applications exist solely to facilitate the manipulation of data. Yet there is little inherent in Visual Basic programming that helps developers become more database-savvy. With this in mind, I have included an overview of database design and related concepts in this chapter. Since relational databases have become the norm in corporate environments, we will limit our discussion to relational database topics. We will review the various constructs and entities in databases and present a few pointers for avoiding common mistakes.

Since your entire application may depend on the integrity of the database, it is imperative to get it right the first time. To this end, we will spend a good deal of time discussing normalization principles and the benefits of a normalized design. We will also discuss denormalization and other strategies for improving the performance of your system. Throughout this chapter, we will also explore both sides of the battle between better database integrity and better database performance.

Relational Databases

Relational Database Management Systems (RDMS) got their start in the 1970s. Prior to the advent of relational databases, data was stored in some proprietary scheme with a very specific access syntax. The most common technique was flat files, often containing homegrown header sections defining indices and record counts.

While they served their purposes, pre-RDMS engines suffered from the following drawbacks (drawn from Mattison, 1998):

◆ They were difficult to scale. While simple database engines worked well for smaller applications that required relatively small amounts of data, developers rarely included the flexibility to accommodate growth. In many cases, no one ever expected them to run more than a few years, so there was little effort put into planning for scalability. (The infamous Y2K problem is another side effect of this lack of planning.) As the needs of the businesses changed, companies found their homegrown databases unable to handle the new features and increased volume of data.

◆ As the databases grew, data corruption and poor integrity became problems. Pre-relational systems had no way of reusing data easily, so it was common to find the same data written several times in different places. Reconciling the discrepancies that inevitably emerged was a real challenge.

◆ The databases were difficult to access from systems other than the ones for which they were originally written. Because of the complexity of the data files, companies had no easy way to access their data for ad hoc reporting, migration to another database system, or for use by a new client application. Accessing the data at all meant writing lots of messy data access code geared specifically for the database in question.

Relational databases help resolve these issues by placing data in a high scalable environment that offers both ease of access and a strong potential for reuse. There are many characteristics that serve to achieve these benefits. First and foremost, relational databases allow developers to store a bit of data once and only once, while keeping it accessible. This has the advantage of eliminating integrity issues and possibly reducing data storage requirements. Relational databases are also easy to scale, since tables have no artificial limit to their size. Essentially, the process for creating and using a table that needs to hold two rows is the same for one intended to hold millions. Furthermore, most full-scale relational database implementations handle multiuser concurrency well, allowing you to add users as needed (see chapter 13 for more information on multiuser issues). Finally, to access data stored in a relational database and to create and modify database structures, developers use Structured Query Language (SQL). SQL is specifically designed to take advantage of the strengths of a relational database.

Database Entities

In this section, we will look at the various database entities commonly found in Relational Database Management Systems. While everyone is familiar with the basics of tables, we'll look into some aspects that are less clear, including picking the right data type and adding constraints. We will then turn to three often underused constructs: Triggers, Views, and Store Procedures.

Tables

Every programmer is familiar with the fundamental database structure known as the table. In the loosest of terms, a table is a grouping of similar data entities. The columns in the table define the structure of each entity, whereas the rows contain the actual data. It is common to find tables with dozens of columns and thousands or millions (or more!) of rows. Tables are the core database structures in the world of relational database systems.

Creating Tables

The first step in creating a good table is to find related data entities in your business domain. Since rows and columns of related data define a table, you need to be sure you understand the relationships that exist between your data elements, at the lowest of levels (see the section "Table Relationships"). There are two primary approaches for accomplishing this. While both are useful independently, ultimately you will probably find that a combination of the two is more practical:

1. *Derive tables (columns and rows) from entities in the business object model.*　While it is common to derive object models from tables, the reverse is also possible. In his landmark book *Object-Oriented Software Engineering*, Ivar Jacobson suggested that tables and business objects are very closely related (Jacobson, 1992). In his method, each class corresponds to a table, with the properties of the class constituting the columns of the table. At runtime, each row in the table corresponds to an instance of the class (an object). If you have a well-defined object model, in most cases, you can leverage it to yield a very good database design. I sometimes find it easier to relate a class to a database view (see discussion later in this chapter), but the idea is the same. As we will see, views allow more flexibility because they provide a layer of abstraction between the tables and your business objects. Your object design may lack the detail to refine your tables very much, though, so you should also consider the data itself.

2. *Examine the raw data.*　If you already have a bunch of loosely organized data (perhaps from an existing system), you should be able to find similarities among elements. Group these similar elements into tables until everything belongs to a table. While this approach is at the heart of what is traditionally referred to as normalization (see discussion later in this chapter), in practice it is usually not very useful for creating large-scale databases—it is simply too difficult to organize lots of data without some overriding structure already in place. However, as just mentioned, this approach remains useful when refining the structure of your tables, since the actual data contains a level of detail not achievable in traditional object-oriented analysis.

As you work through your tables, you are likely to find data that just simply does not belong in the table in which you have placed it. You are also likely to find repeating information and even calculated fields (columns that depend on another column for a value). We'll explore dealing with these situations in the discussion of normalization later in this chapter.

Choosing Data Types

With the tables in your database identified, you can begin the second step, which is refining the definition of the tables as much as possible. Of primary importance in this step is choosing the correct type of data for your columns. You need to choose the base type (usually a number or string) and define the maximum length allowed. Different database systems have different intrinsic types, but usually there is a great deal of similarity between them.

When designing a database to be accessed from a Visual Basic application, be cognizant of how the database's data types map to Visual Basic's data types. I do not recommend choosing database data types based solely on Visual Basic's representation of the same data. However, if you have an opportunity to make your database more VB-friendly, consider it carefully. Doing so will help you prevent unnecessary conversions that always run the risk of corrupting data. Furthermore, consider the following three tips:

1. *Avoid BLOBs and TEXT fields.* BLOBs are large blocks of binary data, used for holding things such as pictures, sound files, cursors, and other binary objects in the database. In Visual Basic, such data usually resides in a resource file. TEXT fields, which go by many names, refer to arbitrarily large blocks of raw text. The problem with these two types of fields is that they are difficult to access from Visual Basic. In fact, depending on the database system and data access mechanism, they are impossible to update through stored procedures called from Visual Basic. In addition, for BLOBs, there is no good matching VB type to hold the data once you have transferred it to VB. (TEXT fields presumably can be put into a string.) You typically will have to use an array of bytes, which can be awkward.

2. *Match string lengths.* Many databases require that you define the lengths of the strings (character fields) in your tables explicitly. While they allow for variable-length strings, you must still supply the maximum size. If you use fixed-length strings in VB, declaring them to be of the same size as the matching fields in the database ensures that you will never try to insert a string field that is too long. Note that different databases may react differently when you attempt to insert a string value that is longer than the defined field: they may truncate the data or even raise an error. The downside to this strategy is that Visual Basic pads your strings with spaces for you. The advantage is that VB always behaves the same, providing consistency. You will want to trim your strings before sending them to the database to avoid storing insignificant spaces (which waste database space). You will also have to be careful how you work with the strings in VB in order to be sure those padded spaces don't cause other problems. Besides making database development easier, fixed-length VB strings are generally faster than variable-length strings, and using fixed-length strings allows you to take advantage of the powerful serialization technique we discussed in chapter 5. See Listing 5.1 for more information.

3. *Do not assume that types will translate well.*   Although a database type and a VB type may have the same name, they may have entirely different storage mechanisms. A good example of this is the Oracle type Date, which is not compatible with the VB type of the same name. Certain number fields also may not have one-to-one correspondence. Ultimately, you may have to translate the value into an intermediate representation to communicate between the two systems. With Oracle Dates, it is common to translate the date into a string (YYYYMMDDHH24MISS format) before sending it to or from the database. Obviously, both VB and the database must understand the translation rules for this approach to be effective.

For more information on choosing data types, refer to chapter 11. While the discussion there focuses on VB data types, the principles are the same for databases.

Constraints

Finally, you must determine what kind of constraints the data in your tables should have. Once the columns in your tables have an appropriate type, you should further refine the definition of how you intend to use the data and what actual values are allowed for each column. There are many kinds of constraints, the most common of which appear in Table 10.1. The first three (primary keys, null constraints, and unique keys) relate directly to a table. Check constraints and foreign keys, while defined on specific columns in a given table, help define the relationships *among* tables more thoroughly.

Constraints are used to help maintain database integrity; they allow you to impose very specific validation rules on your data. If an operation (such as an insertion or an update) on a table causes a rule defined by a constraint to be

TABLE 10.1   Table Constraints and Their Uses

Constraint Name	*Description*
Primary Key	The primary key defines a column (or columns) in the table that uniquely identifies a given row. This is the key you will use to access specific rows in your tables. When more than one column comprises the primary key, it is known as a *composite* key. All tables can have only one primary key (though other unique keys are allowed). Some database systems do not require that you define a primary key for your tables, but you should always make a point to do so, even if it means simply adding a column generated from a sequence. In fact, if you are unable to define a primary key for your table, it is a likely indication of a poorly designed table. Database systems usually build special indices behind the scenes based on your primary keys to improve performance. For obvious reasons, primary keys cannot be nullable columns.
Null Constraint	By marking a column in a table to be nullable, you are indicating to the database management system that no value is required for the column when a row is inserted or updated. These are known as null fields, and they are useful for implementing optional states for your data entities. In general, though, it is a good idea to make all of your columns not nullable by default, since it is generally easy to turn a not nullable column into a nullable one down the road, but not vice versa. In short, if you are making a column nullable, be sure you have a specific business reason. Also, note that some database systems do not allow you to establish foreign keys on nullable columns.
Unique Key	A unique key is a column (or columns) that uniquely identifies a given row. Depending on the database system, the columns comprising a unique key can sometimes be nullable—the constraint is not applied under these circumstances. The primary key of a table is a special kind of unique key.
Check Constraint	While data types help define the usage of the data in your table, you will often want to check the validity of the values in specific columns before you allow them to be inserted or updated. Check constraints can enforce logic at the database level, and are useful for maintaining integrity. Common uses include verifying the validity of two or more columns in the table (e.g., if column XXXXX is null, column YYYYY cannot be) and checking the value against values in another table (though this is usually done with a foreign key).
Foreign Key	A foreign key constraint allows you to verify the relationship between the current row and a row (or rows) in another table or view. The most common example is in a header/detail relationship between two tables (also called a parent–child relationship, see the discussion of relationships later in the chapter). In most cases, you will not want to allow a row to be inserted into a detail table unless there is a corresponding record in the header table as well. To accomplish this, you include a reference to the header table's primary key in the detail table. If a row in the header table matching the foreign key you have established does not exist, the update or insertion will fail. With some database engines, you can even attach conditions to your foreign keys, such as cascading deletes, which allow you to delete child rows automatically when deleting the parent row.

violated, the action will fail. For example, if you attempt to insert a row into a table and that row's primary key already exists in the table, you will receive an error. With relational databases, the burden of ensuring that integrity is not violated resides squarely on the shoulders of the database where it belongs, not on client programs accessing the data. Constraints let the database do the work for you, and you should use as many constraints as you need for integrity.

The drawback to using lots of constraints is that although your data integrity will be solid, there is a performance penalty involved. The database engine must enforce the constraints every time you attempt to insert, change, or delete a row. When you are working with large amounts of data, the performance penalty imposed by the constraints can be noticeable indeed. As we will see later, you always have the option of removing the constraints as part of the denormalization process. While you should be aware of performance issues during the design phase of your database, don't forgo constraints too early in the process.

Triggers

Triggers are routines that launch automatically whenever certain things happen to the database. They are similar to event handlers, firing on the Insert, Update, and Delete "events" of the table in question. Because they are attached right to the table, they fire no matter how the action is initially called. This is especially useful for systems that have multiple front-end applications, since the logic enforced with triggers does not have to be built into every application that accesses the database. There are many advantages to using triggers, as shown in Exhibit 10.1.

There is a big drawback to triggers you should be aware of as well. Because triggers fire for every changing row in the table, like constraints they can seriously degrade performance, especially during batch updates. Because of this, you may want to disable triggers for specialized batch processes. This is dangerous because other processes working with the tables in question will not have the functionality of the triggers in place. You may opt to perform some kind of specialized command lock on the database to prevent other clients from accessing data while your batch process runs. Also, be certain your batch updates leave the database in the state it would have been in had the triggers been in effect.

Views

One of the most powerful, but underused entities in relational database design is the *view*, a logical table that contains no data itself, but allows you to access data from other tables and views. The tables you base a view on are known as

EXHIBIT 10.1 Common Uses for Triggers

1. *Automate logging and auditing.* Triggers provide a simple way of creating an automatic audit trail, tracking who changed what records and when (though this won't work if you are using connection pooling). With more sophisticated database models, you can even log changes made to records, allowing you to review the revision history of your data. Again, since the triggers fire transparently and automatically no matter what application changes the table, they are painless to use.

2. *Encapsulate and centralize complicated business logic.* From security issues to complex validation rules, business constraints can be enforced with triggers easily. Because a trigger can ultimately cause the action triggering it to fail, it can be used as a table-level check constraint, giving you the opportunity to validate the data in the rows in question all together.

3. *Enforce denormalization rules.* If you must denormalize your database, you will want to be sure any repeated data, derived data, or data stored in multiple locations (i.e., replicated data) is automatically synchronized. This will ensure that the database maintains its integrity. Triggers allow you to encapsulate the denormalization rules in one location.

base tables. You create a view by selecting data from your base tables, using whatever derived columns and joins are appropriate. In practice, you can use a view in almost any context in which you can use a table. A view itself can be part of a join and can allow selects, updates, inserts, and deletes. However, note that actions that change data are not allowed if the view's columns do not map back to a single table. Views with complicated joins pulling data from more than one table are rarely updatable.

Views have a variety of useful applications (see Exhibit 10.2). In short, they provide a convenient wrapper around the data in your tables, giving you an opportunity to modify or filter the data before it is returned.

Because views are compiled, the database engine has an opportunity to tweak the performance using established indices and similar constructs. When you are accessing data through embedded SQL, this can provide a performance boost. The biggest advantage of a view is the fact that it provides on-the-fly denormalization of base tables. Your data can remain snug and warm in the base tables while the view crunches away, creating a more context-friendly denormalized version of the data. But the operations the view must perform to return this denormalized data (joins, rollups, calculation of derived columns, etc.) can be very time-consuming. Performance issues get worse as the base tables begin to fill up. There is a temptation to forgo the view and denormalize your database tables immediately. In most cases, I think this is a very bad idea (see the discussion of normalization later in the chapter), and I have had many

EXHIBIT 10.2 Common Uses for Views

1. *Hide the complexity of the definitions and relationships of the base tables.* When accessing data through a view rather than from tables directly, you can change the column names to something more context-friendly, generate derived columns, and leverage foreign key relationships without complicated `select` statements. Changing the name (or meaning) of the data (for example, from `cust_frst_nm` in a base table to `First Name` in the view) is especially helpful when working with users who need to generate their own ad hoc reports.

2. *Add security to your database.* With views, you can automatically restrict access to whatever data you do not want the view to reveal, thus filtering both rows and columns. If users selecting the data do not have permission to select from the base tables, they can still access the data indirectly through a view. This provides you with the perfect opportunity to enforce security. For example, you may want to prevent various people from viewing the `YearlySalary` column from the `employee` table. To do so, restrict access to the table, create a view based on the table but which does not return the salary column, and give the users in question access to the view, but not to the underlying table.

3. *Hide details of implementation.* From the standpoint of developers, one of the handiest features of views is that they allow you to write code that operates on more abstracted renditions of your data. If your VB application accesses the database only through views, the database team can change the design and relationships of the underlying tables without affecting the VB code (provided, of course, the view can be altered to return data in the same format as always). This is especially handy when it comes time to tune the performance of the database, which frequently means shuffling table relationships.

conference-room arguments with other developers on just this topic. If you are experiencing slow performance from your views, be sure to try optimizing with simplified `select` statements and additional indices on the base tables before trying something drastic.

Stored Procedures

Stored procedures are compiled routines that reside in your database. Most database engines provide both stored procedures and stored functions (just like procedures, except they return a value). You can call stored procedures from within Visual Basic or even from within other procedures, making them very reusable constructs. Since stored procedures are compiled (like views), the database engine can optimize their performance using predefined indices. Such optimization can make stored procedures the most efficient mechanism for accessing and changing data.

When performing action queries against a database from within Visual Basic, I find stored procedures to be exceedingly helpful, and they are available from within every common database system. Stored procedures offer many advantages, as shown in Exhibit 10.3.

EXHIBIT 10.3   Advantages of Stored Procedures

> **1.** *Encapsulate complicated logic.*   Stored procedures help to encapsulate complicated data access logic. This is especially useful when you have denormalized your database and want to try to maintain integrity. To ensure that your data integrity remains intact, you should use only stored procedures to access and change data.
>
> **2.** *Perform efficient batch processing.*   Batch processing is more efficient when performed by stored procedures. Stored procedures are most useful when working with large amounts of data, since they allow you to process the rows in your tables individually without transferring the data from the server.
>
> **3.** *Improve transaction handling.*   Stored procedures offer improved performance and transaction processing.

There are very few negatives to using stored procedures. The biggest issue is that not all database engines support the same level of functionality. For example, while MS SQL Server allows you to return rows directly from a stored procedure, you cannot do so easily from within Oracle (in Oracle you cannot compile a stored procedure with a `select` statement unless it also has an `into` clause). Also, different database engines have different syntaxes when called from within VB. Because of these issues, it is likely that you will not be able to run your application against different databases without changing VB code. Embedded SQL offers more flexibility, but generally poorer performance.

Normalization

Normalization is the process by which you define the identities of your data elements more fully. It helps you refine the structure of the database based on the data itself. A database that has been created with normalization in mind (called a *normalized* database) is elegant and natural: the structure of the database itself embodies the relationships inherent in the data. A highly normalized database is a thing of beauty, and normalization is so important that for many people (myself included), a database cannot be considered well designed unless it is highly normalized.

Formally, the primary goals in creating a normalized database are to avoid repeating information that can lead to double-entry database issues; to create simple but well-defined tables; and to ensure that relationships among data elements are clear. I find that in practice it is easiest to describe normalization as making your database as *clean* as possible. It is an exercise in refinement and reduction.

Normal Forms

The degree to which a database is normal is known as its *normal form*. There are four commonly used normal forms (among others), as described in Table 10.2. You start with just a bunch of essentially unorganized, but loosely related data. This is Zeroth Normal Form.

When the data elements in your database are atomic (i.e., they cannot be broken down into smaller data elements) and have been grouped roughly into tables, the database is in First Normal Form. Usually the biggest culprit that causes a violation of First Normal Form is a compound field, for instance, one containing both first *and* last name or both length *and* width. By breaking the compound field into separate fields, you achieve First Normal Form. Repeating information is also forbidden in First Normal Form.

From here, the refinement gets trickier. A database is considered to be in Second Normal Form if it is in First Normal Form and all data in the table relates directly to the table's primary key. In a sense, this is the definition of a well-designed table. Without a strong relationship to the primary key, the fields in the table cannot form an independent, unique record.

Finally, Third Normal Form describes a table that is in Second Normal Form and whose fields are essentially independent of one another. Furthermore, all fields are more or less equally related to the primary key. In technical terms, this means that there can be no transitive dependencies. An example of a transitive dependency would be a table with these fields: BookISBNNumber (the primary key), AuthorsLastName, and AuthorsFavoriteColor. Although the AuthorsFavoriteColor field relates to the primary key (in this case, BookISBNNumber), it is more directly dependent on the AuthorsLastName. As another example, consider a derived column, such as TotalCost, which is the sum of two other columns, UnitPrice and TaxAmount. Since TotalCost is derived, it is dependent on UnitPrice and TaxAmount, rather than the primary key to the table. Derived columns like TotalCost are forbidden in Third Normal Form. In my opinion, Third Normal Form separates the good databases from the wannabes.

There are a few other practices that can help make your databases clean. First, be sure your columns have one and only one meaning. *Do not overload columns by using them to store two or more unrelated pieces of information.* In practice, when a new column is needed for a table, lazy developers often "cheat" and reuse an existing column that is used only under certain circumstances rather than add a new column to the table. There is some argument for doing this: altering a table means changing stored procedures and

TABLE 10.2 Summary of Normal Forms

Name	Description
Zeroth Normal Form	A database with loosely related data elements is in Zeroth Normal Form.
First Normal Form	In this form, the database has elements grouped into tables. There should be no repeating information or compound fields, and the data elements should be logically related.
Second Normal Form	This form dictates the creation of a well-defined table. All data elements in the table must relate to the primary key.
Third Normal Form	When a table has no derived information or internal dependencies (i.e., fields are independent of one another, but relate to the primary key), the table is in Third Normal Form.

embedded SQL, not to mention business objects and user interface elements. However, the alternative of overloading a column adds an element of confusion to your database. Imagine selecting data from a table to discover that the zip code field contains an address under some circumstances and a telephone number under others. Don't laugh—situations like this happen all the time.

Second, avoid columns that contain essentially meaningless data. Here I am referring to columns with vague names that hold data that has no obvious meaning or context. For example, consider a column called status_cd that contains values like D, P, and null. While these values probably have a very important meaning within the context of the business domain (*D*eleted and *P*ending, for instance), they are meaningless on their own. My rule of thumb is that if you cannot easily derive the meaning and use of the column from the data in the column, provide a separate lookup table, referenced by a foreign key. Doing so has two advantages. First, you can associate a meaningful description for the values in the second table, which makes understanding the data easier. Second, you can verify that values fall within the acceptable range for the business domain. If you do not want to provide a lookup table, at least consider using check constraints to verify the values.

The benefits to normalization are simple: no repeating data, well-defined tables (with keys), and exacting constraints to maintain integrity. These drastically reduce the chances that you will have problems with the data in your tables. When all the data is right, your application works correctly: people get paid the correct amount, orders ship on time, and everyone is happy—the world is a nicer place. If after finishing this entire book you remember only one thing, let it be this: *Always make your databases as normalized as possible. Always.* While some denormalization (discussed in the next section) is sometimes unavoidable, there is no excuse for a database with poor data integrity because normalization was never considered. In fact, I have never worked with a database at any company that had solid data integrity without substantial normalization. It is theoretically possible, but not practically.

As we have seen, with normalization there is a trade-off between better integrity and better performance. Highly normalized databases with solid integrity constraints are usually slower than those without normalization. It can also be frustrating to work with normalized databases when developing, since it sometimes takes a lot of time just to enter test data with all the foreign keys and constraints to satisfy. I recommend creating a simple script to enter particularly complex data so that you can reenter the data at a later time as needed. You can also consider temporarily disabling triggers and constraints to enter data. Furthermore, you often have to know a lot about the database you are working with to gain a full understanding of the queries you require. This can be discouraging when you would really need to work only with one or two tables in a less normalized database system. Of course, knowing what you are doing is not necessarily a bad thing. In the end, these disadvantages are really little more than annoyances.

Denormalization

Since normalization is the process of making your data more normal, it follows that *denormalization* is the process of making your data less normal. Note that denormalization implies that you have normalization first. The foremost reason to denormalize your database is to improve performance. However, often normalization is not performed to begin with or denormalization is performed haphazardly, leaving databases in disarray. There are several reasons for this.

First, developers often forgo formal normalization out of sheer laziness. Other times, there is not enough time to perform the normalization required or to do a thorough design. These are the poorest of excuses, but also among the most common.

Second, many VB projects involve converting legacy systems to Windows. Legacy databases (even relational databases) are usually fraught with data integrity issues. Because they may have years of production data, companies may opt not to rework the database, so they concentrate primarily on the user interface. The sexiness of the new UI often distracts from the trouble brewing beneath the surface. Eventually, there will be changes to the existing system (e.g., addition of tables and columns). But when they choose not to overhaul the database, companies are simply inheriting its problems, and there is little incentive to normalize new structures. This decision is usually fatal: it is nearly impossible to have a good overall system with a poor underlying database. If you are adding to an existing database, *do not compromise the design* of new tables strictly to conform to past precedence.

Finally, database designers may try to improve an element, in anticipation of problems, before it becomes a performance issue. They begin creating derived columns and employing other denormalization tactics before the database even has data in it. In my view, such preemptive denormalization is a bad idea. I prefer to take the approach that a performance issue is not an issue until it really becomes one. It is exceedingly difficult to normalize databases after there is a good deal of data in the systems, but denormalization is typically very easy to perform at any time. When deciding whether or not to denormalize, don't jump the gun.

I have several recommendations that should be the foundation of any denormalization effort:

1. Always denormalize only as a last resort. Rework stored procedures and queries and exploit additional indices before even considering denormalization.

2. Document all denormalization techniques (what tables, what columns, and why) thoroughly.

3. If possible, enforce denormalization rules with check constraints, triggers, and stored procedures. This is especially important when storing derived or computed values. The important thing is to concentrate your denormalization efforts at the database level. Visual Basic code should never be concerned with denormalization rules. In fact, if you use views as suggested earlier, you should not have to change your Visual Basic code at all, even if the underlying tables change entirely. The view acts as a layer of abstraction, sheltering VB from the implementation of the database.

4. If you need to remove constraints, remove those that are "safest" first, that is, those with underlying data that behaves well. If your application is designed so that it never violates a given constraint, that constraint is a likely candidate for removal. You can always add it again if needed as development continues.

Table Relationships

To leverage the potential of a relational database, you need to have relationships. As you define your tables and your object diagrams (see chapter 9), you are likely to find some obvious relationships. With databases, there are three kinds of relationships to concern yourself with: one-to-one, one-to-many, and many-to-many. Let's look at each of these in more detail.

One-to-One

The simplest relationship between two tables is a one-to-one relationship. Here, each record in a first table must have a corresponding record in a second table, as shown in Figure 10.1. In many cases, both tables will also have a relationship to another table. Note that you can also implement a one-to-one relationship as a one-to-many relationship (see next section) with the "many" part fixed at one. Although simple, this relationship is rare, because generally you should include all of the information in the same table, since both tables relate to the same primary key. There are specific instances when such a relationship is helpful, though. For example, you may want to have one table be updatable and the other protected by security triggers and constraints (perhaps allowing insertions only). This is common when working with financial applications in which you want to be sure all changes are audited. While you may want to allow updates on some fields (like status and category) in such applications, you will probably want to protect the amount and account fields. In Figure 10.1, the Stock Quantity table contains fields that are likely to change frequently, while the rows in the Stock table itself are likely to be fixed. You could always include all the information in one table and just protect those fields that can't be changed, but the approach shown in Figure 10.1 provides a clearer grouping.

One-to-Many

Perhaps the most common relationship is the one-to-many relationship. Here a detail or child table references a header or parent table, as shown in Figure 10.2. This relationship is enforced with a simple foreign key constraint: every record in the child table must have a corresponding record in the parent table. The child table includes the parent table's primary key (or a unique key) as a column. In Figure 10.2, the Order Item table references the Order Table by means of the `order_id` field. The line drawn between the two tables connects

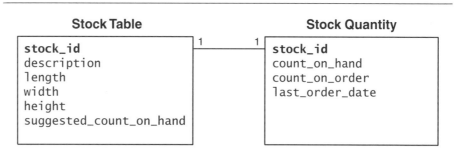

FIGURE 10.1   A One-to-One Relationship

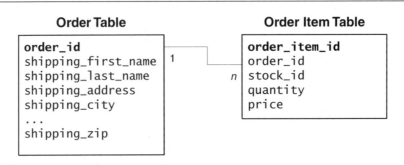

FIGURE 10.2   A One-to-Many Relationship

the fields creating the relationship and explicitly shows that for every 1 Order record there can be *n* Order Item records.

Many-to-Many

The many-to-many relationship is the most complicated of the three. As Figure 10.3 shows, two tables form a many-to-many relationship with the help of a third table. Each of the primary tables (Warehouse Table and Stock Quantity Table) has a one-to-many relationship with the helper table (Warehouse Quantity Table). Each record in the Warehouse Table can have many corresponding records in the Stock Quantity Table, and each record in the Stock Quantity Table can have many corresponding records in the Warehouse Table. Beyond the references to the primary tables, often the helper table has no other fields. In Figure 10.3, each warehouse can hold any number of different kinds of products (identified by stock_id). Similarly, each stock item can be stored in any number of warehouses. This models real life quite well.

It is also possible (in fact, it is common) to make any of these relationships optional. With a one-to-one relationship, one table may have a corresponding record in another table, but both still relate to a third table. In an optional one-to-many relationship, the parent does not need a child record. The principle is the same for many-to-many tables. If there is potential for confusion in your database models, define the nature of the relationship as explicitly as possible. You can indicate an optional one-to-many relationship with the symbols (1 to 0..n) and an optional many-to-many relationship with (0..n to 0..n). These symbols are taken from the Unified Modeling Language, in which you can specify the exact cardinality of a relationship between two entities.

You model your database relationships with an Entity Relationship Diagram (ERD). There are dozens of tools available for creating such diagrams, and many

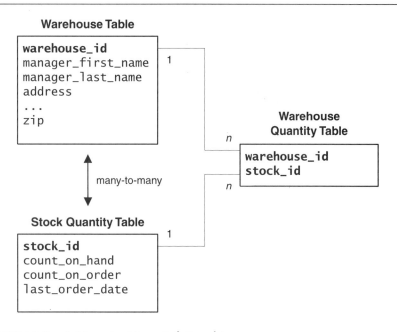

FIGURE 10.3   A Many-to-Many Relationship

even have the ability to generate your database (tables, relationships, and constraints) right from the ERD you define. ERDs give you a visually simplified view of your database and make working with relational databases much simpler. The problem is that there are many ways to demonstrate a relationship graphically, and it may take some time to get used to the notation of a particular system.

Further Reading

E. F. Codd, *The Relational Model for Database Management* (1990).   E. F. Codd is the father of relational databases, and he covers the topic in detail in this book. The concepts of relational databases are now well known, but this book is worth its price for the discussion of normalization alone.

Paul J. Fortier, *Database Systems Handbook* (1997).   Although predominantly theoretical and academic (most of the contributors have associations with universities), this book nevertheless manages to present some useful material.

Deborah Kurata, *Doing Objects in Microsoft Visual Basic 5.0* (1997).   Chapter 8 of this book discusses the basics of relational database design from a VB perspective.

Ivar Jacobson et al., *Object-Oriented Software Engineering* (1992).　Jacobson describes the derivation of classes from tables in this book, and I feel his process works equally well backwards. Furthermore, he focuses on the derivation of business entities from use case analyses, a process that can help you define and verify your database designs.

Rob Mattison, *Understanding Database Management Systems* (1998).　This book discusses most of the major database strategies and includes an excellent discussion of the history of relational databases and relational database topics.

PART III

Implementation

Part III moves the focus from design to implementation. Chapter 11 describes practical coding tips for corporate developers, and chapter 12 looks at the strengths and weaknesses of the new features in Visual Basic 6.

Chapters 13 and 14 concentrate on data access, from the registry to flat files and even to multiuser SQL applications. We will look at OLE DB and ADO to see how they differ from more common data access strategies that use ODBC and DAO or RDO. In addition, we will see how to create an OLE DB provider for your legacy data.

In chapters 15 and 16 we'll explore more advanced topics in Visual Basic. First we'll see how to create ActiveX controls from scratch (and why you might want to), then turn our attention to ways of improving the performance of your applications with multithreading and advanced string handling. Finally, in chapter 17 we will look at two of the most problematic aspects of VB development at corporations, debugging and error handling. We'll discuss ways of making your application both more robust and freer of defects.

Chapter 11
General Coding Practices

In this chapter we'll cover a variety of general topics. We'll start with a brief look at the Visual Basic IDE to discuss some of its more complicated dialog boxes and settings. We'll then turn to a list of good programming practices and examine some of the dos and don'ts of Visual Basic development. We'll cover such topics as choosing good names for variables, understanding data types, binding, and using version control, among others.

Understanding Visual Basic's IDE

Let's take a very brief look at some of the dialogs in Visual Basic's Integrated Development Environment (IDE). Most of these dialogs are easy to understand and their options are clear, but there are a handful of options that are more complex and deserve a few words of explanation. In this section I'll suggest ways of using these dialogs to make coding with a group of developers easier.

The Procedure Attributes Dialog

Visual Basic's Procedure Attributes Dialog is a user interface nightmare (see Figure 11.1) because the fully extended dialog (which appears after pressing the advanced button) is complicated and difficult to use. Bruce McKinney calls it "the dialog from hell" (1997). It is complicated not because its settings are

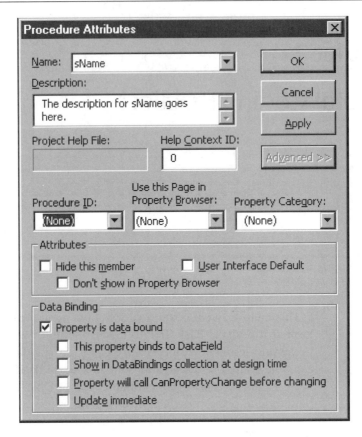

FIGURE 11.1 The Procedure Attributes Dialog

inherently advanced, but rather because it is not laid out very well. It simply tries to do too much, and most programmers I know rarely use it. On the plus side, though, it is reasonably well documented in the help files.

The most useful aspect of this dialog is that it allows you to create descriptions for your methods and properties. When you compile your code into a component and reference it in another project, these descriptions are visible in the object browser. If you are creating ActiveX controls, it is a good idea to set those properties in the Attributes and Data Binding frames. It is relatively simple to add descriptions to the methods and properties with this dialog, although it is easy to forget to do so, especially when under schedule pressure. In short, once you get past the dialog's confusing layout and review the help files on it, you'll see that it is worth your time to use it.

The Object Browser

As with the Procedure Attributes Dialog, a lot of developers forget all about the Object Browser (Figure 11.2) or are not familiar enough with it to use it effectively. I find that for well-documented components and classes, the Object Browser is usually enough to figure out what is going on and provides enough information to use the method, property, or class in question. Also, setting the Object Browser to show hidden members is a good way to discover undocumented features.

Although you can add the descriptions for methods and properties that appear in the Object Browser in the Procedure Attributes Dialog, you can only add a description of the class itself from within the Object Browser (unless you use a third-party tool such as Standards Master). To do this, find the class in question in the Object Browser, right-click on the item, and choose Properties from the pop-up menu. This will present you with a simplified version of the Procedure Attributes Dialog called the Member Options Dialog.

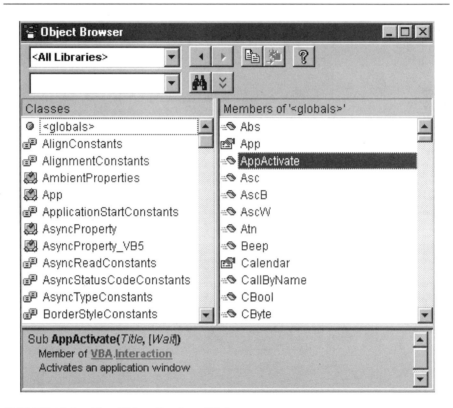

FIGURE 11.2 The Object Browser Dialog

Options Dialog

The general Options Dialog in Visual Basic (under the Tools menu) is easy to use and well documented. I have just a few caveats about problems caused mainly by the VB defaults.

1. *Under the Editor Tab:* First, be sure to check Require Variable Declaration, which is off by default. This forces VB to place the keywords Option Explicit at the top of every new module. Note that it does not retroactively place these keywords in existing modules, so you will need to insert them by hand or with a tool like Standards Master. (See the section "Use Data Correctly" for more information.) Also, in group development, be sure all developers use the same tab width setting. The default (4) is usually fine. Without this consistency, code can quickly become an unreadable mess. (See Figure 11.3.)

2. *Under the General Tab:* You should opt to have all developers on your team turn off both the Background Compile and Compile on Demand options, which are on by default. When these options are checked, VB does not compile

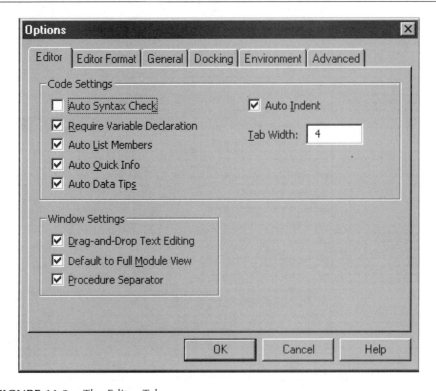

FIGURE 11.3 The Editor Tab

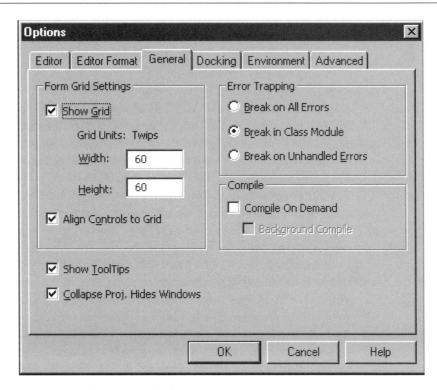

FIGURE 11.4 The General Tab

a function in design mode until it is called (last-minute compilation). This means that it is entirely possible to have code that does not compile in a project without the developer even knowing it. When this code gets checked into a version control tool and retrieved by another developer who has the options turned off, he is besieged by compilation errors. This is frustrating to say the least and can really affect productivity. My recommendation is to keep these options off and comment out any code that doesn't compile (perhaps because it is not finished) before checking it in to the version control repository. (See Figure 11.4.)

Good Programming Practices

Writing solid code is not easy. In fact, I would argue that computer programming is among the most difficult things people do. Although Visual Basic is a relatively easy language to learn and read, writing good VB code at the corporate level can sometimes be especially difficult. Many Visual Basic programmers, even those in senior positions, are self-taught, and VB is often their first (and sometimes only) language. Because VB is so easy to learn and because programmers can create satisfying applications of medium complexity relatively quickly, they are not challenged. Their skill sets reach a productive state relatively quickly (refer to Figure 1.1 in chapter 1), but since they are not pushed or stretched, after that may grow slowly. Furthermore, in the spirit of making things easier, Visual Basic provides many questionable shortcuts that appear helpful at first but in the end are a bad idea. For instance, data-bound controls are the perfect example of an easy-to-learn technology that is too buggy and lopsided to be used effectively on real corporate applications. Yet, some beginning programmers find them indispensable. In short, without formal training in computer science and programming or experience with another language, these individuals may not have exposure to some of the important principles of writing solid code. As a result, they may not be able to separate the good practices from the bad.

Like many developers, I believe there are right ways and wrong ways to program, especially when money is on the line, as it always is in the corporate world. The right way is usually more time-consuming and often involves more planning and rework. The wrong way seems easier at the time but usually manifests its weaknesses at the most inopportune moment. However, because of factors external to the actual coding, such as budget or schedule restrictions, it may be difficult to separate the two.

In practice, corporations often sacrifice principle and do things the wrong way to meet some arbitrary goal. This is especially common during the maintenance period of development when new features are appended awkwardly to a weak foundation that cannot hold them, or when buggy code is patched rather than reworked. The decision to cut corners and implement a quick-and-dirty solution to a problem should be weighed carefully and should never be the result of laziness, sloppiness, or ignorance. Furthermore, if a company must take shortcuts to meet some time constraint, every effort should be made to return to the patched code and make it right (though this rarely happens). It should be noted that only temporary patches are recommended. When code is constantly patched and repatched, it is harder to maintain and scale.

In the remainder of this chapter, I'll discuss my list of the Top Ten Good Programming Practices, which are as follows:

1. Understand requirements
2. Use data correctly
3. Name your identifiers well
4. Practice loose coupling and tight cohesion
5. Comment constantly

6. Think reuse

7. Bind early

8. Limit visibility and duration by encapsulating

9. Debug as you go and use error trapping

10. Use version control

Organized roughly in order of importance, this list is intended to point out some very straightforward techniques for ensuring that your code not only works correctly, but is scalable, easy to maintain, and, most important, easy to read. Individually, none of the entries is particularly earth-shattering, but taken together, they form a powerful paradigm for developing good programming habits.

This list contains items that pertain only to coding. It does not cover database design, object design, software development lifecycles, or other important concepts. Many of these topics are discussed elsewhere in this book and are cross-referenced here.

This list could easily have had hundreds of entries, but the ten here summarize the most important habits of good coders. (For a more exhaustive look at good and bad coding practices, refer to Steve McConnell's *Code Complete* [1993].) In most cases, these practices apply to programming in any language, though a few are VB-specific and I address the others from a VB perspective.

My advice on applying these principles is to follow them to the point that they become habit. Many good programmers may follow these guidelines subconsciously. However, it may take some time for more inexperienced programmers to change the way they think about coding and to gain the most benefit from these suggestions (old habits die hard). In addition, remember that following these guidelines faithfully will not guarantee success, but not following them will likely be detrimental. Let's look at each of the habits of good coders in more detail.

Understand Requirements

Chapters 1 through 4 discussed the importance of developing a solid understanding of the requirements of a project before jumping into development. However, this concept applies not only to entire projects but also to every class, method, and line of code a programmer writes. A project that has been *well designed* and that has clearly defined and documented requirements *is still doomed* if the developers do not take the time to understand what it is they are trying to do, at the most microscopic level.

Before you begin a coding session, be sure you can answer the following simple questions. If you can't, there is a good chance either that the requirements are ill-defined or that you are misunderstanding them. In either case, don't start coding.

1. What is this class/routine/line of code supposed to do? This is basic planning, and can often be answered by thinking ahead and stubbing out the code with comments (see "Comment Constantly" section).
2. How does the code I am working on fit into the bigger picture? Make sure you understand why you are writing this code.
3. Does this code need to be written? Sometimes you may be able to leverage existing code (see "Think Reuse" section).

Use Data Correctly

When it comes to data types, Visual Basic is one of the most paradoxical languages around. On one hand, it is an extremely strongly typed language, offering nine unique simple types (not including object types or user-defined types) to make storing your data easier. On the other hand, when variants are used it is a type*less* language. When you use variants, VB chooses which data type to use for your data automatically. (Incidentally, VB will also convert between types for you.) Just to complicate matters, VB does not even require that you declare your variables in the first place. These two "features" can be frustrating at times and can lead to buggy code. You can avoid complications by following one simple rule: *with rare exception, explicitly declare and type all of your variables*. Visual Basic can enforce mandatory variable declaration when you place the keyword Option Explicit at the beginning of all of your modules, and I cannot think of a valid reason not to use it. This makes following the first part of the rule easy. There is no automatic enforcement of typing, though, so you'll have to watch your declarations carefully (see chapter 19 for more information) or you'll end up with a bunch of variants. You can always use one of the DefType statements to set the default type to something other than variant, but this still will not force explicit declarations.

When choosing a type for your data, there are a number of things to consider:

◆ Is it a number or a string?
◆ If it is a string, how long does it need to be? Is the length fixed?
◆ If it is a number, how big or small does it need to be? What level of precision does it need to have? Will it be involved in complicated calculations? You may end up choosing some floating point or integer representation.
◆ Is the number really a "special" type, like a date, a currency, or a Boolean?

Also, remember that your data is likely to have a lifetime outside of VB. Chances are you will save it to a relational database or flat file or otherwise pass it along for storage. Do not make the mistake of forcing your VB data into a type dictated by its representation elsewhere. For example, if for some reason a number is stored as a string in a database (don't laugh, I have seen this many times), convert it to a number as soon as you read it and convert it back to a string before writing it. You should make such conversions explicit by using VB's conversion functions (`CLng`, `CStr`, `CDate`, etc.). Doing so not only will ensure that VB actually converts the data the way you want it to, but also will provide more readable, self-documenting code with no loss of performance. As another example, consider Oracle's lack of a useful Boolean type. The easiest way to store flags in Oracle is to use some character or numeric representation, often with a check constraint (e.g., "Y" or "N" as `varchar2(1)`, or 0 or 1 as `number` are common). But since VB *does* have a Boolean type, it makes sense to use it.

While data usage may seem to be a very basic topic, a thorough understanding of data types is critical to becoming a top-notch programmer. In my experience, most programmers just get by; that is, they do not think very hard about the data types they are using. Furthermore, many don't understand fully the various data types available in VB. For instance, on more than one occasion I have reviewed the code of experienced programmers and found them using doubles to hold monetary values when the currency type would have been much better. There is no excuse for this kind of error, yet it happens all of the time.

In cases where VB does not provide the simple type you need, you may create your own types, including enumerated types and user-defined types. Enumerated types are just long integers with fancy trim. See the discussion later in this chapter for more information. User-defined types are simply structures composed of individually typed members. They allow you to group related data into one type.

Table 11.1 contains a summary of the data types available to you in VB, describing the size and range of each type. Let's take at look at these more closely. (Note that object types—object, form, control, and so forth—are omitted here, but are discussed in the "Bind Early" section.)

Boolean

Booleans are 2 bytes long and have a range of true/false. They should be used whenever you need to store a value that is an absolute binary. Booleans are commonly called *flags*, which are either raised (true) or not (false).

Byte

A byte is one byte long (go figure) and has a range of 0 to 255. Note that the byte is the only numeric type in Visual Basic that is inherently unsigned. Bytes

TABLE 11.1 Summary of Data Types in Visual Basic

Type	*Size and Range*
Boolean	2 bytes, true/false
Byte	1 byte, 0 to 255
Currency	8 bytes, -922,337,203,685,477.5808 to 922,337,203,685,477.5807
Date	8 bytes, January 1, 100, to December 31, 9999
Decimal	12 bytes, +/-79,228,162,514,264,337,593,543,950,335 with no decimal point and +/-7.9228162514264337593543950335 with 28 places to the right of the decimal. (The smallest nonzero number is +/-0.0000000000000000000000000001.)
Double	8 bytes, -1.79769313486232 E308 to -4.94065645841247 E-324 for negative values and 4.94065645841247 E-324 to 1.79769313486232 E308 for positive values
Enumerated	same as Long
Integer	2 bytes, -32,768 to 32,767
Long	4 bytes, -2,147,483,648 to 2,147,483,647
Single	4 bytes, 3.402823 E38 to -1.401298 E-45 for negative values and 1.401298 E-45 to 3.402823 E38 for positive numbers
String	variable size, theoretical limit of about 4 GB in length
User-Defined	size is sum of constituent types
Variant	16 and 22 bytes in length minimum, range of base type

are most commonly used in arrays to hold chunks of binary data (BLOBs) or strings (see chapter 16 for more information on manipulating strings with byte arrays). In fact, using bytes outside the context of an array is rare and should be avoided, especially since integers and longs are more efficient.

Currency

Incorrect computations involving money always tend to get someone's attention. Traditionally, monetary amounts were stored in floating point numbers (since they have a decimal point) or in some kind of fixed-point integer or long. However, neither of these approaches is very good. Floating point numbers lack the precision necessary to hold large monetary amounts while maintaining significance and are prone to rounding errors in calculations. Integers or longs, while accurate, must be converted to dollars and cents before they can be used practically and are of limited range. VB's currency type provides the best of both worlds. Its eight bytes can hold any number between -922,337,203,685,477.5808 and 922,337,203,685,477.5807, without loss of precision. Always use the currency type when holding values that represent money. Never use a double or a single for this purpose. The currency type can also be used to hold large integer data (larger than the range supported by longs).

Date

The Y2K menace has brought all the problems associated with working with dates front and center. VB's intrinsic date type is eight bytes long and has a range of January 1, 100, to December 31, 9999. It really should be called datetime, since it is precise to the second for its whole range. The date type is really a floating point number, with the number to the left of the decimal point (signed) representing the number of days from December 30, 1899, and the number to the right holding time.

There are two things to remember when working with dates. First, always use VB's date type instead of a string, and second, be very careful when converting to and from the date type (as is common when storing data in a database) to be sure no accuracy is lost.

Decimal

The decimal type is actually a 12-byte variant (the Books Online claim it is 14 bytes), and although there is no decimal keyword, you may use the CDec function to convert to a decimal variant as needed. Its range is +/-79,228,162,514,264,337,593,543,950,335 with no decimal point and +/-7.9228162514264337593543950335 with 28 places to the right of the decimal. Its smallest nonzero number is +/-0.0000000000000000000000000001. You can use this type when arbitrary precision or a huge magnitude are required, but be prepared for atrocious performance.

To be honest, I have found no practical need for this type, but maybe there is one. Moreover, I find the fact that there is no Decimal keyword troublesome. It would seem to me that if Microsoft really wanted to create an arbitrarily large floating point number, they could have created a type called "huge" or something, rather than overloading a variant. This approach to me seems kludgey, and therefore is suspect. When dealing with arbitrarily large numbers, you may want to consider using strings to hold the values and byte arrays to perform the math. While clumsy and slow, this technique has the advantage of allowing you to work with numbers of almost any size.

Double

Doubles are 8-byte floating point numbers with the range -1.79769313486232 E308 to -4.94065645841247 E-324 for negative values and 4.94065645841247 E-324 to 1.79769313486232 E308 for positive values. In my experience, floating point numbers are of very limited practical use. They can be used to hold very large or very small numbers, but are subject to precision and rounding problems, especially in computations. Because of these issues, never perform equality comparisons with floating point numbers. Rather, subtract the two numbers you want to compare and test the absolute value of the difference against some acceptable threshold value. (In other words, if they are not equal, are they close enough?) Consider wrapping this functionality in a simple function, as follows:

```
Public Function bEqual(rdbFirst As Double, _
                    rdbSecond As Double) As Boolean
    Const dbACCEPTABLE_DIFFERENCE As Double = 0.0001
    bEqual = (Abs(rdbFirst - rdbSecond) _
            < dbACCEPTABLE_DIFFERENCE)
End Function
```

With this function, the values 1.00012 and 1.00013 are considered equal while 1.012 and 1.013 are not.

Enumerated Types

Visual Basic 5 introduced the enumerated (enum) type, a subset of the long type (4 bytes) designed to hold specific values. You can think of enumerated types as being Booleans with more than two values or as longs with check constraints. When defining an enumerated type, you may explicitly indicate the allowable values, or have Visual Basic generate them by default.

Ideally, you would want only those values you have defined in your enumerated type to be valid for your enumerated variable, but Visual Basic lets you assign any long value to an enum variable without error. This is a bit annoying, since VB does provide you with the dropdown list of valid values when you try to assign to an enum. For example, if your enumerated type defines etFirst = 1 and etSecond = 2, a variable of that type can still hold a 3 without error. Because of this flaw, enums lose some of their effectiveness. You'll have to place explicit checks into your code to be sure the range of valid values you have defined is not violated.

Enumerated types are used most often to export constant values, since public enumerated types appear as constants in the Object Browser. You can make people-friendly enumerated value names with multiple words by wrapping the words in square brackets, as follows:

```
Private Enum ErrorSeverity_enum
    [Not Bad] = 1
    Bad = 2
    [Very Bad] = 3
    [Hold On To Your Seats] = 4
End Enum
```

Integer

Integers are the workhorses of the data type world. They are 2 bytes in length and can hold any whole number between –32,768 and 32,767. They are most commonly used for indexing and counting when the range of numbers is limited. Integers and longs are the fastest of the data types and therefore are ideal for calculations. If the range of an integer is too limited for your needs, consider using a long.

Long

The long in Visual Basic is 4 bytes in length and has a range of –2,147,483,648 to 2,147,483,647. It can be used whenever integers are too restrictive in range. It is actually a bit faster than the integer type, since on 32-bit machines the long is the "native" type. Longs are commonly used to hold handles to things such as windows (hWnd) or files (hFile). They are also common in API declarations and can hold addresses returned by ObjPtr, StrPtr, and VarPtr.

Single

A single is the smaller brother of the double. It is 4 bytes in length and has a range of –3.402823 E38 to –1.401298 E–45 for negative values and 1.401298 E–45 to 3.402823 E38 for positive numbers. See the previous "Double" section for more information on usage.

String

Strings in Visual Basic can be of almost any length (the theoretical limit is about 4 gigabytes) and are used to hold text data in Unicode format. For more information on working with strings, refer to chapter 16.

User-Defined

The user-defined type (UDT) used to be the staple of the programming world, forming the foundation of abstract data types. This all changed when the object-oriented programming movement became central, combining data and operations on that data into one neat package (a class). Still, user-defined types have their uses. For example, some API calls require specific types to hold information. Also, as we saw in chapter 5, with LSet and two UDTs of the same length, you can copy large chunks of data quickly and easily, which is especially useful when you need to make a copy of the internal state of an object before sending it across a network boundary.

Variant

Variants are designed to hold data of any type and can be between 16 and 22 bytes in length minimum. Variants are slow, and since VB determines how to interpret the data that the variants store, they are subject to misuse. My guideline for using variants is simple: if there is a better type available (99.9 percent of the time there is), use that type. Variants can be used for ParamArrays (variable-length parameter lists), optional arguments (only if you want IsMissing to work—otherwise use an explicitly typed optional argument with a default value of your choosing), and for decimal variants. They can also be used when working with unknown types of data supplied from other components, though it is best to try to figure out what type to use ahead of time and use that type explicitly.

Name Your Identifiers Well

In chapters 19 and 20 we will take an extended look at creating and enforcing coding standards. There we will learn that one of the most common features of coding-standards documents at corporations is a section that defines naming conventions. No matter how detailed the rules for naming identifiers are, they generally all boil down to one essential point: name your identifiers well.

Creating a good name for an identifier is not really that difficult, and I am always disappointed when I review code with poorly named identifiers. Simply put, creating good names allows you to take full advantage of the clarity inherent in VB. Overall, the code becomes much more readable, making your code work for you rather than against you. Whatever it is you are naming, be sure that the name you choose for it is descriptive and accurate. Avoid meaningless, "generic" names (e.g., i, j, k, x, temp, etc.) at all costs, even for identifiers of limited scope, since such names offer no insight into what the identifier means or how it is used. Let's look at some specific types of identifiers and things to consider when naming them.

Variables and Constants

When naming variables or constants, be sure the name accurately describes the data it holds and how you intend to use that data. For example, for a string intended to hold a person's name, a good identifier name would be sName, whereas Temp1 would be a bad identifier. This example may seem unrealistic, since you would think that no one would ever use a variable name like Temp1, but think again—I have seen names like this countless times. Also, consider using a naming convention for your variable and constant names. The best naming conventions are flexible enough not only to provide a descriptive name for the body of the identifier, but also to indicate its scope and type (usage). Also, be sure your naming convention includes a way to distinguish between constants and variables. See chapter 19 for a detailed discussion of these issues.

Specific types of data naturally yield certain types of names, and you should use this fact to your advantage. For example, Boolean identifiers often contain the word "Flag" or "Is" (e.g., bActiveFlag, bIsActive), suggesting some on/off or true/false binary value. Integers are often indices in arrays or loops and therefore may have the word "Index" (e.g., iBookIndex) included in the name. Integers are also used to hold totals or counts of things, so names like nTotalPeople or nCountOfLines are common and meaningful. Consider usage carefully when naming your identifiers.

Subroutines

Since subroutines do things, subroutine names often contain verbs that form the central part of the name (e.g., consider the routines DestroyObjects, Move, and DeleteLines). These names are all descriptive and clear, and each is built on a descriptive verb. If your verb acts on a noun, include the noun, but omit articles like "A," "An," and "The." For example, use ClearForm rather than ClearTheForm. Words like "the" are not detrimental per se, but they contribute little to the meaning of the name.

Be sure the name you choose accurately and fully describes the routine. For example, if you have a routine that computes interest, a good name for the routine would be ComputeInterest. Similarly, if you have a routine that computes interest and updates the total, a good name might be ComputeInterestAnd-UpdateTotal. Note that being as accurate as possible with your names can also help you determine if routines are well designed. A procedure name that is accurate and descriptive but still awkward or confusing is often symptomatic of a bad routine. For example, the procedure DisplayMainFormAndOpenDatabase presumably does what its name indicates, but the fact that its name is awkward shows that displaying a form and opening a database in the same routine is suspect. See the "Coupling" and "Cohesion" sections that follow.

Others (Filenames, Modules, and Such)

Variables, constants, and subroutines will usually be the most important things you will name, but don't neglect your modules (especially classes), filenames, controls, and everything else. Establishing and following a naming convention for these items will make your life easier.

Lengths of Names

I think there is rarely a concern about the lengths of the identifiers you choose, but it is a good idea not to make them longer than necessary. You can shorten names by using common abbreviations. Also, you may want to stick to an 8 × 3 convention for filenames, but this is not a requirement. See chapter 19 for more information.

Practice Loose Coupling and Tight Cohesion

The anatomy of a good function is an important consideration when programming. Not only does a function need to "hang together" well on its own, but it also needs to "play nice" with other routines. Creating routines that can do both can be a challenge.

Coupling

The term *coupling* indicates a dependent relationship between two or more subroutines. Routines that are closely related are tightly coupled, while those that have distant relationships are loosely coupled and those with no relationship are not coupled. Subroutines are considered related if they share common data in some way. This data may be anything from a simple parameter list to a user-defined type to file data or even (gasp) global data. The more data that routines share and the more dependent one routine is on what other routines do with that data, the tighter the coupling. For example, consider the routines `PromptForName` and `LogError`. Because these routines share no data, they would not be coupled. `PromptForName` and `SaveName` would be loosely coupled, since they both presumably work with a name.

Frequently, coupled routines complement one another (the `MoveFirst` and `MoveLast` methods of recordsets are an excellent example of this). Coupling of this type is usually acceptable, but only if the routines do not rely on one another's side effects. When two routines must operate on the same data, it is a good idea to be sure the relationship between them is absolute. Inverse and converse relationships work especially well. That is, one routine should undo what the other does. If you do have such coupling, be certain the nature of the coupling is as exposed as possible (the relationship between `MoveFirst` and `MoveLast` is obvious from the names, for example). Comments can elaborate on less obvious coupling.

In general, strive to create routines that are not coupled or that are loosely coupled. To do so, avoid sharing data between routines whenever possible. If data does need to be shared, encapsulate the coupling to ensure that the data is not more exposed than it needs to be. Data passed by means of parameter lists is a good example of this data hiding.

Cohesion

Cohesion describes how closely related the operations within a routine are. Routines that are strongly cohesive do one thing and do it well. As a subroutine tries to do unrelated tasks, it becomes less cohesive. Routines with strong cohesion are generally more reliable and easier to debug.

For example, consider a function called `Max`, which returns the maximum value of the parameters passed. It does one thing, as is obvious from its name, and therefore it is tightly cohesive. Now consider a routine called `MaxAndMin`, which returns both the maximum and minimum values from the parameter list. It is less cohesive, because although the things the routine does are semantically related, the routine itself no longer does only one thing. Worse still is the function `MaxAndSin`, which returns the maximum value from the parameter list and its sine. This routine's cohesion is horribly weak. Not only does it not do one thing, but the things it does do are essentially unrelated. Routines like this cry out to be split apart judging from the name alone.

When designing a routine, concentrate on making it as atomic as possible. If a routine does more than one logical but unrelated task, consider breaking the routine into two or more routines, each with strong cohesion.

Remember that cohesion applies to entities other than routines as well. It is a good idea to make the functions in a standard .BAS module related, and the methods in properties in a given class also should relate to one another. Strive to make the relationships topical or logical to avoid unnecessary coupling. Even the different modules and classes in a project should be cohesive. For example, a component containing math functions would be more cohesive than one containing both math and string functions.

Comment Constantly

Most programmers will agree that commenting is an important aspect of programming. Unfortunately, many programmers are atrocious at writing comments. Sometimes they do not include comments at all, believing that their code is somehow inherently intelligible (perhaps because it is written in VB). Some believe that because comments do not affect the functionality, it is not worth taking the time to add them. Others add comments gratuitously, perhaps to satisfy some coding standard, and as a result, the code becomes cluttered with worthless, often redundant comments.

Myth 13
Visual Basic code does not need comments because it is so easy to read.

I believe that commenting should not be an afterthought, but rather an art and a philosophy. In my experience, the best programmers take the attitude that comments are the single most important aspect of coding—it is engrained in their nature. Moreover, to be worthwhile, the belief in the importance of commenting must pervade every aspect of coding at all times. I call this commenting constantly.

Many programmers begin writing a routine by stubbing out its functionality with comments. This is similar to a pencil sketch a watercolor artist does before painting. Incorrect assumptions and bad thought processes can be explored in comments, without wasting time coding, debugging, and testing something that is inherently flawed. As coding begins, the programmer reconsiders the original comments, and they form the basis for the actual code, just as the sketch defines the painting. While coding, consider removing or augmenting your comments so that they do not simply repeat the code.

When you have finished a routine, review its comments to be sure they are accurate and concise. Furthermore, as you change the code during ongoing maintenance, be sure to indicate changes and verify that the comments still make sense. The only thing worse than a routine that has no comments is one with incorrect comments. By proactively reviewing the comments in the code every time you visit it, you can avoid this issue.

Ongoing maintenance of comments is usually problematic. Perhaps this is because programmers are expected to make changes to code that was not theirs to begin with and may feel reluctant to change the comments. Perhaps it is just laziness. Whatever the reason, keeping comments up to date can be as important as whatever changes that are made to the code.

Think Reuse

The buzz phrase Rapid Application Development promises faster and cheaper software development. However, the fastest way to write software is to not write it in the first place. Code and component reuse can greatly simplify the software development process. In fact, Microsoft's Component Object Model (COM) is built around the notion that chunks of executable code can be reused in many ways. Component reuse is also at the center of Visual Basic development. Few Visual Basic projects would be possible without using some of VB's intrinsic controls or third-party controls. I have found that the companies that are most successful at software development tend to leverage reuse whenever possible. They draw on a repository of source code and ActiveX DLLs, EXEs, and OCXes to make creating software easier.

Programmers and designers who want to create reusable code and components need to see beyond the routine or module they are currently working on. It takes an understanding of the entire system in question and, more often than not, a thorough understanding of the nature of the business the application is supporting. They not only must know what is potentially reusable, but also have an idea of how (and if) it will be reused in practice. In some cases, they may already have in mind another application that needs the functionality or perhaps just recognize a need for the component in general.

Here are a few questions to ask yourself while programming that will help you create reusable code:

- Is the functionality provided by the code (a routine, class, module, etc.) potentially reusable? Why or why not? Will it be reused in practice?

- If it is not reusable as is, can it be changed to make it more generic or more robust to support reuse? How so? Be sure not to lose track of the original purpose of the code when changing it to make it more reusable.

◆ Is it possible to turn the code into a component (e.g., DLL, OCX, or ActiveX EXE)? The answer to this question is usually yes, but sometimes issues like security and performance come into play.

◆ If the code were put into a component, how would the complexity of the overall system be affected? Using components should simplify the system rather than making it more complex.

If the functionality of the code is potentially reusable, you should then consider how much of an impact it will have on your project to make the changes required to ensure that the code is reusable. This is always the toughest part. Ironically, the intense schedule pressure of RAD projects leaves little extra room for the flexibility and the planning associated with creating reusable code. Anything that does not contribute directly to the finished product is suspect and subject to rejection. Yet in the long run, RAD projects stand to gain the most benefit from taking the time up front to create reusable components and source code.

At the same time, it is easy to take component creation too far. It is possible to make components so generic that they provide little useful functionality and thus in practice cannot be reused. It is also possible to take a lot of time writing extremely robust components that have no potential uses. I call this the "wouldn't-it-be-cool-if-it-did-this" syndrome, and it mostly affects programmers wanting to flex their creative and technological muscles. These components tend to have little focus and often suffocate on their own functionality.

Furthermore, sometimes turning something into a component just does not make sense and actually makes the system more complicated than it needs to be. I once worked on an application suite that had a whole DLL containing only one public class that exposed one simple method, and this library was used by only one application. Its author thought that the library might be expanded in the future for use by other applications. Though his intentions were good, loading this DLL to run the application became an annoyance. Eventually the DLL was removed, and its code was embedded into the one application that actually used it, so ultimately creating the component was a waste of time.

Beyond components, you may opt to have general code that is shared among various projects. As we'll discuss later, many version control tools facilitate this sharing by allowing you to include the same file in multiple projects. When a developer checks out the file in one project, it is checked out in all projects. I find source code reuse most beneficial with files containing general routines and declarations. Shared files are also used with code containing conditional compilation or resource file dependencies, since these may vary from project to project and therefore can be compiled into a DLL.

Bind Early

Many Visual Basic programmers got their first taste of object-oriented programming with Visual Basic 4. Unfortunately, VB 4's object-oriented capabilities were very limited, and developers were forced to use unsavory kludges to achieve some of the benefits object-oriented programming provides in other languages for free. One of the most common tricks was late binding. Late binding occurs whenever the compiler cannot determine the actual type of an object at compile time. As a result, the type is determined at runtime, and the variable is bound to its type then. Late binding offered the advantage of being able to refer to an object and its properties without actually knowing the precise implementation (i.e., type) of that object. In short, it was a way to implement a kind of polymorphism, since it allowed code to work with any object supporting a set of methods and properties. The same code could therefore provide very different functionality, depending on what late-bound object was being called.

However, the flexibility of late binding carries with it a couple of hefty disadvantages. First, late binding is slow. Not only is creating and binding a late-bound object slow, but all calls to methods and properties on that object are slow as well. Second, there is no compile-time syntax checking. This means that you will have no way of knowing whether the methods and properties you assume are on the late-bound object are actually there until runtime. As a result, you have to add extensive error trapping and failure conditions just to make certain your app does not blow up.

So how do you know if you are using late binding? Visual Basic provides several generic object types, such as `Object`, `Form`, and `Control`, that are indicative of late binding. Of these, `Object` is the most generic and the most common. When they refer to objects, variants are also a sure sign of a late binding.

Visual Basic 5 and 6 improve on VB's object-oriented capabilities slightly. The most notable new object-oriented feature is the addition of the keyword `Implements`. This keyword allows you write a VB class that implements an interface created with a type library or a standard VB class. The advantage of this technique is that you can achieve the type of polymorphism just discussed without the penalties of late binding. We looked at this technique in detail back in chapter 8.

Because of the new features provided by the `Implements` keyword, there are very few instances when you will need to late bind an object and continue to refer to the object via its late-bound reference. Never late bind when you know the type. This would be like using a variant when a better intrinsic type is available. Furthermore, strive to make interfaces for your late-bound objects so that you can avoid performance penalties and runtime errors.

Limit Visibility and Duration by Encapsulating

Data hiding via encapsulation is one of the most beneficial features of object-oriented programming. With hidden data elements, objects and components can be treated like black boxes, exposing only those classes, properties, and methods that an external user of the object or component requires. This makes the code easier to maintain and more robust, since you have explicit control over access to internal code and data. Moreover, it becomes impossible for external users of the component or object to alter its state without the component or object knowing it.

Variables

Because encapsulation is such a powerful tool when implemented correctly, it is disappointing to see code with variables that are more public than they need to be. Exposing more of the internal workings of an object or subroutine than necessary weakens the benefits of encapsulation. Most disappointing, though, is that there are no reasons to do so, beyond ignorance and laziness. Admittedly, it can be a chore to write property lets and gets to expose public members of classes, but this really is not a good excuse.

As with many languages, Visual Basic's default visibility for all variables and constants is private within the block in which they are defined. However, when you are working with module-level members, it is still a good idea to indicate the private scope with the `Private` keyword rather than the `Dim` keyword. This has no effect on the scope of the variable, but is easier to understand because it is more explicit.

I always follow a simple rule of thumb when defining variables: make variables *as private and as limited in duration* as possible. You do this by declaring variables as close to the code that uses them as possible, by creating read-only properties, and by avoiding global data. For example, if you are writing a method of a class, first try to declare the variables used by the method as local variables. If a particular variable needs to be accessed by more than one routine in the class, consider passing it between the routines via a parameter list. If this is not practical, make it a private module-level variable. If it needs to be visible (but not alterable) beyond the scope of a class, provide friend or public property get. If it needs to be altered from an external source, provide a friend or public property let or set. As you can see, these steps start with the variable being local and hidden, and they work toward making the variable more public and exposed as required. When working with routines in BAS modules, the rules are similar, except that there are no property gets and sets.

Notice that, although it is possible, the last example doesn't include the step of creating public members in a class. You can simulate this visibility via public property lets, gets, and sets, which provide a way for you to monitor the changes being made to the state of the object by external code. Other than to avoid the essentially insignificant overhead associated with making the call to the property routine, I have not found a good reason not to use property lets, gets, and sets instead of public members.

In fact, creating property lets, gets, and sets is even a good idea for private members that you do not wish to expose to other code. You simply declare the variables privately at the module level and provide private property lets, gets, and sets for them as needed. Whenever you need to access a private member, do so through its properties rather than through the variable itself. While it may seem like overkill, this technique has the advantage of encapsulating validity logic (e.g., bounds checking) in the let, get, and set routines so that you do not have to duplicate it throughout your code.

Also, notice that the steps above never reach the point of making the data 100 percent global. Admittedly, in practice, there are reasons to use global data (global objects with read-only properties are especially useful), but global data should always be a last resort. When making maintenance changes to code, sometimes there is no way to implement a feature without involving global data. Other times it may be very complicated to do so and therefore not practical. Consequently, you must weigh the immediate benefit of using global variables against the potential long-term damage. For instance, using global variables to make a change to code may allow you to finish the task at hand more quickly without major changes, but ultimately you have more complicated code to maintain. Repeated use of global fixes is usually disastrous. When you must have global variables, make certain they are clearly identifiable with comments and an obvious name.

When considering the duration, it is a good idea not to keep a variable around longer than necessary. You usually accomplish this by limiting its scope. Most important, never alter the scope of a variable (by changing it from a local variable to a module-level variable, for instance) just to increase its duration—use a static local variable instead. For example, consider the following code:

```
Private Sub DoIt()
    Dim bNeedsToRetainValue As Boolean
    If bNeedsToRetainValue Then
    '...
    End If
End Sub
```

You could declare bNeedsToRetainValue as a module-level Boolean to be sure it retains its value in between calls to DoIt. However, the better solution would be to make it static and local, as follows:

```
Private Sub DoIt()
    Static stbNeedsToRetainValue As Boolean
    If stbNeedsToRetainValue Then
    '...
    End If
End Sub
```

The one drawback to static variables in Visual Basic is that you cannot set the default value, as you can in C and other languages. This means that you are stuck with VB's predefined default values, and you will have to code around them.

Subroutines

The same rules that apply to variables and constants also apply to subroutines, especially methods and properties on classes. Never make a method or property public when you do not need to. Also, do not forget about the `Friend` keyword. This allows you to make the method semipublic, that is, public to the code in the same project, but private to everything else. It is a useful feature that is frequently overlooked.

Classes

When adding a class to your ActiveX DLLs and EXEs, be sure to consider the class's instancing property carefully. The default instancing value is `MultiUse`, which basically means that the class is as public as it can be. Before relying on this default, consider the other options available to you. Generally, you should choose between `Private` and `MultiUse`, since these are the two most common. Make your classes `Private` unless they need to be visible to external clients. If your class cannot be `Private`, choose the appropriate instancing setting as summarized in Table 11.2. Let's look at each setting more closely.

Private Private classes are visible only within the project in which they are defined. External clients cannot instantiate objects from them or receive explicitly defined references to them. These are the lifeblood of many applications, and I recommend making your classes private unless there is a reason to do otherwise.

PublicNotCreatable External clients can see the class (and thus can declare explicit object references), but cannot instantiate objects from it directly. In order

TABLE 11.2 Instancing Settings for Visual Basic Classes

Setting	Availability
Private	All project types
PublicNotCreatable	All projects except standard executables
SingleUse	ActiveX EXEs only
GlobalSingleUse	ActiveX EXEs only
MultiUse	ActiveX DLLs and EXEs only
GlobalMultiUse	ActiveX DLLs and EXEs only

for an external client to use a `PublicNotCreatable` object, the component must first create the object internally and pass a reference to it to the external client. This type of instancing is most useful when you want to control the creation of objects explicitly. When an external client requests a reference to an object that is `PublicNotCreatable`, you can first check security, the number of objects already in existence, or perform other validation before granting the request.

SingleUse Objects instantiated from `SingleUse` classes each reside in a new instance of the component, providing a type of multithreading. See chapter 16 for more information.

GlobalSingleUse This setting allows external clients to call methods on the class without an object reference (code that is internal to the component must still create an object, however). Component instancing is the same as with `SingleUse`. You can use `GlobalSingleUse` instancing to create traditional libraries—routines that can be called as if they were part of the VB language, without creating an object first.

MultiUse External clients not only can see the class, but also can create as many instances of the class as needed without creating a new instance of the component. For ActiveX components, this is the default.

GlobalMultiUse This setting allows external clients to call methods on the class without an object reference (code internal to the component must still create an object). You can use `GlobalMultiUse` instancing to create traditional libraries—routines that can be called as if they were part of the VB language, without creating an object first. Component instancing is the same as `MultiUse`.

Debug as You Go and Use Error Trapping

Practical experience demonstrates that the code of even the best programmers will have bugs. They are an unfortunate, but unavoidable aspect of programming, especially with nontrivial applications, and developers who think otherwise are just fooling themselves. Once this realization is made, there can be a shift in focus from just eliminating bugs to also setting traps for them. Defensive coding helps by ensuring that stupid, trivial problems never happen and that more subtle problems are exposed and easy to find and fix. The idea of defensive coding comes from the notion that an ounce of prevention up front can save hours of headache in the end. This topic is so important that I have devoted an entire chapter to it (see chapter 17).

Tying directly into the concept of defensive coding is the practice of fixing bugs as soon as they are found. Good programmers gear the whole coding session not toward finishing the code, but toward finishing the code and polishing it to the point that they cannot find anything wrong with it. All too often schedule pressures force programmers to complete a routine quickly, give it a test run, then pass it along to a formal QA team for testing. The problem is that many of the bugs found later by the QA team often could have (and, in my opinion, should have) been found by the developer. Since there is overhead associated with logging, tracking, fixing, and retesting the bug, it is easiest to fix it immediately. The longer a bug remains unfixed (even a trivial one), the more likely it will cause other problems, especially in code that has been modified to work around the bug. I am not suggesting that developers can find all of the bugs in the code, because traditionally they can't. In fact, programmers are among the worst testers, especially when testing their own code. But it also does not mean that developers shouldn't try.

Combining defensive programming with an aggressive and proactive attitude toward finding and fixing bugs early makes software better. It is a one-two punch that makes bug counts smaller, which improves the quality of the software and makes development time shorter.

Use Version Control

Effective use of version control is not really an aspect of coding, but I have included it here as a general good practice for developers. A version control tool acts as a repository for source code, executables, documentation, and just about any other kind of file. It offers a number of advantages to the development experience and is indispensable when sharing code among a group of developers. In the VB world, the two most common version control tools are Intersolv's PVCS and Microsoft Visual Source Safe, which is included with Visual Studio. There are several others available, some as shareware and freeware.

Version control tools offer the following benefits:

- They provide centralized access to code and files, often with security. The version control database typically resides on a network server and benefits from the backup processes and security mechanisms in place for that server.

- They ensure that only one person works on a module or file at a time (a procedure called *change management*), thus preventing one developer from overwriting the changes of another. When a version control tool is installed, the Visual Basic IDE adds convenient menu options to get, checkout, and check-in code. This integration is very helpful, but is still a bit buggy.

- They provide the ability to tag or label related files, such as those source code files used to build a particular version of software. Some version control tools also allow you to pin code, that is, mark a particular version as the latest "good" version, the one to retrieve by default when getting code.

♦ Some have keyword expansion, which allows you to embed keywords into comments within your code. These embedded codes are replaced with actual values when you check in the file. This is handy for maintaining revision histories and even for creating procedure headers.

♦ Most have the ability to display the history of changes to a file. Some even have the ability to show differences in text files visually. Most also provide the ability to "roll back" to a previous version in case of disaster.

There are some drawbacks to using version control tools as well. Some integrate better with Windows and VB than others (I found the Windows version of PVCS to be especially weak), and thus you should expect to spend some time learning. As with any data source, they are subject to internal corruption, and you will likely need to have someone perform routine maintenance on the database to be sure it performs well. These disadvantages are minor, though, and the benefits far outweigh the drawbacks.

For more information on how and why version control can benefit your project, I recommend Aspi Havewala's "The Version Control Process" article (1999).

Further Reading

Aspi Havewala, "The Version Control Process" (1999).   This article provides a convincing argument for using version control. It mentions a number of tools (both for Windows and UNIX) and describes the entire process of managing and using a version control system.

Steve McConnell, *Code Complete* (1993).   This book is full of practical programming tips and should be required reading for anyone even thinking about programming in Visual Basic.

Chapter 12

VB 6: The Good, the Bad, and the Ugly

In this chapter we'll take a detailed look at some of the features new to Visual Basic 6. Although the Books Online introduce most of these features in the "What's New in VB 6" section, the explanations are far from complete. Furthermore, when it comes to the more mundane aspects of day-to-day programming, developers have a tendency to stick with what they know and may not take the time to experiment with the features to become familiar enough with them to use them practically.

To this end, we'll look at the new features, explaining their strengths and weaknesses. Finally, we'll turn to a critique of VB 6 to see how and why it was a disappointing release.

New Features in Visual Basic 6

Overall, besides the new Internet features, there were painfully few new features in Visual Basic 6. However, some of them are worth pointing out. In this section we'll look at the most promising of these features, including the following:

- New string functions
- Data access changes
- The `CallByName` command
- Dynamic control addition

- The dictionary class
- New array features
- CreateObject enhancements
- FileSystem object
- Class enhancements

Rather than concentrate on syntax and structure, we'll talk about practical ways of using these new features to make your life easier. Although some of these features are not advanced, when used appropriately they can help create robust and flexible solutions. We'll end with a quick look at some of the problems with VB 6. You may want to review the "What's New in Visual Basic 6" section of the Books Online before proceeding.

New String Functions

Visual Basic 6 adds thirteen new string functions to an already powerful arsenal. In fact, these new functions constitute the bulk of the enhancements to the VB language itself. They fall into three categories: parsing functions (see Table 12.1), general string manipulation functions (Table 12.2) and formatting functions (Table 12.3, page 209).

These functions are easy to use and reasonably well documented (though not a single example for using them is to be found in the Books Online), so adding them to your tool belt should be easy. However, they do not provide any functionality you could not have coded yourself with other string functions and API calls. In fact, you can often get better performance by writing your own versions. Dan Fergus (1999) discusses these performance issues in his article "Speed Up Your App with New String Functions." In short, you will have to trade power for speed. The functions with lots of extra optional parameters (such as Replace) tend to perform poorly. The simpler ones (such as StrReverse) are more efficient.

Data Access

There are many features associated with data access that are new to VB 6. Most center on ADO as Microsoft's data access model of the week. For a detailed look at data access, especially ADO, OLE DB, and data environments, refer to chapter 14.

CallByName

One of the new functions with the most potential in VB 6 is CallByName. This function allows you to invoke a method or property on an object with a string containing the method or property name. For example, these two lines of code:

TABLE 12.1 Parsing Functions in VB 6

Function	*Description and Syntax*
`Filter`	Returns a zero-based array containing a subset of a string array based on specified filter criteria. You may reverse the intended functionality by returning only those strings that do not meet the criteria. This function is useful for filtering user interface displays. `Filter(InputStrings,Value[,Include[,Compare]]) as String()`
`Join`	Returns a string created by joining a number of substrings contained in an array. A space is used as the delimiter unless otherwise specified. I still haven't figured out why this function is needed, except that it is a partner to the new `Split` function. `Join(List[, Delimiter]) as String`
`Split`	Returns a zero-based string array containing a specified number of substrings. You may opt to limit the number of substrings returned or to set the delimiter explicitly, which is a space by default. The delimiters themselves are discarded and are not attached to any substrings. This is the most powerful of the parsing functions, allowing you to tokenize just about any string. The biggest drawback (and it is a big one) is that you can provide only one one-character delimiter. Practical text parsing frequently requires that you use several (space, period, comma, etc.). Also, be sure to pass only one character as the delimiter, or the function will just return the whole array in one chunk. `Split(Expression[,Delimiter[,Count[,Compare]]]) as String ()`

```
Call moTest.TestSub(Param1, Param2)
nResult = moTest.Result
```

could be called as follows:

```
Call CallByName(moTest, "TestSub", VbMethod, Param1, Param2)
nResult = CallByName(moTest, "Result", VbGet)
```

The `CallByName` function has many uses, including the three that follow.

1. *Consolidating event handler code for common controls such as text boxes:* If the event handler of a control affects a specific object by, for example, setting a property, you could create one common routine that accepts the control, object, and property name as arguments and handles the changes, including error handling. In the event handler, just invoke your new routine using `CallByName` (see Lhotka, 1998).

2. *Table-driving object properties:* VB code is often loaded with repetitive code that simply fills an object's properties from a database or writes them back. With some generic object-processing code and a driver table, you could

TABLE 12.2   General String Manipulation Functions in VB 6

Function	Description and Syntax
InstrRev	Returns the position of an occurrence of one string within another, from the end of the string. You can opt to start from a given position within the string. InstrRev(*String1*, *String2*[, *Start*[, *Compare*]]) as Variant (Long)
Replace	Returns a string in which a specified substring has been replaced with another substring a specified number of times. You can opt to start at any location in the string and set the total number of replacements to be made as well. This is a powerful function, but still doesn't allow you to match by whole word only. It would also be nice if it returned the number of replacements actually made. You can also use this function in unconventional ways in order to search and modify strings without using a loop. For example, the number of occurrences of String1 in String2 is the following: Len(String2) - Len(Replace(String2, String1, Mid$(String1, 2))) Replace(*Expression*, *Find*, *ReplaceWith*[, *Start*[, *Count*[, *Compare*]]]) as String
Round	Returns a number rounded to a specific number of decimal places. There are two things to note about this function. First, though the help files claim it is a string function, it really isn't, since it returns a Double. Second, this routine does not always round in the same fashion. Round(4.5) may return either 4 or 5, in alternating fashion. Dan Fergus claims this may be to prevent loss of significance that occurs when you always round the same way, but I don't buy it (Fergus, 1998). No matter what the reason, this strange behavior is not well documented and can lead to subtle bugs. You are probably better off writing your own rounding routine, just to be safe. Round(*Expression*[, *NumDecimalPlaces*]) as Double
StrReverse	Returns a string in which the character order of a specified string is reversed. This function is very fast, but of limited use. StrReverse(*String1*) as String

easily automate this loading and updating. In the driver table, associate the name of a column in a table with the name of the property it maps to on the object. A generic processing routine then could use this information to fill or save just about any object's values. In short, this trick allows you to table-drive property-to-column relationships, greatly improving scalability and reducing ongoing maintenance costs.

3. *Allowing the user interface to choose the method to invoke:* The discussion of CallByName in the Books Online mentions a mathematics server component with any number of mathematical functions that constantly change. As new functions are added to a server such as this, you would normally have to recompile client-side executables to make the new functions available. With CallByName, however, the user interface can display the available functions (per-

TABLE 12.3 Formatting Functions in VB 6

Function	*Description and Syntax*
FormatCurrency	Returns a string expression formatted as a currency value using the locale settings. You may also override the regional settings to determine the number of digits after the decimal, whether to include a leading digit, whether to use parentheses for negative numbers, and whether to group digits.
	FormatCurrency(*Expression*[,*NumDigitsAfterDecimal*[, *IncludeLeadingDigit*[,*UseParensForNegativeNumbers*[, *GroupDigits*]]]])as String
FormatDateTime	Returns a string expression formatted as a date or time. It will use the vbGeneralDate format unless otherwise specified.
	FormatDateTime(*Date*[,*NameFormat*]) as String
FormatNumber	Returns a string expression formatted as a number using the locale settings. The optional parameters for this function behave like those for FormatCurrency.
	FormatNumber(*Expression*[,*NumDigitsAfterDecimal*[, *IncludeLeadingDigit*[,*UseParensForNegativeNumbers*[, *GroupDigits*]]]])as String
FormatPercent	Returns a string expression formatted as a percentage with the % character, using the locale settings. You may override the regional settings to determine the number of digits after the decimal, whether to include a leading digit, whether to use parentheses for negative numbers, and whether to group digits.
	FormatPercent(*Expression*[,*NumDigitsAfterDecimal*[, *IncludeLeadingDigit*[,*UseParensForNegativeNumbers*[, *GroupDigits*]]]])as String
MonthName	Returns a string containing the month name of the ordinal month provided. If desired, this routine can also return the abbreviated month name.
	MonthName(*Month*[,*Abbreviate*]) as String
WeekdayName	Returns a string containing the name of the ordinal day of the week provided. You may have the function return the abbreviated name and alter the first day of the week as well.
	WeekdayName(*Weekday*,*Abbreviate*,*FirstDayOfWeek*) as String

haps from a table) or even allow the user to type in the name of the method and then invoke the method with its name only. This is complicated to do effectively, since you also have to take into account various numbers of parameters and error conditions, but is useful under certain circumstances.

There are some very serious drawbacks to using CallByName, however. First, because there is no compile-time checking to be sure the string used for the method exists on the object in question, you have to catch everything at runtime. This not only makes the code harder to debug, but also means you will have to litter your code with extensive error handling when you otherwise would not have to do so.

Second, the performance of CallByName is atrocious. The Books Online say it is even slower than late binding. My own time trials show that invoking a method using CallByName is about ten times slower than invoking it the traditional way. In short, keep calls to CallByName out of loops or expect to pay a hefty performance penalty.

For those of you familiar with COM and C++, this performance degradation occurs because CallByName is simply a wrapper around calls to the IDispatch interface supported by automation objects, as indicated in the object browser's description of CallByName. A component that implements IDispatch may be called via late binding. Presumably, Visual Basic first gets the Dispatch ID of the method using IDispatch::GetIDsOfName, then it uses the Dispatch ID with IDispatch::Invoke, which actually calls the function. This amounts to a serious performance hit. Furthermore, all arguments to functions called by IDispatch::Invoke must be variants (hence the ParamArray in CallByName) adding yet another slap in the face to performance. For more information on COM components, see chapter 5 or refer to *Inside COM* by Dale Rogerson (1997).

Dynamic Control Addition

Prior to version 6, the only way to add a control to a VB form at runtime was to load it into a control array. This was a bit restrictive, since it meant that you had to have a representative control on the form as control(0). Adding a different control meant recompiling the code. However, once loaded, a control could be manipulated in any way you wanted. Unfortunately, the events that fired for each control in the control array were handled by the same routine, which included the index of the control that raised the event as an argument.

Even with these limitations, the ability to load and position controls at runtime is a powerful tool. It allows user interfaces to customize themselves based on data, without having to display a different form for each of the various data combinations. Visual Basic 6 expands this functionality by including dynamic control addition. This is the ability to load any control on the PC into the container of your choice without having a representative control on the form or even a reference to one in the project. With this functionality you get true create-on-the-fly capabilities and can table-drive just about every aspect of a form's appearance. This allows you to make complete UI changes without recompiling a single line of code. It also allows you, given information from a table, to reuse a generic form that changes its constituent controls. While Dynamic HTML (DHTML) and friends may outshine this functionality, it is still very cool.

There are two ways to load a control dynamically. If you have a reference to it in the project, you can declare the control `WithEvents` explicitly, load it at run-time, and respond to its everyday events. If you do not have a reference in your project, you must use the type `VBControlExtender`, which has an event called `ObjectEvent`. You use this event handler to respond to all events raised by your control. To access properties and methods that are not supported directly by `VBControlExtender`, access them indirectly by means of the `object` property of `VBControlExtender`. For a simple example of these issues, consider Listing 12.1. It shows how to load a `RichTextBox` at runtime without any prior reference to one in the project. To demonstrate how to manipulate the freshly added control, the example sets the control's position and accesses its `Text` and `TextRTF` properties, and the code in the `mctlNew_ObjectEvent` enumerates the `RichTextBox`'s events as they are raised. To try this out, add the following code to a form, run the project, and watch the debug window as you type in the text box.

Listing 12.1 Dynamically Loading an Unreferenced Control

```
Private WithEvents mctlNew As VBControlExtender

Private Sub mctlNew_ObjectEvent(Info As EventInfo)
    Dim oParameter As EventParameter
    'Enumerate the event name and parameters
    Debug.Print "Name: " & Info.Name
    For Each oParameter In Info.EventParameters
        Debug.Print "Parameter: " & oParameter.Name _
            & " = " & oParameter.Value
    Next oParameter
End Sub

Private Sub Form_Load()
    'Must add the license first
    Call Licenses.Add("RICHTEXT.RichtextCtrl.1")
    'Add the control to the Controls collection
    Set mctlNew = _
        Controls.Add("RICHTEXT.RichtextCtrl.1", "mctlNew")
    'Manipulate as you require...
    With mctlNew
        .Visible = True
        .Width = 2000
        .Top = 200
        .Left = 200
        'Get to the other properties and methods through
        'the object property
        .object.Text = "Hello World"
        Debug.Print .object.TextRTF
        .object.SelStart = 0
        .object.SelLength = Len(.object.Text)
    End With
End Sub
```

```
Private Sub Form_Unload(Cancel As Integer)
    'Remove the control
    Call Controls.Remove("mctlNew")
    'Remove the license
    Call Licenses.Remove("RICHTEXT.RichtextCtrl.1")
    'Clear the reference
    Set mctlNew = Nothing
End Sub
```

There are several peculiarities to this technique. First, you are able to obtain the Library and the Class information when adding the control to the controls collection from the Object Browser. For the RichTextBox control it is RichTextLib.RichTextBox. However, when you use this string to add the control, you get the following message:

> Run-time Error '739';
> Cannot add control 'RichTextLib.RichTextBox'. Dynamically adding
> ActiveX Controls requires the use of the ProgID which can be different
> from LibraryName.Class for some controls. The ProgID for this control is
> 'RICHTEXT.RichtextCtrl.1'.

Switching RichTextLib.RichTextBox to RICHTEXT.RichtextCtrl.1 fixes everything, but why couldn't VB just do this for me? After all, it knew enough to tell me what the correct ProgID was. It would have taken only a couple of lucid comments in the Books Online to clear up the confusion.

The second peculiarity involves licenses. Before you can add an unreferenced control (i.e., one that is not in the toolbox) dynamically, you must first add it to the Licenses collection (see Listing 12.1). Again, this seems like something VB could do for us, except in instances where the control requires a license key. Furthermore, if you attempt to add a license for a control that is already in the toolbox, you will get another polite error, indicating that it is already referenced. For a tool that prides itself on being simple, VB certainly puts up its fair share of hoops for you to jump through when it comes to this functionality.

Dictionaries and Collections

In this section, we'll explore some of the uses for the new Dictionary class in Visual Basic 6. But before we do so, let's look at an old favorite, the Collection class. We'll look at its strengths and weaknesses and ultimately see how it stacks up to the Dictionary.

Collections

With collections, you can add any type of data to a mysterious internal structure, iterate through the items collected, and remove items as needed. The most important feature of collections is that you can access items in the collection by a string key you define. This makes collections more versatile than arrays, with which you can access items only by ordinal index. Furthermore, an array is inherently ordered, whereas a collection is unordered (though it has been shown that iterating through a collection returns items in the same order they were added).

There are two problems with collections. First, they have a limited interface and do not support functionality commonly required by real-world business applications. Second, they are rather slow, especially when working with large collections of objects. We'll address these performance concerns later, but first let's turn to ways of making collections more powerful.

The easiest way to make a Collection behave the way you would like is to create a simple wrapper class around a Collection, and delegate the functionality of the common methods and properties. To this collectionlike class, you can add any number of custom properties and methods, as needed. Furthermore, with an undocumented but now infamous hack, you can have your collection respond to VB's For Each syntax. We'll talk about this briefly later, but for a detailed discussion of this hack, see *Hardcore Visual Basic* (McKinney, 1997).

Listing 12.2 contains the source code for a simple, more specialized collection wrapper class. It delegates the implementation of Count, Add, Remove, and Item to its internal Collection, mclItems. Each of these methods has been simplified a bit, working under the assumption that the wrapper class will be used to hold only keyed objects, not variants. To these standard routines, I have added two new methods: Clear, which completely erases the collection; and FillFromSQL, which takes as arguments an rdoConnection (you can change this to the data access method of your choice) and a string containing some embedded SQL. The connection and SQL are used to query the database for specific rows, which can then be scraped into objects and added to the internal Collection. Note that FillFromSQL is just a stub—a working version would fully implement the code to read the result set and scrape the data into some objects. I present this shortened version here simply to show the potential for expanding VB's basic Collection.

The last function in Listing 12.2 illustrates the technique of enabling the For Each syntax for use with your new collection. The function NewEnum returns an IEnumVARIANT type and simply delegates its implementation to a hidden method called [_NewEnum]. Note that you can override VB's syntax check by enclosing a method name in square brackets. Without the brackets, the method _NewEnum returns a compilation error, since identifiers in VB cannot begin with an underscore. The last bit of magic to make this class behave as a collection is to set the procedure ID of NewEnum to -4. With these changes in place, you can create an instance of the wrapper class, fill it from the database, and iterate through it just as you would a standard collection.

Listing 12.2   A Simple Collection Wrapper Class

```
Private mclItems As New Collection

Public Property Get Count() As Integer
    Count = mclItems.Count
End Property

Public Property Get Item(rsKey As String) As Object
    Set Item = mclItems(rsKey)
End Property

Public Sub Add(roItem As Object, rsKey As String)
    Call mclItems.Add(roItem, rsKey)
End Sub

Public Sub Remove(rsKey As String)
    Call mclItems.Remove(rsKey)
End Sub

Public Sub FillFromSQL(roDatabase As rdoConnection, _
                  rsSQL As String)

    Dim ssResults As rdoResultset

    Set ssResults = roConnection.OpenResultset(rsSQL, _
        rdOpenForwardOnly, rdConcurReadOnly, rdExecDirect)

    'Scrape the results into objects here.
    'Add objects to Collection.

    ssResults.Close
    Set ssResults = Nothing
End Sub

Public Sub Clear()
    While mclItems.Count > 0
        mclItems.Remove 1
    Wend
End Sub

Public Function NewEnum() As IEnumVARIANT
    'In the procedure attributes dialog, set
    'the procedure id to -4 for this
    'method.
    Set NewEnum = mclItems.[_NewEnum]
End Function
```

Though they may be more robust and easier to use than standard collections, custom collection wrappers that merely delegate the functionality to a private collection offer no performance benefits. However, it is possible to overwrite the vtable entries of a COM object to make it look like a collection even if it isn't. Doing so requires using black magic, mysterious type libraries, the CopyMemory API, and a few other tricks, as Bruce McKinney first demonstrated in *Hardcore Visual Basic* (1997). His approach (which he claims is too hardcore to explain thoroughly in his book) allows you to create a collection-like class without having to delegate the functionality to an internal collection. The internal representation can be just about anything, from an array to a linked list. This allows you to improve the performance of a collection class measurably. Nevertheless, the arcane hacks required to make this work are not for the faint of heart and require a detailed understanding of how COM works, especially from the point of view of C++. In Visual Basic 6, there is a simpler way to get a collection's functionality without its performance penalties, namely, the Dictionary class.

Dictionaries

The Dictionary class lives in the Microsoft Scripting Runtime library, which is scrrun.dll. You will have to add this reference to your project to use a dictionary, and you will also have to distribute it with your application. The Books Online claim that Dictionaries mimic the functionality of Perl associative arrays. I find it easier to think of a dictionary as an unsorted basket of things. You may retrieve things from the basket only by key name (or by pulling one out at a time, randomly).

In many ways, dictionaries are a lot like collections. Both can hold any type of data, and both allow items to be retrieved by key. They can both be iterated with For Each syntax, and even their interfaces look a lot alike. Nevertheless, there are numerous differences worth mentioning here. In short, dictionaries are not just better collections, but rather have unique behaviors making them quite different.

Unlike collections, you cannot access elements of a dictionary by means of an ordinal index, unless you use the Item property, described later in this section. The Item property (the default) of dictionaries is accessible by key only. Of course, you can always iterate through all items with For Each. When using For Each, the dictionary will iterate in the order things were added, but since this behavior is not specified in the help files, you should not rely on it, as Microsoft may change it on a whim.

Another, more peculiar difference between dictionaries and collections is that if you attempt to access an item in a dictionary by key and that item does not exist, a new, empty item will be added for you, free of charge. With a collection, you would have received a runtime error. This behavior is indeed strange, and it takes some getting used to, especially if you are accustomed to working with collections. Luckily, dictionaries have an Exists function, which returns a Boolean value indicating whether the key passed is in the dictionary. If you are uncertain about the existence of an element, you should invoke this function first to check.

Dictionaries also provide a handful of other methods and properties not found on collections. The CompareMode property allows you to determine how to define uniqueness among the keys in the dictionary. The Key property allows you to change the key of a given item easily, something that is a real pain with collections. This is an interesting property, since it is write-only, which makes sense, since you have to know the key of an item to access its Key property to begin with. To facilitate housecleaning, there is a RemoveAll method, which is similar to the Clear method implemented in Listing 12.2. There are also two other properties, the Items and Keys properties, which return variant arrays of items and keys, respectively. You can use these properties to assign all of the keys or all of the items to your own variant array or to iterate through the keys or items directly.

Perhaps the handiest feature of dictionaries is that you can modify the value of an element without having to remove it and re-add it, as you have to do with collections. For example, after executing the following snippet of code, the value of dicNumbers.Item("two") is 3:

```
Dim dicNumbers As New Dictionary
Call dicNumbers.Add("two", 2)
dicNumbers.Item("two") = dicNumbers.Item("two") + 1
```

With a collection, the third line would have generated a runtime error. This feature, coupled with the fact that dictionary keys are variants and may therefore be of any type, allows you to use dictionaries in ways that would have been awkward with collections. For example, consider the process of taking inventory of the items for sale at a store. A standard approach is to count the number of items of the same price and record that quantity under a column for that price. These steps are repeated until all items have been considered. To calculate the total, add the quantities in each column, and multiply the sum by the price of items in that column. When done by hand, a complete inventory sheet might look like the one shown in Table 12.4. Here prices appear at the top, and quantities (counts) appear below, along with totals.

TABLE 12.4 Sample Manual Inventory Sheet

	$11.95	$11.99	$12.25	$19.99
	2	3	2	2
	1	4	1	1
		5	2	
Total:	3 ($35.85)	12 ($143.88)	5 ($61.25)	3 ($59.97)

Since the keys can be of any type, you can treat the columns as "buckets" in the dictionary keyed by price (type currency). The values added to those buckets are the quantities (type integer). Listing 12.3 shows a simple inventory-tallying function.

Listing 12.3   Simple Inventory Tallying Using a Dictionary

```
Dim dicNumbers As New Dictionary
Dim iInventory As Integer
Dim vntTotal As Variant
Dim cCost As Currency
Dim nQty As Integer

'Add a few items to inventory sheet
cCost = 10.95
nQty = 2
dicNumbers.Item(cCost) = dicNumbers.Item(cCost) + nQty

cCost = 11.25
nQty = 5
dicNumbers.Item(cCost) = dicNumbers.Item(cCost) + nQty

cCost = 10.95
nQty = 1
dicNumbers.Item(cCost) = dicNumbers.Item(cCost) + nQty

'Show inventory totals:
For Each vntTotal In dicNumbers.Keys
    Debug.Print dicNumbers.Item(vntTotal) & " at $" & vntTotal _
    & " for a total of $" & dicNumbers.Item(vntTotal) * vntTotal
Next vntTotal
```

The output of the routine shown in Listing 12.3 is the following:

3 at $10.95 for a total of $32.85
5 at $11.25 for a total of $56.25

Note that we took advantage of the fact that an item is added for you when you attempt to access it but it is not present. The first time we added the current quantity to the bucket for a given price, an empty item (zero) was created for us. Subsequent additions were made to the existing quantity in the bucket. In short, we didn't have to predefine our buckets, as we would have had to with collections.

Dictionaries versus Collections

In terms of performance, dictionaries fare better than collections on just about every front. Table 12.5 compares the performance of a dictionary and a collection

TABLE 12.5   Performance Trials of Collections and Dictionaries (time in seconds)

Task	Collection	Dictionary
Add Objects	8.25	4.90
Add Integers	1.91	0.59
Iterate Objects by Key	N/A	3.21
Iterate Integers by Key	N/A	0.46
Iterate Objects by Item	N/A	0.88
Iterate Integers by Item	N/A	0.14
Iterate Objects with For Each	0.57	(see iterate objects by key or item)
Iterate Integers with For Each	0.10	(see iterate integers by key or item)
Iterate Objects by Ordinal Index	84.66	N/A
Iterate Integers by Ordinal Index	80.07	N/A
Remove All Objects	2.74	0.02
Remove All Integers	0.21	0.01

when you add 32000 objects or integers, iterate through them, and then remove them. For dictionaries, the For Each iteration can take place by using the Keys property, as follows:

```
Dim vntKey as Variant
Dim oTest as New Dictionary
For Each vntKey In oTest.Keys
    sDummy = oTest.Item(vntKey).sName
Next vntKey
```

Or it can take place with the Items property, as shown:

```
Dim vntItem as Variant
Dim oTest as New Dictionary
For Each vntItem In oTest.Items
    sDummy = vntItem .sName
Next vntItem
```

Since iteration by ordinal index is not possible with dictionaries but is with collections, Table 12.5 omits ordinal index results for dictionaries. For collections, there is only one For Each syntax, as follows:

```
For Each oAny In oTest
    sDummy = oAny.sName
Next oAny
```

As Table 12.5 shows, dictionaries are at least about twice as fast as collections for most tasks. They are particularly good at removing items. Table 12.5 also shows how much faster using the For Each syntax with Collections is than ordinal iteration.

Array Features

Array functionality received a much needed update in Visual Basic 6. First, functions can now return arrays, as demonstrated by several of the new string functions discussed under "New String Functions." This really isn't that exciting, since in the past you could always pass the array by reference in order to fill it with results or otherwise manipulate it. The ability to assign to an array, though, saves some time. This functionality allows a resizable array to be the left argument in an assignment operation. There are some things to watch out for, however. Most important, be certain the array you are assigning to (the left side) is compatible with the array you are assigning from (the right side). As long as the number of dimensions in the arrays are the same, you are fine, but you may run into trouble if you try to work with multidimensional arrays of different types. This functionality will not work with a fixed-length array.

These warnings aside, assigning arrays allows you to make copies of the contents of an array very quickly, without having to copy the contents one item at a time. This is particularly useful for arrays of bytes, which may contain anything from a BLOB of data to a long string. With this new feature, this binary data can be copied very quickly.

CreateObject Enhancements

Keeping with the spirit of making distributed applications easier to write, Microsoft has added an important new feature to the CreateObject command. You may now optionally include the name of the network server on which to create the object. For more information on distributed architectures, see chapter 5.

FileSystem Object

Manipulating drives, folders, and files in VB has long been more difficult than it needed to be. While you could do just about everything you needed to do, there was never any organizational structure to the functions you had at your disposal, unless you encapsulated them into your own classes. With the new FileSystem object and its subobjects, you have a simple but effective and easy-to-use object model for manipulating file systems. The Books Online document this object model well, but you may wish to just review the Object Browser to get a better picture. As with the Dictionary class, you will have to add a reference to the Microsoft Scripting Runtime to access the FileSystem object.

Class Enhancements

Plain-vanilla classes, which in Visual Basic 5 had only two properties (Name and Instancing), have been enhanced greatly in Visual Basic 6. The enhancements fall into three categories: data awareness, MTS enhancements, and class persistence. Let's look at each of these in turn.

Data Awareness

Two new properties have been added to classes to determine the data awareness of objects created from that particular class. While we'll discuss data access in detail in chapter 13, let's take a quick look at these features here.

Use the DataBindingBehavior property to indicate if an instance of the class in question should act as a consumer of data provided by other objects (data sources). A data consumer may be either simple bound (binding to single fields: vbSimpleBound) or complex bound (binding to a rowset: vbComplexBound). When set to vbComplexBound, Visual Basic automatically adds DataSource and DataMember properties for you to fill in. The documentation indicates that when you set DataBindingBehavior to vbSimpleBound, the PropertyChanged event and the CanPropertyChange method are added to the object's procedures, but this is incorrect.

The DataSourceBehavior property allows you to turn an instance of a class into a data source for use by data consumers. When DataSourceBehavior is set to 1 (vbDataSource) the GetDataMember event is added to the object's procedures. Note that the Books Online indicate that you can set the property to yet another value, vbOLEDEBProvider, but this is erroneous. Nevertheless, I'll explain how to write OLE DB providers in chapter 14.

MTS Enhancements

The new MTSTransactionMode property defines the behavior of objects of this class when using Microsoft Transaction Server. In short, this property is used by MTS to determine whether or not an instance of the object can be created within a transaction and whether it requires a transaction. Under VB 5, you had to set these properties by hand once your DLL was added to MTS. With the MTSTransactionMode property, they get set automatically for you.

Class Persistence

The new class property Persistable is available only for public and creatable classes. When it is set to vbPersistable, the InitProperties, ReadProperties, and WriteProperties events appear. The PropertyChanged method also becomes active for the class as well. Developers of ActiveX controls will find these events and methods familiar, since they are how you read and write a control's properties to and from the `PropertyBag`. Since ActiveX controls have a runtime instance at design time, these methods are indispensable for storing properties set at design time for retrieval during subsequent sessions. The property bag used by ActiveX controls is provided for you by VB.

However, classes have runtime instances only at runtime, making these new features decidedly unimportant. Since most classes act as templates for multiple objects and since most developers write their own methods for saving and restoring an object's state to and from a database, I really don't see the need for these new features in the world of classes. I prefer to add logic to the objects that allows them to read and write themselves from the database directly. For example, I provide all database-savvy objects with a `Save` method, and declare internal Boolean variables so that the objects know whether they have been added, deleted, or changed.

Nevertheless, putting the data for an object into the property bag is a good way to serialize data for use with both MTS and MSMQ. Unlike with ActiveX controls, you have to provide your objects with your own instance of a `PropertyBag` object for the `ReadProperties` and `WriteProperties` events to use. This is a bit annoying, but has its advantages. Because you can control the lifetime of the property bag explicitly, you can add data for as many objects as you would like (provided there is a unique key for each object) and then pass the property bag around as needed (Pattison, 1999).

Bugs: An Extended Flame

To close this chapter, I want to mention a few peeves with Visual Basic 6 and Microsoft. I am by no means the first author to complain about Visual Basic. Bruce McKinney's unhappiness with Visual Basic eventually drove him from the language for good (1999a). Other authors have also voiced their complaints. Now it's my turn.

For me, Visual Basic 6 is a major disappointment. Besides the utter lack of substantive new features, perhaps the biggest practical issue is its new help file system. It is decidedly slower, is full of blatant errors, and offers very few examples. It is also difficult to copy code from the help files into Visual Basic—the formatting always seems to be wrong. Microsoft was clearly trying to take a step forward by consolidating the MSDN literature into a common format, but for VB help alone, it has been a huge step backward. The help files in VB 4 and VB 5 were much better.

If the help system were the only thing wrong, I probably would not complain at all. However, it is only the beginning. Many developers look forward to new releases of Visual Basic, not only to use the new technologies but also to escape the bugs of previous versions. Microsoft attempts to fix some of the bugs its finds, but unfortunately never comes close to even acknowledging all of them. As a result, new releases can be a major letdown. As a big fan of Visual Basic 5, I eagerly awaited the release of VB 6. I was disappointed when the feature set seemed limited (the language really didn't change that much at all, unless you are doing Web development), but was even more shocked by the general instability of the product. Not only did it not fix many of the problems with VB 5, but it generated a bunch of new ones.

Myth 14
Visual Basic 6 is more stable and bug-free than Visual Basic 5.

A quick search through the knowledge base Web site reveals entries for hundreds of VB 6 bugs and problems. Admittedly, some of these bugs are minor, but many produce full-fledged General Protection Faults and can only be considered serious issues. At the time of this writing, Microsoft has released three service packs for Visual Studio 6. The first fixed a handful of problems, but the second fixed none. Zero. Zip. The third finally addressed several issues, but there is still a long way to go. Microsoft may come out with one or two more service packs and fix a couple more bugs, but I am not going to hold my breath.

But what is perhaps most frustrating about these bugs is Microsoft's pale attempts to sidestep them, smiling the whole time. I recently submitted a rather nasty ActiveX control bug, along with sample code, to Microsoft technical support. It was a simple VB 5 project that blew up when compiled under VB 6 (if you're curious, the project was actually an early version of the `FormatBox` control discussed in chapter 15). The support technician informed me that it was indeed a problem and that he was able to reproduce it easily on Windows 95, Windows 98, and Windows NT 4.0, using Visual Basic 6.0. "Great," I thought, "now maybe it will get fixed." No such luck. In fact, I was informed that because my sample project contained more than fifteen lines of code, they would not look into it any further (it had about seventy-five lines). Even to this day it has not been logged in as a known issue. While Microsoft aggressively pushes VB into the world of enterprise development, it seems to want to support only applications of the "Hello World!" variety, unless you pay for a special support package. Most companies I know of are well beyond that level. In his defense, it is clear to me that the Microsoft technician I worked with was only following orders, and that is why my problem was dropped. But this just goes to show that in spite of its claims, Microsoft has little interest in making quality software. It's not just the attitude of a few individuals; it's doctrine.

The moral of this extended flame is, never make assumptions about the stability of the products or the quality of the support you will receive. In fact, unless your company spends a wheelbarrow full of money on a specialized support contract, don't count on any support. Furthermore, don't buy all of the marketing glossies and hype—just try the product out on your own first. As I have stated before, because VB 6 offers so few new features and so many new bugs, I recommend that companies hold off on upgrading from version 5 to version 6, unless they are doing extensive Web development.

I mention these issues only in the hope that making them known will eventually get them addressed. Since I am a developer who makes his living using Visual Basic and other Microsoft development tools, some might say that I am biting the hand that feeds me. This may be true, but without exposing such issues, VB will not become a better tool. In the end, improving Visual Basic by making it more stable and powerful is a worthy goal that will benefit all VB programmers.

Further Reading

Don Box, *Essential COM* (1998).   The book presents a thorough discussion of COM, including how to achieve late binding through automation.

Dan Fergus, "Speed Your App with New String Functions" (1998).   This article provides a quick review of the strengths and weaknesses of VB 6's new string functions.

Bruce McKinney, *Hardcore Visual Basic* (1997).   The book (and its on-line update) provides an extended look at collecting objects in Visual Basic. McKinney also compares the Dictionary class to the Collection class.

Bruce McKinney, "Hardcore Visual Basic: A Hardcore Declaration of Independence" (1999a).   This on-line article explains McKinney's defection from the ranks of VB. He covers dictionaries and collections in detail.

Bruce McKinney, "Understand the Dictionary Class" (1999b).   This article contains an overview of the Dictionary Class and how it stacks up to collections. It is essentially a reprint of the material contained in the on-line update to *Hardcore Visual Basic.*

Ted Pattison, "Using Visual Basic to Integrate MSMQ into Your Distributed Applications" (1999).   This article discusses MSMQ and VB in detail, as well as several techniques for serializing object data when using MSMQ and MTS.

Dale Rogerson, *Inside COM* (1997).   Though its focus is clearly on COM from the perspective of C++, this book provides an excellent in-depth look at what COM really is all about, and many Visual Basic programmers will find it indispensable.

Chapter 13

Data Access

Most Visual Basic applications perform some kind of data access, but with all of the different data access methods available, choosing the one best suited to the project can be a real challenge. This chapter will help take some of the confusion out of the selection process. We will discuss general data access issues that you will need to address when creating your data access strategy, including multiuser issues and asynchronous data access. We'll also take a detailed look at the Windows registry and discuss when and why flat files are appropriate. Finally, we'll examine the benefits of embedded SQL and dynamic SQL.

General Guidelines

Data access continues to be the central element of corporate programming. Developers not only need to read data from a variety of sources, but also often need to collect data from the user and store it. When you consider that that data may be stored in any number of locations, in any number of formats, creating reliable and consistent data access is a difficult challenge.

Consider the following questions, which will help you plan your data access strategy at the highest level.

1. Besides data stored specifically by your application, what other data will the application need to access? Where is that data located? Is it readily accessible? How? Answering these questions is critical to determining

what data access technologies you will need (ODBC, OLE DB, etc.) We'll compare OLE DB and ODBC in the next chapter.

2. Will more than one user need to access the data written by this application? If so, will an individual record ever be updated by more than one user at a time? If you answered yes to both of these questions, you will need to carefully consider optimization and locking strategies for multiuser environments. These are covered in this chapter.

3. What kind of supporting data will your application need? By supporting data, I am referring to application settings, user profiles, and similar information. Typically you will need to choose between INI files and the registry, though sometimes proprietary flat files are useful as well.

Multiuser Considerations

In many cases, your data will need to be accessible to many users working simultaneously. When the amount of data stored grows larger and the number of simultaneous users increase, database performance can become a serious issue. As a result, you will have to plan ahead to create an optimized, scalable system. You will also have to worry about the possibility of contention when two users need to change the same data at the same time. In this section we will look at optimization and locking strategies.

Optimizing for Multiple Users

When you have several users accessing data on your system, you will have to make special arrangements for handling the load. You should consider the many techniques for helping improve performance. These range in cost and complexity and include database design considerations, hardware improvements, connection pooling, caching, and stored procedures.

Design Considerations

When you are designing your database, be sure to keep load issues in mind, since the relationships defined in your database can help or hinder both multiuser access and performance. For example, a database structure that relies on only a few high-level tables to control concurrency is unlikely to be able to support many users without frequent contention issues. Also, large, highly normalized lookup tables may yield very poor performance when many users are accessing them for different data.

While I always consider denormalization to be a last resort when trying to improve performance, there are instances when it is the best option available. If all else fails, consider denormalization in heavily trafficked areas of the database. However, don't forget to enforce denormalization rules with triggers and check constraints where appropriate. See chapter 10 for more issues on database design.

Hardware and Network Improvements

One of the common techniques for improving the performance of your database is to throw more hardware at the database server. For example, you often can replace database servers with faster machines or upgrade the disk access systems they use. There is a practical limit to the amount of benefit you can gain from this approach, but nevertheless it is common, especially since no coding is involved.

Another hardware-related approach involves adding more servers to a multitiered, scaled system. There are two general ways to accomplish this scaling: manually or automatically. As Figure 13.1 shows, in a manual system, specific desktops connect to specific middle-tier servers. These middle-tier servers may be application servers or even small-scale databases synchronized with a main data store via replication. To add users to a system manually, you add more servers to the middle layer and point new desktop clients to the new servers.

With an automatic approach to scaling, client desktops attach to a conglomerate of servers, which distribute processing and data access among themselves, as shown in Figure 13.2. Such automatic load balancing requires special software and is difficult to implement successfully. It has the advantage of being automatic and can be made to be relatively fault-tolerant (if one server goes down, the others pick up the slack).

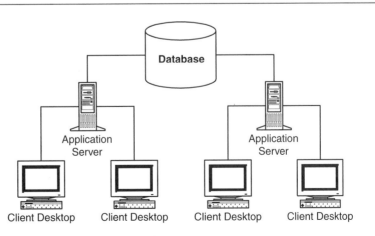

FIGURE 13.1 Manual System Scaling

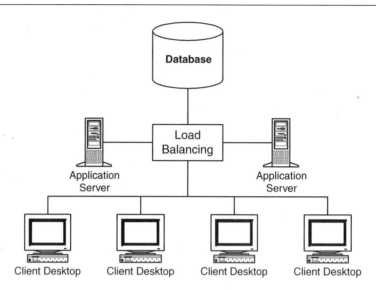

FIGURE 13.2   Automatic System Scaling

The last hardware approach is to upgrade the network that carries the necessary data. However, with 100-megabit and even gigabit networks becoming commonplace, networks are usually not the problem. Still, if your software is running on an older, slower network, the upgrade may be worth your while.

Pooling Connections

Another way to improve the performance of the database system when adding lots of users is to move away from the traditional client/server model of associating a user with a connection. You break this mold by allowing users to share the same database connection. This is most easily accomplished with the connection pooling functionality of ODBC and especially Microsoft Transaction Server. In short, from the perspective of the database, there are actually fewer users, since there are fewer connections. Either of the systems in Figures 13.1 and 13.2 would benefit from connection pooling.

This technique is especially useful in applications that do not have to hit the database very frequently. The more cleanly a client can get to the database and back without multiple calls, the better this approach works. With fewer overall database hits, the number of simultaneous data access requests can remain relatively low, so that sharing technology can distribute free connections more effectively.

Caching

Desktop computers are more powerful today than ever. Interestingly, though, in some cases corporate computers are underutilized: the hard disks and processors are hardly taxed. Caching data on a client system is a good way to make the most of the unused resources on the PC. Client PCs can read data that needs to be constantly accessed and store it locally. While you lose the flexibility of being able to query the data using a language like SQL, the retrieval process itself does not need to access the database, so overall it is faster.

You may also wish to cache data on an application server for client PCs to access rather than retrieve it from the database server. You can create a simple object server and access it via DCOM. DCOM access is generally very slow, so you may want to serialize and even compress the data you send to make accessing it across the network easier. Under this approach, the application server accepts queries from the client systems and performs the database queries itself. It can then cache this data to prevent subsequent database hits. When another client requests the data, it can return the data stored in the cache rather than access it again. This approach is especially useful when several client systems need to access the same data repeatedly. It is important to realize that this type of caching is not very practical with MTS, since MTS objects should be stateless.

Note that depending on your database, you may even be able to forgo the application server and optimize your RDMS to handle such caching automatically. This way, even though the database is being queried for the same data many times, it will not have to hit the disk to return it.

Stored Procedures

We first looked at stored procedures back in chapter 10. There we discussed how stored procedures add to the options that you can use when designing software solutions. Here we'll look at what benefits stored procedures can offer to help improve the performance of your applications.

In addition to encapsulating database logic (including denormalization rules), stored procedures allow for better transaction processing. With proper planning you can wrap several stored procedures into a logical transaction, so that either all of the changes are made (upon success of all parts of the transaction) or none of them are (upon failure of a single part). Smooth and efficient transaction logic can help the performance of a database system by reducing the possibility of multiuser contention.

There are two main types of stored procedures: those that return rows and those that perform actions (inserts, updates, deletes, etc.). In both types, stored procedures can offer substantial performance increases over embedded SQL, for a couple of reasons. First, they are precompiled. This means that the database engine does not have to parse and compile your SQL on the fly, as it has to with embedded SQL. Because stored procedures are precompiled, the database engine has an opportunity to optimize the SQL. It can take advantage of indices and other performance boosters. Second, many database systems have a proprietary language (Oracle has PL-SQL, for example) that allows you to create very robust queries that are not practical with embedded SQL alone. Actions requiring the processing of a server-side cursor are a good example. These languages usually have non-ANSI compliant features, so be sure to weigh the decision to use them carefully.

These advantages may seem minor, but I have found that stored procedures can easily be up to ten times faster than embedded SQL, though on average the performance increase is not as substantial. However, there are some disadvantages to stored procedures that you should be aware of as well. First, different database engines have different stored procedure-calling syntaxes, which means that you lose the biggest advantage of dynamic SQL: the ability to run the same SQL against any database platform. In short, you will have to put your eggs into one basket and write code that works against one database system. For many companies this is not an issue, since they only expect their applications to run against the database platform they have chosen. Second, not all database engines support the same kind functionality, which means that they are not interchangeable. For example, Oracle does not allow you to return rows from stored procedures without complicated hacks. Even so, I recommend using stored procedures for action queries whenever possible. Third, you are often at the mercy of the OLE DB or ODBC drivers you are using to access the database, and these drivers may not support the kind of functionality you require. For instance, it is still surprisingly difficult to access the out parameters returned by stored procedures through ODBC.

Optimistic versus Pessimistic Locking

When two or more users need to access and change the same record in a database, there is the potential for contention. There are two basic philosophies for dealing with this situation. First, you can assume that one user has a good chance of reading the record into memory, updating the data, and then writing the changed record back to the database before another user needs to change it. This is an optimistic view. The more pessimistic view suggests that there is a good chance that more than one user will try to access and change the same record at the same time. If you are optimistic that you can avoid conflicts, you should adopt an *optimistic locking* strategy. Here you check to verify that the data you originally read has remained unchanged when you attempt to update it. When you are less optimistic, you should consider a *pessimistic locking* strategy. Here you must first be given sole claim to a record before you can change it. In effect, you lock the record so that other users cannot make changes to it while you are manipulating it (though they can typically still read it). Let's look at both of these approaches in more detail, beginning with pessimistic locking.

Implementing Pessimistic Locking

To implement pessimistic locking, you will need to develop a mechanism to render the record in question locked (known as *row-level* locking because it only locks one row). Oracle supports this natively with its `Select For Update` syntax. However, prior to version 7, MS SQL Server did not support this functionality out of the box, and many other database management systems do not support it either. If your database does have native support for row-level locking, I recommend using it, because it can automatically help you with the problem of bad networks causing user connections to be dropped, leaving records locked. The built-in system will often automatically unlock the record for you if this occurs.

In the event that you cannot use native row-level locking, you must create your own locking mechanism. The quick-and-dirty approach is to add a column or two to every table that needs to have row-level locking. Use these columns to indicate whether or not the row is locked, perhaps by storing a locked flag and a lock ID. Before attempting to change data, your application must first successfully lock the row by updating the locking information. Later, when your application updates the row, the locking columns are cleared and the row is unlocked.

There are a handful of problems with this brute force approach, though. First, it is easy to forget to unlock a record, thus preventing other users from getting to it. This can also happen if a client with a locked record has some kind of failure and cannot unlock the record at all. As a result, you will have to provide a generic unlocking utility (a skeleton key) to unlock troublesome records. Second, you need to be certain that it is not possible for two clients to think they have the record locked at the same time. Therefore, I recommend using a unique ID to identify the lock—you can generate such a locking ID (key) from a sequence. The only client that can then update the record is the one who has the right key. Third, you will have to be sure all processes that access the data follow your pessimistic locking rules. If even one of your client processes does not follow your rules, it undermines the effectiveness of the mechanism as a whole.

Implementing Optimistic Locking

Practically speaking, optimistic locking is much easier to implement than pessimistic locking, since even a quick-and-dirty approach is essentially foolproof. To begin, you will need to add a column to all tables containing rows you will need to optimistically lock. This column contains what I call a "freshness ID" that gets updated every time a column is inserted or updated. MS SQL has a timestamp type for just this purpose, but a column generated by a sequence works just as well. Avoid using the actual time for this purpose, since it is possible for clients to attempt to update a row essentially simultaneously. When a client first reads the row, it stores the row's freshness ID. Later as it tries to update the row, it first checks the row's current freshness ID, and if it is still the same as the one cached, the update is allowed. The freshness indicator is then updated (it is best to embed this updating logic in a trigger to be certain it always happens). You should also do all data updating by means of a stored procedure encapsulating the freshness-indicator-checking logic. Note that if the freshness ID is different when the update is attempted, the record is stale and must be re-retrieved by the client.

One of the easiest ways to encapsulate the freshness check when performing an update is to include the freshness ID as part of the UPDATE statement's WHERE clause. After the update, you can check the number of rows updated. If none were updated, the freshness check is probably the cause (although you can't be sure). For example, consider the following pseudo-SQL code:

```
UPDATE
    mytable
SET
    column1 = @value1
    /* Set other columns */
WHERE
    keycol = @keyvalue AND
    freshnessIDcol = @FreshnessIDin
If @@rowcount = 0
    BEGIN
    /* Raise an Error here */
    END
END IF
```

Asynchronous Data Access

The most common form of data access is completely synchronous. That is, when a program makes a request for data, it waits until the data is returned before continuing. This technique is efficient and simple, but causes the client application to stop responding while the data access takes place. To remedy this situation, you will need to access the data asynchronously. With asynchronous data access, you initiate a database action that is completed while your application continues to run.

Many of the common data access models, such as Data Access Objects (DAO), Remote Data Objects (RDO), and ActiveX Data Objects (ADO), support some type of asynchronous data access. We won't cover these in detail here, since they are well documented and are straightforward to use. However, it is often not clear exactly when to use asynchronous data access. The important question is really not, "how do I?" but "should I?"

There are many advantages asynchronous data access can offer you. The most important benefit is that it can keep the user interface responsive while performing lengthy database operations such as queries that return large rowsets. In many cases you can also limit the number of rowsets returned, making for a powerful one-two punch in responsiveness. You can easily fill the visible portion of your lists with information returned in the initial rows of the rowset. The remaining rows are not needed until the user tries to scroll down in the list to view more of the items. Also, extended queries and unrelated queries are easier to manage asynchronously. Your application simply kicks off the queries all at once and then moves on to other tasks until they are completed.

However, these advantages are accompanied by some drawbacks as well. First, asynchronous data access usually involves more complicated code than synchronous access. To implement an asynchronous solution, you will have to write additional code to either ping the query's status constantly (e.g., the StillExecuting property of the RDO connection object) or respond to a notification that the query has finished (e.g., by means of the FetchComplete event in ADO). Second, because you cannot predict when an asynchronous query will end, you may have particular difficulty trying to execute a series of asynchronous commands with order dependency. Third, different Database Management Systems have different levels of support for asynchronous queries. This means that a data access solution involving asynchronous queries is likely to be less scalable, since you will not necessarily be able to change Database Management Systems without considerable changes to the code. Last, and perhaps most important, the overall performance of your database queries is likely to be slower, ironically enough. Asynchronous queries provide only the appearance of better performance by providing a more responsive user interface.

Myth 15
Asynchronous queries make database transactions run faster.

In short, my recommendation is not to use asynchronous queries unless you really need to. They are not magic bullets for improving the speed of your applications. There are often better ways to optimize the performance of the user's interaction with the application. For example, optimizing the database (see chapter 10) and preloading forms and data can greatly improve the perceived performance from the standpoint of the user. You should be especially wary of using asynchronous queries just because the technology seems new or flashy. Using asynchronous queries in the wrong instances can seriously degrade the performance of an application and make it more difficult to debug, test, and maintain.

The Windows Registry

The Windows registry is a perfect example of a good idea that has been taken too far. Microsoft wants the registry to be the one-stop shopping center for information about the user's system, whether it is an operating system setting, some COM information, an application's settings, or anything else. In theory, this is a sound idea, but the inclusion of application-specific information makes the registry too confusing to be practical. Rather than turning the registry into a convenient repository for data, such use only turns it into a dumping ground for data that is best stored elsewhere. In my opinion, the registry is best used to hold only relatively unchanging data that users never need to access directly. This amounts to operating system information and COM information only, and I use INI files and database systems for everything else.

But why did the theory fail when applied? In short, the registry never became what Microsoft wanted it to because it has had too many issues and problems. Consequently, developers never learned to trust it implicitly. First, it had a shaky childhood. Under 16-bit Windows there was a 64-kilobyte limit on the registry size—a limit that was often surpassed, leading to strange operating system behavior, including outright crashes. In addition, the initial versions of the Windows NT registry were surprisingly bug-laden. This problematic past gave the registry a bad name before it even got off the ground. Second, to this day the registry remains very difficult to use. The only programmatic way to access it fully through VB is to use a set of rather confusing API calls. In addition, navigating through the maze of keys, subkeys, and values can be daunting, even for experienced computer users. Users who need to tweak a setting can get lost in the registry editor (regedit.exe) easily, and one wrong move can crash a PC irreparably. Third, the registry has a rather weak security model, especially under Windows 95. Because users may not really know what data is stored in the registry, they are less likely to know if someone is accessing it. The fact that it attempts to store all kinds of data in one location makes it a potential security problem. Finally, the registry has made maintaining software installations a true nightmare, and it is common to find applications that leave registry entries behind when uninstalled. These ghost entries may cause other programs to leave files behind when uninstalled, since the applications may think that the files are still shared. Over the course of a few months, the registry can easily become clogged with garbage, and there are few good ways to clean it.

Even with all of these weaknesses, the registry is the ideal stomping ground for COM information. COM entries are created automatically whenever you register a component using `regsvr32.exe`, so there is no manual intervention. In this manner, the registry can approach being the black box Microsoft wants it to be. This is fortunate, since understanding exactly what all those COM entries mean is not a task for the faint of heart. While a complete discussion is beyond the scope of this book, if you are curious about how it all works, I recommend reviewing the COM chapter in Bruce McKinney's *Hardcore Visual Basic* (1997), Dale Rogerson's *Inside COM* (1997), and/or Don Box's *Essential COM* (1998).

Nevertheless, in spite of my pleading, you will still have to know how to access the registry for things other than COM—it is a fact of life in the world of Windows. To make matters worse, the registry functions that VB provides for you give you access only to a small portion of the registry and consequently are of little practical value. This is another one of those times when Microsoft's attempt to make things simpler for VB programmers actually made the functionality worthless. To get around the registry, you'll have to use the Win32 API. You will also have to have a general understanding of organization of the registry (what goes where and why) and an idea of what types of data the registry can hold.

Registry Keys

To begin, there are six primary keys in the registry, as described in Table 13.1. They are the "root" keys of the registry's structure. Keys under the root keys are called *subkeys*. A subkey can have any number of other subkeys and key/value pairs. When viewed in the registry editor, all subkeys appear on the left side in the TreeView, while the key/value pairs appear on the right. (Note that in some cases the information under one root key is repeated in part under another, adding to the confusing nature of the registry.)

Registry Data Types

The registry has several intrinsic data types, but at first glance, there is sometimes not an obvious correspondence between the type in the registry and the type to use when reading the value into Visual Basic. Unfortunately, as Table 13.2 shows, most registry data types need to be stored in an array of bytes, though some, such as REG_DWORD and REG_SZ, work well with standard VB types. Luckily, in practice, the most common types of data you will need to store in the registry for your applications will be strings and longs. You will be most concerned with the odd registry types when reading values inserted into the registry by another application or the operating system itself.

TABLE 13.1   Root Registry Keys

Key	Description
HKEY_CLASSES_ROOT	This key holds information about the classes of the components installed on the system. It also holds associations between file extensions and the corresponding applications. Since COM registration is almost autômatic, you will probably not need to worry about this key very much.
HKEY_CURRENT_USER	This key holds information about the system configuration as it pertains to the current user. It includes control panel settings and network and printer information, for example.
HKEY_LOCAL_MACHINE	This is the key Visual Basic developers use the most. It contains most of the important information about the hardware, software, and operating system settings on the system.
HKEY_USERS	This key is much like HKEY_CURRENT_USER, except that it contains settings for all of the users who have logged into the system and have opted to save settings, not just the current user. There is also a default subkey that contains the settings to use for new users and users who have not saved settings.
HKEY_CURRENT_CONFIG	This key holds general information about the current system configuration.
HKEY_DYN_DATA	This key holds temporary data, that is, data written to the registry since the last login but that will not be saved. This key is generally of no use to the corporate programmer, because there are better ways to store temporary data.

Registry Functions

The registry functions themselves are well documented on-line, so we won't concentrate on them here, beyond the summary in Table 13.3. This table does not include all of the registry functions, but rather just the most commonly used in Visual Basic. We'll look at some of these functions in more detail in the next chapter when we create a simple OLE DB provider for the registry.

Although there are many registry functions you will have to use to get at the data in the registry, there are a handful of things to remember that can make the experience less irritating:

1. Many registry functions have two versions. The first is an older version and the second (ending in Ex) is the more up-to-date and robust version. Stick with the Ex versions for consistency.

2. In order to work with anything in the registry, you must first open its key with RegOpenKeyEx. When finished, close the key with RegCloseKey.

TABLE 13.2 Summary of Registry Data Types

Data Type	Description
REG_BINARY	This value is standard binary data and generally is best stored in an array of bytes. When viewed in the registry editor, REG_BINARY values appear in one-byte hexadecimal segments, as in A3 D1 11 4E.
REG_DWORD	A double word is a 32-bit-long number (4 bytes). To store these values in VB, simply use a long. Note that REG_DWORD values are unsigned in the registry, but in Visual Basic you will see negative numbers instead of large positive numbers because of overflow. In the registry editor, they appear formatted in hexadecimal, with the decimal value following in parentheses, as in 0x0B34A97F (188000639).
REG_DWORD_BIG_ENDIAN	These are also 4-byte numbers, but they are stored in such a way that the high-order byte is at the lowest address. This is the reverse of how Wintel platforms stored data, and if you don't interface with other systems, you won't need to worry about these. See the OLE DB Simple Provider example in the next chapter for more information on conversion.
REG_DWORD_LITTLE_ENDIAN	On Wintel platforms, this is the same as REG_DWORD. With *Little_Endian* values, the low-order byte is at the lowest address.
REG_EXPAND_SZ	This type is used to represent a string value that is an unexpanded environment variable (such as %Path%). Store these values in standard VB strings and expand them with the API function ExpandEnvironmentStrings.
REG_LINK	A link value. These are rare and can be stored in a byte array.
REG_MULTI_SZ	This type actually holds strings that are separated by NULL characters and that end with two NULL characters. While they can be converted to strings, they appear in 1-byte hexadecimal segments, like REG_BINARY, when viewed in the registry. As a result, byte arrays are usually the best way to store them in VB.
REG_NONE	This represents an undefined type, and it is unlikely that you will run into any of these. If you do, a byte array should suffice for representation in VB.
REG_RESOURCE_LIST	This represents a resource list, typically used in conjunction with device drivers. Use a byte array to store it in Visual Basic.
REG_SZ	This is a standard C-style NULL terminated string. You can use a VB string to hold it.

TABLE 13.3 Summary of Main Registry Functions

Function	Description
RegCloseKey	Closes a registry key opened with RegOpenKeyEx. Be sure to call this when you are done manipulating the key.
RegCreateKeyEx	Creates a new key or opens an existing one. This function requires that you first open the parent key with RegOpenKeyEx. The last parameter returns whether the key was already existing.
RegDeleteKey	Deletes an opened registry key. Under Windows 95 and Windows 98, all subkeys are deleted as well. Under Windows NT, it will fail if the key contains subkeys or values.
RegDeleteValue	Deletes a value from an opened key. To delete the default value, pass this routine a null string.
RegEnumKeyEx	This function enumerates the subkeys of an open key. It actually returns the subkey name that is indexed. Use RegQueryInfoKey first to determine how large a buffer is needed to allocate for the string returning the subkey name.
RegEnumValue	This function behaves like RegEnumKey, except that it returns the names and value of the key/value pairs under an open subkey. Again, use RegQueryInfoKey first to determine the length of the longest name under the subkey.
RegOpenKeyEx	Opens a registry key. This function must be called before performing any other operation on the key. Note that this function also controls the registry's security. In fact, you must specify what operation you intend to perform on the opened key while opening it. Indicate the operation desired by combining one or more of the constants beginning with "KEY_".
RegQueryInfo	This workhorse function provides a lot of information about the opened key passed. Items returned include the class name, the number of subkeys it has, the length of the longest subkey, the length of the longest class name, the number of values under the key, the length of the longest value name, the length of the buffer to use for the longest value, and other information.
RegQueryValueEx	Fetches the value indicated from the subkey opened.
RegSetValueEx	Inserts or updates a key/value pair.

3. When working with strings, remember that the registry functions, like most Windows API calls, use C-style strings. This means that you will have to allocate a buffer ahead of time and worry about string length—two things you almost never have to worry about in Visual Basic. Moreover, when using the functions that enumerate keys and values, you will often have to call two functions to get a string value. Use the first call to determine how big a string buffer to allocate, and then fill a string to that length (plus one for the NULL character) with Chr$(0). Use the second call to fill the buffer, then truncate to the actual number of bytes returned.

◆ **Free Wrappers for the Registry Functions**

It is not well known that the Packaging and Deployment Wizard (formally the VB setup toolkit), which includes the source code for the application `setup1.exe`, provides simple VB wrappers around many of the commonly used registry functions. The functions reside in the module `basSetup1`. While you will still have to understand how the functions work and thus will need an understanding of the registry as described in this section, the wrappers are a good place to start. For more information on the Packaging and Deployment Wizard, refer to chapter 21.

Flat Files

In the days of the robust Relational Database Management System, you might expect flat files to be archaic and passé. Admittedly, nowadays the bulk of important data stored by companies usually lives in some large-scale database system, whereas in the past homegrown databases (based on flat files) were the norm. Nevertheless, although flat files have the lost the role of central storage medium, they have continued to thrive, especially as support files for desktop applications (document files) and application developers (INI files, log files, etc.).

I like to divide flat files generated by applications into three primary groups, though there is some overlap among the three. The first consists of generic data files in standard formats, designed to shuffle data between users. Image files (e.g., JPG, GIF, TIFF) are good examples, but there are others. These files can be loaded and edited by a variety of applications. The second group includes document files intended to be edited by the user. Examples include document files generate by Microsoft Word or Excel. These files are in a proprietary format and therefore can be edited only by a select few applications. They usually have some kind of file-name extension associating them with the best app for editing the files. The last group consists of support files. These include traditional data files and INI files. This section will concentrate primarily on this last group, since it is the group most often encountered by Visual Basic programmers in the corporate world.

Local Data Files

In client/server and *n*-tier architectures, one of the most common uses for local files is to store relatively static lookup information on the client to help eliminate numerous trivial database hits. A good example of this is filling list box and combo box entries from a local file that is synchronized with a master list. Microsoft Access databases (Jet databases) are ideal for this purpose: they are relatively fast when local, they consist of only one file so are easy to manage, and they are readily accessible from within Visual Basic. I have worked on several projects that loaded static data once at application startup from the main database to the local Access file (or perhaps even less frequently, with a synchronization tool) and then used the table to read data for static lists (e.g., states, zip codes, countries—information that does not change frequently).

INI Files

In spite of the fact that Microsoft wants developers to use the registry to hold application settings and not INI files, it looks as though INI files are here to stay. As mentioned earlier, the registry is still much too difficult to use for simple application settings. Though the registry has better security (especially under Windows NT) and better multiuser profiling capabilities, in practice I find INI files are a better choice for storing this information for a number of reasons:

1. They are easier to access programmatically (there are really only two simple API functions you will need to worry about).

2. The confusing data types of the registry are not a consideration, since everything stored in an INI file is a string. This is not the most efficient use of space and requires some conversion in VB, but generally these are not problems, especially since performance is rarely an issue when accessing application settings. In fact, if there is so much information that INI files are slow, perhaps a relational database or homegrown flat file would be a better choice—the registry won't be.

3. INI files are much easier to view and edit. With INI files, just about any text editor will suffice, whereas with registry entries you need `regedit.exe` or an equivalent. Navigating through the registry to make changes with this tool is not something you can reasonably expect novices to do, since they can easily damage the system. Editing a text file is much simpler and safer.

4. In terms of physical location on the system, INI files are more readily associated with the application that uses them, since they typically live in the same directory. With the registry, an application's settings may be spread out all over the place, making them more difficult to track when they need to be edited or removed.

5. It is much easier to share application settings among a group of users when using INI files, especially when the INI files reside on a shared network server. Sharing registry entries requires some fancy user profile work that always seems to get messed up and that is exceedingly difficult to troubleshoot.

6. Updating user settings when the application is in the field is easier because with INI files the update is a simple file copy rather than a complicated export/import process.

But don't take my word for it. Even Microsoft has not completely gotten away from using INI files (though they still hide them in the stupidest of places). Consider, for example, the file VBADDIN.INI, which lives in the Windows directory. It contains a list of the VB add-ins installed on the system, along with settings to determine when to load them. This data could easily reside in the registry, but it seems that the designers of VB were not convinced. In short, until Microsoft makes the registry a truly viable option for storing application settings and other information, don't be afraid to use INI files.

Accessing INI file information from within Visual Basic is remarkably simple. Most often you will want to use the API functions that access *private* INI files. These are your own INI files, rather than WIN.INI. While certainly possible, I strongly encourage you not to save your settings in WIN.INI. Under 16-bit Windows, all application settings were stored there, but since it is not required under 32-bit Windows, avoid it.

To retrieve a value from a file, use GetPrivateProfileString as defined by the API viewer. I prefer to wrap this function in a simple VB-friendly version that takes care of initializing the buffer, as in Listing 13.1.

Listing 13.1 A Simple Wrapper for GetPrivateProfileString

```
Public Declare Function GetPrivateProfileString _
    Lib "kernel32" Alias "GetPrivateProfileStringA" ( _
    ByVal lpApplicationName As String, ByVal lpKeyName As Any, _
    ByVal lpDefault As String, _
    ByVal lpReturnedString As String, ByVal nSize As Long, _
    ByVal lpFileName As String) As Long

Public Function sGetPrivateProfileString( _
        rsSection As String, rsKey As String, _
        rsFile As String, Optional rsDefault As String = "" _
        ) As String

    Const nMAX_STRING_LEN As Integer = 32767

    Dim sKeyValue As String
    Dim lCharacters As Long

    'Initialize a buffer
    sKeyValue = String$(nMAX_STRING_LEN, Chr$(0))
    'Get it from the file
    lCharacters = GetPrivateProfileString(rsSection, rsKey, _
        rsDefault, sKeyValue, nMAX_STRING_LEN - 1, rsFile)
    'Trim the excess
    sKeyValue = Left$(sKeyValue, lCharacters)
    'Return the value
    sGetPrivateProfileString = sKeyValue
End Function
```

To write data, use `WritePrivateProfileString`, as defined by the API viewer:

```
Public Declare Function WritePrivateProfileString _
    Lib "kernel32" Alias "WritePrivateProfileStringA" ( _
    ByVal lpApplicationName As String, ByVal lpKeyName As Any, _
    ByVal lpString As Any, ByVal lpFileName As String) As Long
```

This function will return nonzero on success and zero on failure (though I have never heard of it failing). It is rather robust and is actually several functions in one. Nevertheless, the functionality is straightforward, and since it can be called without any preparation, it really does not require a wrapper. If you pass `vbNullString` in for the key name, all of the values under the current section are deleted, as is the section itself. Passing `vbNullString` in for the value deletes the existing value and its key. Also, if you do not provide a path for the INI file, it will search the Windows directory for your file. If it does not find the file, it will create it for you, free of charge.

Data File Access

Beyond INI files, Visual Basic allows you to read and write just about any other kind of information you want to a file. There are three pairs of data access functions in VB, as summarized in Table 13.4. Because each pair is rather tightly coupled, you will have trouble breaking them up. In other words, do not try to read data written with the `Put#` statement with the `Line Input#` statement—it just won't work well.

Before you jump into storing your data with a flat file, be sure that you need to. Practically speaking, there are few times when flat files are the best choice for data storage. Consider placing substantial amounts of data into a database system such as Access, MS-SQL Server, or Oracle. Access databases can be particularly helpful, since they combine the benefits of a SQL database with the versatility of a local flat file. You don't need to have Access installed to use them, either.

I find custom flat files most appropriate when used as follows:

1. *When downloading files from the Internet or another source:* The Internet transfer control allows you to write your cached data to binary files on disk directly, which is quite handy.

2. *As temporary files used to cache data locally:* Caching data in this manner can help reduce network traffic associated with constantly accessing the same data. It can also help to reduce the memory used by VB. However, since in practice most data written to databases comes from the user, temporary files are rare. In short, it is unlikely a user will enter so much data that it will need to be written to a file to save memory.

TABLE 13.4 Data Access Commands Compared

To Write	To Read	Description
Write#	Input#	These two functions read and write values as a series of comma-delimited, formatted values. The data itself is stored as text (and therefore can be viewed with a text editor), but is formatted specifically by Visual Basic depending on the type. For example, strings are enclosed in double quotes, while numbers print plainly. All other types print in a standard format and are surrounded by pound signs (#). Storing data in this fashion is useful when you want to be able to view the data stored easily but do not want to have to worry about binary files or formatting and converting data yourself.
Print#	Line Input#	Unlike Write# and Input#, these functions work directly with display-formatted text. Print# writes data as a string formatted for printing according to locale settings, while Line Input# reads an entire line of text into a string, up until a CR or CR/LF combination. These functions are useful for generating readable text data, as in text files or report files. The big drawback is that once the data is written to a file, it is more difficult to get individual fields on one line parsed back into variables of the appropriate type.
Put#	Get#	These two functions are the only way to read and write binary data in Visual Basic. They both allow random access and can be used along with Seek to read or write data anywhere in a file. They are particularly useful for reading and writing data stored in user-defined types.

3. *When debugging log files:* We'll look at debugging techniques in detail in chapter 17.

4. *As archive files:* One of the biggest drawbacks of relational databases is that they can sometimes get slower exponentially as the amount of data stored in them increases. While it is always possible to optimize the database with indices and denormalization, often the best approach is to remove data that no longer needs to remain "on tap." While most database management systems offer some kind of built-in server-side archiving ability, it is still common for a client application to perform this function. When dealing with legacy systems, it is even more common (homegrown databases, too).

5. *When a RDMS is not available:* This is kind of a lame excuse, as it will generally cost you more to develop a homegrown database system using flat files than it will to license a MS-SQL server. Nevertheless, it still happens.

When deciding what pair of functions to use for your data, consider the following:

♦ *Is the data binary?* Binary data can be stored in any Visual Basic type, but user-defined types are the most common, since they allow you to work with blocks of separate data types simultaneously. Binary data access has a number of advantages over straight text storage. First, binary files usually allow random access, making the files themselves more versatile. Binary data access also takes up less disk space than the same data stored as flat text. This in turn makes reading and writing the data faster, since there is less data to read or write. All of these benefits come at a cost, though. Since the data is binary, it is more difficult to work with the file in other applications. For binary data, use Get# and Put#.

♦ *Does the data need to be display friendly?* Flat files are often used to store report data (typically for file transmission) or actual verbiage meant to be read by people. Consequently, you must decide whether your text data will need to be read by people directly, with a text editor. If so, use Print# and Line Input#. If not, you may consider using Write# and Input#, as discussed in Table 13.4.

In addition to the intrinsic Visual Basic file access functions there are also numerous API functions that allow you to work directly with directories and files. With few exceptions, Visual Basic provides comparable native functions, so we won't cover those API functions here.

Embedded and Dynamic SQL

The terms *embedded SQL* and *dynamic SQL* have confusing definitions, and it is common to hear the two terms used interchangeably. I view dynamic SQL as a subset of embedded SQL. Embedded SQL is simply SQL that lives inside of VB, embedded into some kind of string (constant or variable). Dynamic SQL is embedded SQL that is built on the fly at runtime (dynamically). Beyond this subtle difference, the two terms really are the same.

As mentioned earlier, stored procedures are usually the most efficient means of interacting with a SQL database, and most major SQL platforms support them. Embedded SQL is still appropriate in certain instances, though. For example, consider the following points:

1. Some database systems (e.g., Oracle) do not allow stored procedures to return rowsets easily, meaning that select statements must live in the client code. Although I have seen kludgey workarounds for this shortcoming, I

find that embedded SQL usually does the job and that it is much easier to maintain.

2. Very complicated actions may not benefit from residing inside of a stored procedure. Furthermore, since Visual Basic is a much more robust language than SQL, it may make sense to keep the complicated logic in Visual Basic, for ease of maintenance and readability.

3. Using embedded SQL allows you to keep all code (especially code pertaining to data access) in one place. While this is mostly a logistical benefit, I find it helpful to have data access code right next to business logic code, which usually lives in VB anyway. Note that using both stored procedures and embedded SQL destroys this benefit, so try to be consistent.

4. The most common reason to use embedded SQL is to make data access universal. This comes into play when you expect your application to work against one of any number of SQL database systems, including MS-SQL, Oracle, and even Access. Since each database system has its own syntax for creating and calling stored procedures, making a generic system can be a real nightmare. However, if you stick with ANSI-compliant embedded SQL and do not try to use stored procedures, you have a better chance of succeeding. In practice, I have found that in the end it is very difficult to pull off such systems, since there is usually some database-specific tweaking required.

The biggest drawback with embedded SQL is the potential for horrendous performance. However, if you are working with a relatively small database with a limited number of tables and rows and have relatively few users, the performance impact may not be noticeable. In these cases, embedded SQL will often suffice and actually presents an easier environment to develop in, since all of the code can live in VB.

Further Reading

Dan Appleman, *Visual Basic 5.0 Programmer's Guide to the Win32 API* (1997). This reference provides a good summary of the registry functions, but the chapter on file operations is remarkably light on details and examples. It does, however, contain many good examples of file access using the API, though I rarely find these functions are required.

Don Box, *Essential COM* (1998). This book covers COM from every angle and is helpful when trying to figure out COM registry entries.

Paul J. Fortier, *Database Systems Handbook* (Fortier, 1997). Several of the chapters in the book discuss concurrency issues, though the material is mostly theoretical.

Bruce McKinney, *Hardcore Visual Basic* (1997).   By itself, McKinney's mock-up of what the registry window would look like if COM entries were placed side by side is one of the clearest explanations of the subject.

"Microsoft Data Access Components SDK Documentation."   This on-line documentation is geared toward C++, but is still irreplaceable when you want to create an OLE DB provider.

Dale Rogerson, *Inside COM* (1997).   This is another fine COM reference.

Chapter 14

OLE DB and ADO

Two of the hottest technologies to come on the scenes in recent years are OLE DB and its VB-friendly object model, ADO. Promising cross-platform data access continuity, OLE DB and ADO are every business developer's dream. In this chapter, we'll look at the strengths and weaknesses of the Microsoft Universal Data Access model to see whether it is worth using OLE DB and ADO for your new projects and whether it is worth converting your old ones. In the remainder of the chapter, we'll look at how to create an OLE DB provider from within Visual Basic, giving you the ability to create a custom provider for your own custom data.

Overview

Years ago there was a major shift by companies in the data storage techniques they used. Companies moved from proprietary database systems to more robust Relational Database Management Systems to store, massage, and fetch data. Relational databases promised better performance, more scalability, and easier data access, and they usually kept their promises. However, because different database systems have different specific mechanisms for access, it was difficult to standardize data access. Companies found themselves writing database-specific code, which is exactly what they had to do with their proprietary systems. To help resolve this issue, Microsoft created the Open Database Connectivity standard (ODBC), which consists of API requirements and a minimum

SQL conformance requirement. It allows users to write generic SQL code to access data no matter what kind of relational database it is stored in.

ODBC quickly became the de facto standard in the industry, and it has matured through several versions into a very robust data access technique. Part of its success, when used with Visual Basic, comes from the fact that VB has two common and easy-to-use object models that hide most of the work involved in accessing the ODBC API directly. These are Data Access Objects (DAO) and Remote Data Objects (RDO), both of which are still supported by Microsoft. With these object models, programmers can concentrate more on the data they want to retrieve, rather than on the retrieval mechanism. Simply put, they make data access easier.

Though ODBC offers several advantages, it is unable to access data not stored in SQL-like databases very well. In fact, to access data that is not stored in a relational database, you were usually on your own in the past, with a few exceptions. To remedy this situation, Microsoft has been pushing its Universal Data Access technologies, of which OLE DB is the centerpiece. OLE DB is a standard that is designed to allow access to virtually any kind of data. To make this technology more accessible, Microsoft also introduced a simple but powerful object model to help access data through OLE DB, called ADO. Like ODBC, OLE DB solutions need datasource-specific drivers that implement interfaces required by ODBC and OLE DB in order to make the data visible and to put it into the standard form. Table 14.1 details ODBC's and OLE DB's major similarities and differences.

OLE DB and ADO are both well documented on the Books Online and the Microsoft Web site, so we won't dive into too much detail here. However, it is worth taking a moment to point out some of their weaknesses (information you are unlikely to find on Microsoft's Web site) and then take a detailed look at creating an OLE DB provider.

Weaknesses of OLE DB

In spite of their success and strengths, there are some serious drawbacks to OLE DB and ADO. The very heart of the technology is to allow users to access data in

TABLE 14.1 ODBC and OLE DB Compared

ODBC	*OLE DB*
Standard access to SQL relational databases	Standard access to data from almost any source
Requires specific data providers called *drivers*	Requires specific data providers called *providers*
Data is accessible via RDO, ADO, and DAO	Data is accessible via ADO

a consistent fashion, no matter where it comes from. However, the amount of core functionality the user has access to via ADO is entirely dependent on the database-specific implementation of the OLE DB provider, and providers are wildly inconsistent. If the provider does not implement the functionality, it is not available. We will cover this later in the chapter when we create a simple provider. In short, although ADO is a simple and robust model, using it often requires a very detailed understanding of exactly what functionality the OLE DB provider being used supports. ODBC has this problem as well, but it is not as annoying because there are usually several providers to choose from.

Therefore, in practice, it is impossible to treat all data sources the same, because not all data sources are created equal. However, Microsoft's Universal Data Access strategy wants us to assume they are. If this were really the case, you would be able to change data sources on the fly from, say, Oracle to MS SQL Server, without changing the fundamental data access code. This would be a great feature, but it is just a dream.

Converting to ADO

Recently one of the hottest topics in Visual Basic development has been converting existing DAO and RDO applications to ADO. There have been several articles and newsgroup discussions on the topic, but they primarily focus on the mechanics of how to perform such a conversion and do not address the simple question of whether such a conversion is needed. (See "Make the Leap from DAO to ADO" by Ash Rofail [1999]; and "Converting from RDO to ADO" in the Books Online.)

When deciding whether to convert SQL database access from DAO or RDO to ADO you are not really just deciding on an object model, but on an entire data access strategy. Remember that RDO and DAO rely on ODBC, while ADO uses OLE DB. Depending on your database engine, there may not be an OLE DB provider for your database. Even if there is, it may not expose all of the functionality that your current ODBC solution utilizes.

If you are lucky enough to have a provider that meets your requirements, you must then ask yourself what it is that you hope to gain from such a conversion. First of all, improved speed is usually the main impetus, but ADO is not always faster. Second, companies wishing to expand their software development toolbox with OLE DB–friendly tools such as MTS and MSMQ may believe that the move to these tools is reason enough to convert from older ODBC-centered solutions. I would tend to agree. Third, the ability to create a recordset outside of the context of a connection is extremely useful, opening the door for a variety of implementation strategies not possible with DAO or RDO. Finally, version 7.0 of MS-SQL is specially designed to work with OLE DB clients, making ADO the ideal object model to use in this environment. This is not to say

◆ **DAO and ADO**

If you plan to use both ADO and DAO in the same project, you are likely to run into some issues with type conflicts. DAO has several objects that have the same name as objects in ADO (e.g., `Recordset`). To be sure that you are referring to the correct object in your proj-ects, you may want to clarify the object defin-ition by including the library name before the type, separated by a period. In other words, use `ADODB.Recordset` to declare an ADO recordset and use `DAO.Recordset` to declare a DAO recordset.

that ODBC is obsolete, but rather to say that Microsoft is pushing forward, and you must choose whether or not to follow.

However, I have heard of many programmers who spent days or even weeks converting their apps from DAO and RDO to ADO just to say that they were using ADO. They gained no important benefit from the newer technol-ogy, but rather often had serious problems getting their old code to work. To me, this is not a convincing reason to convert.

In short, be sure you carefully identify what benefits of OLE DB and ADO you plan to capitalize on as a result of converting from ODBC-based solutions. Be sure that your new OLE DB providers supply the functionality you need to realize your plans. Also, remember that the decision whether to use ADO, RDO, or DAO does not have to be an all-or-nothing decision. It is perfectly acceptable to use both OLE DB and ODBC. In my experience, a mixed solution provides the most flexibility. It allows companies to develop new data access code in ADO and rework sections of the DAO or RDO code into ADO as needed, with-out worrying about breaking other data access in the application.

OLE DB Simple Providers

To tie together topics discussed in this chapter and the last, we will look at a de-tailed example of how to create an OLE DB provider that accesses the registry. With this provider, we can easily read and write data from and to the registry using ADO or any other OLE DB access mechanism. To test our provider, I have included an example (see "The Code" sidebar) using ADO to access the registry.

Before we begin, it is worth pointing out that although the method de-scribed here is a bit complicated, it is clear that Microsoft intended to include an easier mechanism for creating OLE DB providers in VB, but for some reason decided against it. The evidence is in the help files—an additional option for the `DataSourceBehavior` property for classes (2—vbOLEDBProvider) is docu-mented but is actually unavailable. Perhaps we'll see it in VB 7.

◆ The Code

The complete listing for the OLE DB Simple Provider is much too long to print in its entirety here. I will, however, highlight important portions of the code within the text. Refer to "On-line Materials" in the preface for instructions on how to download the complete source listing. There are two proj-ects: one called RegOLEDB, which contains the actual OLE DB Simple Provider; and another called OLEDBTest, which provides a simple user interface for testing the provider. You will find it helpful to refer to these projects as you read this section.

The OLE DB Simple Provider Toolkit

To create an OLE DB Simple Provider, you'll need to download the OLE DB Software Development Kit (SDK) from Microsoft's Web site, which is included with the Microsoft Data Access SDK. This SDK includes sample files, help files, and most important for us, the OLE DB Simple Provider (OSP) Toolkit. The toolkit contains several items that help you create an OLE DB provider more quickly:

1. Type libraries providing several interfaces that you can easily implement in VB for creating the functionality required.

2. The OLE DB Simple Provider DLL (MSDAOSP.DLL), which does the bulk of the work of exposing your custom provider to OLE DB consumers. It acts as a go-between between the consumer and your project.

3. Extensive help, though many of the procedure references are in C ++ style. As you go through the documentation, you'll see that the simple OSP Toolkit is not language-specific.

4. Simple examples, including a sample Visual Basic project, implementing a provider.

We'll use this toolkit to create a simple OLE DB provider to access the registry. In doing so, we'll not only see how to create a provider, but also explore the registry functions a bit further. You should be able to create your own simple provider for whatever type of data you need to access after reviewing this section. Note that our Registry OLE DB Provider example is meant to simplify common registry access. However, for extremely registry-intensive programs, you will probably want to write your own functions.

You may be wondering why such a toolkit is needed in the first place. It is to make OLE DB a more realistic and practical technology. When Microsoft began pushing OLE DB a few years ago as the data access method of choice, the company hit something of a brick wall. First, the initial releases of ADO were remarkably bug-ridden, scarring its reputation from the start (as I recall, RDO had a similar, rocky birthing). Furthermore, initially there were very few native OLE DB providers, so developers found themselves using the OLE DB ODBC provider. While this generic provider allowed them to use ADO, it still required them to use ODBC, so it actually complicated the data access model rather than simplifying it. Presented with a questionable object model and few native providers, there weren't many reasons for companies to start using ADO. Rather than make their lives simpler, some companies found that switching to ADO offered many headaches.

Since those early days, ADO has improved greatly, and there are now a number of native OLE DB providers for a variety of common platforms. But for OLE DB and ADO to fulfill all of their promises, developers need to be able to access just about any kind of data source, including proprietary sources. The problem is that creating a full-fledged OLE DB provider from scratch is rather difficult and requires very solid Visual C++ expertise.

Enter the OSP toolkit. This toolkit allows you to create OLE DB providers yourself from within VB, without worrying about the details of providers written in VC++. Although Microsoft has done a lot of the work for us in this toolkit, creating a simple OLE DB provider is still a very complicated process. It requires a thorough understanding of REG files, interfaces, and general data access.

The service providers you can create with the OSP toolkit have a number of limitations, though. The toolkit is designed to provide access to relatively simple data. The OLE DB Simple Provider DLL implements less than half of the approximately sixty OLE DB interfaces. Among the most obvious omissions are those interfaces that support commands and those that support transactions. In short, it's a flyswatter, so don't try to go elephant hunting. If you need to work with complex data or require a fully functional OLE DB provider with all of the bells and whistles, you'll have to resort to creating one in C++.

Luckily, the Windows registry is a relatively simple data model that works well with the OSP toolkit. While we won't be able to support logical OLE DB transactions, with a pseudo-SQL language we can perform actions—we'll just have to expect our actions to return rows.

How It All Fits Together

Architecturally, all OLE DB providers created with the toolkit follow the same basic pattern. Figure 14.1 shows this in a diagram. At the top of the heap is an OLE DB consumer. This is what actually accesses the OLE DB provider. In our RegOLEDB example (see "The Code" sidebar), the test form uses ADO to open a connection to the registry and perform operations against it, though we should be able to use any OLE DB consumer in its place. The consumer inter-

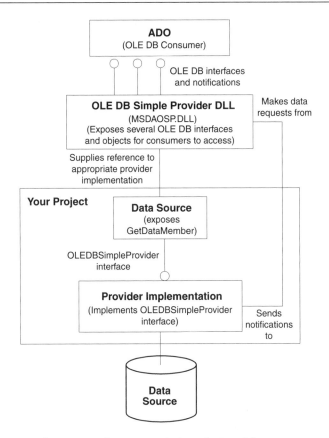

FIGURE 14.1 Architecture of an OLE DB Simple Provider

acts only with the OLE DB Simple Provider DLL (MSDAOSP.DLL). In fact, from the perspective of the consumer, it *is* the provider, and all of the code in the project is merely hidden implementation. The OLE DB Simple Provider DLL exposes objects and interfaces to the consumer and also is responsible for sending notifications.

Hidden beneath the OLE DB Simple Provider DLL is your project, which should be an ActiveX DLL. All projects using the OSP Toolkit must implement at least two public classes. The first is a DataSource class. The OLE DB Simple Provider DLL creates an instance of this class when it needs to access data from your data source. The main purpose of this class is to instantiate and return an object implementing the OLEDBSimpleProvider interface, defined in a type library provided with the OSP Toolkit. This object contains the bulk of the implementation of your provider. The DataSource class passes a reference to it to the OLE DB Simple Provider DLL. From this point on, MSDAOSP.DLL communicates primarily with this object, and the object sends notifications back.

To summarize, there are three main steps for implementing an OSP with the toolkit:

1. Register the OLE DB Simple Provider DLL (MSDAOSP.DLL) using `regsvr32`. Again, from the perspective of the consumer, this is actually your provider. If you have installed the OLE DB Simple Provider Toolkit, this file is already registered. However, when you distribute your completed provider to other machines, you will need to distribute and register this library.

2. Implement the OSP project itself. We'll look at this in some detail later.

3. Register the OSP. Ironically, this is perhaps the most confusing step. Getting an OSP properly registered so that OLE DB consumers can recognize it is a lot more difficult than it should be. We'll look at this in more detail as well.

Creating the OLE DB Simple Provider Implementation

Let's begin by setting up the project, then we'll dive into the implementation. To create your OSP DLL, follow these steps:

1. Create a new project in VB and name it appropriately (for the RegOLEDB example, the project is called RegOLEDB). Your project should be an ActiveX DLL and should contain the following references:
   - *Microsoft OLE DB Error Library* (`oledb32.dll`): This library contains a list of specific error constants to use when implementing your provider.
   - *Microsoft Data Source Interfaces* (`msdatsrc.tlb`): This library contains the data source interface. This reference is not required under VB 6, since you can specify that a particular class is a data source using the `DataSource` property on the class. Under VB 5, you'll need to include this reference. For more information on implementing an OSP in VB 5, refer to the source code in the example.
   - *OLE-DB Simple Provider Type Library* (`simpdata.tlb`): This contains the simple provider interface definition. You will need to implement the OLEDBSimpleProvider interface defined therein.

2. In your project, add two classes. One will be the `DataSource`, and the other will be the OSP itself. In the registry example, these are `clsRegDataSource` and `clsRegProvider`. We'll look at the implementation of these classes in detail later.

3. When you have finished the implementation, compile the DLL. You will need to distribute and register this library when you install your provider.

The DataSource Class

The simpler of the two public classes that you will need to implement is the DataSource class. In VB 6, for this class, set the DataSourceBehavior property to 1 - vbDataSource. Doing so will cause a new event handler, called GetDataMember, to appear under the class. For instructions on how to imitate this behavior in VB 5, refer to the code.

The GetDataMember event handler will fire when your data consumer opens a recordset. The SQL used to open the recordset is passed into the function, and the function should return a reference to your OSP through the Data parameter. Remember that only the Simple Provider DLL accesses your classes, so it is merely passing along the SQL it received from the consumer. Listing 14.1 contains the implementation of the GetDataMember for the RegOLEDB provider.

Listing 14.1   GetDataMember Handler of clsRegDataSource

```
Private Sub Class_GetDataMember(DataMember As String, _
      Data As Object)
   Dim oTstProvider As clsRegProvider
   Set oTstProvider = New clsRegProvider

   'Since we only have one provider in this DLL we can
   'just pass it along. With more than one we would have
   'to determine which one to use from information in
   'DataMember.
   If oTstProvider.lInitialize(DataMember) = glSUCCESS Then
       Set Data = oTstProvider
   Else
       'This is an error - invalid SQL syntax
       'Here we can do nothing. The error will appear
       'as "Table does not exist"
   End If
   Set oTstProvider = Nothing
End Sub
```

This routine creates a new object of type clsRegProvider (more on this class shortly) and attempts to initialize the class by calling lInitialize. If the initialization succeeds, the object is returned via the Data parameter. If the initialization fails, nothing is returned. When the Simple Provider DLL does not get back a valid provider object, it generates the error "Table does not exist," which is fine for our purposes.

The Provider Class

The Provider class contains the bulk of your OLE DB Simple Provider implementation. For the RegOLEDB provider, this class is called clsRegProvider, and like all provider classes, it performs several distinct duties. First, it parses the string passed into the DataSource class from the consumer. In clsRegProvider, this parsing takes place in the function lInitialize, which determines whether or not the data passed in is valid. To use the RegOLDEB provider, I have created an SQL-like syntax that allows you to select, insert, and delete registry keys and values. There are six allowable formats, as shown in Table 14.2. Note that parameters in all caps are fixed, while parameters in italics should be replaced. The square brackets are required. When indicating a RegistryKey value, be sure to provide the entire key, beginning with one of the predefined root keys (e.g., HKEY_LOCAL_MACHINE). The fixed portion of the command determines whether the value for RegistryKey is just a subkey or the name of a value (which in my view, is just another type of subkey).

You may have noticed that there is no syntax for an update command in the SQL-like language. This is because the insert command will also update the

TABLE 14.2 Pseudo-SQL Syntax for the RegOLEDB Provider

Syntax	*Description*
select [VALUES] from [*RegistryKey*]	Returns a rowset containing a list of named values from the key specified. The rowset has two columns, one containing the name of the value and the other containing the value itself.
select [SUBKEYS] from [*RegistryKey*]	Returns a rowset containing the names of the subkeys defined under the registry key specified. This rowset has only one column, containing the name of the subkey.
insert [KEY] into [*RegistryKey*]	Creates the registry key specified. Note that this command actually returns a rowset as well, which contains one row and one column indicating whether or not the key already existed.
insert [*Value*] into [*RegistryKey*]	Inserts the value passed into the key name specified. Because of formatting constraints, this command always treats the value as a string. It will return a rowset with one row and one column, indicating success or failure.
delete [SUBKEY] from [*RegistryKey*]	Deletes the entire subkey indicated. Under Windows NT, this function will fail if the subkey contains other subkeys or values. Under Windows 95/98, it will delete them as well. It will also return a rowset with one row and one column, indicating success or failure.
delete [VALUE] from [*RegistryKey*]	Removes the named value indicated. It will also return a rowset with one row and one column, indicating success or failure.

key if it is already there (this is standard registry function behavior). While it is certainly possible to add the Update syntax, it did not seem worth it in such a simple example.

Implementing the OLEDBSimpleProvider interface is the second function of all provider classes. This interface is defined in the type library simpdata.tlb, included with the OSP Toolkit. It contains several functions and is reasonably well documented in the Microsoft Data Access Component SDK Documentation. Refer to Table 14.3 for a summary of the functions in this interface and for tips on how best to implement them. For more specific information, refer directly to the comments in the implementation of this interface as it appears in clsRegProvider.

In the implementation of this interface in clsRegProvider, there are a number of interesting nuances. First, all data created by a recordset gets generated by the lInitialize command and its helpers, lFillValues, lFillSubKeys, lCreateKey, lInsert, and lDelete. The function lFillValues redimensions the module-level array mavntData() as a two-dimensional array to store the name and value for each key/value pair under a given subkey. While the other functions leverage the same array, they only redimension it to be one dimension (and often will fill only one row). The function lFillSubKeys fills the array with the names of the subkeys under the key passed. The other functions each return one column and one row with a specialized value (see Table 14.2).

The last function that provider classes must perform is the role of notifier. That is, they must keep listeners up to date on the status of the data in the recordset. One of the most important differences between ADO and RDO or DAO is that ADO supports events. When ADO raises an event, it is because it has gotten a notification to do so from the underlying OLE DB provider. When working with the OLE DB Simple Provider DLL, it listens for notifications from your provider implementation and passes them along on your behalf (it also generates several of its own notifications). The OLEDBSimpleProvider interface implementation is expected to raise the appropriate notifications, though there is no way to enforce this.

To pass along a notification to the OLE DB Simple Provider DLL, you must first store any and all references to listener objects that it hands you. In practice, because it passes the notifications you send it along to the consumer, it will only hand you a reference to itself. The OLEDBSimpleProvider functions addOLEDBSimpleProviderListener and removeOLEDBSimpleProviderListener tell you when to add and remove listener reference. In clsRegProvider, I store these references in a collection. Whenever the code performs an action that it should notify the listeners about, it calls the appropriate method on each listener object stored in the collection. The listener methods are summarized in Table 14.4.

After reviewing these notifications, you may think that they seem redundant, since you might assume that the caller knows that calling deleteRows will

TABLE 14.3 The OLEDBSimpleProvider Interface

Function	Description
addOLEDBSimpleProviderListener	Provides a reference to an object of type OLEDBSimpleProvider-Listener. By storing references to listeners, you can notify the listeners when something important happens to the data by calling the appropriate method on the listener object. For example, before deleting one or more rows, you should call the aboutToDeleteRows method.
deleteRows	Called when the consumer wishes to delete rows from a recordset. You should alert all listeners by calling their aboutToDeleteRows and deleteRows methods.
find	Called when the consumer searches the recordset for rows matching the criteria given.
getColumnCount	Returns the number of columns in the rowset being generated. Note that this must be at least one or an error occurs.
getEstimatedRows	For asynchronous queries, returns a "best guess" as to the number of rows the provider expects the recordset to contain. For synchronous queries, you should return –1, but you may return the actual row count. Note that you should not return the final row count if your provider has not already notified listeners with the transferComplete method.
getLocale	Returns the locale of the data set (LCID).
getRowCount	Returns the actual number of rows in the rowset.
getRWStatus	Returns one of four values indicating the read/write status of a given row or column. The values are as follows: $$OSPRW\_READONLY = 0, OSPRW\_DEFAULT = 1$$ $$OSPRW\_READWRITE = 1, OSPRW\_MIXED = 2$$ If the row or column in question is –1, the function should return the status for the entire row or column.
getVariant	Called to return the value in a specific cell (row, column) from the resultset. Note that if the row number is 0, the function should return the column name of the column specified, not the data in that column.
insertRows	Called when the consumer adds rows to the recordset. The implementation should insert empty rows at the start location that is indicated, and it should return the number of rows successfully inserted. You should notify all listeners by calling aboutToInsertRows and insertedRows.
isAsynch	Returns 0 if the query is synchronous and 1 if it is asynchronous.
removeOLEDBSimpleProviderListener	This is called to remove a listener that was added with the addOLEDBSimpleProviderListener.
setVariant	The partner of getVariant. Whenever the consumer changes the values of a particular cell in the recordset, this function is called and is passed the row, column, format, and new value. When implementing this function, be sure to notify your listeners with aboutToChangeCell and cellChanged.
stopTransfer	Cancels an asynchronous query. You should notify listeners using the transferComplete method if some data is returned even though the consumer canceled the query.

TABLE 14.4 The OLEDBSimpleProviderListener Interface

Method	Description
aboutToChangeCell and cellChanged	Call these functions before and after changing a particular cell in your recordset. This usually occurs in the implementation of setVariant. When ADO is the consumer, these two methods will fire the WillChangeField and the FieldChangeComplete events.
aboutToDeleteRows and rowsDeleted	Call these functions before and after deleting the rows indicated from the recordset. Usually you will do this in your implementation of deleteRows. These two methods cause the WillChangeRecord and RecordChangeComplete events to fire in ADO.
aboutToInsertRows and insertedRows	Call these two functions before and after you insert any rows into the recordset. This most commonly occurs in your implementation of insertRows. Like the delete methods, these two methods cause the WillChangeRecord and RecordChangeComplete events to fire in ADO.
rowsAvailable and transferComplete	Use these methods to notify your listeners of the status of an asynchronous query. As your asynchronous query populates internally, call rowsAvailable. When the last row has been loaded, call transferComplete. The implementation of clsRegProvider calls them at the end of lInitialize, just to demonstrate syntax, since our provider is not asynchronous.

cause rows to be deleted. When there is only one listener, this is essentially correct, but in circumstances when more than one consumer is referencing the same data, these notifications are essential in keeping consumers informed of changes the others are making. Overall, these notifications provide the ability to raise events and improve asynchronous functionality.

Note that these OSP notifications are not the only notifications. Under certain circumstances, your DataSource can provide notification to external data consumers, while OLE DB notifications are sent to your primary consumer by the OLE DB Simple Provider DLL. Refer to the Microsoft Data Access Components SDK documentation for more information.

Registering Your OLE DB Simple Provider

Perhaps the trickiest part of creating an OLE DB Simple Provider with the toolkit is getting your new provider registered on the client on which it needs to run. The OLE DB Simple Provider DLL (MSDAOSP.DLL) and your DLL must be registered using `regsvr32.exe`. In addition, you must add numerous entries to be sure that consumers can access the OLE DB Simple Provider DLL and that it can access your provider implementation.

The easiest way to add all of the registry entries required is to create a REG file. Files with the .REG extension are specially formatted text files that you can edit with any text editor. When double-clicked, they insert the values included into the registry in a batch. To make things even easier, there is a template included with the simple provider toolkit.

A template for the REG file is included in Listing 14.2. There are five values you must insert into the template to complete it. They are as follows:

1. *PROG ID of your OLE DB Provider:* To simplify things, make this the same as the name of your project. In our example, it is RegOLEDB.

2. *A name for your provider:* This name will be used to describe your provider to the world. Ours is "Registry OLEDB Provider."

3. *Global Unique Identifier (GUID) for your provider:* You will need to generate a new GUID to identify your provider (see the sidebar "Generating a GUID"). For RegOLEDB it is {826200C0-F0E1-11d2-80B3-006008347170}. You will use this value in almost every line of the REG file.

4. *ProgID for the OSP Data Object:* This is the name of your project followed by a dot and then the name of the DataSource class in your project. For our example, it is `RegOLEDB.clsRegDataSource`.

5. *The path to the OLE DB Simple Provider DLL (MSDAOSP.DLL):* This may vary, depending on where you install the library. For RegOLEDB it is "c:\\Program Files\\Common Files\\System\\OLE DB\\MSDAOSP.DLL."

Listing 14.2 The Template for Registering an OLE DB Simple Provider

```
REGEDIT4

[HKEY_CLASSES_ROOT\<INS: ProgID for OLE DB Provider>]
@="<INS: Name of OLE DB Provider>"

[HKEY_CLASSES_ROOT\<INS: ProgID for OLE DB Provider>\CLSID]
@="<INS: GUID>"

[HKEY_CLASSES_ROOT\CLSID\<INS: GUID>]
@="<INS: ProgID of OLE DB Provider>"
"OLEDB_SERVICES"=dword:00000000

[HKEY_CLASSES_ROOT\CLSID\<INS: GUID>\InprocServer32]
@="<INS: Path to OLE DB Simple Provider DLL>"
"ThreadingModel"="Both"
```

```
[HKEY_CLASSES_ROOT\CLSID\<INS: GUID>\ProgID]
@="<INS: ProgID of OLE DB Provider>.1"    ; NOTE THE ".1"

[HKEY_CLASSES_ROOT\CLSID\<INS: GUID>\VersionIndependentProgID]
@="<INS: ProgId of OLE DB Provider>"

[HKEY_CLASSES_ROOT\CLSID\<INS: GUID>\OLE DB Provider]
@="<INS: Name of OLE DB Provider>"

[HKEY_CLASSES_ROOT\CLSID\<INS: GUID>\OSP Data Object]
@="<INS: ProgID for OSP Data Object>"
```

As an example of how to complete this template, consider Listing 14.3, which is the REG file for the RegOLEDB provider example. When you plug in the five replaceable values defined (in bold) in the list and save the file, you will have a completed registration file. Note that you will need to add these entries not only to your system to test your provider, but also to your users' systems.

Listing 14.3   Completed Registration Template for RegOLEDB

```
REGEDIT4

[HKEY_CLASSES_ROOT\RegOLEDB]
@="Registry OLEDB Provider"

[HKEY_CLASSES_ROOT\RegOLEDB\CLSID]
@="{826200C0-F0E1-11d2-80B3-006008347170}"
"OLEDB_SERVICES"=dword:00000000

[HKEY_CLASSES_ROOT\CLSID\{826200C0-F0E1-11d2-80B3-006008347170}]
@="RegOLEDB"

[HKEY_CLASSES_ROOT\CLSID\{826200C0-F0E1-11d2-80B3-
    006008347170}\InprocServer32]
@="c:\\Program Files\\Common Files\\System\\OLE DB\\MSDAOSP.DLL"
"ThreadingModel"="Both"

[HKEY_CLASSES_ROOT\CLSID\{826200C0-F0E1-11d2-80B3-
    006008347170}\ProgID]
@="RegOLEDB.1"

[HKEY_CLASSES_ROOT\CLSID\{826200C0-F0E1-11d2-80B3-
    006008347170}\VersionIndependentProgID]
@="RegOLEDB"

[HKEY_CLASSES_ROOT\CLSID\{826200C0-F0E1-11d2-80B3-
    006008347170}\OLE DB Provider]
@="Registry OLEDB Provider"

[HKEY_CLASSES_ROOT\CLSID\{826200C0-F0E1-11d2-80B3-
    006008347170}\OSP Data Object]
@="RegOLEDB.clsRegDataSource"
```

◆ **Generating a GUID**

The easiest way to generate a GUID is to use the utility GUIDGEN.EXE, which ships with Visual Studio and is located under the ..\Common\Tools directory. To use this tool to make a GUID for your REG file, simply run the application and choose the fourth format, Registry Format. You can the copy the generated GUIDs and paste them directly into your file.

If you'd rather do it the hard way, you can use the API Call `CoCreateGUID`, but this requires using funky types, and the value returned will need to be translated into a registry-friendly string version before you can use it. The Books Online contain an example illustrating this.

Test-Driving the Provider

The RegOLEDB Provider project group includes a simple application for testing the provider, called OLEDBTest. The application consists of two basic forms: the main application form and a simple prompting form that allows you to enter names and values. The main form has three sections for test-driving the provider. The textbox at the top allows you to enter SQL statements. Pressing the Execute button causes the SQL you entered to be executed, and the results appear in the ListView in the middle. All ADO events that fire are recorded in the textbox at the bottom. Once you have a rowset, you may manipulate it with the Insert, Update, and Delete buttons.

Visual Basic 6 Data Sources and Data Consumers

Before moving on to a discussion of creating ActiveX controls in the next chapter, let's take a brief look at data sources and data consumers that you can create with Visual Basic 6.

As we saw in chapter 12, VB 6 offers two new class properties to help make data-aware classes. The `DataSourceBehavior` property allows you to create data sources, which is useful when creating OLE DB Simple Providers. The `DataBindingBehavior` property allows you to create data consumers. Prior to VB 6, the only types of objects that could be data consumers were controls. Now VB 6 allows you to leverage all of the benefits of classes to encapsulate this functionality.

Originally, data-bound controls (consumers) were designed to make creating simple user interfaces for viewing and modifying tables in a database. By adding a data source control to a form and then binding other controls to fields exposed by the data source, you could create a database application very

◆ **A Word to the Wise**

Before experimenting in any way with the registry, I strongly recommend exporting a backup copy, just in case you suddenly discover that your tinkering has caused your favorite programs to stop running. In fact, it is a good idea to create a test key to use while playing with the registry functions. You can add the key, along with several subkeys and key/value pairs, then export the branch to a REG file. This will allow you to wreak as much havoc on your sample branch as you would like to and then restore it by double-clicking the REG file. In the provider project, I have included a sample test key (along with the subkeys and values) in the file `TestData.REG`.

quickly. However, while they were easy to create, they suffered from two very serious drawbacks. First, performance was generally quite bad. Second, the mechanism of binding the data to the control was unreliable and inflexible. These two issues made using data-bound controls all but worthless in anything other than a trivial application. In short, while simple to implement, interfaces using data-bound controls were not nearly powerful enough for enterprise applications.

Unfortunately, the data consumer classes in VB 6 carry many of these same problems, though things have improved somewhat because of advancements in OLE DB. For serious data access, you should still consider using ADO, DAO, or RDO directly, rather than rely on data-bound classes.

Further Reading

Daniel Mezick and Scot Hillier, "Write a Simple OLE DB Provider" (1998). This article in the *Visual Basic Programmer's Journal* introduces many of the concepts discussed in this chapter. It centers on an OLE DB provider that reads from INI Files.

"Microsoft Data Access Components SDK Documentation." This online documentation is geared toward C++, but is still irreplaceable when you want to create an OLE DB provider.

Ash Rofail, "Make the Leap from DAO to ADO" (1999). This article provides an overview of the relationship between DAO and ADO and suggests a simple strategy for converting to ADO.

Chapter 15

Creating ActiveX Controls

Visual Basic has long centered on using controls to create user interfaces. All versions have provided a whole slew of controls to choose from when making your application. However, invariably you will come across instances when a standard VB control does not behave quite the way you want it to. You may even find that there is no control capable of handling your business requirements.

When this occurs, you have a few choices. You can try to make do with what you have, you can explore using third-party controls, or you can write your own. In this chapter we will look at creating ActiveX controls in Visual Basic. We'll concentrate primarily on how to decide when you need home-grown ActiveX controls and what you stand to gain by implementing them.

Before we begin, it is worth pointing out that most of the skills required for creating ActiveX controls are those you'll already have from working with forms. For a detailed look at the basics, however, you may want to refer to the Books Online or to another source, since we will touch only briefly on the fundamentals here before jumping right into some advanced code that has little to do directly with the mechanics of creating ActiveX controls.

Control Basics

Creating a simple ActiveX control is not very involved technically (though it is time-consuming), as long as you understand the dual nature of controls. When a programmer uses an ActiveX control at design time by dropping it onto a form and changing its properties, she is actually working with a running application. Specific code needs to run to store the properties and provide a user interface (for custom property pages). This is the *design-time* aspect of the control. When a user runs an application containing an ActiveX control, the main functionality of the control comes alive. This is the *runtime* aspect of the control. When designing your control, you must be able to separate these two personalities. At the same time, you must also be able to program and test both aspects.

Other than having to take into account the dual nature of controls, creating ActiveX controls is a lot like adding code to a Visual Basic form, allowing you to leverage the skills you already have in that arena. You add the properties you want (which can be a bit quirky, as we will see later), along with the methods and events you want to expose. You can even use the Control Interface Wizard to help you through the monotony.

There are two fundamental ways to make ActiveX controls in Visual Basic. Either you can design a control that is made up of constituent controls or you can try creating the control from scratch. We'll look at both approaches in this chapter. In practice, most of the controls you will need to make are likely to be comprised of other controls.

◆ Using Third-Party Controls

Fancy ActiveX controls can be very difficult to create, especially if their user interfaces require complicated drawing. Sometimes you are better off buying a third-party control rather than trying to write one yourself. Buying third-party controls is generally a lot cheaper than developing equivalent controls, and there are a large number available. In fact, the creation of Visual Basic components has fostered a whole subindustry of software development—the component creators. Most vendors have demo versions of their controls, so you can try before you buy.

But before you buy a third-party control in the hopes that it will save the day, remember a few basic things. First of all, when you purchase someone else's control, you are buying their bugs—not all component manufacturers test their products very well, and few can anticipate all the strange ways their customers will use the controls. Second, many third-party controls have very steep learning curves, and it can take days or even weeks to figure out how to integrate them successfully into your application. Third, like most shrink-wrapped software, controls often have runtime licensing costs, making the total cost of deployment an issue.

Although buying controls for developers may be cheaper than writing them from scratch, having to purchase licenses for your users may raise the cost considerably. Finally, to create a marketable control, companies have to design them to be either very generic or very robust. In the end, you may find that the control does too little to be practical or does much more than you need it to do.

The other major consideration when creating ActiveX control is that you have to decide whether the control is going to be visible at runtime. Invisible controls are easier to deal with, since you don't have to worry about what the user will see. Drawing controls that are visible at runtime by hand can be a very difficult challenge. To illustrate both of these scenarios, we'll look at one control drawn at runtime and another that is invisible.

Properties

When you are creating user controls, the attributes your control displays in the properties window and those available at runtime are the public properties you define in your user control. However, you may want some properties to be available only at design time. Similarly, you may want others to be read-only at runtime, but write-able at design time, and so on. Let's look at how to accomplish this.

When you need a property that is both readable and write-able at runtime and design time, simply provide the appropriate public get and let (or set) properties. This is trivial, and any one of the full controls discussed later can provide a simple example. To create a property that is read-only at runtime and unavailable at design time, supply only a property get. Without the property let, the property will not appear in the properties window in the Visual Basic design time environment, but will be accessible at runtime as a read-only property. If you want to make the property read-only at runtime, but available at design time, add code to the property let or set to raise an error if you are in runtime mode. You can determine the mode that you are in by looking at the `UserMode` property of the `Ambient` object. This mysterious object is provided to you for free by Visual Basic when you create ActiveX controls, and it contains useful information about the state of the environment you are working in. Listing 15.1 illustrates how to create a property that is read-only at runtime, but completely available at design time.

Listing 15.1 Implementing a Property That Is Read-Only at Runtime

```
Property Let ConnectString(rsNewValue As String)
    If Ambient.UserMode Then
        Call Err.Raise(vbObjectError + 1, _
            TypeName(Me), "Read only property")
    End If
    msConnectString = rsNewValue
    PropertyChanged "ConnectString"
End Property

Property Get ConnectString() as String
    ConnectString = msConnectString
End Property
```

Finally, if you wish to create a property that is completely unavailable at run-time (not very common), check the UserMode property from within the property get of the property as well and raise an error if it is true. For more information on creating properties, refer to the Books Online. Be wary, though; some of the examples have errors, so be sure to try them out yourself.

The Property Bag

We are all familiar with the Control Properties dialog in Visual Basic. Here you can set various design-time attributes of ActiveX controls. Your settings not only remain in effect between VB sessions, but also serve as the default settings when the application containing the control runs. This bit of storage magic is accomplished with the *property bag*. The property bag is simply a storage unit with two methods, ReadProperty and WriteProperty. The idea behind the property bag is that you hand it a value (with WriteProperty), and it stores it for you. You can retrieve the value (with ReadProperty) at a later time. By design, the implementation of just how the property bag stores the information you send it is undefined and presumably unimportant.

In reality, the storage mechanism is no big mystery. If you look at a VB form file with a standard text editor, you will see lots of header information for the controls on the form. This (along with binary information in FRX files) is where VB stores the property bag information. While it is possible to edit the information here directly, I would advise against it, since it is easy to make a mistake that ultimately crashes the control. Also, remember that future releases of Visual Basic may store this information in an entirely different way.

So when and how do you use the property bag to store your control's properties? User controls in VB come equipped with three events that are your cues for accessing properties. The InitProperties event allows you to assign default values to the local variables holding your properties. When you run a control by dropping it onto a form (remember, ActiveX controls run even when the application is not running) or by launching the application containing the control, this event fires first. Sometime after this, the ReadProperties event fires. VB hands you the property bag, full of the properties you have previously stored. You can then use the ReadProperty method of the property bag object it hands you to retrieve the values you need. Finally, when it is time to save the properties of your control, VB fires the WriteProperties event, again handing you a property bag object. Here you can use the WriteProperty method to store your data.

There is a small catch, though. In order for Visual Basic to know that you have changed properties and that it needs to fire the WriteProperties event, you must tell it so. The PropertyChanged command is available to you when working within the context of a user control. It is something of an oddball, since it is a VB language element with only part-time visibility. When you change the value of a property and you want to preserve that value, call PropertyChanged with the name of the value as a literal string argument. Typically, you will put calls to PropertyChanged inside of your public property lets, since this is where you are most likely to change the state of internal attributes. Sometimes you need to do additional work before calling PropertyChanged, though, as we will see in the FormatBox example in the next section. Your call to PropertyChanged is VB's signal to update the value that appears in the Properties dialog, so be sure to call it whenever you want to let the user know the value has changed (especially if it is a side effect of changing another property).

Once you get the hang of using the property bag, it will seem remarkably simple. For most controls, you will have a lot of code that looks pretty much the same, reading and writing properties into and out of the local variables that hold the properties. If you use the ActiveX Control Interface Wizard, VB will generate most of this code for you (it is that redundant), which will make your life even easier.

Examples

Let us turn now to a few examples of ActiveX controls. Each illustrates one of the three main reasons why you might want to create a custom control. First, controls provide an elegant way to encapsulate business logic in an existing control or a group of interacting controls. The FormatBox control is an example of this. Second, sometimes the Visual Basic controls do what you want them to do for the most part, but are missing one or two features that you might need. In this case, you can create an ActiveX control to improve on the standard VB control. The BigTimer control illustrates this. Last, you may find that there is no control that meets your needs and that you have to create it from scratch. We will look at just such a control in the TextButton example.

A Better Textbox

One of the most common practical uses for ActiveX controls in Visual Basic is to encapsulate standard business logic and place it in a reusable package. This notion is at the heart of our first example, the FormatBox control (to get the source code for this lengthy example, refer to "On-line Materials" in the preface). This control is really just a simple wrapper around a text box, but it offers several standard features that are helpful when using text boxes in business applications. For example, consider a simple form that gathers information about an individual. In addition to plain string data (e.g., name and address fields), you will likely use textboxes to gather more specialized information as

◆ **Compatibility Issue**

Note that the `FormatBox` example will work only under VB 5. While it will compile and run under VB 6, it will crash when it fires the `BadKeyPress` event if the parent form does not handle the event. See the extended flame at the end of chapter 12 for more history on this bug. If anyone has a workaround for this bug, please let me know.

well, such as Social Security number, phone number, or salary. These types of data have particular formats and often have simple validation rules that must be in effect (e.g., a phone number field might allow all numbers plus the parentheses characters and the hyphen as valid characters, but would not allow alpha characters). The `FormatBox` is designed to simplify such validations.

There are some quirks about the VB textbox that I just don't like. First, I have never understood why Microsoft defaults the `Text` property to be the same as the name of the control, since in practice this is never actually going to be the control's default value. To remedy this situation, the `FormatBox` clears the `Text` property immediately.

Second, in Windows applications, it is common to find that the contents of a textbox get highlighted when the textbox gets focus, yet you must write the code to do this yourself. Third, the format of the contents of the textbox may change when the textbox loses or gains focus. For example, when users enter phone numbers in your textboxes, you may want them to worry only about the numbers, not the parentheses and hyphens that format the completed number. They should just be able to enter ten numbers and move on. When the users tab to another field, it is helpful to reformat the value they entered with the appropriate formatting, just to remind them that it is a phone number. While this may seem like an unnecessary courtesy to your users, it can be very helpful when they are forced to work with values that are difficult to format. Similarly, when the user enters a field that has formatting applied, it is helpful to remove the formatting, leaving just the raw keystrokes needed to input a value into the field. The `FormatBox` control handles this functionality automatically.

Last, another common requirement of textboxes is to filter out bad entries made by the user. When the users are supposed to enter a phone number, they should not be allowed to enter an alpha character, for example. The best user interfaces verify and filter the keypresses the user makes. This is done through code in the `KeyPress` event that checks the current character against a set of acceptable values. The `FormatBox` control does this automatically by examining the key pressed to see if it is in a string of valid characters (`ValidCharSet`). If the key is in the valid character set, the control raises the `KeyPress` event as you would expect. However, if the key is not in the valid character set, the

`FormatBox` will raise a new event called `BadKeyPress`. It will even eat the bad keypress for you if you would like.

The implementation of the `FormatBox` control is not very involved. For the most part, the functionality (properties, methods, and events) is delegated to the constituent textbox control. Although simple, it is designed to be a useful business tool to add to your toolbox. The example code also illustrates how to include custom property pages into a control, something we won't cover here. More important, though, it illustrates the types of business logic that you can encapsulate in an ActiveX control. While the `FormatBox` provides simple functionality for common types of data as an example, your homegrown control wrappers can be as robust as you need them to be to meet the needs of your business.

So exactly when should you take the time to turn that cluster of controls on a form into a single control? Consider the following two guidelines and prerequisites:

1. *Create a control to encapsulate business logic.* If your constituent controls have some complicated business logic that appears throughout your code, consider wrapping them into an ActiveX control. This is what the `FormatBox` example does on a small scale. Be sure that the functionality you wish to encapsulate is both well defined and consistent. If you need to gather name and address information on several forms in the system, but each form is slightly different, it may not be worth your while to create a control. On the other hand, if you can easily reuse the controls in several places, it is a good idea. Doing so not only saves you time when it comes to coding, but also provides a consistent look and feel to your application with no extra work on your part.

2. *Create a control to use in desktop environments and in Internet applications.* The ability to deploy an ActiveX control in multiple environments means that you can create truly reusable code, even when mixing desktop and Internet development. Nowadays, it is common for companies to provide a Web site for external users and desktop applications for internal users. With a well-designed control, you can capitalize on any functional similarities.

An Extended Timer

The standard Visual Basic timer control has a number of drawbacks. The biggest is that it has only one `Interval` property with a maximum setting of just over 1 minute. This means that if you need a timer to fire every 10 minutes, you need to set the interval at one minute and add code to ignore the first 9 times the timer fires. Also, the timer fires every time the desired interval passes, no matter how long it takes you to handle the `Timer` event. Sometimes this is not desirable, especially when your timer interval is small but the code handling the `Timer` event takes a lot of time to run. You may prefer the timer to resume only after you have finished handling the event.

To get around these issues, I have written my own timer control. It is invisible at runtime, like the standard timer. For the most part, it behaves in much the same way, but it has a few extra properties to make life a bit easier. First, in addition to a `Milliseconds` property (which corresponds to the `Interval` property in the standard timer), I have added `Minutes` and `Seconds` properties. These properties behave mutually, so you can use all three to set one interval. For example, to set the timer to fire every 1 minute, 23.342 seconds, you should set the minute property to 1, the seconds property to 23, and the milliseconds property to 342. (Note that if you would like, you could easily add `Hours`, `Days`, `Weeks`, `Months`, and `Years` properties, but I found these to be less practical.) It also has a `PauseWhenFired` Boolean property to disable the `BigTimer` automatically while you are handling its `Timer` event.

The `BigTimer` project illustrates a few important concepts. First, it is an invisible control built entirely from scratch and is not made up of constituent controls, unlike the `FormatBox`. This isn't particularly earth-shattering, but is worth pointing out since most VB controls have constituent parts. Second, it uses the `SetTimer` API function (and a related function, `KillTimer`). This function creates an internal Windows timer that fires at the appropriate interval. Third, it shows how to use the `AddressOf` operator in a callback scenario. We'll look at callbacks in more detail in the next chapter. The complete source code for the `BigTimer` control is too long to include in its entirety here, but you can find the source for the control and a sample application again at the Web site cited in "On-Line Materials" in the preface. Let's look at some of the code for `BigTimer` in more detail here.

To begin, look at the user control file itself (Timer.ctl). It contains standard code for accessing the public properties, including code to read and write the properties from and to the property bag. The most interesting part of this code is the fact that the property lets for the `Minutes`, `Seconds`, and `Milliseconds` properties each call the function `ChangeTimer`, which computes new timer values, given the current values. This function serves primarily to normalize the properties entered by the user, as shown in Listing 15.2. In short, if you tell the timer to run for 0 minutes, 105 seconds, and 12 milliseconds, it converts the settings to the more user-friendly 1 minute, 45 seconds, and 12 milliseconds. Once these properties are normalized, the world is notified of the new values. You can experiment with this functionality by dropping a `BigTimer` onto a form and settings its properties. For example, if you enter a value for seconds that is greater than 60, it will update the minutes and seconds properties with the correct values right before your very eyes.

Listing 15.2   ChangeTimer Sub of BigTimer

```
Private Sub ChangeTimer()
    mnSeconds = mnSeconds + mnMilliseconds \ 1000
    mnMilliseconds = mnMilliseconds Mod 1000

    mnMinutes = mnMinutes + mnSeconds \ 60
    mnSeconds = mnSeconds Mod 60

    PropertyChanged "Milliseconds"
    PropertyChanged "Seconds"
    PropertyChanged "Minutes"

    If mbEnabled And Ambient.UserMode Then
        Call StopTimer
        Call StartTimer
    End If
End Sub
```

Besides this quirky property implementation, the only other thing that is of note in the user control is the sub RaiseTimer, which is used by the code in basCallBack to force the user control to raise its Timer event.

The real work of the BigTimer control takes place in basCallBack. The sub StartTimer (see Listing 15.3) begins by examining the amount of time remaining before the timer needs to go off. With this information in hand, it chooses the best interval to use for the SetTimer API function, which, like the timer control, expects a long value in milliseconds for its Interval property. SetTimer accepts as arguments the hWnd of the form using the timer, the specific timer ID, the interval (in milliseconds), and the address of the subroutine to call when the interval expires. For this last parameter, StartTimer uses the AddressOf operator to pass along a reference to the function TimerCallbackProc, which determines whether or not it is time to tell the control to raise its Timer event (see Listing 15.4). StopTimer (not listed) releases the timer with the KillTimer API function.

Listing 15.3   The StartTimer Sub in basCallBack

```
Public Sub StartTimer()
    Const nNUM_MILLISECONDS_IN_SECOND As Integer = 1000
    Const nNUM_SECONDS_IN_MINUTE As Integer = 60
    Dim lInterval As Long
    On Error GoTo Error_Handler
    'Create the timer by figuring out which interval to use.
    If mnMinutesRemaining > 0 Then
        lInterval = CLng(nNUM_MILLISECONDS_IN_SECOND) * _
            CLng(nNUM_SECONDS_IN_MINUTE)
    ElseIf mnSecondsRemaining > 0 Then
        lInterval = nNUM_MILLISECONDS_IN_SECOND
```

```
    Else
        lInterval = mnMillisecondsRemaining
    End If

    If lInterval > 0 Then
        'Just to be on the safe side, if the TimerID is not 0
        'then stop the timer before trying to start it
        If mlTimerID <> 0 Then
            Call StopTimer
        End If
        mlTimerID = SetTimer(0&, 0&, lInterval, _
            AddressOf TimerCallbackProc)
    Else
        mlTimerID = 0
    End If

Error_Handler:
    'Not much we can do but fail with grace...
End Sub
```

Listing 15.4   TimerCallbackProc Sub in basCallback

```
Public Sub TimerCallbackProc(ByVal hWnd As Long, ByVal _
    uMsg As Long, ByVal idEvent As Long, ByVal dwTime As Long)
    On Error GoTo Error_Handler
    'Check the results of where we are.  If we are at a
    'threshold, we need to stop the
    'timer and restart it.
    If mnMinutesRemaining > 0 Then
        mnMinutesRemaining = mnMinutesRemaining - 1
        'Did we run out of minutes?  If so, and we are all
        'out of time, fire the event.  Otherwise, the primary
        'interval of the timer has to change to seconds.

        If mnMinutesRemaining = 0 Then
            If mnSecondsRemaining = 0 And _
                    mnMillisecondsRemaining = 0 Then
                Call FireTimer
            Else
                Call StopTimer
                Call StartTimer
            End If
        End If
        Exit Sub
    ElseIf mnSecondsRemaining > 0 Then
        mnSecondsRemaining = mnSecondsRemaining - 1
        'Did we run out of seconds?  If so, and we are all
        'out of time, fire the event.  Otherwise, the primary
        'interval of the timer has to change to milliseconds.
        If mnSecondsRemaining = 0 Then
            If mnMillisecondsRemaining = 0 Then
                Call FireTimer
```

```
        Else
            Call StopTimer
            Call StartTimer
        End If
    End If
    Exit Sub
End If

    'Since it fired because we are in the milliseconds,
    'raise the event.
    Call FireTimer

Error_Handler:
    'Not much we can do but fail with grace...
End Sub
```

To implement large spans of time, the functions in basCallback work together to calculate the appropriate interval to pass to SetTimer, resetting it as time goes by. TimerCallbackProc actually ignores all but the last time it gets called, when it finally calls RaiseTimer. This function calls the RaiseTimer sub on the control, firing the event once and for all. The BigTimer control thus encapsulates the logic of ignoring the callbacks until the specified interval has been reached.

Shaped Buttons

For our last ActiveX control example, we'll look at what it takes to draw controls from scratch. This is not intended to be a detailed lesson in artwork, drawing concepts, or Windows API drawing functions. You should refer to *Hardcore Visual Basic* (McKinney, 1997) or *Visual Basic 5.0 Programmer's Guide to the Win32 API* (Appleman, 1997) for more information on these topics. However, we will see where to put drawing code within the UserControl, and we will spend some time looking at paths and regions. Armed with this information, we will look at a simple example that illustrates how to create misshapen Windows objects, in the form of a TextButton.

Regions and Paths

Most people think of the screen visuals in Windows as square figures. Buttons, textboxes, lists, combo boxes, labels, and so forth, are all rectangular. Prior to Windows 95, this was always the case. Now, though, the area that constitutes a window, known as a *region*, can be of just about any shape and can even consist of separate patches. Technically speaking, regions describe the area of a device context, and use the coordinate system of the device client. In practical terms, a region defines the surface of an object with a device context (like a form or a user control)—the surface that you can see and that you can click.

There are several API functions available for drawing regions, including, among others, `CreateEllipticRgn`, `CreatePolygonRgn`, `CreateRectRgn`, and `CreateRoundRectRegion`. The `TextFill Status Bar` control (not listed here, but available on-line) illustrates how to create a rectangular region for a textbox. This control is like a traditional status bar control, except that it allows you to include text within the bar itself (much like the compile status bar in VB). By generating a rectangular region that grows to the right as the status bar fills, you can set the status bar to any amount, even if it means half of a letter is in the fill zone and the other half is not. (This can be done with a picture box as well.)

When you want to create an arbitrarily complicated region, the easiest way is first to draw a path, then convert the path to a region. A *path* is simply a group of pixels drawn between two points in time. To create a path, you first need to specify to Windows that you are going to start drawing a path with the `BeginPath` API. Then you draw it with standard API calls, which we will look at later. Last, you tell Windows you are finished by issuing the `EndPath` API. Everything you draw between the `Begin` and `End` commands becomes part of the path.

Note that when you issue drawing commands while creating a path, no drawing actually takes place. Rather, Windows buffers the results of the command. Consequently, you must either redraw the same pattern outside of a `BeginPath`/`EndPath` block or use commands like `StrokeAndFillPath` or `Stroke-Path` to draw the stored path. The problem is that these functions destroy the stored path after they are completed, so you won't be able to use it for other purposes (like converting it to a region). As you will see, I find it easiest just to call the drawing functions again outside of the `BeginPath`/`EndPath` block.

Once you have a path, it becomes trivial to convert it to a region using the `PathToRegion` API (like most path functions, this one destroys the current path when finished). The last step is to take the region you have created and assign it to an object with an `hWnd` property and an `hDC` property (like a user control). This is accomplished with the `SetWindowRgn` function.

The TextButton Control

Our last example, the `TextButton` control, demonstrates these commands in a simple button control. This control prints its `Caption` property in the font and color you choose. The interesting part is that the letters that define the caption are the only "clickable" part of the control. Clicking next to a letter (or even inside of one, like in the hole in an "O") has no effect. Most of the code for the `TextButton` control is uneventful, including the property gets and lets and all of the property bag code.

The interesting code is in two routines, `DrawControl` and `SetRegion`, which appear in Listing 15.5. The remainder of the code may be found on-line (see "On-line Materials" in the preface).

Listing 15.5 DrawControl and SetRegion of the TextButton Control

```
Private Sub DrawControl()
    On Error GoTo Error_Handler
    Call TextOut(UserControl.hdc, 0, 0, msCaption, Len(msCaption))
    UserControl.Refresh
Error_Handler:
End Sub

Private Sub SetRegion()
    Dim lRtn As Long
    Dim hRgn As Long

    On Error GoTo Error_Handler
    'Start tracing a path
    lRtn = BeginPath(UserControl.hdc)
    If lRtn = 0 Then
        'Error - may want to raise error here
        'Using LastDLLError information
        Exit Sub
    End If

    'Draw the path of the control
    Call DrawControl

    'Path is finished - end it
    lRtn = EndPath(UserControl.hdc)
    If lRtn = 0 Then
        'Error - you may want to raise error here
        'Using LastDLLError information
        Exit Sub
    End If

    'Now convert to a region and set the control's region to
    'the one created.
    hRgn = PathToRegion(UserControl.hdc)
    If hRgn <> 0 Then
        lRtn = SetWindowRgn(UserControl.hWnd, hRgn, True)
    End If

    'Call draw control again to actually draw the control.
    'The previous call only defined the path.
    Call DrawControl
Error_Handler:
End Sub
```

Let's begin with SetRegion. The purpose of this function is to create the clickable region for the control. It begins by starting a path with the BeginPath function. The actual drawing of the path takes place in DrawControl, which is called next. The function assumes that DrawControl does all of the work required for defining the path, so on its return, SetRegion calls EndPath. It then converts the path to a region with PathToRegion and assigns this region to the user control. Last, the function calls `DrawControl` once again to actually draw the control.

The implementation of `DrawControl` is trivial. It calls the `TextOut` API to turn the text defined in the string `msCaption` into a drawing. However, `TextOut` is only one of many API functions that can be used to define a path. Table 15.1 (modified from Appleman, 1997) lists them all, though not all of these are available under Windows 95/98. You can use these functions to define a path of any shape. The VB drawing functions `Circle`, `Line`, and `Print` can be used within a path definition block as well. These functions presumably call `Ellipse`, `LineTo`, and `TextOut`, which appear in Table 15.1.

The only step remaining is to call `SetRegion`, which must be called whenever there is a potential change in the area of the region. In this example, we call `SetRegion` in the property lets for the `Caption` property, all `Font` properties, and the `ForeColor` property. Each of these may change the area defined by the region or the color of the control.

TABLE 15.1   Drawing Functions for Defining Paths

Function	*Availability*
AngleArc	NT
Arc	NT
ArcTo	NT
Chord	NT
Ellipse	NT
ExtTextOut	NT/95/98
LineTo	NT/95/98
MoveToEx	NT/95/98
Pie	NT
PolyBezier	NT/95/98
PolyBezierTo	NT/95/98
PolyDraw	NT
Polygon	NT/95/98
PolyLine	NT/95/98
PolyLineTo	NT/95/98
PolyPolygon	NT/95/98
PolyPolyline	NT/95/98
Rectangle	NT
RoundRect	NT
TextOut	NT/95/98

Note that our simple `TextButton` control does not behave very much like a button, at least in appearance. For example, there are no `Default` and `Cancel` properties. The biggest omission, though, is that there is no visual indication of a change of state when you click on it, which is one of the prerequisite features of a full-blown button. You can accomplish this easily by drawing a different image when the control receives the mouse down event. You can also add even fancier features, such as some visual indication of a hovering cursor. Again, you accomplish this by drawing a different image when you sense that the mouse has moved over the button. These features are left for you to implement. Remember that once you define a region, you cannot draw outside of it. Also, you should not change the region definition itself for something as cosmetic as a changing picture, so be certain your state change drawings fit within the region.

Further Reading

Guy Eddon and Henry Eddon, *Programming Components with Microsoft Visual Basic 6.0* (1998).   Chapters 6, 7, and 8 take you from the basics of ActiveX control creation to designing advanced controls and controls for the Internet.

Chapter 16
Advanced Topics in Visual Basic

This chapter deals with several disparate advanced programming topics. We'll start with a look at threads and processes and the pros and cons of asynchronous program flow. We'll discover not only how to create multithreaded applications, but also why you might want to. To synchronize the various threads you create, we'll also look at several notification techniques that are useful when working with any kind of asynchronous activity. We'll end the chapter with a quick look at creating NT services in VB.

Asynchronous Program Flow

This section presents a practical discussion of a complicated facet of Windows programming, namely, asynchronous program control through multiple threads and processes. After discussing the whys and hows of asynchronous program flow, we'll look at a variety of ways to implement multiple threads of execution. We'll also examine when and why to use multiple threads and processes and discuss alternatives.

Processes and Threads

In the Windows world, a *process* equates to a running application (either a stand-alone EXE or an ActiveX EXE Server), also known as a *task*. A process has its own private memory pool and consists of one or more *threads*, which are strands of executable code that can run simultaneously (or at least appear to do so when scheduled appropriately). A thread lives in one and only one process, though a single process may have many threads, as Figure 16.1 illustrates. Here Process I represents a standard Windows process, complete with common memory and three simple threads. Process II contains a process with apartment threading, which we'll discuss later.

In Visual Basic, an object lives on one and only one thread, though more than one object may live on the same thread. Incidentally, you may identify a thread by its thread ID, as returned by App.ThreadID. Generally speaking, threads share data local to the process in which they reside, though VB's apartment-model threading is the exception, as we'll see later.

It is best to think of threads and processes as asynchronous entities. That is, you should think of them as bits of executable code that run independently of

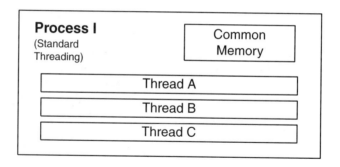

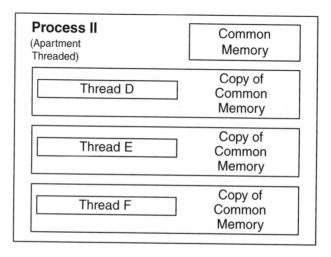

FIGURE 16.1   Threads and Processes

one another, perhaps at the same time, perhaps not. As a result, you should not rely on one process finishing a task before another process finishes a different task, since such a constraint is by its very nature synchronous. Unless you go out of your way to create some kind of synchronization method, assume that the threads and processes you create are running at essentially unpredictable times and speeds. Although you will need to know when a thread is finished, you can't rely on knowing its state or progress while it is running.

In Visual Basic, you normally do not have to worry explicitly about threads or processes, since the compiler handles most of the dirty work for you. And most of the time, it does a pretty good job for the typical application. However, there are specific instances when you will want explicit control over the number of threads on which your applications run. In the remainder of the section, we'll take a look at many of the ways you can create individual threads of execution in your Visual Basic application. But before we discuss how to create multithreaded applications, let's first discuss why you might want to do so.

Performance Issues

There are many instances when creating multithreaded applications is a good idea. Most of these instances center on performance improvements. However, creating more threads rarely improves the computation time associated with your code. In fact, actual performance improvements usually occur only when the application runs on multiprocessor machines, where different processes can run on different processors in parallel. If you have multiprocessor machines (common among servers), you can boost the performance of your applications by making them scalable enough to benefit from more than one processor. The graph in Figure 16.2 (adapted from a similar graph in the Books Online) compares performance of single-threaded and multithreaded applications running on single-processor and multiprocessor machines.

Note that on a single-processor machine, multithreaded applications actually run slower than single-threaded applications, because of the overhead associated with switching between the threads. The operating system schedules time slices for each thread and must store information about the thread when a thread's time slice is up. This information is restored when the thread resumes. This extra work can add considerable overhead, especially if there are a lot of threads. Also, a single-threaded application running on a multiprocessor machine is unlikely to gain much of a performance benefit, since typically only one of the processors is utilized fully by the application.

Looking at Figure 16.2, you might wonder why anyone would ever create a multithreaded application destined to run on a single-processor machine, since it has the worst performance of all. However, while the actual performance of the application is worse, the perceived performance of critical elements may be substantially faster. As an example of this type of perceived performance

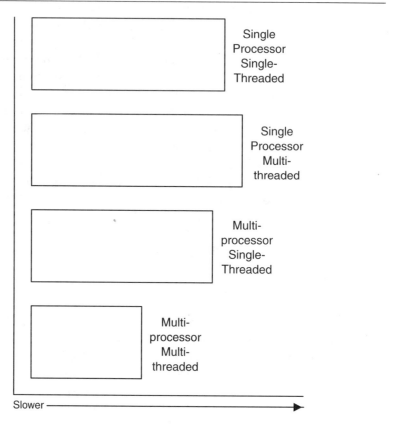

FIGURE 16.2 Average Performance Comparison

increase, consider two functions, Fast and Slow. Fast takes 1 second to run, while Slow takes 5 seconds.

For the sake of simplicity, let's assume that both populate the user interface with information when the user clicks a command button. If the two functions are called in succession, as they must be in a single-threaded application, the perceived time of execution is as it appears in Figure 16.3. If they are running on different threads, however, the perceived time of execution for the function Fast is reduced substantially, as shown in Figure 16.4. Here Fast completes in about 2 seconds, since it relinquishes the processor to Slow on and off for 1 second. Slow completes in 6 seconds, after losing a second to Fast at the start. Note that in Figure 16.4, the times are approximate. There is actually some added overhead resulting from switching between the two threads, which means that the overall time would really be a little more than 6 seconds.

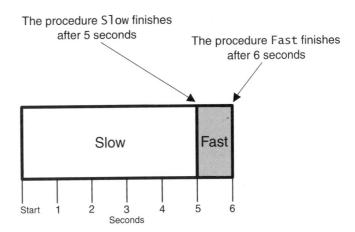

FIGURE 16.3   Perceived Performance of Two Functions in a Single Thread

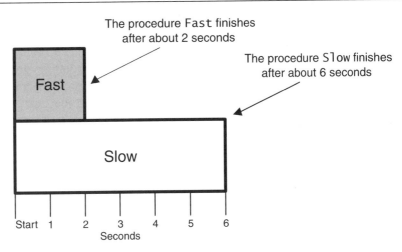

FIGURE 16.4   Perceived Performance of Two Functions in Separate Threads

While this example is trivial, it illustrates an important point: if your application consists mostly of fast operations with a few slow ones (the slow ones often relate to input/output), it may make sense to run the slower operations on separate threads to improve the perceived performance of the faster ones. This advantage becomes most apparent when it causes the user interface to become more responsive. For example, in a single-threaded system, if the function

Slow runs after the user presses the Slow button on the UI, the user has to wait until Slow is finished before pressing the Fast button to execute the function Fast. In the end, the user has to wait until both Slow and Fast have run before seeing the results from Fast. However, if Slow is placed on a separate thread Fast can run immediately after Slow starts, and finish long before Slow does. In terms of the UI, the results of Fast can keep the user occupied while Slow finishes. In a nutshell, this is what Figure 16.4 shows.

Interestingly, this whole plan backfires when you run two functions that take approximately the same amount of time to execute. It is impossible for one of the functions to finish substantially earlier than the other, and consequently the perceived performance benefit is lost. In the end, both functions finish at about the same time, only it seems that they have each taken twice as long to execute.

Concurrency Issues

The other big benefit of creating multithreaded applications is that you can handle the problem of concurrency more easily. One of primary reasons for creating an out-of-process server (an ActiveX EXE) is to allow several client applications (usually standard EXEs) to call objects in the server at the same time. However, if the server application is single-threaded, only one client request can be completed at a time. If two or more clients attempt to use objects in the server simultaneously, only one will win. The others are put on hold until the winner's request finishes, and while on hold the clients are likely to become unresponsive. As we just saw, any mechanism that can improve the responsiveness of an application is likely to be perceived as a performance booster. This is precisely what multithreading provides to ActiveX servers.

Drawbacks of Multithreaded Applications

The benefits of multithreaded applications come at a very steep price, though. Multithreaded applications take much more time to develop and debug, because of the problems inherent with synchronizing threads and determining when threads have finished running. Furthermore, the VB IDE does not allow you to run multithreaded applications directly—you must first compile them into executables. This, combined with the fact that you must typically work with several projects at the same time, makes development a nightmare. For more information on just how involved this whole process can be, I recommend reviewing John Robbins's two-part article "Ingenious Ways to Implement Multiple Threads in Visual Basic 5.0," in *Microsoft Systems Journal* (1997a, 1997b), which is included with the MSDN Visual Studio Library.

Testing also becomes substantially more difficult, because although single-threaded applications usually run on whatever machine you install them on, multithreaded applications may not. Subtle bugs that do not appear when running your application on a machine with a single processor may rear their ugly heads and crash your app on a multiprocessor system. Therefore, you should plan to test your multithreaded applications on every kind of machine on which you intend to run the application.

Creating Multithreaded Applications

There are several ways to create multithreaded applications in Visual Basic, and each has its strengths and weaknesses. In this section we'll take a look at several, roughly in order of complexity. We'll start with the easiest approach, and one that was available to programmers prior to the release of Visual Basic 5.0—Timer routines.

Timer Routines This technique really does not create separate threads explicitly, but rather simulates asynchronous program flow. The timer control that ships with Visual Basic is a wonderful tool for creating very simple asynchronous-like functionality. Tasks controlled by timers are asynchronous because from the perspective of the calling application, they return immediately, and the task itself is performed in the background. By enabling a timer on a form, your code gets interrupted (if it is not doing anything) at a regular interval, providing an opportunity to do a bit of background work. If the tasks you wish to execute asynchronously can be broken easily into smaller, short-lived chunks, you can set up a timer to perform the chunks one at a time until finished. You could, for example, enable a timer and then write code in its Timer event to read data in from a very large file a few records at a time until finished, at which time you could disable the timer. You will want to be careful not to take too long in your Timer event handle, since this may make the application appear to have a sluggish user interface.

Using timers to simulate asynchronous program flow in this way is useful for simple animation or other trivial tasks that need to occur while your application is waiting (such as while a form is displayed). For more substantial asynchronous control, you will need a more robust solution.

Out-of-Process Servers Another easy way to create a multithreaded application is simply to put the code you want to run asynchronously into an out-of-process server (an ActiveX EXE). When you need to run code asynchronously, create an object in the process and call the subroutine in question. You will want the subroutine to return immediately, so you will have to enable a timer in the server process to trigger the task. (It needs to fire only once—the SetTimer API function is perfect for this task.) Since your code runs as a separate task, Windows handles all of the dirty work of making the server application appear to the client to run asynchronously. While this approach is very easy to implement, it is generally going to yield very poor performance, since you must contend with cross-process marshaling, which is even slower than cross-thread marshaling. In short, the solution produces multiple threads only because it produces multiple processes. This is akin to buying an airline ticket to get free peanuts. As we'll see, there are better ways to implement multithreaded applications.

Visual Basic's ActiveX EXE Threading Options Although multithreading by creating an out-of-process server to handle the asynchronous tasks is not necessarily the best way to implement multithreaded apps, there is still a practical reason for creating out-of-process servers. When you create an ActiveX EXE, Visual Basic provides you with options that allow you to make the server itself multithreaded. That is, rather than just the client and the server running in different threads in different processes, the client runs in the first process on one thread while the server runs in the second process on one or more other threads, and this arrangement has benefits.

Apartment Threading Overview. To understand fully how Visual Basic handles multithreading in ActiveX EXEs, you'll have to understand how Visual Basic separates threads from one another. Figure 16.1 shows that normally when threads run in the same process, they share the process's global data. Without getting into the gory details, this can lead to numerous problems and code that is nearly impossible to debug. In short, one thread can change the global data only to return to it to find that another thread has changed it to something else. Since you really don't have control over how fast or slowly

---

◆ Marshaling in Brief

Marshaling is the mechanism that allows you to treat function calls made to objects running in a separate process the same way that you would treat functions on objects in your own thread. With DCOM, the marshaling mechanism is robust enough to make calls to processes on remote machines transparent as well.

COM marshaling is accomplished by first having the server process publish a reference to itself that the client can use. When a function call occurs, all client arguments are serialized and passed to the server process. When the function completes, its return values (including ByRef parameters) are then serialized and passed back to the client. For more information on the intricacies of marshaling, refer to the Books Online.

Although COM marshaling makes life easier for the developer by hiding the details of the mechanism, there is a pretty large performance penalty involved with passing parameters and return values between threads and processes, especially when client and server reside on separate machines. Thus, when considering a multithreaded solution, you must carefully weigh the potential performance impact of the marshaling.

threads run or when the operating system needs to suspend its execution to let another thread have a time slice, you have no way of predicting which of the two competing threads will change what data at what time.

Visual Basic solves this problem by isolating each thread into a separate "miniprocess" called an *apartment*. As the bottom half of Figure 16.1 shows, VB gives each thread its own copy of the global data. Thus a particular thread can change global data to its heart's content and rest assured that no other thread is changing it as well. Microsoft introduced the apartment-threading model in the second service pack for Visual Basic 5, and it has remained in VB 6.

Data that is global to processes includes global environment information (the App object is a great example of this) and all global variables declared in BAS modules. Normally, you initialize global data in the process's Sub Main. Under apartment threading, Sub Main gets run every time an apartment is created. In fact, Visual Basic uses apartment threading even when the application contains only one thread.

In practice, apartment threading can be a real pain. There are circumstances when you will want to synchronize threads with global data, and apartment threading prevents you from doing this. Ultimately, you can always connect your threads together with object references, but this is a lot of work and forces cross-thread marshaling. However, apartment threading does prevent you from making common synchronization errors that are difficult to pin down.

Round-Robin Threading. When you create an ActiveX EXE in Visual Basic, you may choose to have VB create a new thread per object (discussed later) or you may specify an explicit number of threads for VB to create. If you specify only one thread, your ActiveX EXE will be single-threaded. If you specify more than one thread, VB creates threads in round-robin fashion. That is, every new, externally created object will reside in a new thread, until the specified number of threads have been created. At that point, subsequent objects are created on threads already in existence. Remember that this applies only to objects created externally. If an object within the ActiveX server creates another object with the New operator, the second object will live in the same thread as the first.

Note that the Books Online suggest that Visual Basic reuses the threads in the order in which they were created. For example, if you specify that there are to be five threads in your ActiveX EXE, the Books Online suggest that the first object lives on thread 1, the second lives on thread 2, and so on, with the fifth object on thread 5. When you create the sixth object, it will reside on thread 1. However, in reality this is not the case. In fact, the first thread created belongs to the process (the *main,* or *primary,* thread), and your first object will actually live on thread 2. When the specified number of threads have been created, the process cycles *backward* through the existing threads when creating new objects. Thus for an ActiveX EXE with five threads, the object/thread pairings are as they appear in Table 16.1. Here you can see where each of several objects resides (along with sample ThreadIDs) in a round-robin scheme.

I generated the information shown in Table 16.1 using the sample projects MulServe.VBP and ThrdClnt.VBP. The MulServe project is an ActiveX server with three MultiUse classes (and a couple of SingleUse classes, which we will discuss later). Each class has one public property that returns the thread ID of the thread the object lives on. The Sub Main for MulServe does a number of things to let you know when threads are created. First, it initializes the AppLogging feature so that any message boxes you include get written to a log file rather than to the screen during unattended execution. For the sake of tracking, it displays a message indicating that it is creating a new thread and provides the thread ID. It then beeps and pauses to slow things down to a more manageable speed.

The client application ThrdClnt has a simple user interface that allows you to create an instance of any of the objects in the server application. It also has a list box to show you the thread ID of the objects you create. When you run the client application and press one of the first three buttons, the application will create an instance of the object you indicate. The first time you press one of the buttons, it also creates the process itself. As you experiment, keep track of what objects and thread IDs appear in the list box so that you can compare them to what the server application writes to the log file. You may also want to try running multiple instances of the client application to see how the server behaves.

Though I have tested the sample programs on several machines and have gotten consistent results, the details of what object lives on what thread really should not be a consideration in the end. While for trivial applications (like our

TABLE 16.1   Object/Thread Pairings for ActiveX EXE with Five Threads

Object	Thread Created On	Sample Thread ID
(Process)	1	FFF979D3
1	2	FFF911AB
2	3	FFF9148F
3	4	FFF92123
4	5	FFF9244F
5	4	FFF92123
6	3	FFF9148F
7	2	FFF911AB
8	1	FFF979D3
9	5	FFF9244F

client/server example) you may be able to pinpoint exactly what will be created and where, it is not a good idea to rely too heavily on this knowledge, since things can get complicated quickly. Also, Microsoft may change the algorithm that determines which thread to use for the next object at any time, effectively invalidating any assumptions you have made about where a thread is created. Moreover, in an application of any complexity (especially one in which multiple client applications access the same ActiveX server instance), it becomes impossible to predict on which thread an object will be created. More important, you cannot determine which objects will live on the same thread (thus sharing global data in the same apartment). Because of these constraints, you cannot synchronize the states of your objects using global data. The bottom line when working with round-robin threading is that you should make your objects as encapsulated and independent as possible to avoid relying on data provided by or shared with another thread.

If you are using Windows NT, when you choose the number of threads to use in your round-robin model, include as many threads as the machine you intend to run the program on has processors. This will give Windows NT the opportunity to improve performance by distributing the threads among the available processors. Note that Windows 95 and Windows 98 do not distribute workload over multiple processors, which greatly reduces the benefits of a multi-threaded solution on those systems.

Thread per Object. If you choose not to use round-robin threading, you may opt to have Visual Basic create a new thread per object. Under this scenario, every time you instantiate a new object externally, VB spawns a new thread. You can experiment with this type of threading by changing the threading model of `MulServe.VBP` to Thread Per Object and recompiling the executable. Run the client application again and observe the results as you create objects. You will never see the same thread ID twice.

Practically speaking, the thread-per-object model is of limited use. Since in most cases you will want about as many threads as you have processors, it is easy to create far more threads than are practically needed. The overhead associated with managing the threads actually adds to the work the system has to do and thus may ultimately degrade performance rather than improve it. On the plus side, you will rarely have concurrency issues with this approach, since all requests made by all clients live in separate, asynchronous threads.

Single-Use Threading Another way to implement multiple threads is to declare a class to have `SingleUse` instancing. This option is available only in ActiveX EXEs. When you designate a class to be `SingleUse`, every externally created instance of the class lives in a new instance of the process. This is, of course, slow, but nevertheless useful because it offers a better stability model. For example, if your `SingleUse` class has some serious problem and crashes, it will bring down only its process and not the entire application. Windows NT can usually recover from this type of incident well (with Windows 95/98, cross your fingers). In short, by isolating the code in its own process, you implement some damage control.

Note that although they are a bit more stable, you still have to be careful how you instantiate `SingleUse` classes, especially when you have more than one of them or if you are creating a server with round-robin threading. If you experiment with the `SingleUse` threading buttons in the sample project described earlier, you'll see that it is easy to lose track of where the next object will be created. Also, as with our first technique, you must contend with cross-process marshaling. For more information on the `SingleUse` classes, refer to the Books Online.

Creating Threads Explicitly Finally, there is a way to create threads explicitly within a stand-alone Visual Basic application. With the `AddressOf` operator (see "Callbacks" later in the chapter) and the `CreateThread` API, you can activate a new thread on your own. This technique allows you to control every aspect of your thread explicitly, including when it gets created and destroyed, along with how it returns values and shares data. Because these threads are created by Windows and not by Visual Basic, they do not live in separate apartments. If you want to isolate your threads, you are on your own. But beware: such threads have major problems working with Visual Basic COM objects, since such objects are expecting all code to live in some kind of apartment (Pattison, 1998).

While this technique certainly offers the most flexibility, I recommend avoiding it. The biggest problem with using `CreateThread` in Visual Basic is that it really doesn't work very well. The VB IDE does not allow you to debug the threads created, and more often than not simply running a program that uses `CreateThread` from within the IDE causes VB to crash miserably. Also, controlling threads created with `CreateThread` can be a real hassle, and a meaningful control scheme requires knowledge of pipes, mailslots, and semaphores—topics complex enough to merit a book of their own. In short, while it is possible to use `CreateThread` in VB, I have never seen anything except the most trivial of examples work with this technique, and even they didn't work well. My recommendation is that if you really cannot make do with one of the techniques mentioned earlier, choose another language, because VB will only disappoint you on this front.

Still, if you are masochistic enough to ignore my warnings, refer to Bruce McKinney's *Hardcode Visual Basic* (1997) for a simple example of how to use `CreateThread`. Dan Appleman's *Visual Basic 5.0 Programmer's Guide to the Win32 API* (1997) contains a lot of useful information on threads, processes, mutexes, semaphores, and other thread-related issues. Also, Matthew Curland's

TABLE 16.2   Pros and Cons of Various Multithreading Techniques

Technique	*Pros*	*Cons*
Timer routines to simulate asynchronous program flow	Very easy to implement.	Not very robust. Requires manual division of complicated tasks into simple ones.
Thread as out-of-process server	Easy to implement.	Slow, because all calls to thread are across process boundary.
Round-Robin threading	Easy to implement. Simple to match number of the threads to number of physical processors for maximum benefit.	Difficult to predict thread creation, thus cannot predict which objects share a thread.
Thread per object	Easy to implement. Always resolves concurrency issues, since no client calls are blocked.	Of limited practical use, since you can quickly drown the process with too many threads.
SingleUse threading	Better protection of application, since dangerous threads can be isolated in separate processes.	When more than one SingleUse class in a server, difficult to determine exactly which objects' threads will reside in the same process.
Manual thread creation with CreateThread	Offers complete control over threads and thread memory.	Very difficult to implement well. Not recommended.

two articles "Create Worker Threads in DLLs" and "Create Efficient Multi-threaded Apps" (1999a, 1999b) illustrate a technique for creating new threads inside of a DLL using a helper class he provides.

Summary Table 16.2 summarizes the various multithreading techniques available to you, describing their primary strengths and weaknesses. The specific circumstances will dictate which is the appropriate model to choose.

Notifications

If you decide to create multithreaded applications, you will discover that even if you can design your components to behave well asynchronously, you still need a way of controlling them and synchronizing their results. In a client/server relationship, you will want to be sure your client application is notified when an asynchronous server task is finished. There are many ways to accomplish this. We will look at three of the most common approaches.

Active Pinging

Perhaps the easiest way to determine whether a particular component is finished with an asynchronous task is to ask it; that is, actively check a property on the server that returns the status of the asynchronous operation the client has asked the server to perform. As we saw in chapter 14, a good example of this is the StillExecuting property of an rdoConnection. With this property, you can kick off an asynchronous action from within a client application and then wait in a loop (usually containing a call to DoEvents) until the task is finished and StillExecuting returns false. Such an approach makes it easy to run complicated database queries while keeping the user interface responsive. However, you must keep checking the status of the operation, often burning valuable processor time in what amounts to a trivial loop. It would be nice if the client process could launch an asynchronous operation in a server component and forget about it until the server process notifies the client when it finished. This is the idea behind notifications with events.

Events

Windows applications revolve around asynchronous message processing. When you write a Visual Basic application with a user interface, VB does a lot of work for you, filtering the thousands of messages that typically are sent to a window in your application and turning them into simple events for you to respond to. Every VB programmer is familiar with the concept of handling Windows events, and it is this simple functionality that has helped make Visual Basic such a powerful and popular tool.

However, the real power of events goes well beyond simply handling the events of command buttons on forms. With the release of Visual Basic 5, developers could not only handle events generated by components, but could also define and raise their own. While this functionality is most useful when creating ActiveX controls, it is very useful in other ways as well.

For example, consider a simple in-process server component that uses the timer technique discussed earlier to read a file into memory piece by piece. Before the application can start to work on the data read, it must know whether the file is still being read or whether the process is finished. In order to be useful, the second, asynchronous task must be able to alert the client when it is finished. Events provide a perfect way to do this. As Figure 16.5 shows, the calling code first creates an instance of the server and then tells it to read the file asynchronously. The function ReadFileAsynch must return immediately by simply enabling a timer in order to give the calling code an opportunity to do other things (especially process UI events). When the asynchronous task is finished reading the file, it raises the Finished event, thus alerting the calling code to the status of the read.

Although the example in Figure 16.5 is simple, it shows how events can be used to notify the world about the completion of a process. I say "the world" because such a notification technique literally posts its message for the entire

Calling Code

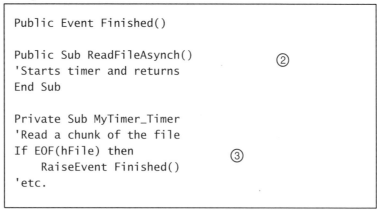

```
Private WithEvents moServer as clsServer
Set moServer = New clsServer          ①
Call moServer.ReadFileAsynch
...
Private Sub moServer_Finished()
'It's Done!
End Sub      ④
```

Asynchronous Task

```
Public Event Finished()

Public Sub ReadFileAsynch()           ②
'Starts timer and returns
End Sub

Private Sub MyTimer_Timer
'Read a chunk of the file
If EOF(hFile) then                    ③
    RaiseEvent Finished()
'etc.
```

FIGURE 16.5 Notification with Events

world to see. The advantage of using events to notify your client code of changes in state is that any number of clients who want to listen to the events of the server may do so with no extra work on the part of the server application. But at the same time, this is also its drawback. The server has no control over who is listening, if anyone at all. Events therefore are primarily an anonymously received notification technique, much like a news broadcast on TV.

Callbacks

The term *callback* in the computer world is somewhat confusing. In a general sense, a callback is the second part of a round-trip communiqué between a client and a server. More specifically, in Windows it has two different but related meanings. The first refers to API calls that accept the address of a subroutine as a parameter (in VB this is accomplished with the AddressOf operator).

The API function uses this address to call back the subroutine, usually multiple times. Examples include the `CreateThread` API and the `SetTimer` API, and there are many others. We saw some callback APIs in the previous chapter.

The other meaning of the term *callback* relates directly to our present discussion. A callback is also a mechanism that asynchronous server tasks use to notify clients of completion. In practice this occurs when a client communicates with the server and provides the server with some mechanism of getting back in touch with it. This is usually through an object reference, sent by means of a property set.

When you use a callback as a notification technique, you are in effect creating the potential for a dialog between two or more explicitly defined participants. Whereas events provide an anonymous broadcast of the state of a component, callbacks are directed at specific listeners, and only at those listeners. While this makes for a more secure model, it also requires more work to set up and is not as easily scalable as using event notifications.

In the most common scenario, the client object creates an instance of the server object, passes the server a reference to itself, and initiates the asynchronous task. The server object then calls some method on the client object when it is finished with the task. In many cases, the different objects reside on different threads and even in different processes. Listing 16.1 illustrates this simple example.

Listing 16.1   Simple Server Notification via a Callback

clsClient:
```
Private moServer As clsServer

Sub BeginAsync()
    Set moServer = New clsServer
    'Handoff a reference to self
    Set moServer.oClient = Me
    moServer.Start 'This returns immediately
End Sub

Public Sub NotifyDone()
    'Called by server when asynchronous task is complete
    Call MsgBox("Done!")
    Set moServer = Nothing
End Sub
```

clsServer:
```
Private moClient As clsClient

Public Property Set oClient(roNewValue As clsClient)
    Set moClient = roNewValue
End Property
```

```
Public Sub Start()
'This function triggers the asynchronous task and returns
'immediately. Later, in another function, the routine issues
'the callback upon completion of the task:
    Call moClient.NotifyDone
End Sub
```

In Listing 16.1, client and server are explicitly typed—that is, the client class refers to the server class by name, and vice versa. In practice this is often not possible, leaving you with a couple of choices. The easiest technique is to use late binding. Under this approach, the client class *assumes* that the server class has a property set called oClient, and the server class *assumes* that the client has a method called NotifyDone. I say assumes because under late binding, there will be no compile-time check, so everything must fall into place at runtime. Because there are usually very few calls between objects for notifications, the ill effects of late binding are usually not a problem. The second approach is to use two simple interfaces (defined in VB or IDL), one for the client and one for the server. The client and server classes can then implement these interfaces and refer to one another by interface name, without regard to the actual class implementing the interface. Like late binding, this has the advantage of allowing polymorphism, but reaps the performance benefit of early binding.

Windows NT Services

Let's switch gears now and take a look at Windows NT services. As Visual Basic comes into its own as an enterprise-level tool, corporate programmers are expecting it to do more and more. While sometimes VB is up for the task, there are other instances when it is nothing but a disappointment. The proliferation of Windows NT servers has pushed VB programmers toward the creation of NT services. As we'll see, this is one of the areas where VB limps along, disappointing all but the most forgiving.

NT Services are daemon processes that run on a server even when there is no one logged in. They are essentially running applications that provide functionality to any number of clients who need it. They are managed by the Services Control Panel, which can start, stop, pause, and resume services for you. A good example is a printing service that allows clients to send print jobs to the server for background printing.

Although services frequently perform generic tasks, there are instances when business-specific services are very useful as well. For example, consider a service that consolidates real-time reporting data from multiple sources. It runs incessantly, polling information from a variety of sources and pooling it into a common location for any number of clients to access easily. Here the service is very specific and will certainly require custom code.

But how do you create such a service? In the days of Visual Basic 3, the answer was simple: not in VB. With VB 4 you can use the service wrapper known as SRVANY.EXE, but it does not provide all of the functionality of a service (Pause and Continue are noticeably missing). Recently, two techniques have emerged that allow you to create NT services in Visual Basic. They are both well documented, so we won't explore their details here. The first technique revolves around a custom OCX that provides the interface required for making your VB application look like a service to NT. For more information on this approach, refer to Mauricio Ordonez's (1996) article "NTService: An OLE Control for Creating Windows NT Services in Visual Basic," available in the technical articles section of MSDN.

The second technique is a bit more difficult to understand and implement, but gives you more control over your service. It uses API calls to load and manage the service directly. Refer to the knowledge base article Q175948, "Running Visual Basic Applications as Windows NT Services," in the Books Online, for more information.

Before you run off to convert your latest whiz-bang application to a service, carefully consider the warnings these articles present. In a nutshell, because Visual Basic does not have the most stable of runtime environments, it is highly susceptible to inconsistencies in threading logic. Furthermore, it is possible for modal dialog boxes to sneak their way into your application in the form of unhandled exceptions, which will hang the service when it is running on an unattended server. There are other inconsistencies as well. Article Q175948 even goes so far as to say that using Visual Basic to implement services, while possible, is not recommended (and this is coming from Microsoft). As an aside, I was able to implement a service using the API calls the article describes easily in VB 5, but the code crashed horribly in VB 6. Unexplained difficulties like this are the norm when trying to create services in VB.

In summary, while there is clearly a need for custom services in some instances and while it is possible to create NT Services in VB, I wouldn't recommend it. Generally, you will want services to be highly stable, maintenance-free tools—it is the nature of the beast. Visual Basic is unable to provide the stability required for a service to be bulletproof. Still, if you can tolerate occasional crashes and unstable behavior, give it a try. I have actually seen a real-time reporting engine similar to the one just described work relatively well, though when it crashed, it meant rebooting the server before the service would start again. For the system in question, this was not too much of a problem. However, for mission-critical servers, this is obviously unacceptable.

Advanced String Handling

To close this chapter, let's look at some ways to improve the performance of Visual Basic's string manipulation. VB provides the most syntactically simple string functions around, but they are much slower than those available to C++ and Delphi programmers. (Delphi in particular is blessed with very fast string manipulation.) VB's functions perform especially poorly when working with large strings. Generally, performance of Visual Basic applications is not an issue, since companies that require extreme performance lean toward C++ or Delphi from the start. There is no reason not to improve VB performance, though, so here are a few points to bear in mind that may help you create faster string functions.

- When possible, use fixed-length strings. This might reduce the number of times VB has to reallocate space for your string and move its contents during concatenations. Reallocating and moving a string are expensive.

- Don't compute the length of string more often than necessary. Instead, store it in a temporary variable. Be careful not to cache the length of a string when it is changing, though. With isolated occurrences, this technique won't buy you much of a performance gain, but in a tight loop, it might make a difference.

- When passing a string to an in-process function, pass it by reference whenever possible. Passing by value forces VB to reallocate room for another copy of the string, wasting valuable time in the process. This is especially noticeable when working with long strings.

- Use the ampersand (&) for string concatenation rather than the plus sign (+). I have heard rumors that the + operator is supposed to be faster, but have found no significant performance difference between the two in my own time trials involving over thirty million concatenations in a tight loop. Since the ampersand converts items to strings before performing the concatenation, you will always end up with a string result. Using the plus sign may yield a string, a number, or even a type mismatch, depending on the type of the operands. If your variables end up getting converted to and from a type other than a string in VB, you will get a performance penalty. Since there appears to be no performance difference between the two, you are better off sticking to the more explicit ampersand.

- Most of the VB string functions have two versions—one that returns a variant (slower) and one that returns a string (faster). For example, Format returns a variant while Format$ returns an actual string. Stick to the string version and you should not only receive a performance increase but also remove the opportunity for unexpected variant conversions that may create bugs.

Supercharged String Routines in VB

Even if you follow these guidelines, however, you are still likely to find that Visual Basic's string manipulations are too slow for your needs. But there is hope, even without resorting to another language. To improve performance even more, consider working with byte arrays rather than strings (Balena, 1998). To convert a standard VB Unicode string to a byte array, you use the CopyMemory API. This function owes its name to VB hacker Bruce McKinney, who discusses its "discovery" in *Hardcore Visual Basic* (1997). It really is the Windows API function RtlMoveMemory in fancy dressing. To convert from a byte array back to a Unicode string, use the function StrConv. Listing 16.2 shows this conversion magic.

Working directly with byte arrays allows VB to work with numbers only, which is much faster than working with the string functions in its internal libraries. However, there are a few drawbacks: you have to be careful to check the length of your byte array buffers, and there is overhead associated with the conversions. Moreover, working with byte arrays forces you to think like a C programmer, which takes some getting used to. Nevertheless, when you are doing serious string manipulation, you can often expect an order-of-magnitude performance increase. Once the string is in a byte array, you can do just about anything to it, then convert it back to a VB string when finished.

Listing 16.2   Converting from a VB String to a ByteArrayAndBack

```
Declare Sub CopyMemory Lib "kernel32" Alias "RtlMoveMemory" _
    (Destination As Any, Source As Any, ByVal Length As Long)

Private Sub ToByteArrayAndBack()
    Dim sTest As String
    Dim abytBuffer() As Byte
    Dim iByte As Integer

    sTest = "This is a test."
    ReDim abytBuffer(0 To Len(sTest) - 1) As Byte

    'The ByVal here forces a conversion from Unicode
    'to ANSI before the copy.
    CopyMemory abytBuffer(0), ByVal sTest, Len(sTest)

    'Enumerate the bytes to prove that they are filled...
    For iByte = 0 To Len(sTest) - 1
        Debug.Print Chr$(abytBuffer(iByte))
    Next iByte

    'Just to show you there is nothing up my sleeve...
    sTest = ""

    'Now convert back
    sTest = StrConv(abytBuffer(), vbUnicode)

    'And prove it
    Debug.Print sTest
End Sub
```

CopyMemory also works well with the undocumented function StrPtr. This function returns a pointer to the first character of a string. So, you thought VB didn't do pointers? You're right, which is why this function is undocumented. In truth, you really can't do much with the return value provided by StrPtr except pass it along to API functions, such as CopyMemory (McKinney, 1997). When used together, these two functions allow you to manipulate strings by working directly with the memory in which they reside—an activity not suitable for the faint of heart.

Consider, for example, Listing 16.3. The function sOverwrite copies characters from rsString2 over characters in rsString1, starting at position rnStart in rsString1. For instance, if rsString1 is "Hello World!" and rsString2 is "Reader" and we want to start at position 7 (i.e., rnLength is 7), then sOverwrite will return "Hello Reader" as its value.

Listing 16.3 Manipulating Strings from Memory with StrPtr and CopyMemory

```
Private Function sOverwrite(rsString1 As String, _
                            rsString2 As String, _
                            rnStart As Integer) as String

    'Note that to start at position rnStart in rsString1,
    'we need to skip (rnStart - 1 )*2 bytes, since Unicode
    'strings need two bytes per character. Also notice we use
    'LenB to determine length, not Len.

    CopyMemory ByVal StrPtr(rsString1) + (rnStart - 1) * 2, _
        ByVal StrPtr(rsString2), LenB(rsString1)

    sOverwrite = rsString1
End Function
```

Playing with strings in this fashion is dangerous, however, and you should expect to crash your programs often during your experimentation. Common mistakes include trying to copy to or from a Unicode offset that is an odd number (not possible, since Unicode characters are 2 bytes) and copying beyond the end of a string. Either may yield a rude response from VB. See Francesco Balena's article "Play VB's Strings" (Balena, 1998) for more information.

Visual Basic has one other undocumented function that helps with string manipulation. It is called VarPtr, and it returns a pointer to the pointer to the first character of a string. (In C, this is known as double indirection.) It is most valuable when used with arrays of strings, which are really just arrays of pointers to strings. As Figure 16.6 shows, given an array of strings (commonly called a string table), asTable(0 to 5) as String, VarPtr (asTable(0)) returns a pointer to the first element in asTable, which is itself just a pointer to the actual location of the string. VB string tables are not necessarily stored in contiguous blocks of memory, so the location of each string in memory is likely to be entirely unrelated to the others.

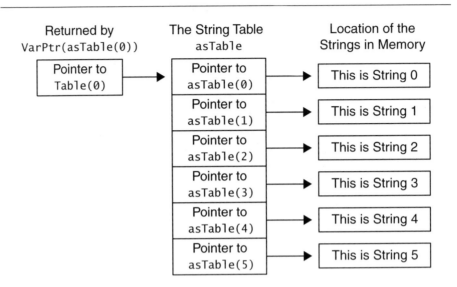

Returned by
VarPtr(asTable(0))

The String Table
asTable

Location of the
Strings in Memory

Pointer to Table(0)		

Pointer to asTable(0)	This is String 0
Pointer to asTable(1)	This is String 1
Pointer to asTable(2)	This is String 2
Pointer to asTable(3)	This is String 3
Pointer to asTable(4)	This is String 4
Pointer to asTable(5)	This is String 5

FIGURE 16.6   Relationship between VarPtr, String Tables, and Member Strings

So what does this level of abstraction buy you besides a headache? It allows you to manipulate string tables without actually touching the strings themselves—you can work with references to the strings instead. This has many useful applications, including sorting and shuffling. Both sorting and shuffling rely on swapping individual elements of an array for others, and with VarPtr, StrPtr, and CopyMemory, you can create a lightning-fast swap function to speed things up. Listing 16.4 illustrates just such a function, and Listing 16.5 uses this function in a simple program that shuffles a string array containing the names of the cards in a deck of cards. The routine ShuffleADeck creates and enumerates a deck of cards (in a string table), then shuffles the deck and enumerates it again to show that it has indeed been shuffled. CreateADeck simply fills in the array with abbreviations of the names of the cards in a deck. The shuffling itself occurs in the routine Shuffle. It is a common algorithm that works its way from the last element in an array forward, swapping the element with a random volunteer from the unvisited part of the array.

Listing 16.4   SwapMembers Function

```
Public Sub SwapMembers(rasTable() As String, _
    riMember1 As Integer, riMember2 As Integer)

    Dim lTempSavePtr As Long

    'Store the pointer indexed by riMember1
    lTempSavePtr = StrPtr(rasTable(riMember1))
```

```
            'Copy the pointer indexed by rnMember2
            'over the one indexed by rnMember1. Pointers are always
            'of length 4 in 32-bit Windows
            CopyMemory ByVal VarPtr(rasTable(riMember1)), _
                ByVal VarPtr(rasTable(riMember2)), 4

            'Copy the stored pointer over the pointer
            'indexed by rnMember2
            CopyMemory ByVal VarPtr(rasTable(riMember2)), _
                lTempSavePtr, 4
        End Sub
```

Listing 16.5   Simple Application to Create and Shuffle a Deck of Cards

```
Public Sub Shuffle(rasTable() As String)
    Dim iMember As Integer
    Dim nRnd As Integer

    'initialize the random number generator
    Randomize

    'Working backwards, replace the current item with a random
    'one from the rest of the array.
    For iMember = UBound(rasTable) To LBound(rasTable) + 1 Step -1
        nRnd = Int((iMember) * Rnd + 1)
        Call SwapMembers(rasTable, iMember, nRnd)
    Next iMember
End Sub

Public Sub CreateDeck(rasDeck() As String)
'Creates a simple deck of cards
    Dim iCardInSuite As Integer
    Dim iSuite As Integer
    Dim sSuiteAbbrev As String
    Dim iCardInDeck As Integer
    Dim sCardName As String

    ReDim rasDeck(1 To 52) As String
    iCardInDeck = 0
    For iSuite = 1 To 4
        Select Case iSuite
            Case 1 'Hearts
                sSuiteAbbrev = "H"
            Case 2 'Clubs
                sSuiteAbbrev = "C"
            Case 3 'Diamonds
                sSuiteAbbrev = "D"
            Case 4 'Spades
                sSuiteAbbrev = "S"
        End Select
```

```
                For iCardInSuite = 2 To 14
                    iCardInDeck = iCardInDeck + 1
                    If iCardInSuite < 10 Then
                        sCardName = CStr(iCardInSuite)
                    Else
                        Select Case iCardInSuite
                            Case 10 'Ten
                                sCardName = "T"
                            Case 11 'Jack
                                sCardName = "J"
                            Case 12 'Queen
                                sCardName = "Q"
                            Case 13 'King
                                sCardName = "K"
                            Case 14 'Ace
                                sCardName = "A"
                        End Select
                    End If
                    rasDeck(iCardInDeck) = sCardName & sSuiteAbbrev
                Next iCardInSuite
        Next iSuite
End Sub

Private Sub ShuffleADeck()
    Dim asDeckOfCards() As String
    Dim iCard As Integer

    Call CreateDeck(asDeckOfCards)
    'Enumerate the deck
    For iCard = 1 To 52
        Debug.Print asDeckOfCards(iCard)
    Next iCard

    Call Shuffle(asDeckOfCards)
    'Enumerate the deck again
    For iCard = 1 To 52
        Debug.Print asDeckOfCards(iCard)
    Next iCard
End Sub
```

Shuffling a simple, small deck of cards is one thing, but repeatedly working on large arrays of strings is quite another. I put Shuffle through its paces by shuffling and reshuffling a deck of 32,000 cards 100 times. I compared this to the same program using traditional swapping instead of CopyMemory, as follows:

```
sTemp = rasTable(riMember1)
rasTable(riMember1) = rasTable(riMember2)
rasTable(riMember2) = sTemp
```

The version of Shuffle that used CopyMemory was almost twice as fast when compiled to native code with array-bounds checking turned off. For even more optimization, you could embed the three lines of CopyMemory directly inline, to avoid the overhead of making the subroutine call repeatedly.

As mentioned earlier, sorting algorithms, which generally rely on two supporting functions, one for swapping and the other for comparing, can also benefit from this fast swap routine. The biggest drawback is that the swap routine shown in Listing 16.4 only sorts strings. However, since there are better ways of working with other types of data, in practice this is not too much of a limitation.

Working with External String Functions

There is yet another way to make VB string manipulation faster: don't do it in VB. Rather, delegate the more complicated functions to routines in DLLs written in another, more string-efficient language, such as C++ or Delphi. You can write your own very specific functions or rely on more generic ones written for you, such as those in the SHLWAPI (shell lightweight API) library.

Microsoft Internet Explorer 3.0 and above includes the file shlwapi.dll, which contains the SHLWAPI Library. This library includes several Unicode-ready string functions that are quite fast, giving even byte arrays a run for their money. Since they work with Unicode strings, they should be highly portable (remember that earlier we had to convert our Unicode strings to byte arrays [ANSI] before using them). The biggest drawback using this library is that, at the time of this writing, it is still unclear whether Internet Explorer and its libraries are part of Windows or not—that is something for the courts to decide. For more information on the SHLWAPI Library, refer to Bruce McKinney's (1997) discussion in *Hardcore Visual Basic* or refer to the Books Online.

Further Reading

Dan Appleman, *Visual Basic 5.0 Programmer's Guide to the Win32 API* (1997). This reference introduces many thread-related topics, including mutexes, semaphores, processes, and, of course, threads. (Coverage of the CreateThread API is mysteriously missing, though.) It also provides a thorough introduction to the Win32 API drawing commands.

Francesco Balena, "Play VB's Strings" (1998). This article in the *Visual Basic Programmer's Journal* explores manipulating strings with byte arrays and CopyMemory for better performance.

Matthew Curland, "Create Worker Threads in DLLs" and "Create Efficient Multithreaded Apps" (1999a, 1999b). These articles describe how to use CreateThread to create and control worker threads to do slower tasks.

John Robbins, "Ingenious Ways to Implement Multiple Threads in Visual Basic 5.0" (1997a, 1997b). This two-part *Microsoft Systems Journal* article describes the creation of a Win32 debugger in Visual Basic. Though the meat of the article is of little use to most VB programmers (Win32 debuggers aren't really all that exciting), his overview of multithreading (in part I) is very good. Also, although he spends very little time describing the `CreateThread` API function, he does include a lot of sample code worth reviewing.

Bruce McKinney, *Hardcore Visual Basic* (1997).   This powerhouse book features an excellent overview of threads and processes and covers drawing functions in gory detail. The author also touches on some of the finer points of string manipulation.

Mauricio Ordonez, "NT Service: An OLE Control for Creating Windows NT Services in Visual Basic" (1996).   This article introduces the NTService control and provides a fine overview of the problems associated with creating NT Services in Visual Basic.

Ted Pattison, *Programming Distributed Applications with COM and Visual Basic 6.0* (1998).   Chapter 7 of this book discusses Visual Basic's threading model and provides a good introduction to Windows threading in general.

Chapter 17

Debugging and Error Handling

As the front line of quality assurance in software development, debugging is a neglected, but important facet of programming. Debugging is a programmer-centric activity and thus directly reflects on the programmers' abilities and the quality of the code the developers create.

A well-defined error-handling strategy leads to software that is robust and reliable. Similarly, programmers with good error-handling habits are more apt to find potential problems in the software before they manifest themselves as full-blown issues, ultimately improving the quality as well.

To this end, this chapter presents effective debugging techniques for you to use in your applications, including ways of setting traps for potential bugs to make them easier to fix. We will also look at standard approaches for finding and handling errors within your applications.

Debugging Techniques

For many programmers, debugging is one of the most mundane tasks associated with creating software. It often means spending hours staring at the same twenty-five lines of code trying to figure out what is going wrong and why the code is not working as it should. Boring as it may be, though, debugging is the most important form of quality assurance a developer can perform. Debugging has two primary goals: seek and destroy. To debug code, you must be able to find potential problems, and then you must devise a way to neutralize them before they grow into serious issues. At the center of this two-phase approach is the notion of fixing bugs now (Maguire, 1994). Errors (and potential errors) found during a typical debugging session are usually easy to fix on the spot. Ultimately, finding potential problems before they become bugs saves time and money.

Like all forms of quality assurance, debugging is valuable only if there is some benchmark to judge quality against. This benchmark can be quite abstract, such as "does it blow up?" Or it can be more specific and demanding. Either way, ensuring your software doesn't blow up is perhaps the bottom line (and a bottom line many companies have a hard time reaching). Nevertheless, there is more to debugging than this.

Let's explore some common debugging techniques for finding bugs and preventing others. While these techniques are applicable to tracking problems in code after its release to production, I cannot stress enough that finding bugs while coding is better all the way around.

Walking through the Code

While there are many weapons available for finding potential bugs, among the most commonly used and most powerful is simply walking through the code: stepping through the code line by line and examining the behavior of the program. This technique is especially useful during the actual coding process and unit testing stages. It allows you to add watches to see how variables change and to examine the call stack to see where you have come from. As you debug manually, be sure to take advantage of all of the options Visual Basic provides for you, including setting watches, examining values in the immediate window, and setting breakpoints and bookmarks. While walking through the code line by line may seem tedious, I have found that it is the best way to find potential problems before they become serious issues. As a team lead, I strongly encourage my team members to execute every line of code they write, especially the error-trapping code, even if it means changing the current line of execution on the fly to reach certain lines. Furthermore, code that is particularly complicated is prone to having more bugs, so spend more time on this code. In practice, schedule pressures (and, sometimes, general laziness) can cause developers to bypass code that may be run only under rare conditions, so they need to be more cognizant of these issues.

Because Visual Basic is an interpreted language, you have a great deal of control over the source code, even at runtime. Use this to your advantage. If while stepping through the code you find something that seems suspicious, you can often add code immediately to fix the problem. However, because you are not really running the program, there are certain things you will not be able to verify, such as the timing of events. However, since most code executes synchronously and inline, this technique is still a solid way of beginning unit testing.

Message Boxes

I used to program in P-System Pascal at my very first job as a professional developer. While I think Pascal is the most elegant of languages, the P-System environment was very difficult to work in. Debugging was an especially difficult endeavor, since the editor and compiler offered little help. When it came right down to it, we had to be creative to debug our code. To aid with debugging, one simple approach was to dump variable information and the function call stack (trace) to the screen. In Visual Basic, debugging with message boxes remains a quick-and-dirty technique for not only tracing the execution path of a program, but also displaying the state of various variables and properties at runtime.

For message boxes to be most effective, they need to display a lot of information. I find it helpful to equip especially problematic classes with a private function that returns a string containing the names and values of all of the important properties in the class (I usually call this function sEnumerateSelf). With such a routine in hand, you can easily check the state of your entire class in one shot by simply calling MsgBox (sEnumerateSelf). I find this technique especially useful when debugging database queries, since you can see exactly what values you are sending to the database ("Hmmm, now which value isn't supposed to be Null?"). Furthermore, you can use this function to log specific information as well, as we will see later. For a simple example of how to create and use a function like sEnumerateSelf, see Listing 17.1.

Listing 17.1   Using sEnumerateSelf

```
Private msName As String
Private mnAge As Integer
Private mnWeight As Integer
Private mnHeight As Integer

Private Function sEnumerateSelf() As String
    Dim sContents As String
    sContents = ""
    sContents = sContents & "msName = '" & _
        msName & "'" & vbCrLf
    sContents = sContents & "mnAge = " & _
        CStr(mnAge) & vbCrLf
    sContents = sContents & "mnWeight = " & _
        CStr(mnWeight) & vbCrLf
    sContents = sContents & "mnHeight = " & _
        CStr(mnHeight) & vbCrLf
    sEnumerateSelf = sContents
End Function

Private Sub ShowError(rsMessage As String)
    Call MsgBox("Error: " & rsMessage & vbCrLf & _
        "Contents: " & vbCrLf & sEnumerateSelf)
End Sub
```

◆ **Generating Your Enumerator Function**

The biggest drawback with routines like sEnumerateSelf is that creating and maintaining them is predominantly a manual process. As you add attributes to your class, you must update sEnumerateSelf to be sure it returns the new values.

However, if you have the time and patience, you can create a simple add-in to automate this process. The VB IDE exposes a list of all attributes in a given class (through the Members collection). By iterating through this list, you can easily build a string containing the lines of code your sEnumerateSelf

routine needs in order to display the names and values of all the members, as shown in Listing 17.1. With this string in hand, delete the old version of sEnumerateSelf and add your new one. There are numerous examples of how to create a simple add-in in the Books Online, so we won't cover it here.

The process of adding template code to a class is helpful to learn. You can use it to add comment headers, generic error-trapping blocks, dynamically generated cleanup code, or just about anything else.

You will want to remove the message boxes before shipping your software, which will require some intervention. You may remove them outright, surround them with conditional compilation blocks, or comment them out. You may find it helpful to begin all message boxes used for debugging with a standard expression, such as Call MsgBox ("DEBUG:"...), which is easy to target with VB's Find and Replace tools for batch commenting.

Logging

Message boxes are handy down-and-dirty tools for debugging code. But because they interrupt the flow of code so dramatically, they are not very useful in projects in which timing is critical. Also, with too many message boxes, debugging can become even more time-consuming. Log files can help solve both of these problems. In short, rather than display the information to the screen while the program executes, you can save it to a log file so that you can look at the results when the application quits. While logging does take up some time and can actually interfere with the timing of your application under certain circumstances, it is far less obtrusive than modal message boxes and can be used in almost any code, including ActiveX servers, which usually do not display dialog boxes.

You can have as many individual log files as you would like, and you can even have multiple users log to the same file. If your log file resides on a shared network drive, you can direct all users to that file and thus can see results from all users when debugging code after release. You may want to add some kind of differentiating tag to tell them apart (Network User ID, computer name, or IP address usually work fine, although you will want to avoid using IP address if your network assigns them dynamically). The trick when deciding how many log files to have and how many users should access those files is to find a balance between the amount of useful information you get and the amount of logging noise (entries that are not immediately useful, but are worth logging since they may be useful under other circumstances).

When employing message boxes to debug, you should use them sparingly and avoid loops, since you don't want to have to dismiss thousands of message boxes just to run the program. With logs you have a bit more freedom, though extensive logging can create huge files that you will need to manage. In addition to logging object state (with a function like sEnumerateSelf, described earlier), it is common to log trace information when program navigation is especially confusing. In fact, you may want to devote a special log file to just this purpose.

Making Bugs Noisy: Assertions

As a student of music, I learned several valuable lessons about ensemble playing. Foremost among these lessons came from an orchestra conductor who said, "Make loud mistakes. If you are doing something wrong, everyone needs to know about it." While it was a real jolt to a lot of egos, he was right: it is much easier to fix a potential problem if you and everyone else know about it.

The same words of wisdom apply to debugging. Programmers spend a lot of time tracking down subtle, hidden bugs, and this can cost companies a fortune in maintenance. The obvious bugs get fixed immediately and ultimately cost much less. The key to making debugging easier is to prepare the code in such a way that any bugs that do work their way into the program are noisy and blatant and therefore easier to find and fix. In this section we will examine several techniques and strategies not only for preventing bugs but also for making the ones that do appear noisier.

When I teach classes in the C programming language, I spend an unusually large amount of time in two areas: understanding the use of data types and using assertions effectively. College textbooks often neglect these topics, yet I feel a thorough understanding of them separates the solid coders from the wannabes. Both of these are important in Visual Basic as well. We discussed appropriate use of data types in chapter 11. Now let's turn to assertions.

In everyday life, an assertion is a declaration that something is true, an affirmation. In programming, an assertion is a syntactic structure that allows the programmer to test the validity of a logical assumption before moving forward in the code. It is a simple Boolean check: an assertion is always either true or false. Proper use of assertions can prevent many problems. Assertions are like land mines for bugs. When code violates documented assumptions, the assertions go off, revealing the exact line of code that is problematic.

Prior to Visual Basic, version 5, developers had to create their own assertion mechanisms. VB 5 and VB 6 offer assertion functionality right off the standard Debug object, though, as we shall see, it leaves a bit to be desired. The best way to learn about assertions is to look at them in action, and Listing 17.2 contains a simple example. The function dbDivide returns the result of dividing rnNumerator by rnDenominator. Since division by zero is a mathematical error, the routine first asserts that the denominator is not equal to zero. If during the course of its execution, this assertion is not true, Visual Basic will halt the program at the line containing the assertion.

Listing 17.2 An Assertion Example

```
Function dbDivide(rnNumerator As Integer, _
             rnDenominator As Integer) As Double
    Debug.Assert rnDenominator <> 0
    dbDivide = CDbl(rnNumerator) / CDbl(rnDenominator)
End Function
```

The idea behind assertions is that they are active only when you want them to be. Assertions made with Debug.Assert become inactive when you compile the code into an executable (just as with Debug.Print), but remain active when running from within the VB IDE. For developers this is ideal, since they can test for conditions in the code that the users don't need to know about.

The drawback to assertions is that because they are not supposed to execute when they are off, their removal may introduce unexpected behavior. If the expression that is evaluated in the assertion has some important side effect (intentional or otherwise), the code will not behave the same when running in the IDE as opposed to the compiled version. For example, consider the code in Listing 17.3. When you run this code from within the VB IDE, you will receive three message boxes: "Hello World," "Is everything o.k.?" and "GoodBye World." When this code is compiled and run from an executable, you receive only two messages: "Hello World" and "Hello World."

Listing 17.3 Side Effect in an Assertion

```
Private msVariable As String
Public Sub Main()
    msVariable = "Hello World."
    Call MsgBox(msVariable)
    Debug.Assert bIsOK
    Call MsgBox(msVariable)
End Sub

Private Function bIsOK() As Boolean
    msVariable = "Goodbye World."
    bIsOK = (MsgBox("Is everything o.k.?", _
        vbQuestion + vbYesNo) = vbYes)
End Function
```

The best way to avoid such confusion is to be sure your assertion expression always evaluates only the value of a Boolean expression or variable, without making a function call or introducing any other side effect. Changing Sub Main as follows fixes the issue:

```
Public Sub Main()
    Dim bOK as Boolean
    msVariable = "Hello World."
    Call MsgBox(msVariable)
    bOK = bIsOK
    Debug.Assert bOK
    Call MsgBox(msVariable)
End Sub
```

The fact that assertions compile out of the code when you create an executable has its advantages, but sometimes you will want to reactivate them on the fly to troubleshoot a particular issue after the software has been distributed. This is just not possible with Debug.Assert, so you will have to turn to your own assertion routine to get the job done. We'll look at just such a routine in the next section.

Note that assertions are not necessarily needed if a program has adequate error trapping. Indeed, if you propagate errors effectively, your application should behave well under just about any circumstances. The advantage to including assertions is that they are proactive, defensive programming. When an assertion fails, you know what is wrong immediately, without having to trace back through the propagated errors to the source. It provides a way for you to identify invalid assumptions that some of your code might be making about other code.

The concept of defensive programming extends beyond the use of assertions. For example, it is also common to include a check for a specific condition before allowing code to execute. The function dbDivide in Listing 17.2 could easily have been written as in Listing 17.4.

Listing 17.4 Safe Divide without Assertion

```
Function dbDivide(rnNumerator As Integer, _
                  rnDenominator As Integer) As Double
    If rnDenominator <> 0 Then
        dbDivide = 0
    Else
        dbDivide = rnNumerator / rnDenominator
    End If
End Function
```

In the code in Listing 17.4 we make an assumption about what the calling code expects in return when it passes a zero for the denominator. If we are confident that the calling code will behave well under these circumstances, then this is a safe bet. However, if the calling code is expecting the routine to return some other number instead, we will have introduced a potential bug. Alternatively, we could have just ignored the potential problem and let the division by zero happen, crossing our fingers that the calling code was ready to trap the error (see Listing 17.5). Last, we could have added an On Error GoTo construct to this routine and changed it to return true or false (success or failure) from the function and the actual answer in an out parameter (see Listing 17.6). All of these solutions are valid under certain circumstances, but all introduce assumptions of how the calling code behaves, which is something a low-level routine typically should not do. Assertions put the burden of judgment on the calling routine itself, where it belongs. In practice, I use a mixture of these techniques, based on how often the code is called and my degree of confidence in the calling routines.

Listing 17.5   Divide without Error Checking

```
Function dbDivide(rnNumerator As Integer, _
             rnDenominator As Integer) As Double
    dbDivide = rnNumerator / rnDenominator
End Function
```

Listing 17.6   Divide with Error Trapping and Out Parameter

```
Function bDivide(rnNumerator As Integer, _
             rnDenominator As Integer, _
             rdbResult As Double) As Boolean
    On Error GoTo Error_Handler
    rdbResult = rnNumerator / rnDenominator
    bDivide = True
    Exit Function
Error_Handler:
    bDivide = False
End Function
```

So when should you use assertions rather than one of the other approaches? Use assertions when you are optimistic that the calling code will behave itself eventually (after debugging and testing), remembering that the assertions will go away when the application is released. Assertions are particularly useful in low-level routines in which you do not want to have explicit If/Then constructs in place (though, to be honest, I have found the performance impact to be insignificant, even in tight loops). They are especially useful in Property Lets of classes, when a calling routine attempts to assign an invalid value.

One final word on assertions: remember that whatever can go wrong in your software will go wrong. When applied to assertion strategies, this means that if your code runs smoothly through testing without violating a single assertion, you can guarantee that there will be violations when in production. You will want to be able to reactivate your assertions on the fly, logging violations while the application runs in production, which brings us to clsDebug.

Combining These Techniques: clsDebug

Although programmers who are good debuggers find that debugging is a disciplined habit, it does not hurt to have a few tricks and tools to make life easier. In this section we will look at a simple, but powerful class that you can use to help debug your Visual Basic applications. Because all of the techniques discussed earlier are useful in certain situations and because the Visual Basic Debug object is not very powerful, I created clsDebug, which combines the features described in the last two sections into one easy-to-use package (see "On-line Materials" in the preface for downloading instructions). The interface for clsDebug includes functions and properties for logging, tracing, asserting, and viewing debugging statements. Table 17.1 summarizes this interface, and in fact it is probably all you will need to get started. Nevertheless, let's take a closer look at some of its features.

On-the-Fly Activation

One of the main problems with using Visual Basic's Debug object is that its methods disappear when the application is compiled. There is no way to reactivate them once an executable is created. This has some obvious drawbacks. For example, in my experience it is common for QA teams working with executables to report bugs that developers have a hard time recreating on development computers. With the ability to turn the program's debugging function on and off at will, developers can activate it on a QA computer. Once activated, the QA team can reproduce the error while the application logs helpful information gleefully (of course, developers still have to write code to log everything important).

TABLE 17.1 Properties and Methods of clsDebug

Property/Method	Description
AlwaysOnTop (Get/Let)	Causes clsDebug's debugging window to appear on top of all other windows when set to true. This setting is useful when you need to view the debugging information while your application switches among several forms.
Assert	An extended version of the Debug.Assert command. Verifies the Boolean expression passed. If the assertion fails, it will log the information to the log file and/or display it in the debugging window. You may also assign a user-defined assertion ID (variant) to the expression for easy tracking.

(continued)

TABLE 17.1 Properties and Methods of `clsDebug` *(continued)*

Property/Method	Description
ClearLog	Deletes the log file specified by the `LogFile` property.
ClearTraceLog	Deletes the trace log file specified by the `TraceLogFile` property.
ClearWindow	Clears the debugging window, but does not hide it.
DebuggingOn (Get/Let)	Activates or deactivates all debugging functionality. This one flag acts as a global kill switch and activation switch for `clsDebug`.
Display	Puts the information passed into the debugging window. You may also optionally force the debugging window to always be on top. You may force the application to pause by setting the last optional argument to True. This will cause the form to be displayed modally, and you will have to press the resume button to continue (you may notice a slight flicker as the form is hidden and re-shown modally). This method will cause the debugging window to become visible if you have closed it.
DisplayAssertionsOn	Returns or sets whether `clsDebug` will display failed assertions in its debugging window. See `Assert` for more information.
DisplayOn (Get/Let)	Activates or deactivates `clsDebug`'s debugging window. Note that activating this flag will not cause the window to show until `Display` is called. Deactivating this flag will hide the window, however.
DisplayTraceOn	Returns or sets whether `clsDebug` will send trace messages to the debugging window.
HideWindow	Hides the debugging window if it is currently visible. Note that this method does not reset the `DisplayOn` flag.
INIFile (Get/Let)	Returns or sets the name of the file holding debugging settings. If no path is supplied, `App.Path` is assumed. Changing this property causes the INI file to be read, and the class will raise an error if the file is not read successfully.
Log	Logs the string passed to the log file specified by the `LogFile` property. Note that you can easily modify this routine to include information like Date/Time, machine name, and user ID automatically.
LogAssertionsOn (Get/Let)	Returns or sets whether `clsDebug` will log failed assertions. See `Assert` for more information.
LogFile (Get/Let)	Returns or sets the name of the file to use to store logged information. If no path is supplied, `App.Path` is assumed. The file will be created if it does not exist.
LogTraceOn	Activates or deactivates the trace log. See `Trace` for more information.
Trace	Potentially displays and logs the trace information passed. Trace information is displayed in the standard debugging window, but is logged to the trace log file rather than the standard log file (though you can make both properties the same). It has two optional flags allowing you to deactivate both the displaying and logging if you wish.
TraceFile (Get/Let)	Returns or sets the name of the file to use to store traced items. If no path is supplied, `App.Path` is assumed. The file will be created if it does not exist.
TraceOn (Get/Let)	Activates or deactivates the tracing commands in `clsDebug`. See `Trace` for more information.

The code in `clsDebug` accomplishes this on-the-fly activation by getting its default instructions from an INI file. This INI file serves as the final check of whether or not a particular debugging feature is active. In fact, activating a debugging feature from within code (see the properties in Table 17.1) will not work if the feature is disabled in the INI file. All of the properties of `clsDebug` get saved to the INI file when the instance of `clsDebug` is destroyed. The INI file even has a master flag, called `DebuggingOn`, which activates or deactivates all debugging in one shot.

A Better Immediate Window

I like the immediate window in VB, and the window provided in `clsDebug` is not designed to replace it. At the same time, however, VB's immediate window has its drawbacks. First, the lack of a `Debug.Clear` command is a frustrating oversight on Microsoft's part, and, second, the window is at the mercy of the rest of the VB IDE, which often gets blocked by your running application. The debugging window in `clsDebug` not only features a `ClearWindow` method, but also has an `AlwaysOnTop` property, which forces the window to the top of the Z order so that it is not covered up by your forms. You can also turn the debugging window into something of a message box, suspending program flow until it is dismissed.

Separate Tracing

Although Visual Basic does not have a feature that tells you the name of a function at runtime (or automatically at compile time, either), the `Trace` function nevertheless remains a useful feature. Just call `Trace` whenever you want to track where you have been in the code. It will write to its own log file or even to the debugging window.

Tracing is most useful when you are tracking down problems that are buried in confusing function-call stacks. Adding a trace statement to each function lets you follow the exact flow of the program. It is especially useful when trying to follow complicated recursions.

Enhanced Assertions

VB's `Debug.Assert` is a bit limited in its features, so I have added my own version. The `Assert` method of `clsDebug` not only tests the expression, but also logs and displays the assertion message upon failure. You can even assign the assertion an ID of your choosing, which is useful when tracking assertions with constants (as with errors).

Using `clsDebug`

Even with these extended features, `clsDebug` won't make your program bug-free overnight. However, it can help set traps for them, as follows: First, you can create one global instance of clsDebug and share it across all components. This gives you the advantage of never having to worry about creating an instance on the fly, since you always have access to a valid reference with a global object. However, this limits your flexibility somewhat because all debugging statements log their results to the same log file. Second, you can change the instancing property of clsDebug to GlobalMultiUse, so you don't have to declare an object at all. Again, you will have to share logs, but this approach has less overhead. The last approach is to have several instances of clsDebug to use as you need them. This approach gives you the most flexibility, but you will have more than one debugging window, which may clutter the screen. Your decision is really going to depend mostly on how you need to use the debug object in a given project.

There are a couple of ways you can include the file clsDebug in your own projects. If you place clsDebug and frmDebugDisplay in a separate DLL, you can reference this DLL from within your projects. This is helpful when you anticipate that you may need to turn the debugging functionality on after the application has been distributed. With this approach, the INI file serves as your source of control. If you want to remove debugging functionality altogether, you can wrap all calls to instances of clsDebug in conditional compilation directives and thus avoid having to ship the DLL. When building the executables, simply remove the reference to the DLL and make sure the conditional compilation turns off the call to the debugging functions.

Alternatively, you can include clsDebug in all of your projects that need it, along with frmDebugDisplay. This gives you the most flexibility, since not only can you control debugging on a per-project basis, but you also can turn the debugging on and off after the application is released.

You are free to make whatever changes to clsDebug you would like to suit your needs. For an example illustrating how to use the class, take a look at the project DebugTester (see "Online Materials" in the preface). This is a good way to see clsDebug in action, since it tests all of the functionality of clsDebug.

Checking for Range Issues

One of the most common types of errors results from passing a value to a function that is outside the range of values the function expects. Out-of-range values can result in strange behavior or even runtime errors. There is no real trick to avoiding range issues, just using common sense. Be sure you understand the practical range of each data type being used (parameters and return values especially). Also, you need to anticipate the potential range from a business perspective. For example, if you are writing a function that returns a person's bonus given their salary and employment grade, how would it respond if the salary value passed were negative?

Fighting Memory Leaks: Tracking Object Lifetimes

Low-level languages such as C and C++ have powerful functions for allocating and releasing memory. The ability to allocate memory explicitly gives the programmer a lot of control over how memory is used in an application. Along with this power comes greater responsibility, though. Programmers in such languages must remember to release any memory they have allocated—failure to do so results in a memory leak. While minor memory leaks often have no noticeable effect on a program, severe leaks can cripple an application and even lock up the operating system.

Microsoft used to boast about Visual Basic's simplicity when its comes to managing memory. Since there is no way to allocate memory explicitly from within VB, one would presume that there is no way to create a memory leak. This is unfortunately not the case. By their very nature, COM objects track their own lifetimes (along with the memory they occupy), and destroy themselves when the last reference to them disappears. It is easy to trick them (accidentally) into thinking that they should live longer than they really should, creating a memory leak that can be very hard to find. If you forget to unload a form in your application, you will usually find the problem during development, because your application won't end when you want it to and the Forms collection will not be empty. With objects, the signals are much subtler (and there is no Objects collection). Although VB is supposed to clean up after itself when your application ends (memory leaks and all), I wouldn't count on it, and it certainly is not good programming practice to do so. Besides, VB won't help you recover leaked memory while your application is running.

Figure 17.1 illustrates a simple way to create a memory leak, using circular references. In step 1, an object of Class A creates an instance of Class B called oB. In step 2, this new object creates an instance of Class C, called oC. If oC gets a reference to oB (by means of a property set, for example) as it does in step 3, the object of type Class B will have two references to it. When the instance of Class A sets its reference to oB equal to nothing, oB does not terminate, since oC still has a reference to it. In this situation, you are left with two objects that are unable to terminate because they have references to each other, and there are no other references to either.

This type of problem can be very difficult to track down, especially in projects that pass object references around all of the time. It is best to avoid this kind of problem from the start by creating explicit Initialize and Terminate methods that you can call directly to force an object to set all of its references to external objects to Nothing. In some cases, though, this just isn't possible or practical. What you need is a way to track an object's lifetime, so that you can be sure all objects that get created get destroyed.

Although you cannot explicitly allocate memory in VB, it does give you a clue as to when objects are actually created and when they are destroyed. The

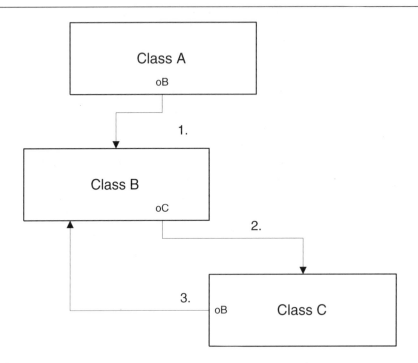

FIGURE 17.1   Creating a Memory Leak with Circular References

Class_Initialize and Class_Terminate events fire whenever an object is created or destroyed and thus are your key to tracking object lifetimes. The strategy is simple: in the Class_Initialize event, generate a unique ID for the object, and store that ID in a private property. Then create a log entry indicating that the object has been created. In the Class_Terminate event, create a log entry that shows that the object has been terminated. Listing 17.7 shows this technique in action. When you run the program with such code in place, you should get two entries for each object ID. If you don't, you'll know which class is the culprit, making the problem easier to resolve.

Listing 17.7   Tracking Object Lifetimes

```
Private msObjectID As String

Private Sub Class_Initialize()
    msObjectID = GetUniqueID
    Call goDebug.Log("Created " & TypeName(Me) & _
                     " as " & msObjectID)
End Sub
```

```
Private Sub Class_Terminate()
    Call goDebug.Log("Destroyed " & TypeName(Me) & _
                        " as " & msObjectID)
End Sub
```

The implementation of the magic function GetUniqueID can be as simple or as complicated as you want, depending on how specific you really need it to be. I have seen successful implementations that used a variety of techniques, such as the following:

- *A routine in a BAS module containing a local static variable that gets incremented upon every call:* This technique is simple and effective, but you'll need to take special precautions for dealing with multiple instances of your project, which will have different instances of the function that could generate the same numbers. Combining the App.ThreadID with the static variable is helpful.

- *A random number generated with* Rnd: While this is not guaranteed to generate a unique number every time, it will probably be different enough for the context, especially when you are creating and destroying lots of objects in a relatively short time span.

- *A GUID generated using the* CoCreateGUID *API with a conversion to a string:* This will give you a unique number every time, but has a messy implementation. Refer to MSDN Knowledge Base article Q176790 for an example of how to accomplish this.

- *A sequence derived from a database:* Since this requires hitting the database for every object, it is a less than optimal approach. However, it does guarantee uniqueness, and you can often use the number generated as the primary key into a table designed to hold an object's information.

For particularly difficult reference problems, you may have to resort to a more aggressive debugging technique. Presumably, if you can ask an object for its reference count, you can add debugging code throughout your app to trace the reference count. You can then watch as references are added and removed. Unfortunately, there is no way to ask a VB object for its reference count. There is, however, a way to steal the count from the object, as shown in Listing 17.8. I am not sure of the original source of this little gem; I have seen it in several places—most notably, Bruce McKinney's *Hardcore Visual Basic*. I am aware of its dangers, though.

This function relies on Visual Basic's implementation of the COM IUnknown interface for its objects, which could change in any future release. Because of this, it may not work (and probably won't) for objects created in another language. Objects created from out-of-process servers won't work either, and

DCOM objects are out of the question. I have used this function in both Visual Basic 5 and 6 with no problems. The good part is that it is relatively crash-proof—it simply copies memory from a specific location to a long. Whether or not the memory it copies is meaningful is another story. Still, save your work often, just in case!

Listing 17.8   Finding a Reference Count

```
Public Declare Sub CopyMemory Lib "kernel32" Alias _
    "RtlMoveMemory" (Destination As Any, Source As Any, _
    ByVal Length As Long)

Public Function lGetReferenceCount _
                    (ByVal voObj As IUnknown) As Long
    Dim lCount As Long
    lGetReferenceCount = 0
    If voObj Is Nothing Then
        Exit Function
    End If
    'Steal the internally stored count
    Call CopyMemory(lCount, ByVal ObjPtr(voObj) + 4, 4)
    'Subtract parameter references
    lCount = lCount - 3
    lGetReferenceCount = lCount
End Function
```

Of course, finding the guilty class is often only half the battle. To fix such memory leaks you need to find out where the stray reference is. As a rule of thumb, always set object references to Nothing explicitly before they fall out of scope. Also, be especially wary of property gets and sets that toss around object references. If you provide one object with a reference to another, be sure to take it away at some point.

The Visual Studio Debugger

For especially tough bugs, you may have to resort to low-level debugging with the Visual Studio IDE. The process involves compiling your executable with symbolic debugging information turned on and optimizations turned off. You can then reference the executable from within Visual Studio and follow along from within the source code. We won't look at this in detail here, but for more information on this technique, refer to Ken Cowan's article, "Swat Tough Bugs" in the *Visual Basic Programmer's Journal* (1998). Rumor has it that Visual Basic 7 will drop the current IDE and use the Visual Studio IDE outright, blending VB and Visual InterDev. This should make such debugging more accessible to VB programmers all around.

Summary

To finish, let's look at several general guidelines to help you write better code. The following list serves as a summary and a checklist for debugging code and preparing it so that potential problems are easier to find. A lot of developers overlook these details, primarily because they lend little to the perception of progress. Not all of these points mandate extra code; rather, they are designed to verify that you have at least thought about debugging.

- Before you declare a chunk of code "finished," be sure you have executed every line of code it contains, including all error conditions and all the "this-should-never-happen" blocks of code. You may have to reset the flow of execution during a break to reach certain lines. For error handling, consider including a couple of `Err.Raise` commands just to see how your routines behave. I mentioned these points earlier, but I cannot stress their importance enough.

- Call all functions with extreme values to verify range behavior. It is usually a good idea to err on the side of being conservative, which means not making assumptions about how the calling code will behave, even if you think you know. If a routine should or does fail under certain circumstances, be sure it fails appropriately.

- Be certain you have addressed error trapping in all nontrivial functions and subroutines. Note that this does not necessarily mean that you have to have some kind of `On Error` construct (though this is usually a good approach). It *does* mean that you have considered (and documented!) how the routine handles errors, and how calling routines can expect it to behave (does it return a value for success or failure, raise an application-specific error, or ignore errors, letting them fall through?).

- Wherever appropriate, include assertions to verify the validity of parameter values and other assumptions the code is making about the state of variables.

- Include tracing and debugging information in any code that is potentially confusing or usually susceptible to problems. This is a good idea even if the code appears to be working correctly. With a tool like `clsDebug`, you can leave the traces and debugging statements in the code lying dormant until activated via the INI file in the face of trouble.

Error Handling

Error handling stands as one of the most problematic areas of application development. Ironically, error handling is really not all that difficult if you have a clear strategy and the discipline to follow through with it. Where projects begin to break down is in the area of discipline—programmers must add error-handling code themselves. It is an aspect of architecture that is everyone's responsibility. But because most added error handling does not contribute directly to the completion of functionality, programmers begin to take short-cuts when under schedule pressure.

Debugging and error handling go hand in hand. Code that has been well prepared with debugging traps is easier to debug, giving it the potential to be of higher quality, with fewer errors. Still, errors are bound to occur in your code. An application's ability to handle errors gracefully directly reflects its robustness, usability, and reliability. The bottom line is that if an application cannot handle errors well, users lose confidence in it. With good error handling, users may even be able to recover from problems on their own, which would reduce support costs and improve user satisfaction.

There are many kinds of errors your applications may run into. Basically, though, there are two categories: expected errors and unexpected errors. By expected, I am referring to those errors caused by conditions that have been identified as having the potential for producing a problem. Unexpected errors are those that pop up without warning and are usually the result of bugs. There is something of a fuzzy line between these two categories, though. If you spend a lot of time exploring the possible errors your code can experience, you reduce the number of unexpected errors. Since it is difficult to handle unexpected errors in a recoverable way, it is in your best interest to anticipate as many errors as you can.

Finding Errors

Before you begin coding your application, you must decide on an error-handling strategy. As we discussed in the "Debugging Techniques" section, you can take a proactive approach and explicitly check for potential problems in your code. You accomplish this with a combination of assertions and preemptive If/Then checks. In most cases, you must take this proactive approach when validating data. Alternatively, you can add more generic error trapping, catching runtime errors in an error-trapping section of a routine. You can even catch an error with runtime error trapping and reraise a more specialized message within the context of your application.

Once you have found an error, you need to decide how you want to handle it. You can log the error, display it to the user, send some external message, or just ignore it. We'll look at logging and external notifications later. More important, though, you need to decide how you wish to propagate the error throughout your code. You can either raise an error (or let unhandled errors fall through) or notify the calling routine by means of a function return value. I find it better to have functions return explicit error codes, an approach that makes no assumptions about the calling code. If you decide to raise errors, the calling code must be able to trap them, or your application may crash. Propagating errors by means of function return values is safer.

Ultimately, most of your errors will need to be displayed to the user. The problem is that an error may occur several function layers deep in a process. Rarely can you (or should you) display an accurate message to the end user so deep within the bowels of the application. Rather, you should log an error that is meaningful within the context in which it occurred. Programmers and users have fundamentally different expectations of error messages. For example, programmers want to know exactly why procedure XYZ was unable to insert a Snarfblat record, while the user is concerned only with the fact that the over-riding "Save Snarfblat" process was unsuccessful and what can be done about it.

One of the best strategies for dealing with this situation is to log an error at every point of failure. The context of the error determines the content of the error message. For example, when a database call fails (in *n*-tiered applications, this is usually in the data services layer), you can log the failed SQL or stored procedure call—information useful to developers but of little use to users. When the error propagates to business objects, you can log a business logic violation error. Again, messages of this type are likely to be of more use to developers than to users. Finally, by the time the error floats up to the user interface, you can display (and perhaps log) a meaningful message to the user, in terms that the users will find helpful. As an example of this, consider the errors in Exhibit 17.1. Here an error occurs in the database layer and floats up to the user interface. Help desk technicians can access the log to see errors 2 and 3, while users see error 1. Some programmers prefer to show all of the errors to the user, but if this is not done very carefully, the error messages become confusing, causing more problems than they help solve.

EXHIBIT 17.1   Error Propagation from the Database to the User Interface

1. **User Level:** Unable to save the Snarfblat record. Be sure that your Snarfblat has a valid thingamabob and save the record again.

2. **Business Object Level:** Unable to save Snarfblat record. A database error has occurred. Aborting save of Snarfblat support record.

3. **Database Services Layer:** Insert Snarfblat failed. A database error has occurred. Primary key constraint violated. SnarfblatID 12345 already exists. SQL is: insert . . . into TblSnarfblat.

Note that, in practice, you are likely to have many more opportunities to log errors, since each layer shown in the exhibit will probably consist of several function calls. As each function call fails and propagates its error to the calling routine, you must decide whether it is worth logging an error. Logging too many errors can be as ineffective as logging too few, since it is easy to lose the real source of the error in all of the noise.

Error Severity

Most errors are the result of invalid data. This is especially true in applications that access databases, which in the corporate world are most applications. Others result from system failures, network problems, or even bugs. Identifying the severity of an error is critical to being able to decide how to handle it. For most errors, you will have to decide what to display to the user (if anything) and whether or not the error should be logged (and where). First, let's take a look at severity.

Table 17.2 illustrates some common error severity levels you may encounter while working on your application. There is some overlap among these categories, and you may discover that your application produces errors that don't fall into any of the categories shown. The levels in Table 17.2 are

TABLE 17.2   Examples of Error Severity Levels

Severity Level	Description
Unrecoverable	Errors of this type usually result in application termination and in extreme cases may require shutting down or rebooting the PC. They are the result of extreme failure (hard disk failure, operating system crashes, etc.). These errors are usually logged and sometimes displayed as well.
Critical	These errors represent some serious problem with your application. Examples include failed networks or databases. Simply put, your application cannot continue to work properly, and as a result you are likely to have to end the application abruptly. Critical errors should be logged and displayed to the user.
Warning	Warning errors inform the users that something might be wrong, often directing them to seek technical assistance. A process that may fail in the future (because of, for example, limited disk space) is a likely candidate for a warning message. Usually these errors are displayed to the user, but may not require logging.
Validation	Validation errors are usually the result of bad data entered by the user. They are of low severity, since the user can do something immediately to remedy the situation. While they need to be displayed to the user, they should almost never be logged, since they are of little use to the developer.
Informational	Informational messages are not really errors, but it is convenient to group them with errors. Informational messages inform the user of some condition that does not represent an error. As a result, they should never be logged.

intended only as examples, so be sure to consider your application's specific requirements.

Logging Errors

When you determine that your code has an error that needs to be logged, you need to call some mechanism to actually log the error. One of the easiest approaches is to call a common function that opens an error log file, writes the details of your message, and closes the file. Useful information to include in your logged errors includes the computer name or IP address of the workstation logging the error; the date and time; the name of the user experiencing the problem; and the name of the application generating the error.

Like debugging logs, you can log errors generated by all of your users to the same log file on a shared network folder or use a local file. Alternatively, you can use the App object's LogEvent function. Under Windows NT, this method writes data to the NT event log. Under Windows 95/98, it logs the information to the file specified by the App.LogPath property. You can use the App.LogMode property to control logging more explicitly. While the App object's logging functions are useful, you may find that they are not quite robust enough for your needs. However, it is trivial to create your own logging object (as we did earlier with clsDebug).

Interactive Alerts

In a system with a large number of users, an error log can fill very quickly. As your application becomes more and more stable, the number of errors logged should decline. Eventually you may discover that your log contains noise errors even if the application is working fine. You can revisit your logging strategy to remove the noise errors if you would like.

The biggest problem with error logs, even after you have fine-tuned your logging strategy, is that you must still monitor the logs to find potential problems. When the support mechanism for your application requires immediate response to critical errors, you will need to be sure that serious errors are dealt with immediately. You can accomplish this with interactive alerts. You can write your error-logging code to send e-mails or pages to the support staff when an error of a particular severity is found. You will want to be sure that critical errors get sent only once (e.g., you will not want to send thousands of e-mails just because the database goes down).

Error-Handling Infrastructure

As your project progresses, you will undoubtedly have dozens or even hundreds of error messages. Managing so many errors becomes a legitimate concern.

One of the most common techniques is to refer to error messages by a constant. When applied faithfully, this is a satisfactory technique. Visual Basic provides a simple mechanism for creating constants. By using enumerated types, you can define any number of long values that are visible in the Object Browser even when your code is compiled into a component. By using an enumerated type to define the constant, you can easily refer to the error number by a named value.

When you create your error constants, it is a good idea to group them by severity. You do not have to supply your enumerated constants with explicit values, so you can insert constants freely into the structure without having to renumber anything.

For each error you will not only have an error constant, but also an error message. Often these messages have replaceable parameters in them, so that you can include values in your messages that are available only at runtime. The decision of where to store these message strings is an important one. I have found that companies rely on one of three storage mechanisms:

1. *Store the error strings in a database.* This technique provides you with all of the power of a database management system. Most important, you can easily change the values of your error messages after the application has been released just by changing the database. However, often database problems are the cause of errors within applications. If you store your messages in the database, you run the risk of not being able to retrieve them in the event of a network or database failure. Also, even if the database is working perfectly, having to make a database read to get an error message is not the most efficient of approaches. To solve these issues, you may consider storing your error messages in a local database (Access is ideal for this use), which should be both faster and more reliable.

2. *Store the error strings as constants within code.* This technique allows developers to have explicit control over the error messages in their code. However, it is difficult to associate error messages with error constants. Although this approach may work well for smaller applications, it is not very scalable.

3. *Store the error strings in a resource file.* Resource files are binary chunks of information that you compile into your application. They can contain string tables (which is where you should store your error constants and verbiage), icons, bitmaps, cursors, and custom resources. The biggest advantage to using resource files is that they are locale-savvy. That is, you can enter different versions of your strings, bitmaps, and such for each locale to which you will release your application. Windows will automatically load the appropriate version based on the locale settings in the operating system. This is a big advantage if you are creating international applications, but is of little use if you are

writing the application for only one locale. While resource files are the method preferred by most companies, they have a couple of big drawbacks. First, you cannot change the value of a resource without recompiling your application. Also, although VB provides you with a simple resource editor add-in, there is still some extra work associated with creating a resource file. In short, they are more difficult to use than constants and database files, but are handy for international applications.

Further Reading

Barry Boehm, *Software Engineering Economics* (1981).   This book contains a section on determining the impact that tracking and fixing errors will have on a project's schedule.

Ken Cowan, "Swat Tough Bugs" (1998).   This article in the *Visual Basic Programmer's Journal* discusses how to use the Visual Studio debugger to track low-level errors in your VB programs.

Steve Maguire, *Debugging the Development Process* (1994).   Maguire covers practical strategies for completing projects on time. Chapter 7 discusses debugging strategies and attitude.

Steve McConnell, *Code Complete* (1993).   McConnell spends a good deal of time discussing finding, classifying, and tracking errors in software. While he does not discuss specific coding techniques, his overviews are highly applicable to Visual Basic development.

Steve McConnell, *Software Project Survival Guide* (1998).   In the chapter on software releases, McConnell discusses how to handle defects you may have created in software, including tracking and measuring severity.

PART IV

Testing, Reviewing, and Distributing Software

In this last part, we will focus on those aspects of development that take place either throughout the development process or after it has been completed. Chapter 18 deals with testing. While much of the book recommends a quality assurance plan that is integrated into the whole development process, this chapter turns to formal testing strategies to help make certain your applications meet their requirements.

Chapters 19 and 20 discuss Visual Basic coding standards in great detail. Many companies have coding standards, but often the standards are either poorly defined or poorly enforced, two fundamental problems that we will explore and learn to avoid.

The last chapter looks at rollout strategies and includes a detailed walk-through of the Visual Basic setup toolkit. We'll see how to customize it to suit the particular needs of your applications and conclude with a discussion of how to maintain your software once it has been deployed to production environments.

Chapter 18

Quality Assurance

Quality assurance (QA) is the process by which you verify that something lives up to your expectations. In the world of software development, QA means verifying that the software you are developing functions as it should. Whenever companies use words like *test*, *verify*, and *assure*, they are talking about quality assurance.

Today, quality assurance is one of the hot catchphrases in the corporate world. Almost every company has some kind of quality assurance program in place, though they are often trivial. However, companies nevertheless insist that quality is their primary concern. (Of course, the same companies will also say that customer service, reasonable pricing, being first to market, and using leading-edge technologies are also each their primary concern, depending on who is asked and who is asking.) In spite of their proclamations, poor quality assurance is the bane of many otherwise successful projects. In this chapter we will discuss traditional quality assurance approaches (the ones that usually do not work very well) and ways of improving them. We'll also discuss metrics for measuring software quality and conclude with a look at the various types of testing that take place during a VB project.

Approaches to Quality Assurance

Few companies will argue that an organized quality assurance plan is not a requirement for successful software development. The one company I know of that has openly rejected quality assurance, under the assumption that it is not "value-added," has had severe problems with software quality. Nevertheless, even in companies that actively embrace it, quality assurance is one of the most problematic areas of software development. Back in chapter 1, I rated poor quality assurance second on my list of the top-ten reasons why software projects fail.

Ex Post Facto, Ergo Splat

Traditionally, most companies consider QA a one-shot, ex post facto prospect. They set aside a block of time, almost always at the end of the schedule, to perform some kind of bulk testing. This last-minute retrospective testing constitutes most of the quality assurance done on the entire project. The amount of time spent varies, but is usually between 5 and 25 percent of the total calendar time allocated to the project. In practice, companies tend to plan more time than they actually spend because of schedule pressure. Some testing, they figure, is better than none at all. Sometimes companies do not spend enough time on quality assurance because they are not sure it is warranted. With Visual Basic projects and Windows programs in general, there is a common misconception that because the software has a user-friendly interface it is easy to test.

Myth 16
Visual Basic projects do not require a lot of time to test.

Short-circuiting the QA process and putting the testing off to the end of the project has a number of potential advantages that perhaps make the option seem attractive to companies. First, the testers only work with the complete system, and they never have to worry about changing feature sets, since by the time they get the software, it is "finished." Consequently, the overall testing time, and therefore the schedule itself, can be shorter, which is always a benefit in the eyes of project management. Moreover, this approach to testing works well if the software has few defects, since the simple brute force verification process it provides is both efficient (does not waste a lot of time) and sufficient (finds the few bugs there are).

In practice, though, these advantages never manifest themselves, and shortened, ex post facto testing generally creates more problems than it solves. As we'll discuss later, an integrated QA plan is much more productive. Here are four of the issues you may run into when you put QA off until the end of the project, rather than address it throughout the development process:

1. *You will find more bugs.* Bugs seem to reproduce exponentially. This is because an undetected bug may hide and create other bugs. Uncovering one

◆ A Bug is a Bug

The computer term *bug* was originally coined back in the days when computers took up vast amounts of space (rooms, literally) and were prone to outages. The story goes that an unsuspecting moth found its way inside one of these huge machines. It flew into some internal doohickey, causing the machine to break down (and also, presumably, signaling the end of the moth). After that incident, when there were troubles with the computer, the operators checked it for bugs. Today we use the term to indicate a problem with a programmer's code.

However, programmers are not the only ones who make mistakes when developing software. A poorly defined requirement that ultimately does not do what it should is just as much a problem as a sloppy subroutine, if not worse. Similarly, poor designs and architectures have cursed many a project. Such

mistakes are, in my opinion, bugs as well. Simply put, a bug is a defect in the deliverable of the current phase of development. It could be one of any number of possible defects, from a requirements bug caused by a mistake in the use case analyses to a design flaw that went unnoticed because of poor proof-of-concept verification to a misprint in documentation. And yes, it could even be an error in the code.

Because the term *bug* sounds so negative, some people refer to such problems with sugarcoated expressions such as "issues," "defects," "undocumented features," or even "opportunities for excellence" in hypersensitive environments. I believe bugs are not bad things per se. Lots of bugs and really serious bugs are, as are ones that go unfixed. But by itself, a bug is really just a bug, isn't it?

uncovers another, which uncovers another. . . . With bug detection delayed until the end of the project, bugs have a lot of time to reproduce undisturbed.

2. *You will find more serious bugs.* Because they have had the time to root themselves firmly into the software, some of the bugs you will find may be particularly nasty. However, not all of these bad bugs are blatant—some may be quite subtle. They may even be mistaken for actual features of the software, having gained legitimacy through longevity. Moreover, when the project is already near its deadline, it is often too late to do much about the problems beyond applying quick Band-Aids. It is unlikely that you can fix serious design flaws discovered in the testing without reworking a large portion of the system. Simply put, delaying problem detection until the end of the project not only makes the problems bigger, but also virtually eliminates any practical chance you have of fixing them within the time frame of the current schedule.

3. *You will have problems with team dynamics and efficiency.* With ex post facto QA, the test group has little or nothing to do during the design and implementation stages and then is swamped at the end of the project. If not carefully managed, this bipolar swing in activity can make for very inefficient use of resources. There is also a strong tendency for the testers and the developers to position themselves in an "us-against-them" mode. When everyone generally acknowledges that the testers test what the developers create, an alienation of the testers can occur and can lead to elitism on the part of the developers, eventually leading to hard feelings all-around. The developers "dump" their product onto the test team and may think it is no longer their responsibility (McCarthy, 1995).

4. *You have no scheduling flexibility.* For most corporations, the delivery date (ship date, rollout date, or whatever they call it) is everything. When the window of opportunity is particularly important, some companies would rather not write the software to begin with if they thought they were going to miss the ship date. If development runs late, the testing cycle must be shortened to hit the target date. This obviously affects the quality of QA. Furthermore, when the bulk of the QA takes place at the end of the project, the company may find out much too late that the software actually is unusable, perhaps because it was ill-conceived from the start. They are stuck with software that they cannot ship but that they have already paid for.

Integrated Quality Assurance

Because of these concerns, I recommend a proactive, integrated QA process that pervades every aspect of software development, as opposed to reactive, lump-sum testing at the end of the project. Formal testing is still a requirement (in fact, we'll spend a good deal of time in this chapter talking about it). However, it should not be the sole or even the primary means by which a company judges the quality of its software.

You integrate QA by ensuring that every step in the development process has some form of verification demonstrating that the results of the step actually are as expected. If you subscribe to an iterative software development lifecycle, as discussed in chapter 2, quality assurance and risk detection are built into the process. Each stage ends with verification of the stage just completed and planning of the stage about to begin. Use case models created in the requirements stage become the baseline for verifying each subsequent stage of development. For example, in chapter 4 we discussed one of the first QA mechanisms in a project: proof-of-concept analyses. Using use case models and scenarios, we showed that right from the start you can verify the system's requirements, at least in theory. A solution for a problem that does not even work on paper will never work when implemented, so these analyses are critical. You must deal immediately with any red flags raised during the proof-of-concept analysis. These are the first indications that the project's quality is not what it should be.

As the project progresses beyond the requirements stage, so should your QA efforts. Design reviews (again pulled from the use case models) help to verify the design. As the actual coding takes places, the testing team verifies the work in progress, while the developers fix bugs and continue debugging new features. It is important to fix bugs as soon as they are discovered in order to prevent them from becoming serious issues. In fact, there is seldom a good reason to delay fixing a problem immediately.

In addition to testing, regular code reviews (see chapter 20) help to ensure that everyone is coding up to the company's standards. Such reviews are more of a general form of quality assurance, since they do not verify specific functionality of the system but rather examine the general makeup of the code itself. Nevertheless, they remain an invaluable source of information about the state of the code.

So why is an integrated QA process better than the traditional ex post facto testing? Integrated QA removes the disadvantages of testing at the end of the project as just described and substitutes corresponding advantages. Compare the four points listed here with the four in the previous section. With an integrated QA process, the following is true:

1. *You will have fewer bugs.* Catching bugs as soon as they are introduced into the system, no matter where you are in the project's lifecycle, allows you to manage them more carefully. Moreover, when the bugs are resolved immediately, they have little opportunity to spawn other bugs. As a result, the overall bug count remains lower. You can also manage ongoing development more carefully, stopping the introduction of new code when the bug count gets too high. Coding can resume when the bugs are under control.

2. *The bugs you do find are smaller.* As with the number of bugs, finding a bug as soon as it is introduced into the system allows you to control it before it gets out of hand. When you address bugs immediately, you are unlikely to find serious problems in the system. With lump-sum testing, you are almost guaranteed serious problems.

3. *You will experience better team dynamics.* When testers, designers, coders, and management are all focusing on quality throughout the project, there is no sense of "us-against-them." It becomes obvious that everyone is working toward a common goal, even if the individual contributions and skill sets are different. Furthermore, everyone on the project gets essentially the same exposure to the software: there is no "ramping up" by the test team as there is for one-shot testing.

4. *You will have better control of the schedule.* Because integrated QA exposes issues that threaten the project as soon as they appear, you gain much more control over the project's estimated effort and, consequently, its schedule. Integrated quality assurance is one of the primary mechanisms of solid risk detection and management (incidentally, poor risk management placed first on my list of reasons for project failure back in chapter 1). If something just isn't going to work, you will know early in the development process, while there is still time to do something about it. This may mean changing the feature set, extending the schedule, or, in extreme cases, even canceling the project altogether. While many companies hate to admit failure, what is worse: calling it quits early on and saving money or proceeding blindly only to have the project canceled at some later date?

One final advantage of an integrated QA plan is that it actually encourages a better attitude about finding problems. With a proactive QA you are happy to find bugs because you can feel confident that the process itself is helping to eliminate them and make the software better. With ex post facto QA, team members are likely to be overwhelmed by bugs, and finding another bug becomes no cause for celebration. In fact, it can be downright discouraging. I have even seen managers and testers cheat by fudging reports and test results to bring down out-of-control bug counts and make things seem better. This may have the temporary effect of fooling their bosses, but in reality, they are only fooling themselves. See the discussion of metrics in the next section for more information.

If this approach to quality assurance seems too simple to work, guess again. Effective quality assurance is not really that difficult to achieve. It is not very glamorous, time-consuming, often entirely unforgiving, and even sometimes downright boring, but with the right approach, not hard. The most difficult part is setting expectations from the start and sticking to your guns. Effective quality assurance requires more than just simple lip service along the lines of "we are dedicated to creating quality software." It requires a commitment on the part of everyone involved in the process, not just a testing team assembled to test the software at the end.

Still, declaring this attitude and actually practicing it are two different things. An integrated QA plan can be difficult to get off the ground because it represents a fundamental change in the way many companies develop software. It is a low-level attitude change that pervades every aspect of development. It means blurring the usual distinctions between testers, coders, designers, and managers. QA can be especially difficult for programmers, who are usually eager to move on to the next challenge before their solution to the first has been proved. Everyone must be committed to the QA plan for it to be successful. Jim McCarthy writes that on successful software projects, everyone participates in design (1995). I would push his statement one step further and insist that everyone also is responsible for quality.

Metrics

No discussion of quality assurance is complete without considering software quality metrics. Metrics are quasi-empirical measurements of various aspects of software development. Quality assurance metrics derive their importance from the notion that, in a corporate development environment, quality should be predictable and must be measurable when it occurs (Jones, 1996). Analysis of quality with metrics is a popular, but complicated topic, as evidenced by the many huge tomes on quality assurance measurement (see especially Jones, 1996). Rather than dive into an in-depth discussion of metrics techniques, which can't be covered adequately here, let's instead turn to the questions of why, how, and when to use metrics.

Reasons to Use Metrics

More and more companies are turning to formal analyses with metrics to help resolve their software development issues. Metrics help to predict or measure (or both) various factors in software development. These include level, origin, severity, and removal efficiency of defects; product complexity, reliability, and maintainability; scheduling and budgeting for projects; and overall portability (Jones, 1996). Corporations often begin using metrics only to help with estimating the complexity of and schedules for their projects (see chapter 4). Later they go one step further and use metrics to determine many of the other factors listed. Altogether, metric analyses help companies gain a better understanding of what they are doing right and wrong, pinpointing more precisely those aspects of development that need particular improvement.

Metrics are clearly an important tool in the world of corporate software development. Capers Jones includes the formation of a software quality metrics program as one of the five important steps to software quality control. He claims that companies with software measurement programs often see dramatic yearly increases in quality for years at a time (Jones, 1996). Steve McConnell (1996) touts measurement as one of his "best practices." However, although it is not necessarily very difficult to create good QA habits, it is surprisingly difficult to establish a meaningful metrics program to measure that quality. Simply put, in spite of good intentions, many companies do metrics poorly. They fall short for any number of reasons, including a poor understanding of what quality really means to the company and unnecessary errors in the mechanical or interpretive aspects of metric analyses. Let's look at each of these issues in turn.

Setting the QA Agenda

The first step in ensuring a successful quality measurement program is to be sure your company has a clear concept of what it means by "quality." The definition will vary depending on the specific priorities of the company: some may be interested most in user satisfaction, while others find robustness more important, and so on. A glance at the numerous definitions in common use makes it clear that defining quality is not necessarily a trivial task. For example, a product is said to be of high quality when it is robust, portable, and fit for use, satisfies users, conforms to requirements, is reliable, is absent of defects, has low complexity, and is on time and within budget (Jones, 1996). Some of these factors are more measurable and predictable than others, but all are accurate definitions of quality in certain circumstances.

A clear concept of what quality means clarifies the corporate agenda for quality assurance and the goal behind the use of metrics. The corporate QA culture may manifest itself in many ways, including use of an integrated QA process as described in the last section (see the "Further Reading" section for more information about the mechanics of setting up a measurement program). However, the agenda must be truly the corporation's agenda and not just the whim of one or two individuals.

Metrics and Management Unfortunately, it is not always the case that the use of metrics is corporate policy. Often one or two members of middle management spearhead the effort. For the most part, these project managers are the individuals who use metrics the most. They have a need for the big picture of the project, and they have access to enough data to create meaningful measurements. People above and below them on the corporate ladder usually have either too focused or too wide a view to use metric analyses directly. Many managers find a metrics analysis useful since it gives them something "concrete" to point to and illustrate how well their project is doing. For them, it provides an empirical description of status when one is otherwise lacking. This description is, in their eyes, both more accurate and more convincing than other status indicators. They use these analyses not only to help manage the project, but, more important, to help support status presentations to their superiors.

Whereas many managers find the use of metrics indispensable, some of their team members (developers, testers, et al.) may have just the opposite opinion and even resent the use of metrics. From their point of view, their manager's analyses miss the big picture. When the team members consider the management weak, they see the use of metrics as a facade covering incompetence. They are also disappointed by the fact that the numbers the managers throw around are perceived to have more value than they may really deserve.

Sometimes the concerns of the team members are justified. If a manager wants to show that a project is successful, it is usually not too difficult to find some measurement that makes even an abysmal failure look sturdy. The interpreters of the data will end up seeing what they really want to see, regardless of the actual data. Furthermore, in some cases the managers just plain manipulate the data to fit their needs. According to Steve McConnell (1996), both managers and developers think that managers fudge data at least one-third of the time. This obviously weakens the merit of any conclusions based on that data.

Nevertheless, even when the numbers are accurate, they are sometimes used in seemingly absurd ways. Employees become particularly discouraged when metric analyses are the primary means management has of evaluating their performance. I once heard a story of a company that used the number of fixed bugs as a metric for evaluating aspects of employee performance. Though intentions were good, this metric ultimately had a negative effect on the quality of the software. In practice, those programmers who submitted relatively bug-free code to begin with were penalized for doing a good job, since they had few fixed bugs on their evaluation. Before long, all coders created sloppy code to have more bugs to fix and ultimately (presumably) get a better evaluation. It was like something out of a Dilbert comic.

However, more often than not it is simply a lack of understanding of the underlying reasons why metrics are being used that causes the confusion. Ignorance spawns contempt—individuals who do not understand the company's take on using metrics may become paranoid. They will think the numbers can be used only against them and that management may just be trying to shift the blame for a failing project with the smoke and mirrors of metrics. As a result, the politics of metrics needs to be handled carefully. When things like raises and promotions are on the line, employees can get justifiably skeptical.

Establishing Guidelines Because of these potential problems, gaining support for metric analysis from all rungs of the corporate ladder is important. Companies must demonstrate that using metrics is part of a larger philosophy concerning quality assurance and explain the role of metrics to all parties affected. Doing so will give the use of metrics more weight and remove the burden of proof from management. Furthermore, potentially resentful individuals can be assured that it is not the incompetence or whim of their managers that is causing their concern. Establishing guidelines up front also helps to clarify what data needs to be gathered, so you will not waste time collecting unnecessary data (McConnell, 1996). You can define and standardize the types of data collected so that categories remain meaningful from project to project for use in making predictions.

Interpretation of Data

No matter what specific goals a company has in mind for metrics, all metric analyses begin with some raw data. Exactly what data is used depends on the metric analysis being done. It could be the count of the number of lines of code or function points, the current defect count (bug count), a comparison of the estimated and actual schedules and costs for the project, or countless other tidbits of information. But data is just data. As Homer Simpson put it, "facts are meaningless. You can prove anything that is even remotely true with facts." To be useful, data must be analyzed. Typically, raw elements are combined, examined, and compared to similar values from past projects and original estimates. For example, useful combinations include number of defects per function point and total cost per function point.

Analyses intended to yield estimates or predictions tend to look most closely at historical data from past projects. Audits and other status checks pull data from the current project and compare it to what was expected. In the end, there are literally hundreds of approaches to metric analyses of software and software development. Choosing the right ones can be a difficult task, so do not be afraid to experiment.

In chapter 4, we discussed several caveats when dealing with formulaic approaches to estimating project size. Many of those concerns hold true here as well. Be wary of quasi-empirical data—numbers generated from weighting essentially subjective criteria. Also, be certain the results of the analyses make sense by performing a simple gut check. When it comes to software metrics, any conclusion that does not feel right probably should not be trusted, no matter how empirically derived.

Testing

Let us turn our attention now to a traditional quality assurance practice, formal testing. There are several different cycles of testing software can go through, including unit, batch, integration, system, beta, and regression testing. There is some overlap between these types of testing, and sometimes people refer to them by different names. But all are important to a successful quality assurance program. We will discuss each in turn.

Except for unit testing, most formal testing is performed by a test team. This team consists of superusers and domain experts from the user community who are familiar with the business needs the software is addressing. They are often the supervisors or trainers of the core group of users. However, companies often make the mistake of forgetting to include average users on their test teams. These are the individuals who will use the software on a day-to-day basis. They can provide down-to-earth suggestions that more advanced users might not even consider.

Test teams develop test plans that specify the paces the testers must put the software through. These plans are best when derived from use case analyses done during the requirements stage. Test plans should be both thorough and consistent in order to be sure the testers test all aspects of the system equally well.

The testing process itself is most productive when the software lifecycle dictates an iterative and progressive series of releases. A release occurs when developers turn a block of executable code over to the testers, because it contains new functionality, bug fixes, or both. Testers evaluate each release, annotating problems and reporting the results to development for resolution. The number of releases will vary from project to project, but it is helpful to schedule them regularly (perhaps weekly) and stick to the schedule until the testing is complete.

Debugging and Unit Testing

Developers perform debugging and unit testing before the code is released to the testers. Usually developers unit-test their own code, though sometimes companies have developers trade code, which has the advantage of getting a second, more objective set of eyes on the code. In our detailed discussion of debugging in chapter 17, we focused on making potential problems with the code as easy to spot as possible (see "Making Bugs Noisy"). Debugging takes you from the first dry run of the program to the point where the code seems to work as expected. Once the code is reasonably stable, unit testing can begin.

Unit testing is designed to verify not only that the code works when used as expected, but also that it is inherently more bulletproof than it needs to be and is capable of handling stress. Stress testing pushes the limits of the software. It tests the extreme ranges of all inputs and outputs of the routines, pointing out where to fortify the code for the unexpected. For example, a thorough unit test verifies that a routine that is designed to work with positive integers behaves well when presented with a negative number. Software behaves well when it handles the bad data gracefully. The routine could ignore it, round it, or generate an error, as appropriate. If after stress testing the code can handle even the exceptional cases well, there is a good chance it will work correctly when called in context and is more likely to withstand the effects of time. Stress testing is the most grueling form of testing. Along with unit testing, it takes place at the lowest level possible—a single line of code.

When you unit-test common routines, business objects, and other potentially reusable components, it is useful to write a separate testing application. Testing such components only from within the context of the actual code that uses them is unlikely to root out the most hidden problems. The testing application should not be fancy, since it ultimately will be discarded. Its goal is to abuse and otherwise mishandle, in every way possible, the code being tested. Sometimes these testing applications have simple user interfaces for entering bogus data. Other times they generate random values for the same purpose. Last, they may call the new code in an unusual fashion, for example, from within a tight loop. Note that Visual Basic is especially well suited for creating these kinds of test applications since simple user interfaces and test code can be written so quickly.

For example, consider a new business class that handles credit card validation. A typical credit card class might have properties to set the card number and expiration date and functions to read from tables to determine whether the card is valid (i.e., passes the mod 10 check common to credit cards) and the card's type (AX, VS, MC, etc.). To test the class, you could create a simple form that accepts the credit card number and expiration date and use this interface to test a bunch of bogus numbers, trying to break the system. You could even write code to generate random credit card numbers in rapid succession, thereby testing the data access.

Another important aspect of unit testing is that it gives the programmers an opportunity to find and fix bugs before the release of the code to the testers. By doing so, developers can save face, and testers are not sidetracked by bugs that should never have been released in the first place.

Batch Testing

Batch testing is really just another term for the day-to-day testing of batches of code as they are released to the testers. This is general testing against a test plan, and it constitutes the bulk of the testing done by the test team. It continues to occur while major pieces of functionality are still being introduced into the system, concentrating on those features of the system that are already in place. When the batch testing of large portions is complete, the testers move on to integration testing.

Batch testing is the time for picking nits. It evaluates data integrity and user interface details. Batch testing also presents an ideal time to incorporate the use of testing tools such as scripts and monkeys, which are discussed later.

Integration Testing

Integration testing begins when individual components are working well individually. It concentrates on validating the relationships among these completed subsystems. For example, if you have created a UI layer and a business rule layer in separate projects, integration testing would be used to verify that they behave well together. Note that integration testing does not need to test the whole system, but rather stress tests each component's interactions with other components and therefore uses only part of a complete test plan. Again, this stress testing involves attempting to "break" the system by using it in ways it is not intended to be used.

System Testing (Alpha Testing)

System testing, sometimes called *alpha testing*, takes integration testing one step further by verifying entire chains of functionality. This is the "day-in-a-life-of" testing, working with every aspect of the system. In theory, system testing should be done with the completed system, with all functionality in place, though this rule is sometimes broken in favor of schedule pressure. For most companies there is a blurred line between the time integration testing ends and system testing begins. But by the end of system testing, the product should be ready for production.

Some companies mark the end of the system testing cycle at the point where the software has passed a thorough inspection by the users. This is often called *user acceptance testing*. It represents something of a first production run of the system, except it involves only users who have been trained on the system and who have very specific intentions for its use.

Beta Testing

Some companies also include a beta testing cycle. In this cycle, the application is distributed to a controlled group of users. The users generally do not have any kind of formal testing strategy in mind, but rather use the software as if it were the "real" thing. The company that develops the software usually solicits feedback from the users to find out what kinds of problems they had and to get a general feeling of customer opinion.

While popular, beta testing has a couple of drawbacks. First, it is usually very difficult to solicit feedback from the testers without some kind of incentive. I have been involved with beta testing products that received feedback from less than 5 percent of the beta testers. And when forced to submit feedback, beta testers often submit very general comments ("I liked it" or "Neat company logo!"). Worse yet, you may get bombarded with wish lists from your testers, things they want the software to do that it currently does not. While this information is important and useful in its own right, it does not help the quality of the product at hand, especially when the requests are farfetched (McConnell, 1998).

Nevertheless, beta testing has its place. It is especially useful when testing applications that must run on a variety of platforms or for very general-purpose applications like operating systems or development tools. It is difficult for one company to anticipate all platform-related problems, so beta testing provides invaluable variety.

Regression Testing

Regression testing is not a separate testing cycle per se, but rather refers to the testing that takes place to verify that new code (enhancements and bug fixes) has not broken code that already works. It focuses on high-level, relatively simple test plans intended to verify the status quo. While it occurs in all cycles of testing, it is most useful during the later stages when it is not practical to retest the whole system completely.

Regression testing is of particular importance in projects using an iterative lifecycle approach. Each new large-scale iteration is likely to have some impact on the functionality of the previous iterations. Regression testing helps to verify that the new code has not broken the existing functionality.

While usually simple to perform, regression testing is often neglected. It is especially important when creating redistributable components that your users will incorporate into their own software (ActiveX controls are a good example). As a user of such components, I have worked very closely with a number of component manufacturers. I worked with a major terminal emulation component provider through numerous versions. It seemed that whenever the company released a new version of its components, my existing code would no longer function correctly. Sometimes it would not even compile. It got to the point where I was reluctant to install a new version for fear of having to rework my code. Taking the attitude that "if it ain't broke, don't fix it," I stopped installing the updates. I soon fell several versions behind and had trouble getting technical support. I was frustrated about the whole chain of events, but mostly because I knew that thorough regression testing on their part could have avoided the problems from the beginning.

Testing and Tracking Tools

There are a number of software tools available to assist with both finding new bugs and tracking them. Tracking tools help manage the history of your bugs, from inception to final fix and beyond. These tools are especially useful when combined with a quality assurance metrics program, since they help provide some of the raw data needed. More sophisticated measurement programs include defect tracking as part of their basic functionality.

Software testing tools fall into one of the following two categories:

1. *Scripting tools:* These tools help to automate the testing process. They usually consist of a simple scripting language that you can use to simulate the activity of a user working with the system. They do things like record and play back the mouse clicks and key presses (and other Windows messages) required to perform specific tasks in a test plan. When used effectively, scripting tools can test and retest basic functionality much more quickly than an actual person could. While not a replacement for a test team, they can make things a lot easier, especially for applications with many user interface elements. They are also useful for taking a "clean" system through its paces to establish baseline data for use in subsequent testing.

2. *Monkeys and other load-creation tools:* These tools automatically bang on systems in ways human testers could not imagine. *Monkeys* are tools that simulate the behavior of quasi-intelligent users who can use a mouse and keyboard but know little else about the system. They interact with the user interface in completely illogical, often random ways, usually uncovering unexpected behaviors of the application in the process. Load simulators help create artificial loads on servers, databases, networks, and almost anything else you can hook a computer to. They are indispensable when testing applications that are expected to handle a large number of users simultaneously, since it is difficult to judge how a system will behave in production when there are only a handful of testers.

Further Reading

Robert B. Grady and Deborah L. Caswell, *Software Metrics: Establishing a Company-Wide Program* (1989).   As the title suggests, this book helps you define and implement an enterprise-level metrics program.

Capers Jones, *Applied Software Measurement* (1996).   This is arguably the most important book on software measurement available. See especially chapter 5, which directly covers measuring software quality.

Jim McCarthy, *Dynamics of Software Development* (1995).   This book provides general anecdotal discussions from McCarthy's days with Microsoft. It provides a good overview of testing.

Steve McConnell, *Rapid Development* (1996).   Chapter 26 covers software measurement as a "best practice."

Steve McConnell, *Software Project Survival Guide* (1998).   This book contains many practical suggestions about quality assurance and establishing a QA plan.

Glenford Myers, *The Art of Software Testing* (1979).   This short book covers the important aspects of software testing. While dated, it remains a classic.

Jon Perkins, *Advanced Visual Basic 5* (1997).   Chapter 10, included with the Books Online, covers some testing basics.

Chapter 19

Coding Standards: Part I

In this chapter and the next, we will take an extended look at coding standards. We will see why standards are important and how they can help reduce the cost of software development. We'll then look at the process of creating a detailed coding standards document and discuss the scope of such a document. Finally, we'll have an extended discussion of naming conventions, including Hungarian notation and naming variables, constants, menus, and modules.

Why Have Coding Standards?

When John Kemeny and Thomas Kurtz designed BASIC, they intended to create a language that was as natural as possible. The language hid the details of the computer's internal representation of the code, and the syntax of the code itself resembled English. They largely succeeded in their goal, creating a clear, people-friendly language that provided the layperson with an excellent introduction to computers and programming. With Visual Basic, Microsoft has made great efforts to keep this concept alive. Although thirty-odd years younger, the Visual Basic of today remains as clear to understand as its great-grandfather.

Perhaps it is because of the inherent clarity of the language that people often think that all code written in Visual Basic is somehow magically readable and maintainable. Though this is a myth, it is certainly one of the main reasons managers and developers choose VB in the first place. The truth is that although the language itself makes writing clear, readable code easier, it is still possible (and unfortunately quite common) to find gibberish written in VB. This becomes particularly true as the problems the code is solving become more complex. Indeed, while Kemeny's BASIC was used primarily as a teaching tool, companies use the VB of today to implement complicated enterprise systems.

Myth 17
All Visual Basic code is inherently readable.

In a corporate world, the general readability of code has significant financial impact on a project. Simply put, code that is more readable is more maintainable. For many projects, most of the overall cost is not the initial development effort but rather the ongoing maintenance of the system. Some studies even claim that the ratio is $2 in maintenance for every $1 in development (Royce, 1998). With as many as 30 percent of new projects being canceled, existing VB programs, though perhaps designed only as temporary solutions, suddenly are faced with an extended lease on life resulting in more ongoing maintenance. The equation is simple:

readable code = maintainable code = lower cost of maintenance = saved $$$

As the programs corporations develop become more complicated and as the programming teams become larger, VB's intrinsic readability has a tendency to wear down, if not disappear. When this occurs, coding standards can help keep code readability on track.

At the most fundamental levels, coding standards are guidelines designed to help programmers write code in a consistent fashion. Beyond this definition, creation and use of coding standards represent a commitment on the part of project managers and developers to strive for readable code throughout the life of a project. In an ideal world, we would not have to have standards at all. In fact, for very small projects or projects with only one or two developers, they probably are not needed. On larger projects with more developers, circumstances change. The bigger the project, the more turnover in management and developers and the greater the discrepancy between the skill levels of the programmers. These factors present greater opportunities for inconsistencies in the code. In short, as the number of programmers on a project increases or as the complexity of the project increases, the benefit of coding standards becomes greater. For very large projects, coding standards are all but required.

Because coding standards are so helpful, one would expect most companies to embrace them enthusiastically, but this is not typically the case. The biggest problem with establishing coding standards at a corporation is that initially it can be somewhat time-consuming (read costly) to do so. Not only does a standards committee need to create the standards, but the programmers need some time to adjust to them. This cost, combined with the fact that the coding standards offer no large immediate or short-term tangible benefit, often leads those in charge of finances to question establishing standards in the first place. Furthermore, most schedules are crunched for time as it is. Taking the time to establish and enforce coding standards cuts into this rigorous business schedule without demonstrating any obvious movement toward the primary goal: a finished product. Without producing something management can point to and say, "this is where our money went," or "this is how establishing coding standards helped move us closer to our goal," a movement to create meaningful coding standards often gathers little momentum. However, projects that succeed in having low ongoing maintenance costs do so by looking beyond the immediate results to the long-term benefits of coding standards. They establish the commitment to strive for readable code.

While coding standards are essential for most projects, they are not without their problems. For example, some coders will relentlessly resist attempts to restrict their freedom as coders. In addition, if unchecked, coding standards often develop a life of their own, and the original purpose is lost, leading to a problem that I call *standards for the sake of standards*. Furthermore, standards are all but worthless if they are not enforced, and enforcement of standards can be a difficult task for some companies. Overall, however, having a set of coding standards, even a trivial one, is better than not having one at all. In the remainder of this chapter and in the next, we will discuss some general strategies for creating coding standards, along with some solid techniques to ensure that the standards are followed. A sample coding standards document, designed for use as a template, may be found on-line (see "On-line Materials" in the preface).

Creating Coding Standards

The single most important aspect of creating coding standards is to be sure that they are formally documented. Place the document in an easily accessible location (perhaps in the version-control repository or on a shared network drive). Developers new to the team should be instructed to review them. The creators of the document should periodically review it to be sure it is up to date and announce the updates to the team (an e-mail list is great for this). Perform this review when a new project begins, when new releases of Visual Basic are made, or when new design or implementation techniques are used.

This being said, implicit standards often exist in code prior to explicit documentation. Developers, especially less experienced ones, will sometimes emulate the style and conventions of the existing code in a project, creating something of a standard. Take into account these informal conventions as you document your formal standards.

Second to documentation, it is imperative to created standards in such a way that they serve to help the development process, not hinder it. While this may seem obvious, all too often standards are so restricting that following them makes the programmers uncomfortable and, in the end, damages the quality of their code. Programming is largely a creative, artistic process. When a programmer's artistic freedom is shackled, it affects his ability to do his job. While the standards must strive to provide uniformity in the code, they must also be unobtrusive. Formalizing meaningful standards that help make code more consistent and readable without restricting the artistic freedom of the developers is a difficult task. Moreover, the suitable degree of strictness on one project may not be applicable to another.

For the formal standards of a project to be followed and respected, the developers must accept them. Generally, it is best to allow the lead developers or a committee of developers to create the standards. These individuals work with code day in and day out, and they are usually the most qualified people in an organization to create the standards. Allowing the developers to author their own standards usually makes for a more thorough and applicable document, and it gives the developers an opportunity to design standards with which they are comfortable. To ensure that developers who arrive after the standards are in place are comfortable with them, it is helpful to explain why the standards were designed the way they were. This explanation can be included in the standards documentation itself.

Last, always remember this rule of thumb when creating coding standards: *readability is everything*. Strive toward including only those guidelines that make the code more readable. If you decide to include standards that make the code less readable, be sure there is a good reason.

Scope of Standards

When developing standards, you must consider the scope of the standards you are creating. Should they apply only to this project? To all projects in this department? To all projects in the company? To legacy systems as well as new development? The contents of your standards will depend greatly on the answers to these questions. There are often cases when it is practical to create more than one set of standards, depending on the requirements of the projects in question. For example, since it may be too time-consuming or expensive to bring old code up to new standards, you might be more lenient on legacy code than you would be on new development. This could result in a relatively loose standards document for the legacy system and a more rigorous one for newer code.

In addition, remember that your team's standards are *your* team's standards, and you should not impose them on others who may need access to your code (while most of the code presented in this book follows the conventions defined in this chapter, some explicitly avoids it for just this reason). This is particularly true if you develop compiled libraries for resale or if others otherwise access your source code. For example, if you have a specialized naming convention for public functions, it is unreasonable, and a bit rude, to assume that developers outside your group and unfamiliar with your standards care about them. If your code libraries meet this description, consider omitting the conventions on public functions and named arguments (optional parameters).

Language Standards

At the core of most standards documents are language standards. These are items that are specific to VB coding and include naming conventions, commenting rules, general code construction practices, and readability guidelines. Your complete standards documentation may also include user interface standards (see chapters 6 and 7) and design standards as needed. You might even have documentation standards for both your technical documentation and your end user documentation (see chapter 3).

Since Visual Basic may not be the only language or environment your system is based on, other standards will probably be needed as well. These include HTML standards (this may end up being a subset of your user interface standards) and database standards (e.g., naming conventions for tables, views, stored procedures, etc.). A full discussion of these topics is beyond the scope of this book.

Naming Conventions

Visual Basic's syntax provides the opportunity to create highly readable code, in the spirit of the original BASIC. Simple but efficient naming conventions for all identifiers (variables, constants, functions, subs, properties, types, modules, constants, files, etc.) can leverage the syntactic sugar inherent in the language. By syntactic sugar, I am referring to the English-like keywords and structures in the language for tasks that can be accomplished with less coating. For example, `With`, `While`, `Then`, `ElseIf`, and `Is` are examples of keywords that could be omitted from the language or changed to a less readable variation, without really sacrificing functionality.

Anatomy of a Good Naming Convention

There are several naming conventions available, and the best of them yield more readable code without much effort on the part of the programmer. One of these conventions, the Natural Language Convention, is designed to make VB read as much like English as possible. In fact, the standard states that "most of the work of creating good names is simply figuring out what a nonprogrammer would call something" (Corwin, 1999). This standard provides conventions for modules, functions, procedures, variables, constants, and classes and is based on the following general rules:

- Use the same vocabulary your customer uses.
- Quality should be built into names, not added on after the fact.
- Use underscores to enhance readability.
- Fix bad names now.
- Avoid cryptic names.

The Natural Language Convention relies on common sense in the creation of names. These five loose guidelines can produce very readable names such as `Grade_Point_Average` and `The_Size_Of_The_Object`. The Natural Language Convention is worth reviewing, but ultimately you will probably find it is not quite thorough enough to adopt wholesale. Conventions of this type are ideal if your code is being read by nonprogrammers, but overall, although they are simple, they lack the rigor and elegance desired by many experienced programmers.

In particular, naming conventions need to address each of the following three areas as well.

1. *Scope of the Identifier:* At a glance, it should be trivial to determine if the identifier is local, passed by reference, passed by value, module, global, static, and so on. Being able to find the scope of an identifier from its name makes it much easier to track down scope-related defects, such as the clobbering of global variables or variables passed by reference into a function or sub. If nothing else, global variables, those capable of causing the most headaches, should be clearly marked.

2. *Type of the Identifier:* Knowing the actual Visual Basic type of the identifier (date, string, integer, long, single, Boolean, etc.) is also imperative. For example, simply knowing that a variable is a number is usually not specific enough, since it could be an integer or some type of floating point number. Not distinguishing can lead to rounding errors, overflow problems, and other debugging nightmares. So first, the appropriate data type must be chosen, though it is common to find programmers cutting corners. It is troubling to learn that there are still many programmers who do not know that VB has a currency type and who use doubles for money instead, fighting rounding problems all the way. Be certain all identifiers have the appropriate type, and include that type in their names.

3. *Usage of the Identifier:* Type and usage are very similar, but there is a subtle and important difference. Whereas *type* refers to the VB intrinsic type of the variable (Boolean, long, string, etc.), *usage* refers to how the programmer who declared it intended it to be used (index, count, rate, etc.). Consequently, the same type can have many uses (and, less frequently, more than one type can have the same usage). For example, an integer can serve as an index in a For loop, a relatively fixed total, and a running total, to name a few of its uses. Under certain circumstances, the type long may be used in a similar manner. Clearly identifying the usage of a variable can help fight a common problem: overloading a simple variable, or using the same variable for two entirely different purposes. An example of this is treating the variable Animals first as an index in a loop and then as a running total of animals in another block of code. This practice leads to confusing, bug-prone code, and it can be avoided by clearly indicating the intended usage from the start.

Some naming conventions do not apply these three items or do not apply them all rigorously. The convention I present in the next section, based on Hungarian notation, is very rigorous. The ideas expressed in the remainder of this chapter can be used as a starting point for your own standards.

Hungarian Notation

Hungarian notation gets its name from the homeland of its creator, Charles Simonyi. Identifier names in Hungarian notation consist of a body (with modifiers) and prefixes. While commonly used in the C programming language, the fundamentals of Hungarian notation apply very well to Visual Basic, with a little modification.

Note that there are a few disadvantages to Hungarian notation. First, since it explicitly ties scope and usage to the identifier name, if either changes, so must all occurrences of the identifier. This normally is not too serious an issue, since Visual Basic has a sophisticated find and replace mechanism, making such changes trivial. Furthermore, taking the time to review each appearance of the identifier in the code to see if the proposed change in scope or usage actually makes sense for every occurrence of the identifier is helpful. The second disadvantage with using Hungarian notation in Visual Basic is that a small handful of developers may not be able to learn it or may take a long time doing so. This happens because old habits die hard, developers are stubborn, or they just plain don't get it. This disadvantage really applies to any naming convention and is seldom an issue if the standards are well documented and clearly presented. Finally, some critics claim that Hungarian notation is difficult to read. This is clearly a matter of opinion, and I believe that most people find a well-formed name in Hungarian notation as clear as any other. If the name is not well formed, however, the critics may be correct to a degree, since the Hungarian aspect of such names (i.e., the prefixes) can get in the way and make the situation worse. In short, use good names.

Before we begin our discussion, it is interesting to note that Microsoft includes recommendations for naming conventions in the Books Online. Those conventions are similar to the ones defined in the following sections and are also based on Hungarian notation. However, they have longer abbreviations than the ones defined here and in general are not detailed enough. The biggest issue with them, though, is that Microsoft's own developers do not usually follow them in sample code, indicating that Microsoft does not take them too seriously. They are by no means an industry standard, but you may refer to them while creating your own standards.

Choosing a Good Body

When naming any identifier, it is best to make the body of the name as descriptive as possible and be sure it accurately describes the thing or action it is supposed to represent. The name may consist of several concatenated words; to separate the words, use either mixed case or underscores (strive for fewer than twenty characters). Use underscores when the parts of the body consist entirely of capital letters. I prefer to use all caps only for the bodies of constants—for everything else I use mixed case. For example, WINDOW_SIZE would be a constant, while WindowSize would be a variable. Whatever you decide, be sure to make the body of the name clear and descriptive, so it is easy to read.

When dealing with variables and constants, consider the plurality of your names carefully. Plural entities should have plural names, and singular entities should have singular names. Plural identifiers are most often associated with collections or arrays, as in a collection of Bottles, but individual variables may be plural as well, as in PeopleInLine or DAYS_IN_A_WEEK. We'll visit this again when discussing naming conventions for classes.

You may also consider adding standard modifiers before or after the body, or abbreviations thereof. Body modifiers, like their English-language counterparts, are adjectives. Modifiers describe how the variable is being used and provide some indication as to its relationship to other identifiers. For example, in the body TotalObjectsOnTable, "Total" helps to decipher usage. In NextPersonInLine, "Next" implies the existence of an opposite—"Previous"—as is the case in PreviousPersonInLine. Where appropriate, establish standard prefixes for your common modifiers. This helps keep the length of the identifier in check. In general, make the body of the identifier as long as needed, but no longer. The abbreviation should be clear and readable and, for short modifiers, may be omitted altogether.

Listed in Table 19.1 are some typical base modifiers along with common abbreviations and examples. Note that many modifiers are tightly coupled to

TABLE 19.1 Sample Modifiers and Abbreviations

Modifier	*Abbreviation*	*Example*
Number	Num	NumberOfPeopleInLine (NumOfPeopleInLine)
Current	Cur	CurrentRecord (CurRecord)
Next	Next	NextRecord (NextRecord)
Previous	Prev	PreviousRecord (PrevRecord)
Last	Last	LastRecord (LastRecord)
First	First	FirstRecord (FirstRecord)
Minimum	Min	MinimumTemperature (MinTemperature)
Old	Old	OldCustomerName (OldCustomerName)
New	New	NewCustomerName (NewCustomerName)
Temporary	Temp or Tmp	TemporarySubTotal (TmpSubTotal)

other modifiers, usually as opposites. Note too that it is also common to find the base portion of the body abbreviated. Most VB programmers are familiar with the abbreviation Wnd (for Window), and there are others. Use these abbreviations to help shorten the names of frequently used bodies, but be sure not to sacrifice readability.

When you document your standards, decide to what degree you wish to standardize your identifier bodies and their modifiers and abbreviations, using the suggestions just discussed as a starting point.

Scope Prefixes

Once you fashion the body of the identifier, it is important to identify its scope. By *scope*, I am referring not only to the visibility of the identifier but also to its duration. Not all variables disappear when they fall out of scope—static variables and variables passed by reference, for example, have lifetimes beyond the procedure in which they are defined, even if they are visible only within that procedure. Ordinarily, Hungarian convention tags the identifier with some type of prefix (usually a single letter to avoid making the name unnecessarily long), though it is also acceptable to use a suffix. If you decide to use suffixes, be sure the suffix is separated from the body of the identifier. This can be accomplished with a leading underscore, for example, _m. To make the scope readily apparent from its prefix or suffix, use a letter or abbreviation that resembles the scope, like g or _g for Global.

There are many kinds of scope in Visual Basic, as determined by where the programmer defines the identifier. When establishing standards, it is important to choose which of these scopes matter to your development team. Some programmers, myself included, find it invaluable to know whether a variable is passed by reference or by value, while others find this level of detail overkill. Likewise, some may want to show that an identifier is static. You must also decide whether to differentiate between public class members and private class members, though this is often not an issue because most programmers avoid public members and use public properties to expose private members. User-defined type and enumerated type members have a peculiar "scope," and you may want to include some reference to the type name in the members themselves (more on this later). Last, functions, subs, and properties can be declared with the keywords `Private`, `Public`, and `Friend`. You may find it helpful to differentiate among them, though I find this unnecessary. As you decide what to include in your standards document, bear in mind that in cases where there is potentially some confusion about how a variable is being used, a comment in the code can clarify.

To return briefly to static identifiers, you can differentiate them by means of an additional prefix concatenated to the base scope prefix or by simply using a prefix for static instead of the scope prefix. Most often, static identifiers are variables declared within a function. However, module-level static variables, which are really the same as module-level variables, are also possible. Static functions, which make all variables local to the function static, can also be found. Listed in Table 19.2 are the scopes you will need to address, along with suggested prefixes and suffixes. Your standards should indicate the use of prefixes or suffixes, but not both.

Usage Prefixes

It is generally good practice to include the type in the declaration of all identifiers. This includes not only variables and constants, but also all properties and all functions. Consider mandating this in your standards document. Furthermore, indicating the usage of an identifier, along with its base type, is perhaps even more important than identifying its scope. As with the identification of scope, employing prefixes (or suffixes) to annotate usage is simple and effective. Remembering that you should describe both the type and the usage in one shot, choose your prefixes carefully. You should choose separate prefixes for every intrinsic VB type, paying particular attention to the most commonly used types—strings, Booleans, and integers—since you will be seeing them a lot. You also should create specific prefixes for all of the controls you intend to use, third-party controls included. A complete list of usage prefixes is typically rather long and may require frequent modification of your standards to be sure it is up to date.

Arrays pose a unique problem, since they actually modify a base usage. Note that this is not true of collections, which are a VB intrinsic object type. To indicate that a variable is an array, consider adding an additional prefix (e.g., a) to your usage prefix or suffix.

TABLE 19.2   Sample Scope Prefixes and Suffixes

Scope	Prefix	Suffix
Global	g	_g
Private Module	m	_m
Public Module (should be avoided)	m	_m
Function parameter passed by reference	r	_r
Function parameter passed by value	v	_v
Static Module	st	_st
Static Local	st	_st
Function declared Static	st	_st
User-defined type member	None[†]	None
Local variables	None	None
All others	None	None

[†]You may also prefix or suffix user-defined type members with an abbreviation of the type name.

Table 19.3 lists several usage varieties, along with suggested prefixes and suffixes. This list provides only a small example of some types, and a more complete listing appears in the sample coding standards document referenced in "On-line Materials" in the preface. As with scope, you should decide on usage prefixes or suffixes, but not both. You should then use your usage prefixes or suffixes for every identifier in your code that has a type: variables, constants, functions, properties, controls, and user-defined type members.

Putting It All Together

Once you have established your prefixes or suffixes, give them a test drive by creating several sample names to be sure the standards produce quality identifier names. When using prefixes for both scope and usage, create the full name by concatenating the scope prefix, the usage prefix, and the body of the identifier. For example, a variable passed by reference (prefix: r), of type string (prefix: s), and with the body FirstName would produce the identifier name rsFirstName. Table 19.4 presents several more examples, including the names of constants. I find it easiest to read suffixes with the usage placed before the scope, though I prefer prefixes in the first place. Consider removing extra underscores or other characters used to separate your suffixes from the body— one will suffice. If you are using scope prefixes and usage suffixes (or vice versa), the concatenation rules should be obvious.

There are a couple more issues to consider when reviewing the complete names of your identifiers. First, be certain there is no confusion in the meaning of the name after the prefixes or suffixes have been concatenated. For example,

TABLE 19.3   Sample Usage Prefixes and Suffixes

Usage	Prefix	Suffix
Array	a	_a
Byte	byt	_byt
Boolean	b	_b
Single	sng	_sng
Double	d	_d
Integer	n for relatively fixed values, i for indices	_n or _i
Object	o	_o
Long	l for relatively fixed values, h for handles	_l or _h
Currency	c	_c
Date/Time	dt	_dt
String	s	_s
Variant	vnt	_vnt

TABLE 19.4   Sample Identifier Names

Identifier Name	Description
sFirstName	A string variable with local scope
rsLastName	A string variable passed by reference into a procedure
vsTable	A string variable passed by value into a procedure
avntArgs	An array of variants with local scope
gsCOMMA	A string constant with global scope
mnImages	An integer variable used as a count with module scope
mdEXCHANGE_RATE	A constant double with module scope
rdtDateOfBirth	A date variable passed by reference into procedure
stbBeenHere	A static Boolean variable with local scope
viCurItem	An integer variable used as an index passed by value into a procedure
rasNames	An array of strings passed by reference
mnMAX_AGE	A module-level integer constant used to hold a fixed value

the prefix rs for a local RecordSet or ResultSet might be confused with a string (prefix s) passed by reference (prefix r). Does rsCustomer refer to a customer's name passed by reference or to a RecordSet of customer information? While situations like these may be clarified with a more accurate body for the identifier, it is best to avoid these conflicts by choosing your prefixes carefully. Second, it is important to insist that the identifier names make sense within the context of the code. Names that are technically correct according to the standards may be utterly confusing if presented in the wrong context. For example, the variable vnTotalCost implies an integer used to hold a relatively fixed value that has been passed by value into a subroutine. To then use this variable to count rows in a RecordSet is confusing.

Naming Menus

Menus are really just another type of control and should receive a usage prefix (e.g., mnu) or suffix along with all other controls in your standards document. Since menus are hierarchical, however, it is helpful to show the relationship in the name itself. Typically, this is accomplished by concatenating the child menu's caption onto the name of its parent. Attach the appropriate prefix or suffix for the usage, and you have the complete name. For example, under this standard, the File menu would be called mnuFile. The Exit option under the File menu would be called mnuFileExit. Table 19.5 includes some more examples.

There are a couple of caveats when employing this technique, though. First, the menu names can become quite long. This is especially true if your applications have menus that cascade several layers deep. While deeply buried submenus should be eschewed in the first place, they are sometimes unavoidable. For these long names, consider abbreviations. Second, when a menu option changes parents (a common and simple procedure in VB), its name (and all occurrences of it) must change as well. This can be a real pain, and you may want to use simplified versions of the names until your user interface design is complete.

Naming Modules

Visual Basic has many types of modules from which to choose. Though they have individual iconic representations within the VB project explorer, it is handy to provide a simple prefix to further distinguish one module type from another. The most common prefixes are derived directly from the default file

TABLE 19.5   Sample Menu Names

Menu	*Name*
File|Exit	mnuFileExit
File|New|Customer	mnuFileNewCustomer
Edit|Paste	mnuEditPaste
Help|About	mnuHelpAbout
Reports|Status|By Period	mnuReportsStatusByPeriod
Tools|Language|Hyphenation	mnuToolsLanguageHyphenation

TABLE 19.6   Module Types and Prefixes

Module Type	Prefix	Example
Standard Module	bas	basStartup
Class	cls	clsOrder
User Connection	con	conDatabase
User Control	ctl	ctlFormatBox
Data Environment	dat	datWorkspace
Designer	dsr or des	dsrConnection or desConnection
Form	frm	frmMain
MDI Form	frm	frmDocument
Property Page	pag	pagCustom
Resource File	res	resErrors

extensions that VB generates for you when saving the files and are listed in Table 19.6.

Most of the individual modules also refer to types within VB. That is, you may declare variables to be classes, forms, property pages, designers, and so on, within your code. For this reason, you need to consider naming conventions not only for the modules themselves but also for the variables declared to be of the type the module represents. These types should receive their own usage prefixes or suffixes, as defined with the rest of Visual Basic's types.

Plurality again is a consideration with module names, particularly with class modules. A class often acts as a container or collection of objects or private user-defined type variables, and in this role, it should have a plural name or a singular name describing something that has a plural meaning. Consider, for example, a class called clsDatabaseTable. As we all know, a table is a collection of zero or more rows (clsDatabaseRow). In this example, the name of the class, though not plural itself, implies plurality. Similarly, clsRows implies a collection of rows and makes a poor name for a single row.

Naming Files

Filename conventions are often overlooked by developers, but filenames can lead to headaches if not given sufficient thought. Long filenames, for example, may be shortened to their tilde (~) equivalents when copied by some programs, and this can leave you with two filenames for the same file. Here are five other questions to consider when devising standards for filenames:

1. *Are the Visual Basic default filenames acceptable?* The VB default names consist of whatever you named the module, plus its standard file extension. These extensions are listed in the VB help files, but most developers know them cold. The problems with accepting the default names are that the file-names may be quite long (see next) and the file extension appears in both the file prefix and extension, if you follow the convention just described. This is from the office of redundancy office, and you may wish to omit the prefix.

2. *Are long filenames allowed, or should developers always stick to an 8 x 3 format?* Your answer to this question will depend on whether all aspects of your system support long filenames. On older systems with 16-bit network drivers, filenames not in an 8 x 3 format may be abbreviated by the system, as mentioned earlier. In general, though, it is best to treat filenames like identifier names—make them as long as needed, but no longer. Ultimately, filenames longer than twelve characters or so can become unwieldy.

3. *Are spaces in the filenames allowed?* While Windows is delighted to let you use spaces in your filenames, they are best avoided, for the reasons in the preceding item.

4. *Are any specific prefixes or suffixes required for the files?* You may want to include a standard prefix in your filenames. For example, consider adding information about the project to the filename, perhaps as a very short abbreviation used as a prefix. Be careful with such conventions, though, because when files are shared across multiple projects, project-specific refer-ences can become confusing.

5. *Are there any other restrictions?* You should also consider other restric-tions, such as forbidden characters, a versioning convention used to date or ver-sion the filenames, and any other conventions applicable to your projects' files.

User-Defined and Enumerated Types

The last topic to address when defining naming conventions is standards for types defined by programmers. Visual Basic allows developers to declare both enumerated types and user-defined types within code. Again, you can distinguish the type by using prefixes or (more commonly) suffixes. If suffixes are used, be sure to include a leading underscore as needed for clarity. For enumerated types, consider _enum or _Enum. For user-defined types, try _udt, _type, or _Type.

It is common with enumerated types to include an abbreviated reference to the type name as a prefix for each of the member elements, as in the follow-ing declaration:

```
Public Enum ErrorStatus_enum
    esInformational = 0
    esWarning = 1
    esSevere = 2
End Enum
```

Here the suffix _enum is added to a complete base name ErrorStatus. In addition, each member of the enumeration is prefixed with a shortened, two-letter version of the type name (es). This convention is particularly rewarding if the enumerated type is public and declared in a DLL. The Object Browser in Visual Basic shows the base type, with each of its members as constants, and conveniently enough, they all resemble one another.

With user-defined types, it is less common to include a reference to the type name in the members. Rather, the members are given a unique scope prefix or, more commonly, no scope prefix at all. Usage, however, should be clearly indicated by an appropriate prefix or suffix. Here is an example:

```
Private Type EmployeeInfo_type
    sFirstName as String
    sLastName as String
    dtStartDate as Date
    nAgeInYears as Integer
    cSalary as Currency
End Type
```

As with modules, you must take into account the conventions not only for the types, but also for the variables declared to be of these types. Again, variables of these types should receive their own usage prefixes or suffixes, as defined with the rest of Visual Basic's types. I prefer e for enumerated types and t for user-defined types, as in the following:

```
Dim eErrorSeverity as ErrorStatus_enum
```

and

```
Dim tEmployeeOfTheMonth as EmployeeInfo_type
```

Further Reading

See "Further Reading" section of chapter 20.

Chapter 20
Coding Standards: Part II

Continuing our discussion of coding standards, we will switch gears slightly, in this chapter, to focus on commenting and general code construction standards, as well as general readability guidelines. We'll then discuss how to manage your coding standard document and end with a look at how to enforce the standards you create with code reviews.

Commenting Standards

No standards document can call itself complete without thoroughly addressing comments. In my opinion, comments are the single most important element of computer programming, typically more important than the code itself. A single well-written comment can help make sense out of hundreds of lines of gibberish code. Yet, many programmers simply do not use comments effectively or do not comment code at all. Steve McConnell (1993) presents a concise summarization of why some developers do not comment their code in a humorous section of *Code Complete*. People refuse to write comments for the following reasons:

- They think their code is clearer than it could possibly be.
- They think that other programmers are far more interested in their code than they really are.
- They think other programmers are smarter than they really are.

- They are lazy.
- They are afraid someone else might figure out how their code works.

As harsh as these criticisms may be, they hit home with many coders.

To be fair, while generally very helpful, sometimes comments can be problematic as well. Inaccurate comments are typically worse than no comments, and comments do have a tendency to become inaccurate as code maintenance continues. Some comments merely echo the code exactly, adding no clarification or insight into the code at all, and can be annoying if too prevalent. The bottom line is that a good comment always clarifies the code, while a bad comment may do just the opposite.

This being said, there is no substantial reason not to add good comments to your Visual Basic code, and your standards should both encourage the use of comments and explain the anatomy of a good comment to clarify any confusion. There are three general types of comments: *procedures headers*, which help document a whole module or routine; *revision history comments*, which track changes in the code; and *inline comments*, which provide a running commentary. When creating commenting standards, be sure to address each of these types.

Before continuing our discussion, it is worth pointing out that VB has two ways you can begin a comment: with the keyword REM or with an apostrophe (single quote). It is generally easier to read comments beginning with an apostrophe, and it is actually rare to find programmers still using the REM keyword, which is really a throwback to the old days of BASIC. You may wish to specify one of these two comment indicators in your standards.

Procedure Header Comments

Procedure headers, or flowerboxes, help to explain the purpose of a routine or module and provide other general information about the code. They usually appear at the top of a procedure, before or after the declaration. However, if some of your developers use VB's procedural code view, rather than the full module view, you may find it best to insist that all developers place flowerboxes after the declaration of the procedure. This is because programmers may forget to leave a blank line before the comment, causing the comment to attach to the previous routine and making it invisible when the routine in procedural view is being edited. Placing the flowerbox after the declaration eliminates this problem.

Flowerboxes also provide the opportunity to present some general data about the routine or module. Elements often found in flowerboxes include the following:

- *Name of Module or Routine:* While it may be redundant to identify the name routine right after its declaration, it is sometimes helpful to see the name along with the rest of the comment block.

- *Short Description:* A short description explaining the purpose of the routine is helpful. For functions, it is useful to describe the return value here. Also, consider using this value for the procedure's description in the Procedure Attributes dialog.

- *Long Description:* A detailed description may not be needed, but can sometimes be beneficial when explaining a complicated algorithm.

- *Parameter List:* If the parameters require additional explanation, put it here. It is often advantageous to know what "out" parameters there are in the routine, that is, those parameters that are passed by reference with the intention of returning a value.

- *Author's Name:* This is the name of the individual who originally wrote the routine.

- *Author's Company:* This item is invaluable for projects employing contractors from different companies, but is probably not needed for in-house development.

- *Date:* It is usually helpful to know when the code was originally written.

- *Detailed Notes:* A notes section provides additional space for the developers to elaborate on unusual aspects of the code or anything that might require some additional information.

- *Side Effects:* Side effects, usually in the form of modified global data, should be avoided, but unfortunately are sometimes inevitable. If your function has a side effect or can be affected by a side effect, a clear comment can help to clarify. You may also choose to annotate side effects in the detailed notes section.

- *Revision History Block:* If you track changes in a routine or module, a flowerbox is a good place to gather summaries. (See the section "Revision History Comments" for more information.)

- *Copyright Information:* Many companies have copyright information in all modules, including all the legalese required to protect the company's interests.

- *Anything Else That Seems Appropriate:* There may be project-specific information, such as tracking numbers and the like, to add to the flowerbox as well.

When defining your flowerbox templates, decide which of the items in this list are most applicable to your project. Also, remember that depending on the level of detail you consider, three types of flowerboxes are possible: those at the module level, those for procedures and subs, and those for properties. Because of this, it is possible to have three separate templates, or even more, that differ in level of detail. For example, you will probably want to include copyright information only in the flowerbox for the whole module, since repeating the notice for each procedure and property is overkill.

The format of the template can impact its readability greatly. Consider beginning and ending the flowerbox with a thin border created with hyphens or some other character and use these lines to separate major portions of the flowerbox as needed. This border should define the maximum width of the flowerbox, so be sure it is not so wide that programmers will have to use horizontal scrolling all of the time to read the contents of the flowerbox. The text in the comment will be easiest to read if it is contained within the boundary. To create a more boxlike flowerbox, add some kind of end marker to the end of each line, right justified. Usually a single quote will do fine, for symmetry, and leave a space before it so the text does not run into the marker.

I normally do not recommend interfering with the way developers set up their VB editor, since to many this is a highly personal aspect of coding. However, those developers using very small fonts and those with large monitors may have a tendency to create flowerboxes (and code in general) that stretch far beyond the horizontal boundary of the page as it appears on smaller monitors or in a larger font. This causes other developers to scroll to read and maintain the code, and many developers find this annoying. Simple guidelines can prevent this.

When completing the contents of the flowerbox, consider labeling the sections and indenting their values consistently. Set up the indented sections of the flowerbox so that the default tab settings your team uses fall in the appropriate spots. It is annoying to tab to a particular spot just to find the cursor off by one character in the line above and the line below. Last, avoid capital letters in large blocks of text because they are more difficult to read and give the appearance of shouting. Developers should use capital letters for added emphasis when needed, however.

In Figure 20.1 is a sample flowerbox. It is simple and efficient and can serve as a model. While it would clearly stand out in code, it is not too loud—the decorative characters are thin and simple. Fields are clearly labeled, and the field values have wrapping text that indents appropriately. Note that the two revision history line items would not be part of the template (nor would the sample field values), but are provided here to show the overall appearance of the flowerbox.

Revision History Comments

On large projects, projects with long development cycles, and projects with changing feature sets, a clear and accurate record of revisions is indispensable. This revision history can include any level of detail you desire, but you want to be sure the programmers spend more time coding than they do completing

```
'-------------------------------------------------------------'
'  Procedure:    TestProcedure                                '
'  Description: In this field, enter a brief description of    '
'               what the routine is supposed to do.           '
'  Parameters:  Describe the parameters here, along with their '
'               types. Also indicate any out parameters.      '
'  Author:      Dan Petit                                     '
'  Company:     My Company, Inc.                              '
'  Date:        XX/XX/XXXX (today's date, Y2K compliant)      '
'  Notes:       Additional notes about the routine go here. Use '
'               as much space as needed, but be sure you are  '
'               not simply repeating the code.                '
'-------------------------------------------------------------'
'  Revision History:                                          '
'  Name:        Date:      Description Of Changes:            '
'  ---------    --------   ----------------------------------- '
'  Dan Petit    XX/XX/XXXX A description of the revision goes  '
'                          here.                              '
'  Dan Petit    XX/XX/XXXX Another revision history comment.  '
'-------------------------------------------------------------'
```

FIGURE 20.1   Sample Procedure Header

revision history comments. Items to consider including in your revision histories are as follows:

- Name or initials of the programmer
- Date of revision
- General description of what was changed
- Purpose for the revision, perhaps including a tracking number for a bug report or change request form
- A brief note about the scope of the change

You can place revision history comments throughout the code, as inline comments (see next section), thus serving to identify the exact lines changed. However, in addition to (or instead of) these inline comments, I recommend placing a summary in the flowerbox for the procedure changed and/or for the whole module (see Figure 20.1). Placement here allows developers to identify what has been changed in the code and by whom. They can do so at a glance, without having to search the code line by line.

There is one other important issue to weigh. Although it is simple to add a revision history comment, in the heat of the coding moment, many coders forget, which results in an incomplete revision history. In some cases, the impact on the history is minimal. However, in cases in which the incremental nature of the history is important to understanding the individual elements, the effect can be more severe, rendering subsequent comments less effective. Version control tools that provide a visual comparison of two versions of the code can be used to track these instances and find those coders with memory lapses. Alternatively, use a stiff rap on the knuckles with a wooden ruler (just kidding).

In addition, some version control tools offer automatic keyword expansion for specific types of files. You simply embed keywords into your source code (inside of comments) and the tool replaces them with the checkin comments when you check in the code. You can then use the source code control tool's commenting and labeling functions to maintain your revision history.

Inline Comments

The last of the three types of comments are inline comments. These refer to any other comments placed in the code, in the approximate location of the actual lines of code on which they are elaborating. An inline comment may be placed on the same line as the code it describes, or it can go on the line immediately above. Avoid long end-of-line comments that cause the code to scroll horizontally. Rather, push them to the line above for enhanced readability.

When dealing with descriptive comments, some coders prefer to add inline comments first, before the actual code, to give them a clear overview of the routine they are coding. This is a useful technique because when the code is finished, the comments remain. Along with well-named identifiers, the whole process leads to self-documenting code. The only issue with this is that having a one-to-one relationship between lines of comments and lines of code can be overkill. This is especially true if the comments merely echo the code, as mentioned earlier, or worse yet, if they are inaccurate (after all, who is going to maintain *both* code and all of those comments when making changes). You may want to point out such practices in your standards document, with this caveat as well. The bottom line is to insist that the comments are good comments, not just filler.

Besides elaboration on the code, inline comments can also be used as markers to indicate unfinished sections of code (to dos) or the code involved in a revision. It is common to see large blocks of code with begin and end markers before and after, along with a comment intended for the whole block. It is helpful to tag these markers with the initials of the programmer and the date for easy reference.

Last, it is not unusual to find old code commented out, even in large blocks. In fact, this is a helpful debugging technique, since it allows programmers to try different versions of the code as they work through a problem. In addition, because of constantly shifting user requirements, a programmer may not be very confident about whether a change made will last very long, and leaving the old version commented out makes restoration simpler. However, large blocks of code that have been commented out for some time can hinder the readability of a program. I recommend including in your standards document instructions to delete commented-out blocks of code that have become stale, especially at major project intervals, like a new release of code.

Code Construction Standards

Programming styles are like opinions: everybody has one. In no other aspect of programming is style more individualized than the body of a routine—the very bowels of the code. With as many styles as there are coders, some uniformity, defined by coding standards, is in order. However, care must be taken to allow some breathing room for the coders.

Because of this variety, this section of your standards document is the one most likely to raise eyebrows and stir opinions. Here are ten suggestions of things to consider.

1. Use of `Option Explicit`
2. Use of "magic" numbers
3. Use of string literals
4. Use of `GoTos`
5. Use of archaic language elements
6. Implicit versus explicit Boolean comparisons
7. Variables after `Next` statements
8. Multiple variable and constant declarations on one line
9. Use of single-line `If/Then` constructs
10. Use of type declaration characters

Although I have an opinion on each of the topics, in most cases there is no cut-and-dry right or wrong practice, and I provide these merely as points to consider. They are certainly worthy of discussion by your standards creation team, even if the team makes no formal decisions on them. Let's look at each of these in more detail.

Use of `Option Explicit`

It seems that every book that has ever been written about VB has preached the virtues of the `Option Explicit` setting, so why is it programmers still do not use it? Do the future VB authors of the world a favor and require use of `Option Explicit` in your standards.

Use of "Magic" Numbers

A magic number is any hard-coded literal number in your program. Usually these numbers actually have some significant meaning and should be given a good name (via a constant). For example, nDAYS_IN_A_WEEK is a lot more meaningful than a "7" by itself in code. Using well-named constants for magic numbers not only makes the code more readable, but also makes maintenance easier, since if the number changes, only the constant declaration, not every occurrence of the number, has to change. However, the "no magic number" rule can be applied to the level of absurdity. For instance, having a different constant for every array index starting from one or zero is overkill, since the index name and the context make the number's meaning obvious. In your standards, decide on the degree to which you will allow magic numbers. A good rule of thumb is that if the same number appears in more than one place with the same meaning, make it a constant.

Use of String Literals

String literals are like magic numbers in that they may have some significant meaning that is not obvious from the literal alone. For this reason, consider making them constants. String literals usually fall into two categories: verbiage to display in a user interface (message boxes, captions, etc.) and internal data (fixed keys in collection or default data to write to a database, for example). I am more inclined to recommend using constants for the latter group, since they can benefit most from it. Besides, if you are not putting your verbiage into a string table in a resource file or database, there really is no other option besides hard-coded strings. Remember that the string properties you set on controls and forms at design time (like the caption) count as string literals.

Use of GoTos

Rather than present yet another religious argument over whether or not GoTos should be used in code, let me just restate the main reason for having coding standards in the first place: to make code more readable. If the use of GoTos by the coders on your project makes the code less readable (and GoTos can do this easily), simply do not use them. You may decide to take a firmer stance one way or the other in your formal standards, but this will likely depend on the opinions of the developers on your project. In my experience, it is best allow the use of GoTos only in error-trapping syntax and to make error trapping mandatory in every function that might fail. Also, don't forget about the Resume command, which can help direct the code to labels marking cleanup blocks. When companies create standards, use of GoTos is always one of the most heatedly debated topics.

Use of Archaic Language Elements

Visual Basic still supports some archaic language elements, throwbacks to the earliest version of BASIC. These include some keywords, like GoSub, Return, and Rem, and some general programming elements, such as line numbers. Visual Basic is likely to continue to support these elements for backward compatibility, but it is unlikely that Microsoft will expand on them. They are seldom used in newer code and are essentially dead. Consider the degree to which your standards will allow using these elements. While you may not want to convert existing code, you should probably discourage their use in new development.

Implicit versus Explicit Boolean Comparisons

When writing comparisons for If/Then statements or other conditional constructs, the net result is always something that is either true or false. Always. Therefore, it is redundant to test your expression against the Boolean constants True or False explicitly. Rather, try rewording the expression so that the comparison is implicit. For example, consider using:

```
If nTotal-iTest > nThreshold Then
    DoSomething
End If
```

instead of:

```
If (nTotal-iTest > nThreshold) = True Then
    DoSomething
End If
```

When a comparison to false is needed, take the converse of the entire expression by placing the keyword Not in front of it. A typical expression like this:

```
If (nTotal-iTest > nThreshold) = False Then
    DoSomething
End If
```

then becomes:

```
If Not (nTotal-iTest > nThreshold) Then
    DoSomething
End If
```

The second expression is a bit more readable, and it may be slightly faster in a tight loop. On the whole, either approach is acceptable, but it is often helpful to spell out the preference in a standards document to make the code as consistent as possible.

Variables after Next Statements

I have heard a rumor from several sources that omitting the variable after the Next keyword when ending a loop makes the code run faster. Despite my best efforts, I have not been able to substantiate this rumor, and in fact, my own research with nested loops yields the opposite result. One thing is certain, though: omitting the Next variable makes the code less readable. I suggest requiring variables with Next statements and forbidding multiple Next variables on one line. The expression:

```
For iIndex1 = 1 To 100
    For iIndex2 = 2 To 200
        For iIndex3 = 3 To 300
            DoSomething
        Next
Next iIndex2, iIndex1
```

becomes:

```
For iIndex1 = 1 To 100
    For iIndex2 = 2 To 200
        For iIndex3 = 3 To 300
            DoSomething
        Next iIndex3
    Next iIndex2
Next iIndex1
```

If you feel compelled to omit the Next variables, at least add references to them as comments, as in the following example:

```
For iIndex1 = 1 To 100
    For iIndex2 = 2 To 200
        For iIndex3 = 3 To 300
            DoSomething
        Next 'iIndex3
    Next 'iIndex2
Next 'iIndex1
```

Multiple Variables and Constant Declarations on One Line

Like most of the issues in this list, this one has two sides. Physically grouping related variables or constants by declaring them on the same line helps clarify the code by providing a visual cue for the relationship. This in turn improves readability. However, it is just as easy to declare variables that are not related on one line as well. What is worse, though, is that unless the declaration is complete, Visual Basic makes the variables variants, leading to hard-to-find bugs. For example, in the following declaration, nTotalPeople is actually a variant, while only nTotalWomen is an integer:

```
Private nTotalPeople, nTotalWomen as Integer
```

The correct version is as follows:

```
Private nTotalPeople as Integer, nTotalWomen as Integer
```

At a glance, the first version looks correct and, under most circumstances, will behave as intended. But not always. The second is more clearly and accurately defined. However, perhaps the best approach is to separate the declarations and list them one per line, with inline comments to describe the relationship between them. This approach provides the best of both worlds, as in the following example:

```
' Variables to hold head counts
Private nTotalPeople as Integer
Private nTotalWomen as Integer
```

The trade-off here is of course clarity for brevity. Declaring every variable on a different line consumes more space. However, the benefit of the gained clarity typically far outweighs the damage caused by a few extras lines.

Use of Single-Line If/Then Constructs

Some developers prefer single-line If/Then constructs for one statement Then clauses, while others find them a bit distracting. There is no noticeable difference in performance, so stick with the more readable format.

Use of Type Declaration Characters

Another one of the more archaic language elements is the use of type declaration characters as abbreviations of the full type names when defining variables and functions. Unlike some of the other relics, this one seems to have stuck around. API declarations in particular seem to favor this approach. Though they do shorten the code slightly, before you decide whether to allow developers to declare variables with these abbreviations, consider the following:

◆ Not all of Visual Basic's intrinsic types have abbreviations (there is none for Boolean, for example). This means that if you allow type declaration characters, you will also have to allow traditional declarations, making for an inconsistency.

◆ Some type declaration characters are a bit obscure (an "@" for the currency type? Come on, Microsoft, really!) and will be difficult to remember. The full type names are easier to read.

Readability Standards

Whereas code construction standards refer to the view of code from the trenches, readability standards represent the view from about 150 feet. Instead of line-by-line specifics, these standards deal with the overall flow and appearance of blocks of code, whole routines, and even whole modules. The visual appearance of code can greatly influence its readability. Psychologically, things that are presented together visually can be grouped (chunked), simplifying the structure of complicated code. If items in code are supposed to have some relationship, this relationship can be made clearer with visual association.

Formatting is at the heart of making source code maintainable. A lack of rigorously applied formatting can render even the most well-designed routines unreadable. No matter how clever the naming conventions or how prevalent the comments, bad formatting can ruin it all. Formatting code includes indenting and outdenting block structures, using white space appropriately, and thinking carefully about odd-sized lines of code and function lengths.

Indenting Block Structures

Most programmers are accustomed to formatting their code in some way, and the most common technique is recursive indentation of block structures. Furthermore, most programmers even agree as to what defines a block structure. Yet, code from two people with the same basic understanding of indentation can look entirely different. One of the causes of this discrepancy is a difference in the number of spaces used when indenting. Some programmers always use three spaces, some stick with the default of four spaces, and others use a different value. Still others mix and match the number of spaces, depending on the context. They may indent a `Case` statement by one space from the `Select` statement it belongs to, but indent the lines following an `If/Then` statement by three spaces. All find their own code readable, but will often reformat someone else's code when working on it. On a project where everyone edits everyone else's code, this leads to a great deal of formatting and reformatting.

This busywork is needless if the appropriate standards are in place, but it means all coders must accept a few compromises to meet on middle ground. Decide on one length for tabs and stick to that length. Multiple tab widths wreak havoc with VB's automatic indenting and outdenting features and are more difficult to standardize. Once you have a defined tab width, decide which keywords begin and end block structures. Summarize your findings in a simple table, like Table 20.1 (we'll discuss the white space columns of this table later). Lastly, consider whether you want to put the keyword As in a particular column when defining variables and constants. Aligning the types sometimes makes the code easier to read, but pulls the type away horizontally from the variable for short identifier names.

Inline comments should be indented along with the code they describe. However, flowerboxes and other major sections of comments are more readable if they remain against the left margin.

Use of White Space

When logically related chunks of code are physically separated by white space (a blank line), the individual chunks stand out visually, thus making the code

TABLE 20.1 Formatting Rules

Block Structure	Begins Block	Ends Block	White Space	White Space
Keyword	Indent next line by	Outdent this line by	Before	After
#Else	1	1	No	No
#ElseIf	1	1	No	No
#End If	N/A	1	No	Yes
#If	1	N/A	Yes	No
Case	1	1	No	No
Do	1	N/A	Yes	No
Else	1	1	No	No
ElseIf	1	1	No	No
End Property/Sub/Function/Enum/Type	1	N/A	No	Yes
End Select	N/A	2	No	Yes
End With	N/A	1	No	No
End If	N/A	1	No	No
For	1	N/A	No	No
If	1	N/A	No	No
Loop	N/A	1	No	Yes
Next	N/A	1	No	No
Property/Sub/Function/Enum/Type	1	N/A	Yes	No
Select Case	2	N/A	Yes	No
Wend	N/A	1	No	Yes
While	1	N/A	Yes	No
With	1	N/A	No	No

easier to comprehend. The simplest way to standardize the use of white space is to associate it with the keywords defining the block structures. In addition to listing the block structures and indentation rules, Table 20.1 shows suggestions for the addition of white space for each block structure keyword. In practice, larger blocks (whole routines, large loops, and cases) need white space before and after the block, but you may wish to define other instances as well. To add emphasis to a particularly important block of code, use more white space, but be aware that after two or three blank lines, the extra white space is redundant and may actually hinder readability. In your standards document, consider adding guidelines for instances where white space is useful.

Long Lines of Code

Depending on the font size of the editor and the resolution of the monitor, it is typical to find one logical line of code that cannot fit on one physical line and still remain entirely visible while editing. Since horizontal scrolling is best avoided, line continuation characters invariably appear in the code. The problem becomes even more complicated as many developers with different monitors and different tastes in fonts are added to the picture. Overall, long lines damage the readability of code, and line continuation characters help only a little. The best bet for making long lines of code more readable is to avoid them in the first place. Here are some suggestions for keeping line length under control:

- Always include just one thought per line. Avoid multiple statements on one line, single-line If/Then structures, and multiple declarations on one line.

- When concatenating strings, break up the concatenation across multiple lines whenever possible. This may have a minor effect on performance, but generally improves readability greatly.

- Like strings, break down complicated mathematical expressions into smaller subexpressions that fit comfortably on one line.

Unfortunately, the reality of the matter is that even if you try these suggestions, you are still likely to run into instances where the line is simply too long, and breaking it apart is not practical. I find this to be true especially of long parameter lists for functions and subs, and I prefer to split them out with one parameter per line whenever possible. Because you are likely to encounter long lines in spite of your best efforts, consider adding a few simple guidelines to your standards to address how to handle line continuation characters. Be sure to include both line indentation and maximum line length guidelines.

Indentation

You'll probably want to indent continued lines to distinguish them from normal lines. Consider indenting all continued lines in a group by one tab, as in the following example:

```
Call LotsOfParams(Param1, Param2, Param3, _
    Param4, Param5, Param6, Param7, Param8, _
    Param9, Param10)
```

With procedure declarations, try placing one or two parameters per line, and line them up as much as possible:

```
Private Sub LotsOfParams(rnParam1 as Integer, rlParam2 as Long, _
                rnParam3 as Integer, rlParam4 as Long, _
                rnParam5 as Integer, rlParam6 as Long, _
                rnParam7 as Integer, rlParam8 as Long, _
                rnParam9 as Integer, rlParam0 as Long)
```

Maximum Length

Because of the variety of fonts and monitors that is typical in a group of developers, you may want to place a maximum line length on your code (e.g., 80 or 100 characters) to help keep things consistent.

Function Length

Long functions can be as difficult to read as long lines of code. In general, keep function lengths in check. Some sources provide statistical limits for practical functions, but I believe it is truly a matter of taste and can vary from situation to situation. Common sense is the best standard in these cases. Rather than provide a hard-and-fast limit to the number of lines in a function, concentrate on the following in your standards:

- Longer functions are generally difficult to follow. This being said, shorter functions that exist only because a longer function has been broken apart are even harder to read. Do not break apart functions artificially.

- Longer functions generally have weaker cohesion. *Cohesion* is the ability of a function to stick together. A routine that is strongly cohesive does one thing and does it well. While it's possible for a long function to do one task, in general it is an indication that the code is beginning to become less cohesive.

- Too many short functions can affect performance. This is sometimes difficult to judge, but calling several short functions, especially ones with lots of parameters, can make an application slower, since all of that information has to be passed to the stack repeatedly. If it makes sense to combine two similar routines to aid performance, do so. Typically, though, the end solution is less readable, and this is likely to be a difficult trade-off.

Project and Company Standards

The language standards you create from the guidelines in the last section and from the previous chapter are likely to comprise the bulk if not all of your standards document. By design, those suggestions are generic and can be applied to all projects equally well. Furthermore, they concentrate primarily on the particulars of Visual Basic code. Nevertheless, you should also consider providing standards that apply to your project (as opposed to other projects) and even standards for the whole company. There are many types of things to include in this section, and the following five samples are merely suggestions.

1. *Third-Party Controls:* List the acceptable third-party controls your developers may use. Limiting the variety allows companies to keep better track of the licenses that are typically required and helps standardize applications to provide a uniform look and feel.

2. *Design Standards:* If your programs fit into some large-scale system architecture, you will need to document the entire system and fully describe the hooks to which additional applications are supposed to attach. A summarization of this design can be put into your standards document. The summarization may be quite brief, referring the reader to other documentation, such as, "All classes must implement the ICommon interface as described in (cross-reference)." Note however that it is possible to take this direction too far. Coding standards should not dictate application design, except on the highest of levels.

3. *Data Access:* Visual Basic offers several different data access methods, from text and binary flat files to advanced database access via ODBC and OLE DB. With all of the different data access methods out there, you will probably wish to standardize as much as possible. For example, you may insist that all new database coding use ADO as the object set for access. Or perhaps you do not yet trust ADO and want to stick with more proven technologies, like DAO or RDO. You may even want to allow any type of data access and to provide rough guidelines for using each.

4. *Dictionary of Terms:* If you are writing software with a very business-specific vocabulary, you will want to standardize the names of common business entities and their abbreviations. This will ensure that different coders refer to the same entity in the same way throughout the code.

5. *Coding Habits:* There are many nuances of coding in VB whose explanations are also likely candidates for standardization. Consider adding the following to your standards document:

- To prevent performance problems, always explicitly close RecordSets and databases and set them to nothing.
- Explicitly unload all forms and set all object references to `Nothing` when finished with them.
- Always use error trapping.

Before we conclude our discussion of coding standards, I would like to provide one final caveat. You may be tempted to include any number of items in your coding standards document that should really be omitted. Remember that the goal of the standards document is to provide guidelines for coding in Visual Basic, not to teach Visual Basic syntax. Avoid prolonged discussions of topics programmers should already know; this will make a more consistent (and shorter) document. If you are concerned about the level of expertise of your developers, provide training materials. You may even create a separate company-sponsored handbook for an introduction. Alternatively, suggest (or even require) specific readings about programming. For example, Steve McConnell's *Code Complete* (1993) is an outstanding source for polishing the skills of all coders.

Alternatively, provide two versions of your standards document, being certain to keep both up to date. For the first, provide all of the detail and explanation you would like, including notes on "the way we do things around here." This can be read by new employees and those unfamiliar with your standards. For the second, create an abbreviated version of your standards document to be used as a handy reference. You may want to make this a full-blown document, or you may create a simple "cheat sheet," including only those items that may require more frequent consultation.

Changing Coding Standards

Once you have a completed standards document, you will need to provide a mechanism for amending it. You should strive to make the standards document as stable as possible. Guidelines that change frequently are usually ignored, since the followers lose faith in the designers of the guidelines. Sometimes, however, amendments need to be made.

To help ensure that your standards are stable, do not invite an open debate every time there is a question about standards. Defer these to a standards committee for discussion. New suggestions should not be ignored, but they should not be given such immediate attention as to weaken the overall usefulness of the standards. The committee (often the same one that created the standards) can discuss and amend the standards document as needed.

Major changes to the standards document should be difficult to make in your maintenance mechanism. However, minor changes, such as the addition of a new usage prefix, should be approved more easily, since they will have less of an impact on the coders. Most important, though, whenever a change to the standards is made, be sure to inform the programmers.

Enforcing Coding Standards

Unfortunately, many companies pay a lot of lip service to programming standards. They openly agree that coding standards are important and may even create and document them. In the end, though, many show an utter lack of commitment to them and provide no enforcement mechanisms. Even with those who do, pressing deadlines often cause them to cut corners, and coding standards are one of the first things to go. Eventually, the standards are completely forgotten, and after a period of time the code looks like the standards never existed. If this happens, all of the time and energy spent creating and maintaining the standards in the past were wasted. This does not mean that all code must always be 100 percent up to standards for the standards to be effective. It is unrealistic, if not impossible, to expect that to happen. It does mean that measures must be in place to ensure that the code always stays at some acceptable level. Specific procedures can come into play when the standards fall below that level.

Since coding standards are all but worthless if they are not enforced, this section presents enforcement techniques. Remembering that coding standards are not a means unto themselves, I have presented methods here that are as simple as possible.

Code Reviews

There are several techniques to ensure that the standards an organization has defined are followed, but the most straightforward is the code review. *Code reviews* are simply regularly executed checks of the source code. They are best carried out by a small group of individuals who have been instructed on how to find violations in the code. The reviewers may themselves be coders, and, in fact, rotating reviewing duty among members of a team is often productive, since everyone gets to be both a reviewer and a reviewee. Alternating this duty also helps everyone become more familiar with everyone else's code and provides a chance to become more familiar with the company's standards.

Reviews also provide an opportunity to perform a gut-check on the state of the code. Having a second (and third and fourth) set of eyes examine code is always a good idea, and the reviews act as a quality assurance technique (McConnell, 1993).

Deciding on how to run your code reviews can be a complicated process, though. You can take one extreme and have very formal reviews, with clearly defined roles (moderator, secretary, etc.) for all programmers who attend the meeting. Alternatively, you can choose the other extreme of a more informal approach, treating the review session as a type of group therapy. Overall, it is best to make your review mechanism as formal as needed, but to avoid going overboard. The code review process represents a proactive manifestation of the commitment to more readable code discussed at the beginning of the last chapter. It should be as pleasant and simple an undertaking as possible. The process should be a positive experience for all involved.

You may opt to allow the programmers to polish their code for the review before the review takes place. It can be frustrating for a programmer to be criticized on a work in progress. If it is not practical to review all of the code, when the review begins, pick some of the reviewee's code at random from a pool of code (source code control tools facilitate this tremendously). Have at least a semipublic review session, with the reviewers and the reviewees in attendance. Your reviewers then examine the code for violations, annotating them for the programmers to correct. The programmers eventually address the problems, and the code gets re-reviewed to be sure the violations have indeed been fixed. Depending on the schedule and the number of programmers, sometimes it is helpful to have a completely public review session. Here all programmers attend the review and examine someone's code together, with the premise that everyone can learn from the mistakes that are found.

No matter how you decide to run your reviews, it is important to schedule them regularly (weekly to begin with) and ensure they have a clearly defined agenda. Some standards violations may not be as serious as others, and the agenda the reviewers follow should clearly reflect this discrepancy. To ensure that the reviewers actually have some authority, incentives may be presented to programmers who consistently do well at reviews and perhaps disciplinary measures can be established for those who do not. Establishing these reward and punishment guidelines can be a real test of the company's commitment to the process, though, and the whole process needs to be handled carefully to avoid the appearance of heavy-handed management.

Although a formal review process is usually successful when carried out faithfully, there are some obvious problems with it as well. First, no matter how much the reviewers may try to be objective, sometimes programmers may take the comments of the reviewer as personal attacks. This is clearly counterproductive and should be addressed as soon as it arises. Second, because of human error, reviewers may miss violations in the code. Third, code reviews may be time-consuming, since not only do the reviewers have to spend the time doing the review, but often the programmer whose code is being reviewed has to revisit the same code. This code may actually function correctly, even if it is not up to standards. These second visits take more time and actually may increase the opportunity for bugs to enter the code. Ideally, the whole process would be better if the code were written up to standards in the first place.

Coding up to Standard

In the end, it is less time-consuming to write code up to standards from the start than it is to try to bring code up to standards after the fact. To accomplish this, coders must develop programming habits that are consistent with the coding standards and apply them to every line of code written. Old habits may be difficult to break, though, and some coders may need some assistance. Luckily, there are programming tools available to help ensure that coding standards are followed.

These tools provide a consistent, neutral, objective view of the code. My own product, Standards Master, is specifically designed to help keep code up to standards while the programmer is coding. A demo copy is available on-line (see "On-line Materials" in the preface). It is an add-in, appearing as a dockable tool window from within VB, so the programmer always has access to it. Standards Master is extremely configurable, allowing you to check most of the elements of coding practice discussed in this book. In fact, it also serves as a handy reference for many common standards, allowing programmers to review them on-line.

While coding, programmers can activate Standards Master, and it will generate a list of standards violations and provide suggestions on how to fix the errors. In some cases, it can automatically fix the errors it finds. In addition, it provides commenting functions for creating uniform flowerboxes, revision histories, and inline comments. Standards Master also includes an automatic formatter that inserts white space and indents code according to the block structures you define.

Your reviewers can use Standards Master during code review sessions to decrease the time of the review. However, tools like Standards Master are not designed to replace the traditional code review, though they do simplify the process greatly. Programmers with access to the tool can see their violations immediately. Reviewers can use it to check the code more quickly, thus saving time. Formal reviews that had to take place weekly may now become biweekly or even monthly.

Further Reading

Deborah Kurata, *Doing Objects in Microsoft Visual Basic 5.0* (1997).   While this book's discussion of coding standards (naming conventions, commenting, error handling, etc.) is not detailed enough for my tastes, it does provide a good overview to help get you started on the contents of your standards document.

Steve McConnell's *Code Complete* (1993).   Chapter 9 provides an excellent summary of the creation of good names for variables. The author also discusses the role of code reviews in the quality assurance process in chapter 24.

Walker Royce, *Software Project Management* (1998).   This book provides a comprehensive assessment of the poor state of software development, stressing the need for standards and metrics (see especially appendix A).

Chapter 21

Distribution of Software

Distributing software has often been as difficult as creating it. Complex interfile dependencies, obscure but required DLLs, and version conflicts plague even the best Windows applications. This chapter enumerates various methods for moving Visual Basic programs into production. We'll start with an overview of planning your installation strategy, then move onto specific techniques for realizing the rollout.

When it comes to installing your software, you should expect your users to need all the help they can get. More often than not, you will have to create a setup program. In this chapter, we'll also look at Visual Basic's setup toolkit in detail, along with third-party tools to make the job easier.

It is common for a company to have thousands of computers, all with different hardware and software. Managing existing software, ensuring that specific usage guidelines are not broken, and installing new software is the job of tools like SMS and login scripts. In other instances many of your company's computers may need to be exactly the same (such as in a customer service department). In such cases, you have an important edge, because supporting a rollout for one known platform is much easier than supporting one for a mix of computers. Cloning entire computers may be valuable for you. We'll look at both SMS and cloning in this chapter.

Last, if your application requires frequent updates, you may want to develop a home-grown updater application that ensures that the applications on the end users' computers are always kept current. We'll discuss patches and updater applications at the end of this chapter.

Planning the Rollout

So you are finally finished with that new application—or are you? An application is nothing without an end user, so you have to roll out the application to really be finished. Unfortunately, under heavy schedule pressure, many developers forget all about setting aside enough time to plan, test, and implement a rollout strategy. For them, the completion date is that day on which the last line of code is written, and that's where their focus stays. Nothing could be further from the truth, and creating a practical rollout strategy (including plans for initial installations and subsequent updates) as early in the process as possible is critical. One way to ensure you are ready to roll out your software on its due date is to make testing installations of your software part of your iterative quality assurance plan, as discussed in chapter 18.

Things to Consider

Several parameters can impact your rollout plan, and it helps to have a good idea of exactly what you are dealing with from the start. As you formulate your rollout strategy, consider the following:

1. Is the application for internal company use only, or is it shrink-wrapped software to send to unknown customers? You will have more flexibility when it comes to installing and maintaining internally used software.

2. If it is for internal use, how many computers need the software? The scope of the rollout is important. Obviously, distributing software to 10,000 computers is more complicated than installing it on one.

3. Other than end-user PCs, are there other computers that need software? Does your application require application or database servers? How many? How will these be installed? Do you have Microsoft Transaction Server (MTS) components?

4. Are there any special considerations about the architecture that could affect the rollout? Do certain pieces need to be in place before others?

5. What are the system requirements for all computers that will get the software? If hardware upgrades are required, when will they take place?

6. Does your application have to go through any external certification processes before going live? These include such things as Y2K testing and getting certified for the Win95/98/NT logo? If so, how will these processes affect your rollout plan?

Careful consideration of these questions from the start can help prevent rollout troubles down the road. No matter what your long-time rollout plan may be, software distribution begins with the compilation of the applications. For this, you will need a solid process.

The Buildmaster Process

Compiling and building executables can be real chores, especially for larger projects. Add in complications like code that will not compile and DLL version conflicts, and the process becomes a nightmare. To help with these issues, I strongly encourage using what I call a "buildmaster" process, which involves both a dedicated build computer and an individual who is responsible for overseeing the build process. The buildmaster concept centers on having a "clean" environment for building the code and a snag-free process for correcting the issues that inevitably occur.

The buildmaster computer is a single computer used solely for compiling and distributing your software. This PC has Visual Basic, Visual Source Safe (or whatever your version control tool is), and all supporting software (third-party OCXes, etc.) installed on it, but nothing extra. It should be kept as clean as possible and really should not be used for any purpose other than building code. Although the source code for your project lives on this PC, no changes to the code should be made from here. Rather, developers should make code changes on their own PCs and check the changes into the version control tool, which is then used to retrieve the latest pinned version on the buildmaster PC for compilation. Usually changed code must go through some review (to verify that it is up to standard) and formal pinning process (to indicate that the version is the latest "good" version). These steps should be completed before attempting to create the build.

Using a buildmaster PC has a number of important benefits. First, since all of your software resides in one place, setting version compatibility options is more reliable, and you won't have to worry about incorrect GUIDs causing missing references in your project files. A buildmaster also helps avoid conflicts with other software, since only software that is directly related to building your application resides on this PC. Last, a buildmaster PC offers a consistent source platform for creating setup programs.

The buildmaster individual is responsible for babysitting the buildmaster PC. When the time comes, she also performs the actual builds (often by means of a build script, discussed later). This individual must thoroughly understand the application's dependencies and know when to recompile all code or just specific projects. Furthermore, the buildmaster hunts down and resolves any issues that may break the build (code that won't compile is the most common problem). It is important for this individual to have the power to get people to correct problems as they occur, and she will require the full support of the team. If the buildmaster finds a problem with the build, she identifies the person responsible and has that person fix the problem. The buildmaster should not fix coding problems herself, since this would contradict her primary role as over-seer and would likely create some bad habits among developers. Nor should she perform any significant testing, beyond a spot check to verify that the application launches correctly. Rather, code should be turned over to a formal testing team for complete verification. See chapter 18 for more information.

In order for the build process to be successful, everyone involved must be dedicated to the cause, not just the buildmaster. Each developer must do his part to ensure that everything goes smoothly on build day. In particular, developers need to verify that their code compiles and runs before checking it into the version control repository. Although this may seem obvious, sometimes the pressure of deadlines makes developers cut corners. There really is no good excuse for checking in code that does not compile, but in my experience, it happens frequently, especially on larger teams. This can wreak havoc on the process, making it take much longer than it should.

At build time, here is what the buildmaster typically will need to do:

1. Verify that all code for the new build has been checked in and that the appropriate versions have been pinned (if you are using a pinning strategy).

2. Label the code in the version control tool so that developers can continue working on other issues. Bear in mind that if any corrections need to be made to the code because of a problem with the build, developers should apply them to the labeled or pinned version of the code file, not the latest version.

3. Check out the project files (VBP files) and executable files for all projects in the application.

4. Compile the code and build the executables, making the appropriate changes to the projects' versions and verifying that all references and version compatibility options are set correctly.

5. Save the project files and check everything back into the version control tool.

6. If required, create the setup package and distribute the software.

Build Scripts

Since Visual Basic does not have a very fast compiler, you will want to automate the build process as much as possible, which you can do with a *build script*. Build scripts are batch files that perform much of the grunt work associated with the build process. Visual Source Safe, the Packaging and Deployment Wizard, and even Visual Basic have command-line interfaces you can use to build a batch file. The command-line options for each are well documented in the Books Online, so we will not cover them in detail here.

Generally, your batch file will automate each of the steps just listed (Label, Get, Checkout, Compile, Checkin). However, although VB has a command-line

◆ **A Look Under the Hood: Visual Basic's Compiler and Linker**

When Visual Basic kicks off its secondary compiler, c2.exe, it passes a number of command-line parameters along for each file to be compiled. Among other things, the parameters determine what compile-time optimizations to use for each file. These are normally set in Visual Basic's Project Options dialog and its advanced subdialog, and you get the same optimizations applied to each file in your project. However, it is possible to change these to optimize differently at the module level. Bruce McKinney mentions a handful of techniques for doing this in "A Hardcore Declaration of Independence" (1999a). His big beef with Microsoft on this issue is that the only reason Visual Basic does not let you apply the optimizations on a file-by-file basis right out of the box is that Microsoft simply did not provide a user interface to allow you to do so.

To see what all the fuss was about, I followed his advice and examined the command-line arguments passed to c2.exe with a simple logging program. I renamed c2.exe and wrote my own version. The new application simply logs the command line passed to a text file and then shells out to the renamed real c2.exe with the same command line. Note that this simple trick also works for Visual Basic's linker, link.exe. I then tried every optimization setting I could find to see how the command line changes. Unfortunately, only the "Favor Pentium Pro," "Create Symbolic Debug Info," and "Remove Safe Pentium FDIV Checks" were affected, which means that the bulk of the optimizations are actually done directly by the VB executable itself (e.g., vb6.exe).

In short, the most important runtime optimizations for Visual Basic are not provided by the compiler or the linker. As a matter of fact, it appears that c2.exe and link.exe are actually Microsoft's VC++ compiler and linker, so it is not surprising VB-specific optimizations do not come into play. For more information, check out "Advanced Visual Basic," included with the Books Online.

switch to compile a project into an executable, it is difficult to use in a batch file for two reasons:

1. The buildmaster individual may need to specify version information by hand, since this cannot be supplied via the command line.
2. The main VB executable (vb5.exe or vb6.exe) actually shells out to other programs, its secondary compiler (c2.exe) and linker (link.exe). When this occurs, the main Visual Basic application ends while the compilation finishes. As a result, the batch file will begin to compile the second project before the first has finished, which is problematic when there are dependencies.

Because of these issues, after checking out the projects and executables, I have the batch file launch VB and open the first project to build. I follow this command with the pause batch command and then move on to the next project, and so on. While the batch file pauses for each project, I verify the references, set the version number, and compile the executables before moving on to the next project by resuming the batch file.

You may find it possible to include all of your projects in one group file. You can then simply compile the whole group from the command line in one shot with the default build options. This is handy for smaller projects, but for larger ones it tends to consume too much memory and is often too slow. To build a whole project group, use the /make switch followed by the group name.

Setup Tools

Because Visual Basic applications have so many dependencies (the VB runtime files, files for additional controls, etc.), it is not possible simply to compile the application into an executable and copy it to the user's machine. A more sophisticated solution is required: a setup program. To install your application, the user will run the setup program you provide. This program will copy the files needed to the user's computer (perhaps from the Internet or a network share folder), register all files requiring registration, create shortcuts and program groups, and make any other changes to the user's computer that are necessary to run your application. In this section, we'll look at the much neglected setup toolkit provided with Visual Basic and then turn to other tools that help make installing your program easier.

VB's Setup Toolkit

To facilitate the installation of applications, Microsoft has included a tool for creating setup programs with Visual Basic. In VB 4 and VB 5 it was called the Application Setup Wizard, but has been expanded and renamed the Packaging and Deployment Wizard in VB 6. Early versions of the toolkit were difficult to use—so difficult, in fact, that a whole genre of third-party applications, the installation program builder, arose to placate programmer frustration. In VB 6, things have improved, and it is worth taking a closer look at this tool to see what its strengths and weaknesses are.

The Packaging and Deployment Wizard has three primary functions. First, the Packaging Wizard allows you to create installation packages, which consist of one or more cabinet (CAB) files and a setup program directed by a setup list file. With a setup package completed, you use the Deployment Wizard to send your package to the Internet, a shared network drive, or even floppies. Last, there is an option that allows you to manage the packaging and deployment scripts you created in the process of making and distributing your package. The Packaging and Deployment Wizard is well documented and simple to use, so we will not discuss how to use it in detail here. Rather, let's focus on what the wizard does for you.

First, compile your finished VB project(s) into the appropriate executable files. If you forget to do this, or if your VB projects appear newer than their executables, the Packaging and Deployment Wizard will ask if you want to compile the projects.

Second, run the Packaging Wizard against each supporting project. Usually these are DLL or OCX projects you have created for your main application to use. If you wish to distribute your supporting files separately, as is common with OCXes, create separate setup programs for each. More often, you will want to install all supporting files along with your main executables, so you should simply generate dependency files initially. Store these dependency files in the same directory as the DLLs to be sure the wizard can find them during subsequent setups.

Note that you must work with your supporting projects in lowest to highest order in the chain of dependencies. For example, if your main application references `first.dll`, which in turn references `second.dll`, you should create the dependency file for `second.dll` first, then the dependency file for `first.dll`.

There are a number of details we have skipped here, including special conditions for DCOM servers, Remote Automation, and MTS. Be sure to review the on-line help for more information. In the end, you should have a dependency file for each of your supporting projects.

In the third step, run the Packaging Wizard against your main application's project. As you work your way through the wizard, it automatically performs several important functions. First, it identifies your application's required files and compresses them into one or more CAB files, as you specify. Second, it generates the file `setup.lst`, which is easily modified by hand for custom installations. We will look at this file in more detail later. Third, it moves a copy of `setup.exe`, the bootstrap application, from its home on your PC (usually `...\VB98\Wizards\PDWizard`) to the destination directory. The completed package's destination directory will have one or more CAB files, `setup.exe`, and `setup.lst`. The CAB files will contain the following:

- Bootstrap files needed by `setup.exe` (listed in the bootstrap section of `setup.lst`)
- The file `setup1.exe` (the main setup program, discussed in detail later)
- The file `st6unst.exe` (the application that runs when the user uninstalls your application)
- Your application's files

Last, and perhaps most important, the Packaging Wizard creates a directory called Support that resides immediately under the directory you told the wizard to put the package into. This directory contains the files included in your CAB file(s) in uncompressed form and a batch file (`projectname.bat`) that allows you to recreate the CAB files for your project without having to run the wizard again. The batch file itself uses another file with a DDF extension (projectname.DDF), which you will also find in the support directory. You can run the batch file whenever you make a change to one of your project's files or to setup1.exe, as we will later.

With the package complete, you can deploy it as you desire with the Deployment Wizard. This fourth step is generally simple, and since it is already well documented, we won't cover it here.

For simple projects, the Packaging and Deployment Wizard and a bit of patience will generally suffice to create working setup programs. If you have more complicated applications or if you require a more finely tuned installation process, you will have to make modifications to the VB setup program (setup1.exe) and setup.lst or turn to a third-party tool. We will discuss third-party tools later, so first let us turn our attention to expanding the setup1.exe project.

Two common features of setup programs missing from those created out of the can with the Packaging Wizard are as follows:

1. The ability to display a ReadMe text file following the installation.
2. The ability to break the installation up into components, to allow the user to select which pieces of the software to install. This is useful for larger applications when the user may not want all of the files installed.

Since we have the source code to setup1.exe, we will customize it and add these features in the next section. By doing so we will not only extend the functionality of setup1.exe, but also see what makes it tick. Unfortunately, Microsoft did not ship the source code for the Packaging and Deployment Wizard. This means that after creating our setup program as usual, we will have to manually modify the setup.lst file to support our new features and then remake the CAB files with our new setup1.exe and setup.lst files.

Before we begin, a small flame is in order. The code for setup1.exe remained relatively unchanged between versions 5 and 6 of VB (even with the additions of Service Pack 3), and as I remember, it was essentially the same in the previous versions as well. Microsoft has had many opportunities to clean up this code, but it nevertheless remains rather choppy and confusing. It can be difficult to expand since adding a new feature frequently means digging deep into it. While there has been some improvement from version to version, the code still does not follow any kind of consistent coding standard, especially when it comes to variable naming conventions. Finally, although Microsoft has touted the object-oriented capabilities of Visual Basic since version 4, not a single class is to be found. As the only nontrivial project shipped with Visual Basic, it is the ideal candidate for a polished application. But once again, Microsoft disappoints.

On the plus side, the code is generally well commented (though there are some inconsistencies). Also, there are a number of useful functions in several modules that you can readily reuse. In fact, with a few notable exceptions, the `setup1.exe` contains everything you should need to create an impressive installation package—you just have to figure out how.

Modifying `setup1.exe`

The `setup.exe` (bootstrap) application performs some initial file copies and then spawns `setup1.exe` or whatever is specified in the `setup.1st` file under the key Spawn. Since `setup1.exe` is a VB application, it requires several supporting files to run correctly. It is the job of the bootstrap application to install these files (they are listed in the `Bootstrap` section of `setup.1st`) before spawning `setup1.exe`. Note that `setup.exe` is not written in VB, and its source code is not shipped with Visual Basic.

The code for `setup1.exe` is contained in the project `setup1.vbp`, which resides in the directory ...\VB98\Wizards\PDWizard\setup1. Before you make changes to any of these, remember to make a backup copy of all of the files in this directory. In fact, you may want to copy and rename the project something more appropriate for your application.

Setup1.vbp Most of the work in `setup1.exe` takes place in the `Form_Load` procedure of its startup form, `frmSetup`. The program begins with some general initialization. It creates the font structure it will use on all forms, loads some user interface strings from its resource file, initializes global variables to use for the various directories on the target PC, and processes the command-line arguments. It reads a handful of settings from `setup.1st` and then shows the main backdrop window (a full screen form with a blue wash) and the welcome screen. Note that all user interface elements can be turned off at the command line, so keep this in mind if you intend to add UI elements of your own.

After the user dismisses the welcome screen, the program displays the Begin dialog, allowing the user to choose the destination directory for the installation. The routine checks the user's computer for required disk space and then begins the grunt work of the installation. The destination directory and all program groups are created, with a prompt from the Create Program Group dialog as appropriate. The function displays the Copy Status dialog and the copying begins. When finished, all executable files and licenses that require registration are processed, followed by a few operating system-specific functions. Finally, the application creates the individual shortcuts and performs some general cleanup before ending.

Command-Line Arguments and Logging Normally, the user installing your application will simply double-click on the icon for the bootstrap application (setup.exe) and follow the prompts generated by the spawned setup1.exe to complete the installation. However, it is also possible to run the setup.exe from the command line, with or without a silent mode switch to turn off the user interface. The switch syntax is /s filename, where filename includes the full path and name of the file to use for logging silent messages.

setup1.exe itself takes several command-line options. Although they are of little use to the user, these parameters are important to developers. If the silent switch and log file are sent to the bootstrap application, they are passed along to setup1.exe as the first command-line option. After this, setup1.exe requires the source directory, the path and filename of the removal log file, and the path and filename of the removal application. These three options are provided by the bootstrap application as well. The source directory is, of course, where the setup files reside.

The bootstrap application creates a log file of all changes made to the user's computer during installation, in case the installation fails or the user wants to uninstall the application. This file is in the Windows directory (or WinNT) with the filename st6unst.000, where 000 is the first available three-digit extension. When setup1.exe begins, it uses this same file to continue its own logging. If the setup process completes successfully, setup1.exe copies the log file from the Windows directory to the destination directory of the application, renaming it st6unst.log. If the installation fails, setup1.exe uses the removal application specified by the last command-line argument to undo the changes to the user's computer.

When you are debugging and testing changes to setup1.vbp, it is helpful to specify the three required command-line arguments under the properties for setup1.vbp. Note that the application will not run if the removal log file and removal application do not actually exist, so be sure to specify a real directory with real files, even if they are copies.

Adding a ReadMe Dialog Let's begin with the easier of the two new features mentioned earlier, and add a ReadMe dialog to the end of the installation process. These dialogs are commonly used to display release notes, information about updates, late-breaking news, or information about bug fixes.

◆ **Getting the Source Code**

The source code for all of the code discussed in this section is available on-line. See "On-line Materials" in the preface for information on how to download it. Although I highlight important changes here, be sure to search all the code for "DWP" to find all of my tagged changes.

To include such a dialog, we will need to add a new form to setup1.vbp. The form I have added is frmReadMe, and it contains a multiline textbox with a vertical scroll bar, a simple icon for consistency of appearance, and an OK button. The form has one public property, sReadMeFile, which assigns the name of the file containing the ReadMe text to load into the textbox to a local variable, msFile. The complete source code for frmReadMe is contained in Listing 21.1.

Listing 21.1   Source Code for frmReadMe

```
Option Explicit

'This file displays a standard ReadMe file from the text in
'the file set by sReadMeFile.

Private msFile As String

Public Property Let sReadMeFile(rsNewValue As String)
    msFile = rsNewValue
End Property

Public Property Get sReadMeFile() As String
    sReadMeFile = msFile
End Property

Private Sub cmdOK_Click()
    Unload Me
End Sub

Private Sub Form_Load()
'----------------------------------------------------
'    This function prepares the form by loading the
'    text in the file specified by msFile and
'    putting it into txtReadMe. It also prepares the
'    fonts, captions, and position of the form. The
'    form remains loaded until the user presses
'    the OK button.
'----------------------------------------------------
    Dim hFile As Long
    Dim sText As String
    Dim sLine As String

    On Error GoTo Error_Handler
    If Not FileExists(msFile) Then
        Unload Me
        Exit Sub
    End If

    SetFormFont Me

    cmdOK.Caption = ResolveResString(resBTNOK)
    Me.Caption = gstrTitle
```

```
On Error Resume Next
Err.Clear
hFile = FreeFile
Open msFile For Input As #hFile
If Err.Number <> 0 Then
    Err.Clear
    Exit Sub
End If
On Error GoTo Error_Handler
sText = ""
Do While Not EOF(hFile)
    Line Input #hFile, sLine
    sText = sText & sLine & vbCrLf
Loop
Close #hFile

txtReadMe.Text = sText
Call CenterForm(Me)
Me.Refresh
Exit Sub

Error_Handler:
    'This is not critical to the installation.
    'In fact, the installation is finished,
    'so just unload the form and exit.
    Unload Me
End Sub
```

Most of the work in this form takes place in the Form_Load event handler. After the program checks that the ReadMe file specified by msFile exists, the font for the form is set by a call to the routine SetFormFont. This function is in the Form_Load event handler of all of the forms in the project. It iterates through all controls on the form and sets the font property (if there is one) to the best font to use given the computer's locale settings, as returned by GetFontInfo. This is a handy bit of code to steal for your own projects, especially if you ship software to multiple locales.

With this form created, the only remaining step is to add code to frmSetup1 to display the new ReadMe form. I have opted to place the display code in a new procedure called ShowReadMeForm, which is called just before the exit setup code in the Form_Load event handler of frmSetup1. The source code for ShowReadMeForm is in Listing 21.2. It resembles several of the other routines designed to display dialogs already in the setup program. It checks the global flag gfNoUserInput first to see whether the form can be displayed at all. If you want to add dialogs to this setup program, be sure to check this flag before displaying anything. Note that gfNoUserInput will be true if the installation is running silently (i.e., gfSilent is true) or if the installation is running via SMS (i.e., gfSMS is true).

Listing 21.2   Source Code for ShowReadMeForm

```
Private Sub ShowReadMeForm()
'----------------------------------------------------
'   DWP - added this routine to display the ReadMe
'   form if needed.
'   If user can see dialogs, find out if the ReadMe
'   dialog is supposed to be shown, load the filename,
'   set the ReadMe dialog's property, and show the
'   dialog.
'----------------------------------------------------
    If Not gfNoUserInput Then
        If ReadIniFile(gstrSetupInfoFile, gstrINI_SETUP, _
            gstrINI_SHOW_README) = "1" Then

            'Load the path of the ReadMe file and set the
            'property on the ReadMe form
            frmReadMe.sReadMeFile = gstrDestDir & _
                ReadIniFile(gstrSetupInfoFile, gstrINI_SETUP, _
                gstrINI_README_FILE)
            frmReadMe.Show vbModal
        End If
    End If
End Sub
```

If the form can be displayed, ShowReadMeForm checks setup.1st and uses ReadIniFile to see whether the file actually should be displayed. The constant gstrINI_SHOW_README refers to a new key in setup.1st called ShowReadMe under the Setup section. This key will contain a value of "1" if the ReadMe file should be displayed. If the flag is on, the routine reads the name of the file to display from setup.1st (again using ReadIniFile) and sets the property on frmReadMe accordingly. Note that the application is expecting the ReadMe file to be copied into the main destination directory (as specified in gstrDestDir). You may easily change the location, but it is as good as any. Finally, frmReadMe is displayed modally, at which point the Form_Load handler just described kicks in.

With this code added, including a ReadMe dialog in your setup programs simply entails adding two lines to the setup.1st file under Setup, as follows:

```
[Setup]
ShowReadMe=1
ReadMeFile=ReadMe.txt
```

If you set ShowReadMe to 0, or omit it, the dialog will not display. Nor will it display if the file specified by ReadMeFile does not exist. You will need to add your ReadMe.txt file to the list of files to install in the Packaging Wizard for everything to work correctly.

Adding a Component Selection Dialog   Throughout the code for setup.exe, there are numerous hints, sometimes contradictory, on how to expand its functionality. One of these suggestions is to add a Component Selection dialog that allows the user to select the components to install, which is what we'll cover in this section. Setup programs for larger applications frequently have separate components for things such as the main application, supporting applications and files, help files, and examples.

To implement this new functionality, there are some basic requirements. For each component, we need to do the following:

1. Provide general information to display in the Choose Components dialog, such as a short and long description and whether the component should be installed by default

2. Store information about what files to install

3. Know what program groups and icons to create

The first of these requirements is straightforward. We simply need to create a new section in the setup.1st file to contain display information for each component, as shown:

```
[Components]
CompLongDesc0=This is the long description of the 1st component.
CompShortDesc0=This is the short description.
CompInstallByDefault0=1 (or 0 if false)
CompLongDesc1=This is the long description for the 2nd component.
```

For each component, there are three keys. The three keys for the first component end in "0," and this number gets incremented for each subsequent component. This technique allows us to store what would be rows and columns in a relational database using rows only in a flat file. It is the method used throughout the setup.1st file, albeit inconsistently. For example, program groups start with Group0, icon listings start with Icon1, and files start with File1.

Implementing the second requirement is a little more complicated. Normally, the setup.1st file contains one file information section called Setup1 Files, stored in code in the constant gstrINI_FILES. It contains a list of all of the files to install (File1, File2, and so on). We need to remove this one-only restriction and create several sections, one for each component, and list the files to install for that component. This approach has a couple of advantages. First, it provides an easy way to separate the files for each component in the setup.1st file. But more important, it allows us to reuse some heavy-duty routines in setup1.exe, especially CopySection (in basSetup1), which takes the name of a section in the setup.1st file and processes all of the files listed there. Normally, this routine is called once, with the section gstrINI_FILES. Under our new system, we will want to call it for each component to be installed. Therefore, for each component, we need to know the name of the section containing its list of files. We can add this to our components section in setup.1st, as shown:

```
[Components]
CompSectionName0=Name of section listing files in first component
CompSectionName1=Name of section listing files in second component, etc.
```

We will also have to add a whole new section for each component, with meaningful and unique names. Ideally, the Packaging Wizard would create these sections for us, and all we would have to do is follow some simple user interface that allows us to create the components' names and assign files to them. Since Microsoft does not ship the source code to the Packaging Wizard, as mentioned, we are stuck making these changes to setup.1st by hand. Of course, you could always create your own wizard to handle this for you.

Figuring out what program groups and icons to create, the third requirement, is more complicated still. Normally, another section of the setup.1st file, IconGroups, contains information about each program group that needs to be created. For each program group needed, three lines are keyed: GroupN, ParentN, and PrivateGroupN, where N is an ordinal index starting from 0. The value keyed by GroupN is a reference to the name of yet another section in the setup.1st file containing the icons for that group. The value for PrivateGroupN is a flag indicating whether the program group is private under Windows NT. Last, the value under ParentN refers to the name of the group's parent group, which will be either the Start Menu program group or the Programs program group. The relationship between the IconGroups section and its supporting sections is a complicated one, but should become clearer after reviewing the file.

Luckily, we need to modify this arrangement only slightly to add our component functionality. For each component to be installed, we need to know what program group and icons to create. Like the section for files, this can be accomplished by adding a reference to the name of the section containing the icon groups for the component, as follows:

```
[Components]
CompGroupSectionName0=The group name for the first component
CompGroupSectionName1=The group name for the second component
```

Before looking at the Choose Components dialog itself, we need to address how all of this new information in the setup.1st file is accessed. My solution is a new routine called LoadComponentInformation. It resides in basSetup1 and is called in the Form_Load event handler for frmSetup1. The source code for this routine appears in Listing 21.3. To make the data for the components available in the several places in which it will be needed, it is stored in a global array (gatComponents) of a user-defined type (ComponentInfo_type) also defined in basSetup1 and shown in Listing 21.3.

Ideally, this data would be loaded once, and read (but not changed) many times. This is possible with specific objects and provides all of the benefit of a global variable without all of the headache. With such a simple application, however, it did not seem worth the trouble, though if things were to get more complicated (following substantial changes), it would be a good idea to implement this functionality.

Listing 21.3 Source Code for ComponentInfo_type and LoadComponentInformation

```
'DWP - This type holds the information about
'the components to be installed
Public Type ComponentInfo_type
    sSectionName As String
    sGroupSectionName As String
    sShortDesc As String
    sLongDesc As String
    bInstall As Boolean
    bInstallByDefault As Boolean
End Type

'These two variables hold the component information
'itself and the number of components in the setup.lst file.
Public gatComponents() As ComponentInfo_type
Public gnComponents As Integer
'End DWP

Public Sub LoadComponentInformation()
'--------------------------------------------------------
'   DWP - added th is routine to load all information
'   about each component into the array gatComponents.
'--------------------------------------------------------

    'Get list from setup.lst - populate udt and list box

    Const sCOMPONENT_SECTION As String = "Components"
    Const sCOMP_SECTION_NAME As String = "compsectionname"
    Const sCOMP_GROUP_SECTION_NAME As String = _
        "compgroupsectionname"
    Const sCOMP_LONG_DESC As String = "complongdesc"
    Const sCOMP_SHORT_DESC As String = "compshortdesc"
    Const sCOMP_INSTALL_BY_DEFAULT As String = _
        "compinstallbydefault"

    Dim iComp As Integer
    Dim sName As String

    On Error GoTo Error_Handler
    iComp = 0
```

```
        sName = ReadIniFile(gstrSetupInfoFile, _
            sCOMPONENT_SECTION, sCOMP_SECTION_NAME & CStr(iComp))
    While Len(sName) > 0
        'Found one. Get all of its info
        gnComponents = gnComponents + 1
        ReDim Preserve gatComponents(1 To gnComponents) _
            As ComponentInfo_type

        With gatComponents(gnComponents)
            .sSectionName = sName
            .sGroupSectionName = _
                ReadIniFile(gstrSetupInfoFile, _
                sCOMPONENT_SECTION, sCOMP_GROUP_SECTION_NAME & _
                CStr(iComp))
            .bInstall = False
            .sLongDesc = ReadIniFile(gstrSetupInfoFile, _
                sCOMPONENT_SECTION, sCOMP_LONG_DESC & _
                CStr(iComp))
            .sShortDesc = ReadIniFile(gstrSetupInfoFile, _
                sCOMPONENT_SECTION, sCOMP_SHORT_DESC & _
                CStr(iComp))
            .bInstallByDefault = _
                (ReadIniFile(gstrSetupInfoFile, _
                sCOMPONENT_SECTION, sCOMP_INSTALL_BY_DEFAULT & _
                CStr(iComp)) = "1")
        End With
        iComp = iComp + 1
        sName = ReadIniFile(gstrSetupInfoFile, _
            sCOMPONENT_SECTION, sCOMP_SECTION_NAME & _
            CStr(iComp))
    Wend
    Exit Sub
Error_Handler:
    'Not much we can do about it...
End Sub
```

LoadComponentInformation simply looks in the setup.1st file for components under the Components section. It loads all corresponding information into
the user-defined type for each component found. When all information is
loaded, the variable gnComponents contains the count of all components.

As with the ReadMe dialog we added earlier, implementing the Choose
Components dialog entails adding a new form to the setup1 project. Again, this
form is simple: it contains a checkable list box, a label for displaying a detailed
description of the component, and OK and Exit buttons. Add a simple icon and
an instructional label, and the form is completed. As always in setup1.vbp, the
actual verbiage of the captions for all controls, including the instructional label,
resides in the project's resource file or somewhere in setup.1st. No verbiage is
hardcoded.

The code for our new form, frmChooseComponents, appears in Listing 21.4.
The code behind the OK and Exit buttons mimics the code behind these but-

tons as they appear on other forms. The OK button simply unloads the form, and the Exit button calls the subroutine ExitSetup, which verifies that the user really wants to stop the installation, and, if so, handles any cleanup, undoing any changes made to that point. The Form_Load event handler sets up the fonts and captions as before. With the component information buffered in the array gat-Components, the routine fills the list box, using the components' short descriptions for the list text. If a component is supposed to be installed by default, its checkbox is preselected automatically.

Listing 21.4 Source code for frmChooseComponents

```
Option Explicit

Private Sub cmdExit_Click()
    ExitSetup Me, gintRET_EXIT
End Sub

Private Sub cmdOK_Click()
    Unload Me
End Sub

Private Sub Form_Load()
'------------------------------------------------------
'    This routine sets up the form's font and captions,
'    then fills the list box with data from the global
'    array of component information.
'------------------------------------------------------
    Dim iComp As Integer

    SetFormFont Me

    cmdExit.Caption = ResolveResString(resBTNEXIT)
    cmdOK.Caption = ResolveResString(resBTNOK)
    lblInstructions.Caption = _
        ResolveResString(resCUSTOM_SELECTCOMPONENTS)
    Me.Caption = gstrTitle

    'At this point all the information about the
    'components is stored in the global array.
    'Fill the list box and proceed.
    With lstComponents
        For iComp = 1 To gnComponents
            Call .AddItem(gatComponents(iComp).sShortDesc)
            If gatComponents(iComp).bInstallByDefault Then
                .Selected(.NewIndex) = True
            End If
        Next iComp
    End With

    Call CenterForm(Me)
End Sub
```

```
Private Sub Form_Unload(Cancel As Integer)
'------------------------------------------------------
'   Save the components to be installed by checking the
'   list box to see which options are checked.
'------------------------------------------------------
    Dim iComp As Integer
    For iComp = 1 To gnComponents
        gatComponents(iComp).bInstall = _
            lstComponents.Selected(iComp - 1)
    Next iComp
End Sub

Private Sub lstComponents_Click()
'------------------------------------------------------
'   When the user clicks on an item in the list, display
'   the long description in the label to the right of the
'   light box.
'------------------------------------------------------

    If lstComponents.ListIndex > -1 Then
        lblDescription.Caption = _
            gatComponents(lstComponents.ListIndex + 1).sLongDesc
    Else
        lblDescription.Caption = ""
    End If
End Sub
```

The `Form_Unload` event handler cycles through our array of components, setting the flag `bInstall` on `gatComponents` if the corresponding item in the list box is checked. In the `Form_Load` event of `frmSetup1`, we will process only those components in the array that have this flag set to true (more on this later).

Note that in addition to having components that are installed by default, it would be simple to expand this functionality to allow for components that *must* be installed. These components would not appear in the list at all (or could be checked and disabled) and would have the `bInstall` flag set automatically. A new field would have to be added to the user-defined type `ComponentInfo_type` and to the `setup.lst` file to indicate this mandatory installation.

To complete the Choose Components functionality, we need to make numerous small changes to the code in `frmSetup` and its supporting subroutines. We'll discuss the important changes here, but for a complete list, you can search the source code for my comments, which are all tagged with DWP, or use a visual comparison tool such as the one provided with Visual Source Safe.

The first change that is to be done in `frmSetup1` involves making a call to `LoadComponentInformation`, followed by a call to a new subroutine to display the Choose Components dialog at the appropriate time. Per the suggestions in the comments in the code, I have placed these lines immediately after the call to ShowBeginForm. The new subroutine to display the dialog (see code in Listing 21.5) is called ShowComponentsDialog.

Listing 21.5   Source Code for ShowComponentsDialog

```
Private Sub ShowComponentsDialog()
' -------------------------------------------------
'   DWP - added this routine to display the Choose
'   Components dialog if needed. If no UI is to be
'   shown, the routine forces everything to install
'   by default.
' -------------------------------------------------
    Dim iComp As Integer

    If gfNoUserInput Then
        'Load everything.
        For iComp = 1 To gnComponents
            gatComponents(iComp).bInstall = True
        Next iComp
    Else
        'Let the user pick the components
        frmChooseComponents.Show vbModal
    End If
End Sub
```

This routine is straightforward. If the setup application is not supposed to display a user interface, we force all components to install by default by setting the bInstall flag to true. Note that the routine can easily be modified to set the bInstall flag to true only for those that have the bInstallByDefault flag set. If the UI is used, only those components actually chosen by the user will have this flag set.

Continuing through the Form_Load event handler for frmSetup1, we find the next change just a few lines later. Normally, the setup program verifies that the destination PC has enough disk space by calling CalcDiskSpace for the setup.lst section contained in gstrINI_FILES. In our new system, we need to call this routine repeatedly, using the file section name (sSectionName) for each component to be installed. Note that CalcDiskSpace has the side effect of setting the variable mlTotalToCopy, which contains the total number of bytes to copy to the destination computer. This total is used later when the files are actually copied in order to calculate the percentage completed for the copying status bar.

Further down in Form_Load, the setup program calculates the number of program groups and icons that need to be created. This code is a bit awkward, since later the count is used in calculations that assume that there is only one component being installed. I have modified this code to provide the total number of icons and groups for all components to be installed, as the comments suggest. To do so, I used the sGroupSectionName field of the user-defined type for each component rather than the default section name (gsICONGROUP).

Immediately after calculating the count, the setup program does some simple checks to verify if we really need to create groups and, if so, creates them, prompting the user for the name as needed. I have modified this code to loop through each component to be installed and use its sGroupSectionName field to create the program groups. The existing code assumes that the keys for the group information to install would always be sequential. Since our users can select what they want to install, this assumption is no longer valid. A simple check to verify that the group information exists before trying to access it solves this problem.

The next change takes us to the meat of the functionality of the setup program, namely, installing the files. The routine CopySection takes as a parameter the name of a section in the setup.1st file. It goes through each file listed in the section, performs the necessary verifications, and installs the file as required. Our change is simple: rather than calling CopySection only once for gstrINI_FILES, we call it for each component we are installing, using the sSectionName field of ComponetInfo_type.

The last change is to create the icons for each component. Again, a single function, CreateIcons, does the bulk of the work. It takes as a parameter the name of the section in the setup.1st file that contains information about the program groups. It then searches through the values in the section to find the corresponding information about that group's icons. Luckily, we need to be concerned with only the call to CreateIcons, since as long as we fill in our setup.1st file correctly, everything else takes place automatically. The change I have made calls CreateIcons for each component to be installed, using the field sGroupSectionName.

Additional Functionality

Expanding setup1.exe even further is certainly a possibility. For example, the functionality of the Choose Components dialog we added is trivial. We could expand this by defining both subcomponents (e.g., Component A consists of subcomponents B and C) and intercomponent dependencies (e.g., if user installs Component A, then Component B must be installed as well). It would also be nice to remove the restriction that one component has only one program group and that a program group can only belong to one component.

The following are some other suggestions for expanding the functionality of setup1.exe:

1. Make specialized changes to the registry (add, remove, or change keys and values as needed).

2. Make specialized changes to any INI file (add, remove, or change sections, keys, and values as needed).

3. Create ODBC entries automatically.

4. Shell out to other installation programs.

5. Display an end-user licensing agreement (EULA) and request that the user accept the terms of the agreement before continuing.

6. Associate file extensions with your application.

Some of these changes (#1, #3, #6) can be done with registry hacks using the registry functions provided to you in `basSetup1`. The others require more customized code. Altogether, changing `setup1.vbp` to add these suggestions is not difficult. The problem is that it can be difficult to record how to undo the changes you make to the user's computer, since the uninstalling logging of `setup1.vbp` is limited.

Briefly, the logging functions used by `setup1.exe` are used by `setup.exe` also, and they reside in the file `vb6stkit.dll`. In `setup1.vbp`, a standard module, `basLogging`, declares the functions in the DLL and provides simple wrappers for them. Before making any change to the user's system, logging is enabled (see the `Form_Load` event handler of `frmSetup1`). For each change, a simple transaction is started. As the changes are made, the specific logging functions write the information to a stack. If all items in the transaction are successful, the stack is saved in the file `st6unst.log`, otherwise it is rolled back. As mentioned before, the application removal program (`st6unst.exe`) uses `st6unst.log` to uninstall the application by undoing the changes logged therein.

In addition to these wrapper functions, more practical functions are provided by the module `basSetup1` to do the work that typically needs to be logged. However, even with all of this help, there are a number of things that are still never logged and therefore cannot be undone. These include the following:

♦ Changes to the registry made by calling RegEdit to install a .REG file

♦ Changes to and deletions of registry keys and values

♦ Changes of any kind to any INI file

The registry limitations are not very serious, since generally you will want to add only keys and values to the registry (an action which is logged), not change or delete existing ones (actions which are not logged). However, the INI file limitations are a problem. Microsoft has tried to get rid of the usage of INI files by forcing the registry down everyone's throat, but they live on, even at Microsoft (just try installing a VB add-in without changing the file `vbaddini.ini`). You could create your own logging functions, but you would have to create a new `st6unst.exe` clone to understand how to undo them. This is, to say the least, messy. If you need to make such changes, you will probably want to consider using a third-party utility, our next topic.

Third-Party Utilities

Even with the extended functionality you can provide with modifications to `setup1.exe`, you may still opt to use a third-party tool to perform your installations. Likely candidates include one of the Installation Suites from Wise Solutions or one of the products from InstallShield, and there are many others. Some of the available tools are very robust and may even include a miniature visual IDE, complete with scripting language, compilers, and linkers. Be wary, though. They can also take some time to learn to use. With the more advanced tools, using the tool effectively can mean learning a whole new scripting language. In short, when choosing a third-party installation package, you will need to balance ease of use against power required.

Luckily, most of these tools also have wizards to assist with creating the setup script. These wizards behave very much like the Packaging Wizard, only they are more robust and generally easier to use.

SMS and Login Scripts

If it is not reasonable to expect your users to be able to run your installation program on their own, you can turn to more subtle ways of ensuring your software gets installed correctly. Microsoft's Systems Management Server (SMS) is one such tool for simplifying the management of corporate PCs. It handles such tasks as hardware and software inventories, software scheduling, and installation and distribution of software. Simple login scripts can also be used to launch installation programs and, when run in silent mode, are all but transparent to the user.

The main benefit of these techniques is that users with no expertise can still use the software without having to know how to install it. This means fewer PCs have to be visited, and troubleshooting the rollout in general becomes simpler. Microsoft touts SMS as a key part of its mission to lower the total cost of ownership of computers. However, even with the benefits, there are a number of drawbacks.

Many users see such silent control of their computers as an invasion of their privacy. It gives them the impression that Big Brother is watching, and many find it unnerving. Some companies have clearly defined (and well-distributed) policies regarding computer use, including use of the Internet, e-mail, and the physical PCs. Users who violate company policy and are upset about it really don't have a leg to stand on. However, in many instances the policies are unclear.

Furthermore, it may even be common practice (and therefore seemingly acceptable) for users to use the company's systems for nonwork-related activities, even during business hours. If you consider the computer to be an extension of the desktop, this is reasonable—most companies allow personal items such as pictures and coffee mugs in the workplace. These individuals have a right to be upset if SMS suddenly becomes intrusive.

To avoid these touchy issues, be sure your company clearly documents its policies regarding computer use. If personal items can be on computers, describe the limitations. If certain programs (such as games) cannot be run during business hours, indicate this. Also be certain to inform users about changes to this policy. Last, if you are using SMS or a similar tool, let your users know about it. Be sure they understand the capabilities of your tools so that if they have a problem, they cannot say they haven't been properly warned.

Cloning Systems

If you are writing programs for very specific computers and need to distribute exactly the same software to all computers in question and only that software, consider a cloning tool. These tools work by copying an image of a master computer's hard disk to the destination computer. There are several packages to choose from, including Ghost from Symantec, SCSI Mechanic from Corporate Systems Center, and a shareware package called HDCP.

To clone a system, set up one computer (I call this machine the dropmaster) exactly as you want all of them to appear, right down to the desktop icons. You should test your software thoroughly on this computer to ensure that it behaves as expected on the given platform. You then make a compressed image of the dropmaster's hard disk using one of these tools, storing the image on a CD-ROM or network drive. When completed, you may use these tools and your image to overwrite the hard disks on any number of destination computers.

Though ultimately you erase the destination computers' hard disks and therefore this method is not applicable in all instances, cloning has a number of advantages:

1. Cloning removes the possibility of incompatibility as a result of software conflicts, since you know exactly what is on the destination computers when you are finished.

2. With cloned systems, ongoing troubleshooting of the destination computers becomes greatly simplified. If there is a problem with a particular computer, simply reapply the image, and the machine is restored to working order. This will not help with hardware issues, but it takes the headache out of software problems. Note that this means training the end users not

to leave important materials on their hard disks. Such information should be written to removable storage or to a network share, since it will be completely overwritten in the event that the PC needs to have the image reapplied.

3. Cloning systems is a great way to restore a computer to a "pristine" state when testing complicated setup programs. You can create an image of a PC as it exists *before* you mangle it with installations to be tested, then restore it as needed to retest. Some of the cloning tools can place an image onto a destination computer in less than half an hour, depending on the size of the image. This is substantially faster than having to reinstall Windows and all of your base software.

There are a few limitations to cloning that you should be aware of as well:

1. Because Windows modifies its setup based on the hardware, you will find it difficult to install a master on a different kind of PC than the one on which the image was created. In general, you must have the same PC type (right down to the monitor) to get the most out of this approach.

2. Some tools have a hard time with NTFS and NT installations, though all the ones I have worked with handle FAT 32.

3. Some packages do not handle IP addresses very well, and you may still have to do some last-minute tweaking on each PC to get things right.

Patches and Updater Applications

Once you have installed and distributed your application, you may need to make frequent modifications to it. For simple changes to one or two files, you probably will not want to have to go through the trouble of creating a setup package and distributing the whole application and all of its parts again. When there are only one or two files that need to change, it is often easier to create a homegrown solution that updates just those few files than it is to do something more extravagant.

There are two basic approaches for handling these issues. First, you may create a simplified setup program that installs just the files that have changed. Some of the third-party installation tools even have patching options to simplify this process for you. The second approach is to create a simple VB application that searches a network share or the Internet for new files and copies, and registers them as needed. If you have applications that change many times a day and the users must always run the most current version, you could have the application periodically checked for updates and update itself automatically.

Further Reading

There is not a lot of good material available on distributing Visual Basic applications, so I have little to offer here in the way of further reading.

Bruce McKinney, "Hardcore Visual Basic: A Hardcore Declaration of Independence" (1999a). This on-line article contains material McKinney would have put into the VB 6 edition of his book *Hardcore Visual Basic*. Unfortunately, he decided not to write this edition, but included a lot of the material here instead.

Appendix

Developer Resources

As a supplement to the bibliography at the end of this book, here are some additional sources covering Visual Basic development I have found useful. For updates, refer to the on-line listing at

http://www.awl.com/cseng/titles/0-201-61604-1

On-line Resources

1. Perhaps the most important VB resources come directly from Microsoft, although the information can sometimes be difficult to get at:

- I usually start with the Books Online, which have become integrated with the MSDN Library in Visual Studio 6. The shortcomings of the VB help files are well known: very few examples, inaccurate text, and atrocious performance. Nevertheless, there is a wealth of information, and the search engine is reasonably complete and quick. The MSDN Visual Studio Library also contains numerous periodicals, complete and partial books, and white papers to add to the material provided directly by Microsoft.

- Microsoft's MSDN Web site offers updated versions of the MSDN library and is a helpful starting point for researching an issue on-line.

- While Microsoft technical support is expensive and leaves something to be desired in terms of problem resolution, the staff is very good at searching the on-line information for you. If you have a particular question and are willing to pay for the service call, try contacting Microsoft's technical support staff. They search through incidents and articles for a living and have often found information I was certain did not exist. They certainly do not consider themselves librarians, though, so you'll have to pose your questions carefully!

♦ Microsoft also offers numerous e-mail letters containing updates to the knowledge base, news about patches and service packs, and the like.

2. If you cannot find the answers to the questions you have through Microsoft's resources, there are other Web sites to consider. Here is a list of those I have found most useful:

♦ Carl & Gary's (*www.cgvb.com*). This site contains lots of links to VB-related sites.

♦ VBOnline Magazine and Catalog (*www.vbonline.com*). This is a monthly on-line magazine aimed mostly at promoting products, but also providing detailed how-tos and interesting articles.

♦ The Development Exchange (*www.devx.com*). DEVX covers many different languages and is the support site for Fawcette Technical Publications magazines (*Visual Basic Programmer's Journal* is among them). It contains articles, white papers, downloads, e-mail lists, and more.

♦ *Advisor Magazine* (*www.advisor.com*). This is the support site of the Access-Office-VB Advisor magazine.

♦ Advanced VB Website (*vb.duke.net*). This site has lots of VB-related details and is updated regularly.

♦ VBXtras (*www.vbxtras.com*). This site is primarily a catalog, but has event announcements, links to other resources, and so on.

3. Finally, don't forget the newsgroups. Perusing the newsgroups, I have had numerous questions answered by folks for free.

Journals

Several journals contain a wealth of information about programming and some journals focus on Visual Basic. My favorites are the following:

♦ *Visual Basic Programmer's Journal.* This magazine contains VB articles for all levels of programmers. It is probably the best Visual Basic magazine around. The layout of the magazine (especially the code examples) could be better, but content is always solid.

- *Dr. Dobbs.* This journal is more academic in nature, so you'll find articles about algorithms, security, programming, and just about anything else related to software. The magazine rarely has VB-specific articles, though.

- *Microsoft Systems Journal.* This magazine is aimed at developers working with Microsoft technologies. It often contains advanced articles about Visual Basic.

- *Access-Office-VB Advisor.* While the focus of this journal is clearly Access, it nevertheless contains many fine VB-related articles.

Bibliography

Appleman, Dan. 1997. *Visual Basic 5.0 Programmer's Guide to the Win32 API*. New York: Ziff-Davis.

Balena, Francesco. April 1998. "Play VB's Strings." *Visual Basic Programmer's Journal*, 8(4):109–112.

Boehm, Barry. 1981. *Software Engineering Economics*. Englewood Cliffs, N. J.: Prentice Hall.

Boehm, Barry. May 1988. "A Spiral Model of Software Development and Enhancement." *Computer*, 21(5):61–72.

Booch, Grady, et al. 1999. *The Unified Modeling Language User Guide*. Reading, Mass.: Addison Wesley Longman.

Box, Don. 1998. *Essential COM*. Reading, Mass.: Addison Wesley Longman.

Brooks, Frederick P., Jr. 1995. *The Mythical Man-Month*. Reading, Mass.: Addison-Wesley.

Codd, E. F. 1990. *The Relational Model for Database Management*. Reading, Mass.: Addison-Wesley.

Cooper, Alan. 1995. *About Face: The Essentials of User Interface Design*. Foster City, Calif.: IDG Books Worldwide.

Cooper, Alan. June 1999. "14 Principles of Polite Apps." *Visual Basic Programmer's Journal*, 9(7):62–71.

Corwin, Alan Brice. 1999. "The Natural Language Convention." Available on-line at *www.processbuilder.com*

Cowan, Ken. July 1998. "Swat Tough Bugs." *Visual Basic Programmer's Journal*, 8(8):117–119.

Curland, Matthew. June 1999a. "Create Worker Threads in DLLs." *Visual Basic Programmer's Journal*, 9(7):120–123.

Curland, Matthew. June 1999b. "Create Efficient Multithreaded Apps." *Visual Basic Programmer's Journal*, 9(7):116–119.

Eddon, Guy, and Henry Eddon. 1998. *Programming Components with Microsoft Visual Basic 6.0*. Redmond, Wash.: Microsoft Press.

Fergus, Dan. October 1998. "Speed Your App with New String Functions." *Visual Basic Programmer's Journal*, 8(12):124–132.

Fortier, Paul J., ed. 1997. *Database Systems Handbook*. New York: McGraw-Hill.

Grady, Robert B., and Deborah L. Caswell. 1989. *Software Metrics: Establishing a Company-Wide Program*. Englewood Cliffs, N. J.: Prentice Hall.

Havewala, Aspi. May 1999. "The Version Control Process." *Dr. Dobb's Journal*, 299:100–111.

Homer, Alex, and David Sussman. 1998. *Professional MTS and MSMQ with VB and ASP*. Olton, Birmingham, U. K.: Wrox Press.

Jacobson, Ivar, et al. 1992. *Object-Oriented Software Engineering: A Use Case Driven Approach*. Reading, Mass.: Addison-Wesley.

Jacobson, Ivar, et al. 1999. *The Unified Software Development Process*. Reading, Mass.: Addison Wesley Longman.

Jones, Capers. 1996. *Applied Software Measurement*. New York: McGraw-Hill.

Kruchten, Philippe. 1999. *The Rational Unified Process: An Introduction*. Reading, Mass.: Addison Wesley Longman.

Kurata, Deborah. 1997. *Doing Objects in Microsoft Visual Basic 5.0*. New York: Ziff-Davis.

Lhotka, Rockford. 1998. *Visual Basic 6 Business Objects*. Olton, Birmingham, U. K.: Wrox Press.

Maguire, Steve. 1994. *Debugging the Development Process*. Redmond, Wash.: Microsoft Press.

Mattison, Rob. 1998. *Understanding Database Management Systems*. New York: McGraw-Hill.

McCarthy, Jim. 1995. *Dynamics of Software Development*. Redmond, Wash.: Microsoft Press.

McConnell, Steve. 1993. *Code Complete*. Redmond, Wash.: Microsoft Press.

McConnell, Steve. 1996. *Rapid Development*. Redmond, Wash.: Microsoft Press.

McConnell, Steve. 1998. *Software Project Survival Guide*. Redmond, Wash.: Microsoft Press.

McKinney, Bruce. 1997. *Hardcore Visual Basic*. Redmond, Wash.: Microsoft Press.

McKinney, Bruce. 1999a. "Hardcode Visual Basic: A Hardcore Declaration of Independence." Available on-line at *www.devx.com*

McKinney, Bruce. July 1999b. "Understand the Dictionary Class." *Visual Basic Programmer's Journal*, 9(8):50-61.

Mezick, Daniel, and Scot Hillier. August 1998. "Write a Simple OLE DB Provider." *Visual Basic Programmer's Journal*, 8(9):115-117.

Microsoft Corporation. 1995. *The Windows Interface Guidelines for Software Design*. Redmond, Wash.: Microsoft Press.

Myers, Glenford. 1979. *The Art of Software Testing*. New York: John Wiley.

Norman, Donald A. 1990. *The Design of Everyday Things*. New York: Doubleday.

Ordonez, Mauricio. June 1996. "NTService: An OLE Control for Creating Windows NT Services in Visual Basic." Available in the MSDN library.

Pattison, Ted. 1998. *Programming Distributed Applications with COM and Microsoft Visual Basic 6.0*. Redmond, Wash.: Microsoft Press.

Pattison, Ted. May 1999. "Using Visual Basic to Integrate MSMQ into Your Distributed Applications." *Microsoft Systems Journal*, 14(5):37-48.

Perkins, Jon, contrib. 1997. *Advanced Visual Basic 5*. Redmond, Wash.: Microsoft Press.

Robbins, John. August 1997a and September 1997b. "Ingenious Ways to Implement Multiple Threads in Visual Basic 5.0." *Microsoft Systems Journal*, 12(8-9). Available in Books Online.

Rofail, Ash. April 1999. "Make the Leap from DAO to ADO." *Visual Basic Programmer's Journal*, 9(4):30-38.

Rogerson, Dale. 1997. *Inside COM*. Redmond, Wash.: Microsoft Press.

Rosenberg, Doug, with Kendall Scott. 1999. *Use Case Driven Object Modeling with UML: A Practical Approach*. Reading, Mass.: Addison Wesley Longman.

Royce, Walker. 1998. *Software Project Management*. Reading, Mass.: Addison Wesley Longman.

Rumbaugh, James. 1996. *OMT Insights*. New York: SIGS Books.

Rumbaugh, James, et al. 1999. *The Unified Modeling Language Reference Manual*. Reading, Mass.: Addison Wesley Longman.

Schneider, Geri, and Jason P. Winters. 1998. *Applying Use Cases*. Reading, Mass.: Addison Wesley Longman.

The Standish Group. 1995. *The CHAOS Report*. Available on-line at *www.standishgroup.com*

Index